Dear [...]

May G[...]

and forever.

Jerri Dobbins

Take My Hand!

Your Personal Retreat Companion

By
James H. Dobbins, Ph.D.

Copyright © 2004 by James H. Dobbins

ISBN 0-7414-2326-X

Published by:

INFINITY
PUBLISHING.COM

1094 New De Haven Street, Suite 100
West Conshohocken, PA 19428-2713
Info@buybooksontheweb.com
www.buybooksontheweb.com
Toll-free (877) BUY BOOK
Local Phone (610) 941-9999
Fax (610) 941-9959

Printed in the United States of America

Printed on Recycled Paper

Published March 2005

Dedication

This book is dedicated to my loving wife, Mary Beth, without whose constant support and encouragement my life would be very different and this book would never have come into being. Next to my relationship with God, her coming into my life and accepting me as her husband is the most wonderful and most important thing that has ever happened to me.

I also dedicate this book to my five children, Maureen, Kathleen, Nathan, Daniel, and Fr. Michael Dobbins, a priest in the diocese of Arlington, Virginia. I pray that each of them finds something within that can serve as a key to unlocking a deeper relationship with God.

To the members of our prayer group which met every week in St. William of York Parish Church, for whom much of this work was originally created, I owe my eternal thanks.

To those who continued to encourage this work, especially Fr. Michael Duesterhaus, I owe my thanks and prayers beyond any measure I could ever describe. I also owe special thanks to all my friends on the Spirit-L and CINCARM internet discussion groups, whose many and valuable contributions helped me enormously in my own developing relationship with God. Special thanks go to Fr. Tim Hayes, Elizabeth Stevens and Lonnie Sorensen for their help and constant support.

To these, and many others who have helped me along the way, I offer my prayer and thanksgiving.

I would be remiss in not offering my thanks and gratitude for the help and encouragement of the wonderful staff at Infinity Press, without who dedication and expertise this book would never have become a reality.

James H. Dobbins

Foreword

The spiritual life is a mysterious reality. As a child, I recall thinking once that it was so difficult to know how to respond to the call of the spiritual life, especially since no one told you "what it was like." I thought to myself, "*If I ever go there, I will tell others what it is like so it won't be so difficult for them.*" In later years, of course, I discovered that there are indeed a whole host of friends on the journey who are willing to tell you "what it is like."

The Saints John of the Cross, Teresa of Avila, Therese of Lisieux, Catherine of Siena, Thomas Aquinas, Faustina, Padre Pio, and many others, do offer us their understanding of the spiritual journey. They communicate the Wisdom of the Spirit in very personal human images and stories. They share their own experience of God and His ways so that we can all discover them for ourselves. Dr. Jim Dobbins brings home the message of these masters and others as he presents his version of an "at home" retreat for the busy people of our modern age in his book Take My Hand. From the very first chapters, you are invited to visit with those who have walked the journey of faith quite literally through the centuries. The landscapes of the spirit are outlined with a map that is readable. You can find your own way because the map is presented clearly and with down home descriptions of familiar landmarks.

The call to conversion is a daily call. It is in the midst of life itself that we encounter God and come to understand His will for us. Ask any "old Catholic" this question: "*Why did God make me?*" Almost without thinking, he or she will recite some version of this statement: *"God made me to know Him, to love Him and to serve Him in this life, and to be happy with Him forever in the next."* Then ask, *"What does this mean?"* Most likely, the very first response will be something like, *"I don't know. That's what the Sisters taught me."* Take My Hand is an invitation to unpack the meaning of the expressions of Faith that were learned by rote and to discover their hidden depths. You are invited to come to know something of your own spiritual journey while you are on the way. Whether you were educated in the days of Latin, with the Tridentine Mass and the Baltimore Catechism as your religious food, or you are—as I am—"a child of the Second Vatican Council," fully at home and familiar with the Mass as it celebrated today, insights into the inner meaning of these "holy things" are offered for your reflection.

Catholic Christians often doubt their own knowledge of the Sacred Scriptures because they are unable to cite chapter and verse. However, when the events and persons who are in the Scriptures are mentioned, they will recognize them and they find they know the stories well. Reflection on human experience will show that this is a common way of knowing other human beings. You know them in their place of work or recreation, but can you give their address by memory? As Take My Hand calls to mind particular Biblical figures, you will meet some old friends. Implicit is the invitation to get to know them better. Citations and footnotes offer details concerning where you can find them (their Scriptural "address"), but the encounter and the reflections offered take you to a deeper way of knowing. Many questions that arise in the midst of the topics discussed jump right off the page and into your heart. Like Mary, you are invited to ponder them and to respond, "Let it be done to me according to Your Word."

God first loved us. Our journey of faith is our response to the God Who reaches out to us in the depths of our being. You are being invited to "take a look inside" your own soul and into the intimacy of God Who is Father, Son and Spirit and with Whom you have a living relationship. Dr. Dobbins offers reflections, suggestions, guides for prayer and meditation, many practical approaches to your life of prayer. Much of what is offered in Take My Hand can be found in other spiritual books. What is unique is the manner of offering. This little treatise puts into contemporary language for persons engaged in a complex world the fruits of contemplation by one of their fellow travelers who has studied and prayed and is still on the way. A father of a family, who has journeyed through the life of today's world, invites you to walk with him. The natural desire of every child who walks along an unfamiliar path is to reach up to hold the hand of a parent. Dr. Jim Dobbins says "Take my hand." Enjoy the journey!

Rev. Timothy M. Hayes
Pastor, Church of the Blessed Sacrament
Newark, Ohio
Feast of St. Therese of Lisieux,
1 October, 2004

Table of Contents

Why Make a Personal Retreat?

Before answering this question, let me introduce myself. My name is Jim Dobbins. Like you, I have a life in the world. Before beginning a retreat, we should have some idea of why we want to make a retreat. A retreat is a form of withdrawal from the world to spend concentrated time with God. We have to ask ourselves, "Who is this "me" who wants to make a retreat?" We usually have two kinds of identity. We either think of ourselves in terms of what we do, our job, or we think of ourselves in terms of our roles or vocations.

For example, with regard to what I do, I work for a contractor supporting the Department of Defense and the Department of Homeland Security. Before that, I spent twenty-one years with IBM Federal Systems Division and several years with the government teaching at the Defense Acquisition University. My first assignment with IBM was working as part of the Apollo flight support team at the Manned Spacecraft Center in Houston. I am also an attorney licensed to practice in Virginia. I received my bachelors degree in physics from Loyola University in New Orleans, a master of science in information systems, and a Ph.D. in the Management of Science, Technology and Innovation from George Washington University. I have been in school, or teaching adults for one reason or another since 1962. In 1985, and 1986, I participated in the exchange of distinguished engineers and scientists program and visited France as a state guest to discuss the work I was doing in software reliability. I have belonged to several professional associations and I am a member of Mensa. That is a brief summary of what I am. It is not a description of who I am. We always have to ask, "So what?" None of this has any relation to why I might want to make a retreat or become a spiritual person.

i

If I want to consider who I am, I look at different things. I look at my vocations in life and who I am before God. My family lives in Goldvein, Virginia and we have a second home on the island of Chincoteague, Va. Our primary home is in the middle of a fifty eight acre forest and we have a herd of dairy goats and various birds such as chickens, peacocks, turkeys, geese and ducks. So I have a role as steward of part of God's creation as well as the role of husband and father.

I am a cradle Catholic, and my vocation is to be a husband, and father of five children. I grew up in St. Stephen's Parish in New Orleans, and was taught by the Daughters of Charity who ran our parish grade school. These good sisters also taught us to be altar boys, and this was where I first developed a special appreciation for the Mass. I spent my first two years of high school in a minor seminary in Cape Girardeau, Missouri - now closed, but then known affectionately as The Cape. I graduated from Jesuit High School and Loyola University in New Orleans. At Loyola I had three years of philosophy and four years of theology.

I am a member of St. William of York Parish in Stafford, Virginia. I am a fourth degree Knight of Columbus, and have led a parish prayer group or taught adult education since 1994. My wife, Mary Beth, and I have also team-taught CCD classes at St. William of York. I have served as spiritual director for several lay persons and one priest. One of my five children, Fr. Michael Dobbins, was ordained to the priesthood in May 1999 for the diocese of Arlington, Virginia. My two youngest children, Nathan and Daniel, were born in 1987 and 1989. Both are altar boys at our parish and served the first Mass of their brother, Michael.

Since 1992 I have been quite involved with internet discussion groups, primarily the Carmelite Spirituality Discussion Group (CINCARM), and the Catholic Spirituality Discussion Group (Spirit-L). On the CINCARM discussion list, I was privileged to lead a four month study of St. Teresa of Avila's book, Interior Castle. So, when I begin a retreat, I do so as Jim, a child of God by His grace, a husband and father and teacher by vocation, who tries to serve God in several ways. I should have some sense of what I hope to gain or achieve by making a retreat. It might be something as simple as to grow closer to God, or understand my role better as His child.

Now, let me address the opening question. Because retreat centers are so few and so widely scattered, many of our Catholic family members lack the opportunity for that special time devoted exclusively to spiritual growth normally afforded by the experience of making directed retreats. They also have little guidance in how to grow in prayer at home and during periods of time in church outside the liturgy. I have encountered many life long Catholics who have never been on retreat. The value of retreats was made evident to me when I saw the response of my wife to her first retreat, made at a Trappist monastery in 1995. A convert, Mary Beth had never had the opportunity to spend time alone with God this way. Recognizing this need, and after returning from a pilgrimage retreat to Medjugorje, I decided to write Take My Hand as a personal retreat guide and companion. It was also written so that sections could be used by retreat masters guiding short retreats of a few days or less. Each section includes reflections designed to address issues I have encountered in myself and others as we walked our paths toward God. It is intended to be useful for adults, teenagers, and those participating in RCIA and other adult education programs.

The objective of meditation is to come closer to God; to come as close to God as possible during this life. The reflections in Take My Hand are intended to help you read, meditate, and grow a little each day. Anyone can use Take My Hand as a guide for making a personal retreat wherever they may be; whether at home or even on a business trip. It was not written with any presumptions of prior theological education.

So, what is an at-home retreat? An at-home retreat is a self-directed period of prayer and reflection undertaken to gain a more intimate relationship with God. It is often difficult to do this without guidance. Proper guidance can come through a spiritual director, or can be a written guide such as this book. There is no set length for how long an at-home retreat should be or must be, or how time must be spent each day in the retreat activity. You could decide to devote an hour a day for a week, a month or a year. You may also decide to visit a retreat center for a week or a weekend with Take My Hand as your companion. I ask that you pray beforehand to see what kind of retreat plan would work best for you. The retreat should be undertaken in measured steps. Reflection on the reading is the key to success. It is better to find a quiet place to read a little each day and reflect much on what has been read, than to read voraciously and not have time to meditate on or contemplate what has been read. It is also a good practice to engage in the retreat with notebook and pen always handy so that thoughts which come to you during periods of reflection can be captured immediately. It is also advisable to have a bible handy in order to read and reflect on the references included.

The purpose of Take My Hand, therefore, is to offer guidance for those going through a deeper discovery of God and their relationship with God. The objective is for you to attain a loving intimacy with God himself. In the process, you will not only come to know God better, but yourself as well, for self-knowledge and humility are both key elements of spiritual progress.

Before progressing in your relationship with God, let me share with you a few general considerations about getting close to God within the framework of our daily lives. Those of us immersed in the world tend to lose sight of our relationship with God. Our lives are so filled with activity related to family, jobs, social responsibility and recreation that we often have difficulty fitting God into the picture. It is easy to get sidetracked and put God on a schedule. We "do" God like we do lunch. He becomes an event for Sunday morning, some note made in the schedule planner, and forgotten the rest of the week.

We must get ourselves away from this misdirected focus, for God cannot be first in our lives if we give Him so little of our time and effort. How can we expect Him to give us eternity if we hardly give Him an hour a week? How do we break out of this mold and still meet our other responsibilities?

There are as many facets to the relationship with God as there are individuals seeking God. We search for God until He finds us. He has guaranteed we will find Him if we seek. We will never find Him if we put everything else first, for each other thing we put in first place serves as a barrier to reaching and embracing God. Once God is found, or we at least have the desire to find Him, we can begin exploring our relationship with Him and embark on the most exciting journey of our lives.

We will explore God for eternity and never finish, the marvels of His life and love in us unfolding layer by layer the more we dig. The seeking and exploring process begins with rearranging our lives to put God in first place and reorienting our personal priorities. It does not mean we stop doing the ordinary things of life, but rather we do the ordinary things of life from a different perspective and with a different motivation. We learn to live our lives with the understanding of our place as children of God. The more we explore, the more intimately united to God we become.

We must eventually recognize that, regardless of who we are or what our job is or what our vocation may be, there are only three things which should drive everything we do. These are (1) to know God, (2) to love God, and (3) to do God's will in everything. It is a simple picture, but a tall order. We cannot love God until we know God, and we will not be concerned with His will unless we love Him. Therefore, our relationship with God is one which builds over time, progressing from a relationship of curiosity or perceived need to one of intimacy. It is an iterative process and, like a spiral, keeps expanding throughout our life.

Discovering God, and ourselves in Him, is a process which continuously repeats the Know/Love/Do-His-Will cycle. We know Him a little, love Him a little, and try to do that part of His will we perceive. By doing this, we discover more about Him, are able to love Him more, and so it continues. It is a journey of discovery which has no end, for no matter how much we know and love God, we can always know Him and love Him even more. But we must care enough to seek Him, care enough to begin this process of discovery. It is my hope that what you find within these pages will give you the incentive to seek Him if you are not already doing so, and will help deepen your relationship if you are already experiencing the excitement of discovery.

Everything we encounter in our lives has some relationship to the plan God has for us. All that happens in our lives is the result of our cooperation or lack of cooperation with His plan for us. There is no such thing as coincidence. All is God directed or God allowed. God will encourage us in one direction, but, using our free will, we may go some other way. If we do, we bear the consequence of that choice, and then God again encourages us to move in His direction. And so it continues; a pull from one side, resistance, and another pull, until we are finally enlightened enough to cooperate and allow our soul to soar with the angels.

Each time you pick up <u>Take My Hand</u>, pray to the Holy Spirit first. Ask Him to help you gain what you need at this moment from what you read. Try to do the reading in the morning if possible, and then meditate on what you have read during the day. When you go to bed in the evening, let your meditation guide your night prayer. You will discover that <u>Take My Hand</u> is a kind of map to aid you in exploring God and His love for you individually, and your response to that love. You are the explorer. Along the way you will capture a heavenly storehouse of treasures to hold in your heart. These treasures form the basis for the growth of your soul in God, and of the predominance of God in your soul. As this happens, you become one with Him, just as Jesus asks of us in the gospel. God is always calling us back from the death of sin. In the gospel of Mark we read the account of the cure of Jairus' daughter. This little girl was dead, and Jesus brought her back to life. He called out to her, "Talitha cumi", rise up and live, and held out His hand for her to take. Listen, now, in the quiet of your soul as He calls you. Reach out to Him and respond as He says to you

"Take My Hand"

jdobbins@nishanet.com

jhdphd @ gmail. com

Knowing God

**If you know Me, then you will also know My Father.
Whoever has seen Me has seen the Father.**

John 14:7

**You know neither Me nor My Father. If you knew Me,
you would know My Father also.**

John 8:19

The God of Revelation

Our God is a God of revelation. All other "gods" have been invented and made by man. God reveals Himself to us in nature, as Paul tells us in his letter to the Romans, and in Scripture, so what we know about God today is the sum of what He has thus far revealed about Himself. With the incarnation of Jesus, we have the fullness of revelation until the Second Coming. Jesus completed God's revelation about Himself. There is nothing we need to know about God to believe in Him beyond what Jesus revealed.

Our discovery of God begins with scripture. Through scripture we can begin to contemplate the attributes of God. Jesus told us through St. Faustina Kowalska[1] that the greatest attribute of God is His mercy. St. John tells us that God is love (1 Jn 4:8). Therefore, as we explore the unfolding relationship between God and man in scripture, we should be aware of these two attributes of God in particular.

When we read scripture, we do not just see things God did, as if it is merely a history book or a compilation of events, nor do we learn mere facts about the nature of God. Scripture is our key to the mind and heart of God. God's Love is the heart and soul of scripture. When we read God's word, we discover an unfolding relationship of love between God and man, and in so doing we discover many things about both God and ourselves. It is a true relationship into which God calls each of us to participate as fully as possible. Our retreat goal is to enter into that relationship with God as deeply as we can.

---

[1]St. Faustina Kowalska, Divine Mercy in My Soul, Marian Press, Stockbridge (1987) par 301.

2

In each case, it is an individual relationship, unique to you and God. True, God has a universal relationship with all of us through His Church, the Sacraments, and because we are members of His Mystical Body. But He also desires a personal and unique relationship with each of us. He desires to sanctify you to such a degree that you can encounter Him in the deepest recesses of your soul. He wants to have an encounter with you in that secret place in your soul where St. Teresa of Avila tells us no one can go but you and God[2]. There, in that hidden place, that sacred place to which God must bring you for you cannot go there on your own, you will experience a spiritual intimacy with God unlike that enjoyed by anyone else in heaven or on earth. But to be brought there you must be properly disposed and prepared, and that is what a developing prayer life is about. Not many people are willing to prepare to go this far in their relationship with God.

When we receive the Eucharist, we should enter spiritual union with God. The only thing which prevents this union from being experienced by us in its full depth is the degree of imperfection of our response to His invitation of love. Pray that the Holy Spirit will perfect this response in you. Begin at the beginning, by getting to know intimately the God who loves you so dearly.

---

[2]The Collected Works of St. Teresa of Avila, Vol 2, trans Kieran Kavanaugh, O.C.D. and Otilio Rodriguez, O.C.D. Interior Castle, Seventh Dwelling Places, Ch 1, par 5, pg 49, ICS Publishers, Institute of Carmelite Studies, Washington DC, (1980)

The Second Bridge
Becoming a Spiritual Person

Many who desire to begin a spiritual journey, to get closer to God, are not sure just where or how to begin. There is so much to consider. They hear about Jesuit spirituality, or Carmelite, Dominican, Carthusian or Franciscan spirituality, and others, and it can be confusing. What do they mean and how do they differ? Is one right for me?

Those already on a spiritual journey often wonder where they are, where others are, and how to recognize the more evident signposts along the way. The answers are found among the prominent works on spirituality which the church has provided through the centuries. Examples are the Dialogues of St. Catherine of Siena[3], the Spiritual Conferences of Johann Tauler, O.P.[4], the works of Fr. John Arintero, O.P.[5], Fr. Reginald Garrigou-LaGrange, O.P.[6], St. Ignatius of Loyola[7], St. John of the Cross[8], St. Teresa of Avila[9], St. Francis de Sales[10], any many others. All, in one

---

[3]The Dialogue of St. Catherine of Siena, http://www.ccel.org/c/catherine/dialog/dialog1.0.txt, 1995.

[4]Johann Tauler, O.P., Spiritual Conferences, TAN Books, Rockford, (1978)

[5]Fr. John Arintero, O.P., The Mystical Evolution, Vol 1&2, TAN books, Rockford, (1978)

[6]Fr. Reginald Garrigou-LaGrange, O.P., The Three Ages of the Interior Life, Vol 1&2, TAN Books, Rockford, (1989)

[7]The Spiritual Exercises of St. Ignatius, trans Anthony Motola, Ph.D., Image Books, N.Y., (1964)

[8]The Collected Works of St. John of the Cross, trans Kieran Kavanaugh, O.C.D. and Otilio Rodriguez, O.C.D., ICS Publ., Institute of Carmelite Studies, Washington DC, (1991)

[9]The Collected Works of St. Teresa of Avila, Vol 1&2, trans Kieran Kavanaugh, O.C.D. and Otilio Rodriguez, O.C.D. ICS Publishers, Institute of Carmelite Studies, Washington DC, (1980)

way or another, try to help us along the way. The writings of these great saints should be part of your spiritual library, and read regularly.

It is worthy of note that St. John of the Cross and St. Teresa of Avila are extensively referenced in almost all other works on spirituality which followed them in time, and therefore they, together with St. Catherine of Siena, are a very rich source of advice. We must also recognize that these giants of spirituality often did not work in isolation. St. John of the Cross was, for a time, the spiritual director of St. Teresa of Avila, and we can only guess as to how they must have helped each other, both having become Doctors of the Church. And we know that St. Teresa of Avila was also quite influenced by the works of Ignatius of Loyola and Louis of Grenada. St. Francis DeSales and St. Jane DeChantal worked closely together, as did St. Francis of Assisi and St. Claire. We can all benefit from these spiritual masters, whether we are lay or clergy.

In almost all of these works we find an understanding of the three major levels of conversion we must go through to reach perfection, those bridges we must cross from one level to the next, to reach the ultimate destiny desired by Our Lord for all souls, namely that state generally described as the transforming union, or spiritual marriage of the soul with God. The intent here is to try to summarize what the spiritual masters have told us about those three conversions, why they are necessary, and the signs to look for which tell us when they are necessary.

First, we must recognize that conversion is not a single discrete event. Even when St. Paul was stricken blind on the road to Damascus, that was only the beginning of his conversion process, not the complete event. We do not say

---

[10]St. Francis de Sales, Introduction to the Devout Life, Image Books, New York, 2003

we are converted, bur rather that we are in the process of conversion. It may begin with a discrete event, but it is a progressive state characterized by a desire of the soul to come ever closer to God, coupled with the grace through which God communicates Himself to the soul to some level and degree. The whole process is fueled by one thing; love. Love of the person by God, and love of God by the person, is the force which draws the two beings, God and His creature, together like opposite poles of magnets until, resistance by the soul overcome, the two eventually unite spiritually while also preserving the individual identity and function of the soul. How close we come to spiritual marriage, and by what path, is the spiritual diary, the spiritual record, of our life.

As you explore your relationship with God, the soul is largely the determinant of the rate of progress. It is the soul's cooperation with grace that will determine whether it experiences all three levels of conversion, or even any meaningful conversion at all, for God never interferes with His gift of free will.

As you progress spiritually, it is helpful to remember that if you go all the way to the final destination, the soul will enter into three stages of relationship with God, each often being characterized and initiated by a defining conversion experience. It is similar to what happens between a man and woman. They first get to know each other, then love each other and become betrothed, then commit completely to each other in marriage. We begin as strangers to God, possibly engaged in serious sin, and, being such, we are generally in that category of souls St. Teresa of Avila would describe, in her *Interior Castle*, as being outside the walls of the castle[11]. How far outside, how far away from the castle - which she uses as a representation of our soul as we

---

[11]The Collected Works of St. Teresa of Avila, Vol 2, Interior Castle, First Dwelling Places, pg 283, ICS Publ., Institute of Carmelite Studies, Washington DC (1980)

enter a life of prayer - we are depends on how much we have rejected the grace of God and embraced the temporal gods of this world. If we respond to the call of grace and desire to enter into the castle, into a life of prayer, we may then progress in our relationship with God from stranger to servant, from servant to friend and beloved, and, finally, from beloved to the spouse of God, the transforming union.

Take a moment now and try to describe for yourself, to yourself, the characteristics of the relationship you have with God right now. Write them down as best you can. Do you have a blank page? A full page? Several pages? What does the content of what you have written tell you about your relationship with God? Is it a relationship of passing acquaintance, love, or spiritual intimacy? How well do you know God right now?

Three Plateaus

Being one who tries to simplify things in my own mind, I tend to think of this whole process of spiritual growth as if the world were a large, flat plain teeming with souls, each preoccupied with the delectable things of this world. Rising out of this plain are three plateaus all in a line, each successive one higher than the preceding. The first and lowest plateau has a ladder from the ground to the top. Between the three plateaus there are two connecting bridges that one must cross to get from the top of one plateau to the top of the next. The ladder and the two bridges represent conversion processes we must go though to get to the next level of our relationship with God.

Climbing the ladder

Two hundred years before St. Teresa of Avila wrote Interior Castle, St. Catherine of Siena wrote her Dialogue, the opening paragraph of which is:

The soul, who is lifted by a very great and yearning desire for the honor of God and the salvation of souls, begins by exercising herself, for a certain space of time, in the ordinary virtues, remaining in the cell of self-knowledge, in order to know better the goodness of God toward her. This she does because knowledge must precede love, and only when she has attained love, can she strive to follow and to clothe herself with the truth. But, in no way, does the creature receive such a taste of truth, or so brilliant a light therefrom, as by means of humble and continuous prayer, founded on knowledge of herself and God; because prayer, exercising her in the above way, unites with God the soul that follows the footprints of Christ Crucified, and thus, by desire and affection, and union of love, makes her another Himself.[12]

Occasionally, someone living on the plain will look up from their all-consuming preoccupations with the world, notice the ladder leaning against the first plateau, wonder what is on top, and perhaps hear joyful sounds coming from the top of the first plateau. They begin to look at their surroundings and notice things, perhaps for the first time. People smile, but there is no inner joy showing in the smile. People hurt each other in many ways, with no regret. Newspapers are full of violent things people do to each other. It is rare for a newspaper headline to proclaim a joyful event. Holidays are dominated by commercialism. Tomorrow will be more of the same. So, this person climbs the ladder, dragging with him or her the things of the world to which they are so very attached and believe they cannot exist without.

This first conversion occurs in those who respond to the grace by which they climb the ladder to the top of the

---

[12]The Dialogue of St. Catherine of Siena, Trans. By Algar Thorold, Treatise on Divine Providence, TAN Books and Publishers, Rockford, 1974, pg 26

first plateau, to enter into the first mansions of St. Teresa's Interior Castle. This can be likened in many ways to the call of the apostles by Jesus in Matthew 4:18-22. "Come after me and I will make you fishers of men," He told them, and they responded. The analogy was apparently not lost on these fishermen as they responded to grace. They knew that fish were living, but when caught they died. However, when these apostles would fish for men, the men would be spiritually dead through sin and by the grace of Jesus administered through His apostles they would be given the grace to become children of God and gain eternal life. At this initial stage, when first called, the person is in an exploratory and searching mode. His or her relationship with God is one of servitude, possibly one of fear, and the punishment of hell may be a major initial motivator. These people also drag up the ladder with them a sack full of the things of the world to which they have become attached, and which seem so important. Esteem in the eyes of others, wealth, material goods, and so on.

However, regardless of the initial motivator, those of us on this first plateau eventually come to the realization that the development of an interior life is essential, even exciting, involves the whole person, is an exploration that will take a lifetime, and thus must be a life's work. You now have a different set of goals for your life. The work of spiritual development of the soul begins and we realize conversion is not a one time event, and that once embarked on the journey we are changed, and continue to change forever. We will never be again what we once were. Even if we revert, we will still be changed, for we will know what we have turned away from. We know we had a chance to gain eternal life and chose enticements of the world instead. As we respond to grace on this first plateau, we hear the call of St. Paul to "put on the new man." (Eph 4:24)

On top of this first plateau we meet others who were similarly curious and who are exploring what is there. The more we explore and discover God's treasures, the more we consider discarding our worldly treasures, usually one at a time, in exchange for more of the spiritual treasures God provides. It is as if we lug our large sack around and occasionally put something in, and, less frequently, remove something and discard it.

Here we also begin to explore ourselves because we are not just exploring God, but our relationship with God. It is here the soul must begin to both explore who he or she is before God, and gain an understanding of the degree to which the virtue of humility is part of our identity. It has been said that humility is the key that unlocks the door to all the other virtues. It begins with an awareness of how the people on this first plateau are treating each other. Those who are responding to grace help one another. They smile and the smile is genuine. They are happy when something good happens to someone else. They genuinely care about each other.

However, these souls still hold fast to many of the worldly treasures they brought with them. The more they explore, and the more they experience God, the heavier the sack feels. As they find the treasures of grace, these are added to the bag and the worldly junk gets even heavier. But in the beginning they are still reluctant to throw anything away, to start setting aside the things of the world to which they are so attached.

At this stage, theology is very important, although it will become less important later. It is very important now because it serves as a foundation and framework, and a scaffolding so to speak, that helps shape the structure of our growing interior life, and keeps it from collapsing because of bad design and error. The principles of theology taught through the ages in Scripture and entrusted to the apostles by Jesus, and the framework Jesus gave us of His Church and its teaching magisterium, give us the governance and

10

guidance we need to build a spiritual life on solid foundation. This will be very important as we encounter resistance from the world and later as we approach the time of our second conversion.

We find the serious beginner developing a zeal for souls, for in loving God we desire that all men do likewise, and we love those whom we know God loves. We cannot separate ourselves from the love for others without separating ourselves from the love of God. We find that the more we share God with others, the more we possess Him ourselves. We can paraphrase what Garrigou-LaGrange teaches us by saying that a desire for material possessions divides us, and interferes with the love we owe each other, for no two of us can fully possess the same material thing. But the possession of God unites us, for the more we possess Him the more we share Him, and the more we share, the closer we come to fully possessing Him. Thus the search for God in our lives becomes a primary motivator. We appreciate the role of love, for love always increases in proportion to how much we love others. The more we love, the greater our capacity for love becomes. We appreciate more fully the gospel promise at Mt 7:7, "Ask and it will be given to you; seek and you will find; knock and it will be opened to you." Jesus did not just hold out a possibility, but rather gave us the certainty that if we truly seek Him out, we will find Him, and this is so because of His immense love for each of us individually. And so we must "seek first the kingdom of God." (Mt 6:33) When we find God, we have found Love.

As the soul progresses during its time on this first plateau, it often enjoys certain consolations from God, given by Him to inspire and encourage the soul to continue its journey of discovery. We sometimes even experience physical signs, such as rosary chains that turn gold, people see the spinning sun, and other such phenomena. They may have all manner of spiritual experiences that are not

11

explained by the laws of nature. They correspondingly feel the interior call of God deep within them and the desire to respond. This is what God is really after; our response and commitment to Him because He is God. For what may be the first time in our life, we understand God has a personal interest in each of us as an individual, not just as part of the collective human race.

While exploring the first plateau, we look down at the plain below and see more clearly the nature of a world trying to live without God. On the plain, we had lost the sense of what love is about, and found ourselves 'loving' things; possessions, power, fame, and especially self, above all else. On the plain God is not loved. Therefore, part of our exploration is a discovery of self, while also being a discovery of God. We think of the name of God and recognize that our own name identifies who we are among so many others. But God's name identifies both what He is and who He is, for He is unique. There are no others like Him. He is I AM (Ex 3:14; Jn 8:58), the Ancient One, the Creator, the Almighty One, and He is also Our Father.

Our Father, my Father. My Holy God, my Mighty God, and my Eternal God who loves me infinitely and who offers to bring me into the family of God, to make me His adopted child. As these words sink in, the implications and awesomeness of the filial relationship He offers out of love for me, and the opportunity to partake of His nature through sanctifying grace, begins to gel within as I see references throughout scripture to the possibility of this new way of being, of becoming what I was created to be.

The excitement mounts, and as we seek to do what we must for God to close the gap individually between us and Himself, to draw us to Himself (Jn 12:32), we also become so much more aware of the vastness between us and God. We see how far we have to go, and how dependent we are on God and His grace to reach our goal. We finally realize that our principal activity will be cooperation with God, for only in that way can we come to Him. All the marvelous qualities in ourselves we may have taken such pride in when we lived on the plains, now pale in comparison to even an iota of the power and majesty and beauty and love of God upon whom we realize we are completely dependent. And yet we are also filled with hope, for we realize the infinite love He has for us which has brought us here, and how much He wants to unite us with Himself. We begin to contemplate the possibilities inherent in this relationship, and they are awesome.

The hope we have in God propels us to continue exploring ourselves and our relationship with God. As St. Teresa of Avila would say, we explore the various rooms of the first, second and third mansions of our soul. We learn some of how God works in our lives, and we learn the necessity of cooperation with His grace so that we might love Him more. We develop a growing desire for spiritual cleanliness, a desire for sanctifying grace. Our attendance at Mass, which might have been done, if at all, once a week through a sense of duty, is now done as often as possible, out of a desire to grow in grace and wisdom as we partake of the gift of the Eucharist and the gifts of the Holy Spirit. We now have a new goal, "be ye perfect as the heavenly Father is perfect" (Mt 5:48), and we are profoundly aware of the possibility of reaching this goal, and the absolute dependence we have on God to achieve this state of perfect love. We can help through cooperation with grace, but God has to bring us to that state. No matter how gifted we may be, we cannot get there on our own (Mt 19:26).

We approach God through the eyes of faith, not through the clarity of the Beatific Vision. The closer we come to God, and the more of Himself He communicates to us, the more insignificant we understand we are compared to Him, and the more we understand the power and extent of His infinite Love for us as an individual. The more we grow in humility the more easily we are able to discard the worldly baggage we brought with us. Therefore, we begin discarding things from the sack we still carry, even if reluctantly.

It is important we understand this process of growth in humility and the effort it takes on our part on this first plateau. We do not compare ourselves to others, but rather we compare ourselves with God. In doing so, we focus on how far from God we are and how dependent on His love we are. We must do this rather than succumb to the temptation to assess that we are, for example, in the fourth mansions as described in St. Teresa of Avila's Interior Castle. Knowing where we are is less important than recognizing where God is, and what we must do to cooperate with His will for us. Each person follows God's light to walk his or her individual path on the way to the embrace of God, so we should not be comparing ourselves and where we are to others and their place on the journey to see if we are ahead of them or behind them. To do so implies a level of self-focus, and possibly pride, we should be discarding. All we need care about is doing all we can to love God and do His will. Our only reason for considering others on the path is to either seek their help or offer them our help. Our consideration of others should never be motivated by trying to see if we are ahead of them, at least in our own eyes. Even when looking only at yourself, it is better to let your spiritual director or confessor consider where you are in your journey than to try to decide that for yourself. We tend to give ourselves too much credit, and may think we are farther along than we are.

Having moved from the plain to the first plateau, we have thus undergone our first conversion. We have passed from living oblivious to God's love or in mortal sin, to living in a state of sanctifying grace as our norm. We have grown from indifference toward God, or lukewarmness towards Him (Rev 3:16), to a growing fervor and desire to possess Him as fully as possible. It is still a struggle to maintain our life of grace, but we are going beyond ourselves to make

God the new center of our lives. We live for Him, and all the while we grow in love for Him and for each other.

When contemplating love, we realize that, in contrast to the worldly treasures of which we had been so desirous, the more we give the more we gain. Love is one of the few things that increases in us in proportion to how we give love to others. Love is self-generating through the activity of love. This is one reason why Satan will fail. Satan is void of love, and is consumed with hatred for God. Hate is self-consuming. Hate feeds on itself. Hatred is unable to increase in the face of constant love. It needs responsive hatred on which to feed. When confronted with constant love, hatred eventually burns out; it runs out of fuel, consumes itself, eating away internally the one who hates. This is why Jesus said, "Love your enemies." (Lk 6:27)

The more we love the more we understand it is actually God's gift of love for us that we experience, for all love comes from Him and true love itself is always His supernatural gift; a gift of part of Himself. By giving us love, He is sharing Himself with us and communicating knowledge of Himself to us, for God is Love itself ("Beloved, let us love one another, because love is of God; everyone who loves is begotten by God and knows God. Whoever is without love does not know God, for God is love." 1 John 4:7-8).

We have learned the meaning of seeking God first and we keep progressing in this endeavor. We begin to understand what the gospel is telling us: "Instead seek His kingdom and these other things will be given you besides." (Lk 12:31) "But seek first the kingdom of God and His righteousness, and all these things will be given to you besides." (Mt 6:33) "For where your treasure is, there also will your heart be." (Lk 12:34, Mt 6:21) None of this will happen if we turn away from love and continue to seek first the things of the world, for in doing so we still place self first. For many, it is a wrenching, even unnatural, experience.

In this first state, beginning in spiritual infancy, we have been going through an active purgation. It has been hard, and took a lot of effort on our part. We have been maturing toward spiritual young adulthood, toward a committed relationship with God, shedding our attachments to the world as best we could, and replacing them with a different set of attachments and values, ones more fitting to a spiritually mature person. We have been developing attachments to God, becoming more concerned with His will for us than our own will, replacing activities which are world-focused with activities directed toward God, and have been developing an active life of prayer and meditation.

By our response to the action of grace, God has been positioning us, through self-knowledge, humility and love for God and fellow man, for a transition, a second conversion, from beginner to proficient. This entire process on the first plateau may take along time, even years, depending on our disposition toward God when we begin. Finally, we believe we are ready to enter the gate leading onto the first bridge, the one which will bring us to the second plateau. In the Interior Castle[13], St. Teresa identifies this as entering the fourth mansions.

Naturally, during each stage of conversion there is a progressive spiritual advance. The spiritual masters previously mentioned all tell us that there is no such thing as standing still in one's relationship with God. One either progresses or one falls back. There is no marking time in place. We each take different periods of time to move through a given stage depending on how fully we cooperate

---

[13]The Collected Works of St. Teresa of Avila, Vol 2, trans Kieran Kavanaugh, O.C.D. and Otilio Rodriguez, O.C.D. ICS Publishers, Institute of Carmelite Studies, Washington DC, (1980)

with the graces we receive. Some may get so far and not be able to progress farther toward the next plateau because of their preferential attachments to things other than God. Their situation is similar to that of the rich official in the gospel of Luke (Lk 18:18-23). He kept the commandments, and lived a good life, but could not turn his back on his worldly treasures. In such a case, these souls must content themselves with seeking whatever grace and virtue they can find among the treasures on the first plateau. But if they do not continue to deepen their search, they find themselves in danger of moving backward toward a preoccupation with the things of the world and may resume their former life, always with a tinge of guilt. They still hear the call of God, but are afraid to answer, afraid of what it will demand from them.

Some on the first plateau may progress very rapidly, and may even move almost immediately to the third plateau, into the spiritual union, because of a special call and grace for a task God has for that soul. This rapid progress is the exception, not the norm.

It is important to note here that it is possible, in fact it is the desire of God, that all souls reach the final destiny of the transforming union with God, regardless of their state and vocation in life. This mystical union is not a state reserved only to those in the monastic community. All are called. How many respond is almost exclusively a function of cooperation with grace. No one has the excuse that he or she was not called. They who do not respond can only acknowledge their preference for things of this world, or their fear of what might be requested of them in order to complete the journey. This fear is usually a characteristic result of a lack of trust in God, the result of a diminished knowledge and understanding of His infinite love for the soul. We fail to realize that God will never ask anything of us that is not the best thing for us spiritually at that point in our growth. This may be our own fault, or the fault of those who were our teachers. It is usually only through prayer and meditation that this hesitation can be overcome, and to reach the fulfillment of God's desire for us we must pray unceasingly.

The soul working its way to the first bridge finds it has a serious concern for the interior life. This person avoids mortal sin, avoids deliberate venial sin, begins to practice forms of both interior and exterior mortification, and develops a serious prayer life. Without prayer, this spiritual growth cannot happen. For some, usually only a few, this purgation of the senses, the turning away from the appetites for the world in preference for God, is intense, while for others it is more subtle.

Having discarded many of the treasures of the world, the soul finds itself at the point at which a crucial decision has to be made. You must decide what is more precious; whatever treasures from the plain you still drag around, or the spiritual treasures you have been accumulating on the first plateau, with an expectation of greater treasures on the second plateau. You must do a self-examination and ask, "What are the treasures I hold most dear?" Are they the kind that will help me love more? Do I love these things of the world more than anything else, even God?" Before I answer this question, I must consider whether, for example, I would give up my house or my car or my job if I had to make a choice, for whatever reason, between them and God. If choosing God would mean changing my standard of living and no longer spending lavishly to keep up with the Jones', or if it would mean living a moral life, or being faithful to my marital vows, or making sacrifices for my children, which choice would I make? If I would choose the world instead of God, why?

Many souls remain on the first plateau for the rest of their earthly existence, unwilling to shed enough of their attachments to the world to move on to the second plateau. Others, mindful of Jesus' admonition in Mt 10:38 and Lk

9:23 that we must take up our cross if we wish to come after Him and be worthy of Him, fear the purgations they may be asked to endure. Their fists are still tightly wrapped around the sack. They never respond to grace in the way necessary to grow in the virtue of courage sufficiently to cross that first bridge over which they must pass to become a spiritually mature adult. They choose to remain spiritual infants or adolescents.

Eventually, having explored most of the first plateau, the soul properly disposed will feel the call to move to the next plateau, and will join others making their way toward the first bridge. The closer they get to the gate granting access to the first bridge, the heavier their sack of worldly treasures become. They arrive at the gate, but to get through the narrow gate they must leave behind many of the worldly treasures still in the sack. The gate, and the bridge itself, is just too narrow for it all to fit through.

Relatively few souls choose to cross the first bridge, hopeful for the deeper relationship with God awaiting them, and hopeful they will be ready to endure any cross necessary to progress there. The rest remain clustered around the gate, hopeful that one day they may have the courage to cross. Others wander back onto the first plateau to continue exploring what they have already found, content with the familiar and fearful of the unknown.

The First Bridge

For reasons not always well understood by the soul, the treasures found on the first plateau seem to fit through the gate quite easily, are not heavy, and are no hindrance in crossing the bridge. It becomes increasingly apparent that we must purge ourselves of the appetites for the worldly treasures and seek the new, spiritual treasures which we now understand will be on the second plateau.

If we do cooperate, we begin our second conversion process experiencing a more passive purgation of the senses. If we are successful and do cross over the first bridge, we step upon the surface of the second plateau and enter what is referred to as the illuminative way. To go all the way across this bridge, we have a spiritual crisis to handle, and thus we have a need for a second conversion. John of the Cross speaks of this in Dark Night[14], and this second conversion is one of purgation of egoism.

God's love for us brought us from being a stranger to being His servant, and now we perceive He wants to make us His dearest friends, if we will but cooperate. We understand the need for humility, for we have a clearer knowledge that the awesome power of sanctifying grace, which is gradually divinizing our souls more and more, is a purely gratuitous gift of God's love and not something we deserve or to which we are entitled as a matter of right on our own merits. We are now passing from spiritual immaturity to spiritually mature adulthood. In this as yet unfamiliar terrain, Tauler tells us to "Cling to those who cling to God, so that they may draw you with them to God. And may our loving God Himself help us to this end."[15] Note he does not say they will stop their progress and come backward to get us, but rather he tells us to cling to them so we can progress faster. We do this by paying attention to how they pray, how they relate to others, and how much they love. We seek to learn what they have learned by following their example. We ask them to discuss with us their relationship with God. After doing so with several individuals, we marvel at the steadfastness of God's love and the infinite variety of relationships He has formed with those He loves.

---

[14]The Collected Works of St. John of the Cross, trans Kieran Kavanaugh, O.C.D. and Otilio Rodriguez, O.C.D., ICS Publ., Institute of Carmelite Studies, Washington DC, (1991)

[15]Johann Tauler, O.P., Spiritual Conferences, TAN Books, Rockford, (1978), pg 63

Once on the second plateau we are transitioning to proficient. This process takes time. Generally, it is not a quick process, but each of us is different. When we approached that first bridge we had questions. How do I cross over onto the second plateau? Do I have the courage? Once across, we find that it was only with the help of God that we arrived on the second plateau.

Initially, we were able, through only our reason, to come to a knowledge of God as first cause. Having done so, we could come to a relationship with God characterized as master-servant. On our own, through reason, we cannot go much further. We are His servant, His creation, not His child. We will have admiration, awe, and respect for God, all the things that characterize a relationship of servitude. But through revelation and by operation of sanctifying grace received through the sacraments, His free gifts to us, we are able to discern the true natural end of the soul, that of a filial relationship that grows into a spousal relationship with God. And even more, we learn that even while here on earth we can come to union with Him. God brings us to a condition of friendship with Jesus, our Savior, and we inherit with Him the filial status of an adopted son of our heavenly Father. We enter into a Divine life through which we have a relationship with God and encounter the indwelling Trinity (John 14:23). In Heaven, we will see God as Himself ("Beloved, we are God's children now; what we shall be has not yet been revealed. We do know that when it is revealed we shall be like him, for we shall see him as he is." 1 John 3:2), in all His glory, in all His aspects; all united in one simple, supreme, uncreated and infinite Being whose force and power is communicated always through His infinite Love. It takes time to grasp all this. It takes development on each succeeding plateau.

We saw a genuine need to cast away all that hinders our unification with God, all that acts as a barrier to His Love. We began as a opaque pane of glass almost impervious to light, one that needed to be scrubbed. The more we purged ourselves of the things of the world and the more grace we obtained, the cleaner the glass became, until finally the power and light of God's love for us streams through and fills the soul with His grace and nature. Thus His love not only fills us, but is now able to pass through us into others, so when they encounter us they really encounter Jesus acting through us. We become His effective instruments. This is accomplished within the framework provided by our growing knowledge of God gained through scripture, tradition, theology and the teaching magisterium of the Church, coupled with our growth in humility and self-knowledge through prayer. These shape and mold our growing understanding of the way God intended for us to come to Him, for these are the tools He gave us to use. It is also necessary to live a life of virtue.

Tauler tells us in his Spiritual Conferences that the three virtues we should concentrate on are humility, love and prudence. He says, "Humility must be the foundation and we must build on it with love and reason and prudence. Children, there are many who have gone far in developing their intellectual powers, and made great reputations for themselves as scholars, but have not traveled along this way. They will all tumble down, and fall into the abyss. The higher the mountain, the deeper the valley."[16] He tells us further that even though many have attained the state of proficient, "they go on indulging in the activity of their own intellect, and take such great pleasure and joy in this that they cannot attain to the highest truth."[17] If this condition persists, they cannot progress beyond the second plateau. They will never come to union with God. Tauler calls them God's false lovers who do all things, not for pure love of God, but always with an eye for their own advantage.

---

[16]Johann Tauler, O.P., Spiritual Conferences, TAN Books, Rockford, (1978), pg 47

[17]Ibid, pg 50

The second conversion, like the first, has its own scriptural counterpart in the apostles. It occurred for them at the time of the Passion. The apostles, fear overcoming trust, concerned more for self than for God, abandoned Jesus in His hour of need. The conversion experience occurred for Peter when he, who denied Jesus three times, saw Jesus look at him when the cock crowed. Peter wept bitterly, humiliated by his weakness. He recognized himself more at that moment than ever before. He saw his true self, and experienced profound contrition.

Just prior to Peter's second conversion, he and the other apostles, having been prepared by Jesus for three years, listened to Jesus' lesson on friendship during the Last Supper. In John's account of the Last Supper, Peter and the others refer to Jesus several times as Master, not brother or friend. During the washing of the feet, Jesus tells the apostles, "You call Me 'teacher' and 'master', and rightly so, for indeed I am." (Jn 13:13) But a little while later, during the discourse on the vine and the branches, Jesus gave them their lesson on becoming His friend. He gave them the commandment to love one another as He has loved them, and says, "You are My friends if you do what I command you. I no longer call you slaves, because a slave does not know what his master is doing. I have called you friends, because I have told you everything I have heard from My Father." (Jn 15:14-15). Thus, Jesus has set them apart, He has prepared them in everything necessary, He has brought them up from the status of servant to the status of friend of God. The condition for this friendship is that they do as He commanded them. One among them would not. Judas excluded Himself from the friendship of God; God did not exclude Judas. After their second and third conversions which would soon follow, all of the apostles but one would suffer martyrdom for this love. These martyrs, and John, too, proved their friendship; they passed their test. They loved God more than self. We must do the same.

The need for the second conversion often comes as a surprise for us, usually because we do not know ourselves as well as we think. Jesus predicted His Passion several times, so it should have come as no surprise to the apostles. They should have been preparing themselves for it. Jesus, at the Last Supper, also predicted the apostles would not remain faithful during His Passion. Peter, thinking he knew himself and believing he loved Jesus enough, vehemently denied that he would ever do such a thing. Jesus then told Peter that before the cock crowed Peter would deny Him three times. Peter was incredulous. However, as we now know, Peter had weaknesses he was not aware of. He had to go through his fear and humiliation to see the depths of his conviction and experience his true self. He had to find the limits of his own inner strength, to recognize his dependence on God, and to affirm within the depths of his soul how evident was his dependence on God and his love for God. Realizing what had happened within himself, the gospels tell us that Peter wept bitterly. It was another beginning for Peter. His conversion experience here set him up for his third and final conversion at Pentecost, the conversion that would give him the strength for leading the infant Church, and for martyrdom. St. Catherine tells us in her Dialogue that the soul always fears until it arrives at true love[18].

John, too, had his second conversion. He had initially abandoned Jesus with the rest, but by a powerful conversion experience he was called to witness the Passion, called to the foot of the cross so that he could stand there with Our Blessed Mother to be the proxy for us all as Jesus gave us to her as her children, and gave her to John as Our Mother. He was the only apostle to be with Jesus as He completed His act of perfect redemption, the only one to witness this consummating act of Divine love.

---

[18]The Dialogue of St. Catherine of Siena, A Treatise on Discretion, Section 49, http://www.ccel.org/c/catherine/dialog/dialog1.0.txt, 1995.

For most of us, we recognize that we have been trying to lead a Christian life, following the teachings of the Church. We have thought seriously about our salvation, and have done what we thought was our best to become companions of our God within us, to be a true temple of God, to do as Jesus asked of us - to walk in His Way, and to accept our daily cross. Nevertheless, many tend to revert to our former state in time of stress. It is almost as if what we have done is somewhat artificial and now we tend to revert to our 'real' self, our natural self. We are in need of the passive purgation of the senses spoken of by John of the Cross. We must come to grips with our need to love God for Himself, not for His consolations. We must learn to put Him first; always, not just some of the time. We must love God because He is God, whether or not He ever gives us consolations. We must trust that He loves us infinitely, regardless of the obviousness of His intervention in our life. St. Catherine of Siena also speaks of this second conversion in her Dialogue[19]. One result of this second conversion is that we will desire to devote ourselves more fully to the service of God for His sake, not for our personal gain. This desire is one of the fruits of the conversion. It is also a supernatural state, for being concerned with self is the most natural state we have.

What about us who live everyday lives in the world? What signs do we have that a second conversion is necessary, and what signs tell us it is happening? What prevents us from simply walking across the bridge, so to speak? Even the apostles, formed by Jesus Himself, had need of this second conversion, and so in all probability we will also have a like need.

---

[19]St. Catherine of Sienna, The Dialogue of St. Catherine of Sienna, A Treatise on Prayer, section 12, http://www.ccel.org/c/catherine/dialog/dialog1.0.txt, 1995.

This second conversion affects the soul at much greater depths than our first conversion. God is digging out, spooning out, the things that are barriers between Him and us, but He will not leave us empty. For each spoon of 'self' He removes, He will replace the void with Himself. But for many, this digging out, this purging, hurts. We still have attachments to our ego and to some of the things of this world that stand between us and God. It actually takes great courage to undergo this purgation, this emptying out. Peter had the courage, Judas did not.

The more tightly we hold onto things of this world in preference to Christ, the more wrenching an experience it will be and the longer the bridge will be to get to the second plateau. It is usually the sole result of our own negligence, fear and lack of trust in God that we do not successfully go through this second conversion or that it takes a very long time. We cry "Uncle" too quickly, for we do not trust in God enough. We trust ourselves too much, desiring to maintain control rather than giving God control. We have not developed enough of the virtue of patience. Jesus had promised, even before His Passion, He would send the Holy Spirit to the apostles, yet they still cowered in the upper room, doors locked, huddled in fear.

St. Catherine, in her Dialogue, tells us some of the faults we typically have that require a second conversion experience. One fault she notes is an egoism, perhaps much stronger than we realize ourselves. This manifests as self-love, especially when consolations are removed. She describes it as the mercenary love of the imperfect. Because of it, we still fall prey to numerous habitual faults and venial sins, even if we remain free of mortal sin. Some characteristics are that such a soul,

"... inasmuch as she has not yet arrived at great perfection, she often drops sensual tears, and if you ask Me why, I reply: Because the root of self-love is not sensual love, for that has already been removed, as has been said, but it is a spiritual love with which the soul desires spiritual consolations or loves some creature spiritually. (I have spoken to you at length regarding the imperfections of such souls.) Wherefore, when such a soul is deprived of the thing she loves, that is, internal or external consolation, the internal being the consolation received from Me, the external being that which she had from the creature, and when temptations and the persecutions of men come on her, her heart is full of grief. And, as soon as the eye feels the grief and suffering of the heart, she begins to weep with a tender and compassionate sorrow, pitying herself with the spiritual compassion of self-love; for her self-will is not yet crushed and destroyed in everything, and in this way she lets fall sensual tears."[20]

St. Thomas Aquinas speaks of it as the mixture of sincere love of God and inordinate love of self. In a sense, it is like a mixture of two competing loves, a sort of alloy. This description of St. Thomas will become more important in the third conversion. We still have to learn how to love God for His sake alone. It takes patience. It takes time to develop a sense of the continual presence of God.

In Catherine's Dialogue, we find that even among those who have a sincere love of God and devote themselves to His service, many do so for their own profit and satisfaction, and not for the sake of God alone[21]. This imperfection is not obvious and shows itself more clearly when the consolations of God are withdrawn. When this happens, "their love fails and can no longer survive. It becomes weak and gradually cools..." as the consolations are withdrawn. Yet God does this to show the soul how

---

[20]St. Catherine of Siena, The Dialogue of St. Catherine of Siena, Treatise on Prayer, section 13, http://www.ccel.org/c/catherine/dialog/dialog1.0.txt, 1995.

[21]Ibid, section 9

imperfect its love is, and to bring the soul to perfection. He sends difficulties and afflictions to help us know ourselves, just as He did for Peter, and to learn that "of themselves they have no grace." If the soul does not recognize its imperfection, and if it does not thereby develop a desire for perfection, and do what is necessary to attain perfection, it will certainly fall back and progress no farther. It generally must do a lot of ego-shedding. Through the adversity we face, we should, if all is going as God wills, seek our refuge in Him, not in ourselves. Our only other solution is to fall back on ourselves, to rely on self to satisfy the void we feel when the consolations are withdrawn. However, to rely on self is trusting in a house built on sand. We must become another Peter, not another Judas. We must run to our Father, fall at His feet, praise Him, thank Him, worship Him, and only then beg His beneficence, forgiveness, and our daily bread. We must grow to love Him for Himself, not because of the consolations He gives us.

If a child does not continue to grow, we say it is stunted, or has arrested development. The same analogy can be said of the soul. The soul does not merely stop, but rather it experiences stunted development. And it all depends on how we respond to the lessons God sends us. Perhaps this is why Jesus said so very often, "Be not afraid."

John of the Cross, in Book I, Chapter 9, of Dark Night[22], gives us three signs by which we can recognize that the second conversion, this purging of ego, is taking place so that we can cooperate with this grace rather than resist it. "(1) The soul finds no pleasure or consolation in the things of God, or in any thing created. (2) Ordinarily the memory is centered upon God, with painful care and solicitude, thinking that it is not serving God, but backsliding, because it finds

---

[22]The Collected Works of St. John of the Cross, trans Kieran Kavanaugh, O.C.D. and Otilio Rodriguez, O.C.D., ICS Publ., Institute of Carmelite Studies, Washington DC, (1991)

itself without sweetness in the things of God. (3) The soul can no longer meditate or reflect in its sense of the imagination. ... For God now begins to communicate Himself to it, no longer through sense, as He did aforetime, by means of reflections which joined and sundered its knowledge, but by an act of simple contemplation, to which neither the exterior nor the interior senses of the lower part of the soul can attain." God Himself now feeds the soul directly. In this regard, St. Catherine of Siena warns the imperfect soul to take great care, for these souls often try to seek the Father alone, without following the way of Jesus crucified, because they have a strong aversion to the suffering they know is required. In modern parlance, they try to reach the Father by doing an end run around Jesus[23]. Yet Jesus has told us plainly that we can only come to the Father through Jesus (Jn 14:6).

Why put ourselves through all this? What are the requisite motivations? One motivation is because the primary commandment is to love God with our whole heart, soul, strength and mind. We reserve none of these for ourselves. We must do it void of any inclinations to self-love or self-attachment. Our whole focus is on love of God. We do what it takes for that to happen. We do not love God from the position of a servant, but rather as a faithful child. We love our Father because He is our Father, not because He gives us gifts. Thus, in the second conversion, through operation of sanctifying grace, we progress from servant of God to child of God. As we become conscious of our life as His true children, He communicates Himself to us more deeply through the gift of contemplation, a special knowledge communicated directly to the soul by God.

Another motivation for us is the price Jesus paid for us to be united to Him, the price of His blood. The value of

---

[23]The Dialogue of St. Catherine of Siena, A Treatise on Prayer, Section 5, http://www.ccel.org/c/catherine/dialog/dialog1.0.txt, 1995.

His precious blood is understood in terms of what it opened up for us, what it allowed us to become, for only through this blood shed for us are we enabled to become children of God (Jn 1:12). The realization of what this truly means to us is part of the conversion process and motivates us to endure the passive purgation of the senses that accompanies this second conversion. We learn to love the God of consolations, not the consolations of God.

But if we are motivated by this love, we will also have an increased zeal for souls as an accompanying motive, for how can we love God and not love Him in other souls, not love those souls for whom He paid such a high price, not love those other souls He also loves so much? We have the examples of many souls who have been selected by God to be victim souls just for this purpose. This zeal for souls is a result of God's infinite mercy working in us, and an act of His love by which He allows us to participate in His redemptive work through the operation of the Mystical Body.

We see Him now with the eyes of Faith and we love Him with the love He gives us, which we recognize as His own divine love acting in us. We realize, perhaps for the first time, we can only love Him with His own gift of love. When we reach Heaven, we will see Him in the beatific vision, and will love Him with the same love with which He loves Himself.

In undergoing this second conversion, as we enter into the illuminative way, we reap further benefits of God's love. One such benefit is an entry into contemplative prayer. We begin to contemplate the great mysteries of our faith; the great mysteries of the incarnation, the cross, redemption, the Mass, the Eucharist, and the indwelling Trinity. We gain an even greater appreciation of the price of His blood paid for our individual soul. Our relationship with God, our encounter with Him, now becomes more personal than ever, more continuous as opposed to occasional. We have become His constant friend and companion, and He ours, not just a servant who comes when beckoned. We become much more aware of God always with us, of God within us, of God's constant presence dwelling within our soul. We become more aware of His intense interest in and governance of our lives and we encourage His governance. The statement we have heard so often, that in a life with God there are no coincidences, now takes on real meaning. We experience the reality of becoming not just sanctified, but sanctified in Him. The burning in the heart the apostles experienced on the road to Emmaus (Lk 24:13) should also be our experience as we encounter God more fully.

Love is the key to contemplation. In contemplating the indwelling Trinity, we are reminded of the promise of Jesus in Jn 14:23, "If any one loves me, he will keep my word, and my Father will love him, and We will come to him and will make Our abode with him." As the Father and Son love each other, that Love is personified as the Holy Spirit. If they love us, and dwell within us, because we keep His word, we are the temple of the indwelling Trinity. But this infinite love is so powerful that when we are the object of that love and open to accept it, we, too, are transformed and take on the nature of that love, we take on the divine nature, for only by operation of our free will can we reject the effects of the power of the love of God who desires to unite us to Himself. How it must hurt Him when we turn our backs on this love through sin. In the first letter of John, he tells us that "he who abides in love abides in God, and God in him." (1 Jn 4:16) Luke tells us, "For lo, the kingdom of God is within you."(Lk 17:20) St. Thomas Aquinas tells us that God's love does not presuppose that there is anything in us which is loveable, but rather creates that lovableness in us.

The life of contemplation is one of growing intimacy with mystery. The great mysteries of our faith are the subjects of our contemplation. In the incarnation we might contemplate the awesome desires in the heart of God that led the Creator of the universe to become a tiny embryonic human, a most helpless being, all for love of us. Mary has just spent the last several years immersed in study in the Temple. Suddenly, the angel Gabriel addresses this young teenage woman by the title given to her by God, not by her familiar name. He addresses her with the salutation, "Hail, full of grace." She already has the fullness of grace before she becomes pregnant. She is told by the angel that she will be the mother of God. She does not panic, but simply asks the pivotal question. How? What infused knowledge of the Trinity must she have received for her to give her fiat? What trust she must have had in God to give this fiat before being married. What infusion of grace and knowledge had to occur only six weeks later for Elizabeth to so readily recognize Mary as "the mother of my Lord"(Lk 1:43) without Mary even saying she is pregnant? When Mary and Joseph went to Jerusalem for the presentation, what joy, humility and awe was in Mary's heart as she presented Jesus to Him whom she knew to be Jesus' Father; as she considered her selection and her role in this pivotal event in salvation history? How much of all this did she understand? Did she wonder what else God would ask of her?

In contemplating the passion, in addition to the suffering of Jesus, we might contemplate the extent to which Mary understood it was her spiritual children who were the players in what her only-begotten Son was suffering, and what that did to her heart. We might contemplate what Jesus saw from the cross; the multitude of expressions in the faces around Him, the walls of the city soon to be destroyed, the temple that would stand no more.

If we contemplate the Eucharist, we might ponder the essential relationship between the Eucharist and the indwelling Trinity, and to what extent love affects the level of grace received during reception of the Eucharist or during Eucharistic adoration.

We can also let our eyes scan the pages of scripture until some word or phrase reaches out and grabs our heart. When this happens we stop, and continuing to look at this passage, we let God work within us.

Our life of contemplation grows without need for consolations from God, almost in replacement of consolation. For some, the purgation suffered is very hard, at least in the beginning, for the crutch of consolation has become a focal issue. We have been taught by the saints not to love the consolations of God more than the God of consolation. That is very difficult for some, because they feel that God withdrawing His consolations means He does not love them or care about them any more, or is somehow rejecting or punishing them. Yet all of the spiritual masters tell us He is closer to us during this time of purgation than at any other time. He is calling us to love Him for Himself, because of who He is, not because of what He does for us. He is God, the almighty One, and we owe Him our love and devotion regardless of consolations or the lack of consolations. And He loves us as His child, because we are His child, in spite of our warts, sins, and all of our imperfections. He is trying to bring us to perfection.

Sometimes the hold of the world is still strong, even though not fully realized. As God begins to act in our lives, He may withdraw not only His consolations, but also those things we hold dear. He has to bring us to a state where we truly live the commandment to love God with our whole being so we can completely turn our backs on attachment to material things. Sometimes we have to lose something to both understand the grip it had on us, and to understand how we can get along without it if we place our trust and hope in God, and place our lives and future in His hands, at His disposal.

In some cases, God may remove either things, or people, or both from our lives. He may remove a loved one, or remove personal health, or social status, or the esteem in which we are held in the eyes of others. As these things happen, the suffering soul may cry out and try to hold on even tighter to the things to which he is attached, holding on so tight his knuckles turn white. Then He may remove the knuckles.

He continues until finally the soul falls to its knees, and looking up at God cries out, "Why me? Why now? What more will you take from me? What else do you want from me?" He will look on the soul with love and reply, "Whatever it is you prefer to hold onto instead of holding Me." Then He will say, "Take My hand," and if we are able to respond to this grace and place our hand in His, He will draw us into His embrace, fill us with Himself and we will finally understand what He has been trying to offer us for so long, and we will have our 'Peter' experience. We have finally stopped denying Him, stopped preferring self or others, stopped fearing the opinion of others, and have accepted His mercy and love. We desire to love Him above all else, so now, finally, He can work in us largely unimpeded.

In this period of mixed trial and ecstasy, we learn the intimate relationship between Divine love, suffering, and conversion. They come together, and are held together, because of God's desire for us. We cannot do an end run around to avoid any one of the three: love, suffering or conversion. The degrees may vary among us, but, because we love God, we march through, we endure, and we persevere - as St. Teresa of Avila so often advises us. We come out the other side, we get to the other end of the first bridge, whole, purified, and more fully converted, more fully in love with God, than ever. We literally fall in love with God, with the Eucharist.

During this time, you also understand how difficult it is to speak with those still on the first plateau and communicate to them a true understanding of what you have become after this second conversion. We see this in St. Teresa's Interior Castle. She will say at about the fourth mansions, and again at the sixth, how she cannot explain what she really means, but those who have been through it will understand. It is like a seventeen year old trying to have a meaningful conversation about teenage kinds of things with a three year old. You can understand what they are experiencing but they cannot understand what you are experiencing, for they have no experiential basis for absorbing what you say. Nowhere is this more true than when you contemplate Divine Love, or the indwelling Trinity, and then try to explain to someone on the first plateau what has been communicated to you about them. All you can say is something like, "God loves you", or "God dwells in you", and the more you try the more frustrating it becomes, for no words exist to convey what you know interiorly with such certitude and in such depth. It is reminiscent of what Jesus told His disciples in the account of the washing of the feet in the gospel of John, when He said, "What I am doing you do not understand now, but you will understand later." (Jn 13:7)

I once went to a healing Mass at Our Lady of Angels Church in Woodbridge, Virginia offered by an elderly and very holy priest. In the homily, he was trying to help us understand how much God loves us and how important it is for us to understand this. He kept saying, "You must understand how much God loves you." The tears were streaming down his face and you could hear the frustration in his voice as he struggled to find words to express the depth of what he wanted us to understand, but there were no words capable of doing so.

The proficients on this second plateau observe those on the first plateau and see some of their brethren perhaps still enamored with the latest car, or fashion, or vacation spot, or picture phone, or Palm Pilot, or any of the hundred other things that seem so very important. People are collecting thousands of sports cards, as if they had real intrinsic value. People devoting enormous amounts of time and money to all sorts of things having no spiritual value whatever saddens you, not only because of the waste of time, but because of the energy and funds, that could be doing so much good for others, going to waste on things having no real intrinsic value at all.

You sometimes see priests who view themselves as the object of servitude from others instead of being the servants of souls; whose zeal for souls has waned; who are so focused on self they have completely missed the whole concept of being a good shepherd, of the obligation they have to bring the beauty and truth of the faith home to rest in the hearts of those souls entrusted to them, a beauty and truth given life by love. They fail in their duty to teach, but more importantly they fail in their duty to love. These people of God never seem to understand why they are still beginners in spirituality, even after many years in the priesthood or religious life. Tauler, in his Spiritual Exercises, explains it as follows:

Secondly there are the people who are devoted to religious life, enjoying great esteem and a reputation for holiness. They think that they have left the darkness far behind them; and yet in their hearts they are Pharisees, full of self-love and self-will, and in fact interested in nothing but themselves. If you judge only by externals you cannot see them for what they are, but if the Spirit of God is within you, you will know them. In fact, even outwardly there is one way of distinguishing them from those who truly love God: you will always find them sitting in judgment upon other people, even upon God's true lovers, but never upon themselves; whereas those who truly love God judge only themselves.[24]

[24]Johann Tauler, O.P., Spiritual Conferences, TAN Books, Rockford, (1978), pg 59

In our journey through the conversions we see many along the roadside, like broken down cars, souls whose real journey has come to a stop, some permanently. We even see committed Catholics - lay, professed religious brothers and sisters, even some priests - who are like the shallow soil in the gospel. They hear the message, become enthused for a time, but the commitment is not there, the love does not run deep. They receive the seed, it sprouts in them, but the commitment has not been nourished by mortification, prayer of the heart, and love of others instead of self. Love of self is still too strong to release, and yet it is like spiritual poison.

Tauler tells us that to overcome self-love, "the only thing which works is for God to take possession of you and inhabit you; and this He only does for those who love Him."[25] These misguided souls will wander always on the first plateau, or will slide back down the slope to return among the masses on the plains. Vocations are lost or never fulfilled. Work in the vineyard is left undone, or has to be done by others already overly busy in the vineyard.

The greatest value some of these misguided souls have in the Kingdom, unless they convert, is to be someone to love who is not easy to love, an opportunity for others to live the gospel. These souls with stunted growth remain too fixed on what is being left behind to appreciate what is to come. Jesus said, "No one who sets a hand to the plow and looks to what was left behind is fit for the kingdom of God." Lk 9:62

The Second Bridge

But even the faithful proficients on the second plateau are not always ready to cross that second bridge bringing them to spiritual marriage with God. There is a still

---

[25]Johann Tauler, O.P., Spiritual Conferences, TAN Books, Rockford, (1978), pg 59

another spiritual crisis facing them. There is one last bridge to cross, one last conversion to experience.

It is not inappropriate to ask at this point why a third conversion is necessary, why that second bridge has to be crossed. What is there that is left to correct? In this state, the soul must undergo another purgation. This time it is not a purgation of the senses, but a purgation of the spirit. The focus here is on the intellect and the will, the deeper parts of the soul. In order to receive the graces of Pentecost, the apostles had to have a purgation of the spirit to be fully prepared to be filled with the Holy Spirit. In receiving the Holy Spirit as fully as they did at Pentecost, the apostles experienced the gift of illumination, and they received the power of the Holy Spirit. This conversion was a complete transformation of the soul, and was necessary for them to exhibit the subsequent courage they did. In this conversion, the apostles were filled with infused contemplation of the profound mystery of what they had recently experienced, the profound mystery of the Cross and Resurrection, and full understanding of their mission as apostles. They had to go out and bring the message of the gospel to the whole world, even at the cost of their own lives.

The effects produced in them flowed out from them and into those they encountered. When we obtain the grace of contemplation, we contemplate the mysteries of Faith. When we receive the grace of infused contemplation of these mysteries, are we not on the normal path to sanctity, just as the apostles? What then are the remaining faults which must be purged before we can enter into complete union with God?

In Dark Night - Book II, St John of the Cross enumerates a few which deal only with the inner soul. He tells us that if he were to try to list all the faults, the list would be endless. The list will also be filled with faults we would never recognize on the first plateau, some which we then might even have considered semi-virtues. This final preparation is necessary because at this level, where the soul passes from proficient to perfect, in fulfillment of Christ's command to be perfect as the Father is perfect (Mt 5:48), we must have a true purity of soul, humility, and must gain a much more profound understanding of the theological virtues of faith, hope and charity. St. John of the Cross calls this final purgation the removing of rust from the intellect and will. Some of the faults and signs he enumerates which still need purging are:

- Roughness and impatience;

- A strong attachment to our own point of view;

- We imagine we have received a special inspiration from God, but in reality we are victims of Satan or our own lively imagination;

- We are puffed up with presumption, spiritual pride, and vanity;

- We depart from the true path or lead others astray;

- We are filled with the sisters of spiritual pride; intellectual pride, jealousy, and hidden ambition.

We might stop now to consider whether we recognize these faults as our own. Have we ever considered them as faults to overcome, or have they been on the back burner, to be dealt with later? Have we tried to rid ourselves of them? If not, why? If we find them present, what can we do to remove these faults and move forward in perfection? Is there someone we know who could help?

In her Interior Castle, St. Teresa of Avila tells us in chapter nine of the sixth Mansions that some souls who think they have intellectual visions of God in reality have an "imagination that is so weak, or their understanding is so nimble, or for some other reason their imagination becomes so much absorbed, that they actually think they see everything that is in their mind. If they had ever seen a true vision they would realize their error beyond the possibility of doubt." One clue she gives us that the soul has fallen for this trick of the mind is that a true vision will be extremely brief. She tells us that "When the soul is able to remain for a long time looking upon the Lord, I do not think it can be a vision at all. It must rather be that some striking idea creates a picture in the imagination: but this will be a dead image by comparison with the other [a real vision]." She tells us that a true image is very fleeting, often like lightening, during which God communicates great and secret things about Himself instantly through infused contemplation.

In this third conversion, from child to betrothed to spouse, we recognize very powerfully the work of the Holy Spirit. Just as it was His work with the apostles at Pentecost, so it is His with us. As He works in us and digs deeper within our soul, purging it of all that is not of God, He must, for a time, darken our intellect and control our will through aridity. The dryness we experience is characteristic of the work of the Holy Spirit. When this happens, we must reach down in the very depths of our soul and find that rock upon which Jesus built everything. We must find that anchor of faith, that vessel of hope, that wellspring of life which is His love. The solid spiritual structure of the soul formed much earlier through the scaffolding and mortar of sound theology and teaching, now withstands the test. It endures the spiritual storm. When we experience our aridity, just as the apostles did between the Ascension and Pentecost, we fall back on what He has given us. We hunker down and wait for Him in hope to rescue us.

In the purgation required for our third conversion, we are being tested in the spiritual fire. Earlier, I referred to St. Thomas Aquinas' description of the mix of self love and love for God within us; that alloy of loves. Now, in this final purgation, the self-love must be purged. The soul is tested with the fire of God's love. The gold of God settles, and the impurities of self-love are skimmed off the top. All that remains is the gold, which is love for God. We are finally prepared for union with Him Whom we love above all others, above all else, including self. We hold ourselves as nothing, God as everything. He now gives us all; He gives us Himself. "How much more will the Father in heaven give the Holy Spirit to those who ask Him?" (Lk 11:13)

The intellect is filled with understanding as God now communicates Himself to the soul, the gift of infused contemplation. The will is filled with divine love for God. We experience God as we have never before experienced Him. We have an experience similar to that of the apostles. An example is in Acts 2:22-36, where Peter now understands the mystery of redemption, now understands why Jesus had to be a willing victim, finally understands the value and merits of the precious blood for him and for each one of us. Priests who reach this level develop such a profound love for the Mass that they experience it as they never could have before. They truly live the Mass. We see this in the autobiography of St. Ignatius Loyola and in the Masses offered by Padre Pio. The beauty of God's love is that now we, too, can live the Mass.

Many who read and think about the Pentecost story tend to focus on the outward signs, the tongues of fire and the gift of tongues in particular, since the account in Acts emphasizes it so. It is not the gift of tongues that was the real gift, but rather the profound understanding of the mysteries of faith, an understanding and faith which God charged the apostles with spreading. Thus, the Holy Spirit gave them the gift through which they could do this most readily. This is why St. Paul tells us the gift of tongues is the least of the gifts.

Another gift we often don't think much about, one Jesus mentioned many times in His conversations with the apostles and others, is courage. "Be not afraid," He told them. Courage is one thing. Courage to the point of martyrdom is truly a gift of the Holy Spirit.

And so as we stand on this third plateau, we will each be called by God to some task of love. The tasks are many, the trials many and in some cases severe, but there is one common objective and motive for us all. That objective is love for God, and Him alone. We cannot have a higher call. We cannot accomplish a greater work. We cannot have a greater work accomplished in us by Him. And we arrive here by being little, by serving, by being willing to be the least among others; by faith, hope, humility, love, courage and prudence.

The Consummation Covenant

Why did Jesus have to give us a new covenant? Why is it the everlasting covenant?

These two questions are so very fundamental to our interior relationship to Christ and His Church, and to Christianity in general, that we must give them great consideration. We begin by reflecting on Psalm 139 and two passages from the gospel of St. John.

Psalm 139

O Lord, you have probed me and you know me; you know when I sit and when I stand; you understand my thoughts from afar.

My journeys and my rest you scrutinize, with all my ways you are familiar. Even before a word is on my tongue, behold, O Lord, you know the whole of it. Behind me and before me, you hem me in and rest your hand on me.

Such knowledge is too wonderful for me; too lofty for me to attain.

Where can I go from your spirit? From your presence where can I flee?

If I take the wings of the dawn, if I settle at the farthest limits of the sea, even there your hand shall guide me, and your right hand shall hold me fast.

Truly you have formed my inmost being; you knit me in my mother's womb. I give you thanks that I am fearfully, wonderfully made; wonderful are your works.

My soul you also knew full well; nor was my frame unknown to you when I was made in secret, when I was fashioned in the depths of the earth. Your eyes have seen my actions; in your book they are all written; my days were limited before one of them existed.

Probe me, O God, and know my heart; try me, and know my thoughts;

See if my way is crooked, and lead me in the way of old.

Gospel of St. John

The One who sent Me is with Me. He has not left Me alone, because I always do what is pleasing to Him. (Jn 8:29)

Whoever loves me will keep my word, and my Father will love him, and we will come to him and make our dwelling with him.

(Jn 14:23)

The doctrine of the Indwelling Trinity is founded in this last quote from the fourteenth chapter of the gospel of John. But if we meditate on all three of these selections, we can see how beautifully the doctrine expresses the intended effect revealed to us by God through His chosen people. Psalm 139 is so incredibly beautiful, and lays down such a marvelous foundation for the doctrine of the Indwelling Trinity. Read Psalm 139 slowly and see how wonderfully the relationship between God and David is expressed. David is absolutely awestruck by his realization of the continual loving presence of God with him. He sings that God is always with him, before him and behind him; God's hand is always on him. God knew David intimately before he came into existence. God knit him in his mother's womb. His every thought is known by God before it is ever expressed. God knows the depths of his soul; every action he has ever taken is known and remembered by God, and even the number of his days is known. And how does David respond? He says "Probe me, O God, and know my heart; try me, and know my thoughts; See if my way is crooked, and lead me in the way of old." What a beautiful expression of trust, fidelity and love.

What is so striking to me in Psalm 139 is David's understanding of the inseparability of God's intimate knowledge of him and God's uncompromising love for him as an individual. In our everyday life we encounter so many different people, and there is hardly anyone in whom we would confide all of the innermost secrets of our heart and life. We value their feelings toward us, and we instinctively know that their love for us is usually dependent to some extent on their knowledge of us. So we hide parts of our inner self so as not to jeopardize that love, for we crave to be loved. But in this beautiful psalm, David tells us that God knows us intimately, completely, down to the core of our being, body and soul, and still loves us no matter what He knows about us. He wants to be with us. He wants us to want Him to be with us. The profound knowledge God has of us, and His simultaneous infinite love for us, cannot be separated. He will love us infinitely in spite of anything we might do, for He already knows what we will do and loves us anyway. What we do is never a surprise to Him, even if it is a surprise to us. David tells us how we, too, should respond.

He does not tell us to act as we do toward men, trying to hide parts and parcels of our inner self. Mindful of God's infinite knowledge and love, David says, with full confidence, "Probe me, O God, and know my heart; try me, and know my thoughts; See if my way is crooked, and lead me in the way of old." How different from the willful and self-centered condition so prevalent in our world. Probe me, and lead me; submission to the will of God because of confidence and trust in God's inseparable love and knowledge. David also understands how much God desires this intimate and loving relationship with each of us individually and what He is willing to forgive to achieve it.

The possibility of punishment, demanded by justice, evokes fear. God much prefers that we respond in love, for He is love. When He responds with punishments, it is only because we have forced that response demanding His justice. His greatest attribute is mercy[26], and He always prefers to exercise mercy before justice, but we must do our part to open the door to His mercy. His mercy is a gift, not our right. We must seek His mercy, preferably in humility rather than from fear. The confidence we should have in the love of God for us, seen in Psalm 139, is mirrored when Jesus speaks to us in the eighth chapter of John. The Father is always with Him and has never left Him alone. Why? Because He always does the Father's will. "I always do what is pleasing to Him." (Jn 8:29)

In Jesus' statement, we see a parallel to Psalm 139 in that both speak of the continual presence of God with them, but they also speak of the desire to submit to the will of God as a condition of that intimate relationship. In David's case, he recognizes the failings of his human nature and begs God to probe him, determine the errors of his ways in every respect, and then lead him on the right path. In the case of Jesus, isn't He telling us that He has never failed, has never sinned, has never been separated, even for an instant, from the Father? Jesus always does what is pleasing to the Father. What a beautiful expression of intimacy in His relationship to the Father. He does not say He tries to do the will of the Father. He says He does; no exceptions. He does not ask to be corrected by the Father, for there is no need. How could any other man say this? Jesus is leading us into the doctrine of the Indwelling Trinity. He is leading by example.

All of the above leads us into the full teaching of the Indwelling Trinity found in Jn 14. We see the same conditions, the same filial relationship expressed in Jn 8.

---

[26]Divine Mercy in My Soul, paragraph 301, Marian Press, Stockbridge (1987).

However, this new revelation of the indwelling presence of the Triune God in our soul is the essence of the New Testament covenant relationship established at the Last Supper, the essence of being the new chosen people of God who respond to those who went into the whole world to preach the gospel (Mk 16:15-16). The central key to the Divine intimacy called for by the new covenant is the indwelling Trinity. The new objective is not just to have God always near us, but always within us; to be intimately united with God, in what St. John of the Cross calls the transforming union; to ultimately have the infinite God within our finite soul in such a way that we become one with Him by participation. As we saw before, this level of transforming intimacy is not common, but we still have the indwelling Trinity when we are in a state of grace, for we have loved Jesus enough to have kept His word at least to that extent. We are true temples of God when we are in the state of grace. (1 Cor 3:16)

The character of being chosen by God means much the same thing to us today as it meant to the Jews. God has extended to us the same chosen-ness He had extended previously only to the Jews. He had made covenants with the Jews, covenants which were repeatedly broken by man, but He will not abandon them.

At the Last Supper, Jesus made a new covenant, an everlasting covenant, not with one nation, but with a borderless nation made up of all, Jew or gentile, who desire to accept Christ and be a part of His new nation, His new eternal kingdom. He made this covenant with His apostles and those who would follow His teachings given through them (Jn 17:20-21). It is a covenant sealed in His Blood. It is everlasting, and thus will never be repeated or replaced. It is the final covenant between God and man. Thus we have the words of the consecration in the Mass of Pius V, "This is the chalice of My Blood, of the new and everlasting covenant: the Mystery of Faith. It will be shed for you and for many for the remission of sin." The Eucharist is the central mystery of faith and the binding instrument of the New Covenant.

The significance of this, and the role and responsibility we have as a chosen people in the life of the Church, is to recognize the importance of this gift, and to live our part of this new covenant. It was sealed in the blood of God, not the blood of an ox or goat or sheep. It is the fullness of the covenant relationship with God. Accepting this offering of His blood on our behalf gives us the power to become children of God (Jn 1:12), His chosen ones. "When the Son of Man is lifted up, I will draw all men to Myself." (Jn 12:32) All are given the opportunity. All are called. Those who respond to the call of the Father are given to Jesus as His own, and He is their Savior (Jn 6:44).

In His final prayer to the Father, Jesus said, "I pray for them. I do not pray for the world but for the ones you have given me, because they are yours, and everything of mine is yours and everything of yours is mine, and I have been glorified in them." (Jn 17:9-10) Those the Father gives to Him are the ones who respond to the call (Jn 6:44). It is they who bear the responsibility to live the covenant life. It is they to whom Jesus referred as the "many" for whom His Blood would be shed when He said at the Last Supper, "... which is poured out for many...". (Mt 26:28)

To do this, we must keep the Commandments. This will let us enter Heaven, as Jesus told the rich young man. But Jesus also calls us all to a life of perfection. In His encounter with the rich young man, "Jesus said to him, "If you wish to be perfect, go, sell what you have and give to (the) poor, and you will have treasure in heaven. Then come, follow me."" (Mt 19:21) He calls each of us to a state of being where we can meet His challenge to "be you perfect as the Heavenly Father is perfect." (Mt 5:48) He is calling us all to put aside everything of our own making that stands between us and God, that creates a veil or division between us, and walk with Him, taking His hand, letting Him lead us into His kingdom to share in His inheritance.

The Church, recognizing the responsibility to which it is called, and recognizing the leadership provided by the Holy Spirit since Pentecost, assumes a role which is both teacher and minister. The Church is obligated to do what it can to lead us and prepare us spiritually to receive the Holy Spirit so He can make us holy, divinize our souls, and make us true children of God. Our responsibility is to acknowledge this Spirit-led mission, and respond faithfully. To do otherwise is to behave as the grumbling Israelites in the desert, never satisfied, always wanting something different and more to their own liking. God said that for forty years He endured these people, and not one of the adults entered the promised land (Num 32:13).

To live the covenant life is to live a life of submission to God's will - His plan for us. That is the life and mission of the Church. Our manna is the Eucharist. Our life is the Holy Spirit, for Jesus said "I am the Way, the Truth, and the Life." (Jn 14:6) We follow, He leads. We submit, He sanctifies.

In reflecting upon the idea of chosen-ness and what it means to the Church, there are some additional things to consider. In Psalm 139, in that beautiful prayer of love, David is almost mesmerized by God's infinite love for us and His knowledge of us. Nothing David can do will make God stop loving him. And so David says 'probe me and lead me'. This psalm epitomizes the height of the expressible relationship the Jews had with God. It is a betrothal, but not a marriage, even though He called Israel to spiritual marriage (Is 54:5), and characterized Israel's unfaithfulness as adultery (Jeremiah 3:6-9; Hosea 1, 2).

This developing relationship of love is seen in the chain of covenants God established with man. God established His covenants with Noah (Genesis 9), Abraham

(Genesis 15) and then Moses, whose covenant was ratified by Israel (Exodus 24). Each covenant describes a closer and more intimate relationship. This relationship is paralleled in the marital relationship between a man and woman. There is first an acquaintance and a desire to get to know each other better. This progresses to a relationship of affection and growing trust. This leads to a betrothal in love where the man and woman make certain promises and commitments to each other. Finally, the relationship is consummated in marriage where the fullness of the relationship can be explored without limit for the remainder of their lives. There can be no further covenant between them that would bring the relationship between them any closer.

We cannot effect this intimacy with God, this closeness, without the Church. It was Christ Himself who established the Church and He gave no alternatives. It was only through the Church that Jesus provided the one instrument of His mercy instituted for the forgiveness of sin (Mt 16:18-19; Jn 20:21-23), effected through His own sacrifice (Mt 26:27-28). If we desire to know God and do His will, we become part of His Church and serve Him as a member of His Mystical Body. To do otherwise is to put our will ahead of God's will, and if we do that we serve self first, and then God. In so doing, we fail the test of the First Commandment. His commandments are commandments of love, even though none of the Ten Commandments contains the word 'love'. Jesus told us that all the commandments and all the law are founded on the two great commandments of love. It is only through the Church that God gives us the greatest fruits of His love: forgiveness of sin and the Eucharist.

In the same way the relationship between a man and woman progresses, we see the relationship between God and His chosen people progress; from acquaintance to affection and, with Moses, to a form of betrothal. We hear in the words of consecration of the chalice at Mass, "This is the chalice of My Blood, of the new and everlasting covenant...". In Jesus Christ, God brought the covenant relationship to full consummation, to union with God, to the level of spiritual marriage. It can go no further on earth. That is why it is the new and everlasting covenant. Everything in the Old Testament was the shadow of this fulfilling reality of intimate divine love.

The covenant of betrothal through Moses was also the time when God gave us the Ten Commandments. Jesus told us that all the Commandments and all the Law were founded on His two commandments of love (Mt 22:34-40). This tells us how the Ten Commandments should be read by our hearts and lived; not legalistically, but as expressions of how people who love each other should behave toward each other. They are commandments of love that should not require enforcement.

In Jn 8 Jesus expresses His relationship with the Father. It is not just a filial relationship as we think of it, but one which is so deep and so intimate that, unlike David, He never has to ask the Father to probe Him and lead Him in right ways. He always does the will of the Father. He does not try; He does. And He knows He does. Every moment of every day He knows and does the will of the Father.

In Jn 14:23, Jesus finally reveals the doctrine of the indwelling Trinity, "If any man loves Me, he will keep My word, and the Father will love him, and We will come to him and make Our abode in him." This one thing is what the covenant relationship of the Church is most characterized by; it is the fruition of our chosen-ness. We cannot separate chosen-ness and covenant. This fruition, when taken to completion, is the spiritual marriage with God that takes place in the innermost depths of the soul. It brings to the state of spiritual marriage that betrothal relationship described by David in Psalm 139.

In Psalm 139, God was seen as close but outside, caring for us, leading us, guiding us, protecting us, teaching us. The God who is committed to us and we to Him by covenant, the God who was always by our side, can now, in Jesus, become the bridegroom of our soul. The betrothal is over, the spiritual marriage can be consummated through Jesus and the Holy Spirit. Just as marriage is as far as the relationship can go between man and woman, the spiritual marriage of our soul with the indwelling Trinity is as far as we can go this side of Heaven. There is no spiritual relationship more intimate than that which exists within the Trinity itself. It is only through the activity of Jesus and the Holy Spirit that the spiritual union between our soul and our Triune God can take place.

In marriage, the union intent and reality is externally symbolized by the rings and the ceremony. These things are symbols and signs for others to see because they are external to the relationship. But the real marriage takes place within the couple as they give themselves to each other, and is consummated later, when the two give themselves completely, each to the other. The consummation is real, not symbolic. There are no stand-ins, no proxies. Consummation is the giving of self, one to the other, in the most intimate way possible. It seals the covenant relationship. Thus, when Jesus determined to give Himself to us in the spiritual union between man and God, it was an individual union and giving of Himself, living and complete, which had to be, and has to be, real and total, not symbolic. He will not enter into spiritual marriage with our soul by proxy, or only symbolically. When He brings us to the state of spiritual marriage, He gives Himself to us completely, and we give ourselves to Him; He consummates the union between man and God the only way He could; in the Holy Eucharist. No other way would work, for the consummation must be experienced and known by both. The consummation has to be the union between the individual soul and the living God, and thus the Eucharist must be real, not symbolic, and the union must be with a soul He has made to be like Himself. The external appearances of bread and wine are like the wedding rings, symbols of the reality taking place within the soul, the outward sign of the consummation. The consummation with God cannot be by proxy, not even through the apostles. It has to be real, with us and within our soul. It has to be effected through our individual and willing participation. This is the reality St. Teresa of Avila is describing for us in the seventh mansions in Interior Castle. It cannot happen merely because we are in a state of grace, and cannot happen merely by our receiving the Eucharist, for our soul may not be sufficiently prepared, sufficiently purified for this union. It happens when we have progressed sufficiently through prayer for our soul to be brought by God into spiritual union, and only He knows when we have reached that state of purification.

Consummation with God must be individually entered into, just as it must be between and husband and wife. It is not just living a covenant entered into between your spiritual ancestor and God. It is the fruition of the development of your personal relationship with your God and Savior. It is that which makes your union with God real and substantial and requires your divinization. Like must consummate with like. God must make us like Himself to consummate the union with us. If the consummation were merely symbolic, it would be like an exchange of rings with no wedding night, and the substantial union between your soul and God would not take place. The true potential effect of the indwelling Trinity could not become real, could not progress beyond a promise. We would be no further advanced individually in the man-God relationship than the Jews who wandered the desert. We would know more, and more would have been revealed to us, but we would remain in a state of perpetual betrothal. The covenant with Christ would have no meaning, for the Messiah had already been promised and the betrothal had already been accomplished. No new covenant was needed for the Messiah to come. The new covenant was needed for more than just salvation to be accomplished. It was needed for substantial union between man and God. This cannot happen if the Eucharist is only a symbol.

In the consummation between the perfected man or woman and God, effected through the Eucharist, the Indwelling Trinity and man become spiritually one. The fullness of revelation found in Jesus brings with it the fullness of the relationship, the fulness of what we should be, the fullness of the chosen-ness and the consummation of the covenant relationship. That is why Jesus said what He did at the Last Supper. This Eucharistic union, this consummation, is *The* Mystery of Faith. It is the new and everlasting covenant, sealed in His Blood, because it is the culmination of the entire history of covenants, from acquaintance to spiritual marriage. That is why the Jews should have recognized the importance of this. They should have seen that a betrothal without a marriage is just teasing; a promise of unity that would never come without Jesus. The marriage had to come, it had to, for the fidelity of God demanded it. God even told them He desired this consummation with Himself (Ezekiel 16:1-14), told them how they would betray Him (Ezekiel 16:15-58), but also told them He will still forgive them in spite of their sin (Ezekiel 16:60-63). He told them, and us, through the Messianic prophet Isaiah "The One who has become your husband is your maker; his name is the Lord of hosts; your Redeemer is the Holy One of Israel, called God of all the earth." (Is 54:5)

In looking only for an earthly king, a Messiah who would restore Israel to earthly power, the Jews who rejected Jesus missed the most important event in the entire covenant relationship. The consummating covenant is what Jesus brought, doing so through the lineage of David who had expressed the betrothal so beautifully in Psalm 139.

In hindsight, the link between God's desire to consummate the God-man relationship and the revelation of the indwelling Trinity is so clear. Jesus brought to completion the chain of covenants, brought to fullness the revelation of God to man, brought to maturity the relationship between God and man, and granted us a familial unity with God, through the gift of the indwelling Trinity. Jesus accomplishes this through the gift of the Eucharist and its effects on our soul. The natural end of consummation between man and woman results in new life as the expression of their love. In like manner, the consummation between man and God, through the effects of the Eucharist, results in new Life, Divine Life, in man, transforming him. He does not become God, or a god, but participates in the Trinitarian life of God through this gift of God.

At the time of the original Passover, the mark of protection was the blood of the lamb on the doorpost. The indwelling Trinity is the mark of our chosen-ness today, the net effect of the completion of the covenant relationship. The Life of the Trinity acting on our soul is the evidence of our belonging to God. This is what separates us from all other people who are, or who ever were. It is our indelible mark of uniqueness in salvation history. It is the ultimate gift to all those who respond to the call of the Father and for whom Jesus prayed to the Father in Jn 17.

But we must do more than attend Mass and receive the Eucharist. We must develop the relationship and we do that principally through prayer. We must be open to prayer if we are to truly know and love Jesus in a perfect way. Without prayer, our spiritual growth comes to a grinding halt. It is through prayer that we develop the relationship that allows us to reap the full benefits of the Mass and the Eucharist.

Relationship is an essential concept here, for it is a true and intimate relationship, not a one-sided authoritarian relationship. We, as a covenant people, living temples of God (1 Corinthians 6:19), true children of God (Jn 1:12), intimately united with the God within us (Jn 14:23), are, as a priest friend once told me, "chosen to be extensions of the Divine kenosis (self-emptying) and, thereby, to be an active 'Divine invasion' into fallen Creation."

All this is continually happening as Jesus develops a distinctly unique and intimate relationship between you and Him deep within your soul as you progress in prayer. It is distinctly your own relationship, responsive to that which makes you unique. He brings Himself to you in a unique union of individual love, and brings us all into union with Him and with each other in the Mystical Body, a union whereby we are all spiritually united to each other through Him. The all-encompassing Mystical Body of Christ, the Church and all of its members, in all of their roles - Church militant, Church Suffering, Church Triumphant - are spiritually united in love through Jesus Christ, the common Head of the Mystical Body. This sense of collective spiritual union with each other, as well as individual union with Christ, requires us to pray for each other, to offer prayer and faith inspired good works for the spiritual healing of each other. These prayers and good works, offered to Jesus, become the spiritual salve used by Jesus to heal those in need.

The richness of the doctrine of the Indwelling Trinity, the importance of it, cannot be probed fully by reason and logic alone. It requires an infusion of grace communicated by the Holy Spirit, a change in our understanding of who we are, and why we are, and what we are. We are each God's child, loved by Him. We are each a being holding the infinite Triune God within. We are each a being made to love God with our whole soul, our whole mind and our whole will. This filial relationship is His gift to us so we can participate in Him as He dwells in us (Jn 17:20-21). All He asks in return is that we love Him, and obey Him. Our love of God and obedience to His commands must be inseparable, just as in Him knowledge of us and love for us are inseparable. We need time with God; time away from the sitcoms, parties and other time consumers which give little or nothing in return. We would never try to develop a relationship leading to marriage if the only time we ever spent together was at parties or large gatherings. We need time alone to talk, discuss ideas, get to know the other's heart, mind and soul; to get to know who the other is, not just what they are. We must do the same with God, and we do that through prayer.

If we love Jesus, if we keep His word, then the Father will love us and They will dwell within us (Jn 14:23). That is Jesus' promise, not just a possibility. The difference now, compared to the old covenant relationship as it was understood before Jesus, is the explicit statement that God dwells within and is not just close at hand watching us from outside and probing our minds and souls. He is in us and we are in Him (Jn 15:5; Jn 6:56; Jn 17:20-21). That same combination of inseparable, intimate and infinite knowledge and love perceived by David, is now united with the very substance of our soul.

Seeking God

A friend of mine wrote, in response to a question asking the difference between seeking God and pursuing God, "Thank you for posting such a thoughtful question. The difference I see is the commitment. To seek God is to look for him in your everyday life, in the people and in the "details". I think you seek God first; you learn the more passive, openness to God's presence. But God calls some to the' chase' - and their hearts do not rest until they rest in God."

When we seek, we look for signs, perhaps for a trail. A hunter may hear that deer are in an area, so he wanders about looking for signs. Similarly, on hearing something about God, some people seek Him. They look for signs that tell them He is real. They search for a spiritual environment, looking for a trail that might lead to evidence He truly exists.

Some people never seek God, for they are afraid of what they will find. They are afraid He might ask too much of them. They would prefer not to have their cushion of comfort disturbed. Nor do they want to see themselves for what they are, for in discovering God they will also discover themselves. They would rather maintain their own notion of who or what God is, and keep Him wrapped up in the cocoon of their own image of Him. They would rather delude themselves into believing they are in control, even in control of how much they will let Him affect their lives. By not seeking to know God they can use the excuse of ignorance to convince themselves they remain in control.

God told us that all we have to do is seek. He said that if we do seek Him genuinely, we will find Him (Mt 7:7). If we knock on the door of His Heart, He will open it for us to enter. He loves us too much to refuse. The only thing we must be concerned about is the genuineness and humility of the inquiry. If we only seek a god to fit our mold, one who will meet our requirements, we are putting ourselves above all else, and God will remain hidden from us. We might just as well build our god out of wood or stone and put it on the mantle next to the incense sticks. When we seek God, we must be ready to accept Him as He reveals Himself to us. What we find is in His hands, not ours.

If we seek Truth, we will find Him, and He will reveal Himself to the heart, for when He reveals Himself, He necessarily reveals His nature, which is pure and infinite Love. If you have pure and unselfish love within you, then you feel the hand of God on your heart. This leads you to seek the one Who is the source of that pure unselfish love, for such a love as He showers upon you and calls forth from you is not a natural thing for any person; it is supernatural. In experiencing this kind of love, you discover that although you seek Him with your mind, you find Him with your heart.

Once we begin our search for God we invariably gain a glimpse of Him, sometimes close and sometimes at a distance. When this happens the natural inclination of the soul is to possess Him and to be possessed by Him. Thus the pursuit begins, just as a hunter who finally spots a deer, or fresh signs of the deer, will pursue his prey. Our objective in pursuing God is to possess the Holy Spirit so He may possess us. We must become docile in His hands so He can do in us what He knows must be done for His great work, for the plan of the Father for us, to bear fruit. To the extent we fail to cooperate, we deprive ourselves of the wonders God had planned for us, the supernatural wine cellar of the mansion Jesus said He was preparing for us in His kingdom, the delights of which, as Jesus told us, the mind of man has not conceived.

Fr. Luis Martinez, the late archbishop of Mexico, said of the Holy Spirit:

"His ideal is to produce Jesus in us, and through Jesus and with Jesus, to take us to the bosom of the Trinity and glorify the Father with the supreme glorification of Jesus. ... To be devoted to the Holy Spirit is to open our soul for Him to dwell there, to dilate our heart that He may anoint it with His divine charity, to deliver our whole being up to Him that He may possess it with His gifts, to give Him our life that He may transform it into a divine one, ... To be devoted to the Holy Spirit is to possess Him and to let ourselves be loved and moved according to His good pleasure; ... to let Him infuse into us a new life, the marvelous participation in the life of God." [27]

All of this means that if the Holy Spirit is to come to us and perform His works in us, He can do so to the extent we are disposed to receive Him, to the extent we have done what we must to prepare for Him. Each of us has what we might call our own little Pentecost, and the extent to which we receive the Holy Spirit, the power of the results of this little Pentecost, is a function of the degree to which the soul is prepared to receive Him. When properly prepared by turning away from the temptations and attachments of this world, when we die to self to live in God, we become those who

"... receive Him [the Holy Spirit] not by way of any mere mode of experience, but within the secret abyss, the hidden kingdom, in the blissful depths of the soul where the noble image of the Holy Trinity lies concealed. The soul has nothing more precious than this." [28]

All of this preparation we make to possess God, to be possessed by God, often requires forsaking a temporal and immediate delight available to us now, in favor of an

---

[27]Martinez, Rev. Luis, The Sanctifier, Daughters of St. Paul, Boston, 1982, pp. 44-45.

[28]Tauler, p. 109

unknown delight in God. Our minds cannot conceive of the treasures God has waiting for us, and it is very hard to desire something about which you know little or nothing, or so it seems. But what is the greatest treasure we could receive? It is God Himself. He gives us Himself, He shares Himself with us out of love for us, and nothing is more precious. Our task is to recognize and prepare for God's gift of Himself.

It is hard to appreciate what we have not sought, desired and pursued. Without pursuit, God remains conceptual and elusive. We have no inner fire of love that fuels a desire for union. God, for us, is distant, uninterested and aloof. He is someone to whom we pray out of obligation, not love, who we think may or may not hear us. We give Him attention occasionally, amidst the many temporal delights toward which we are continually drawn. He is not someone to whom we are willing to make a commitment or a consecration.

But when the soul seeks God, it finds Him. When it asks for the grace to know Him, it will receive. When it knocks on the heart of God, His Heart will open to receive the soul. He refuses no one. When this happens and the Holy Spirit works in us unimpeded, then our pursuit is rewarded as we discover the Trinity within.

"... the image of the Trinity lies in the most intimate region of the soul, in its most secret and inmost depths, where God is present essentially, actually and substantially. Here God acts, makes His home, and rejoices in Himself, and it would be as impossible to separate God from this inmost depth of the soul as it would be to separate Him from Himself. This is by God's eternal decree; He has ordained that He will not and cannot separate Himself. There, in the depths of the soul, the soul possesses by grace all that God has by nature....

There are three who give testimony in heaven, that is, in the interior heaven of our soul: the Father, the Word, and the Holy Ghost. These are your witnesses, who give you true testimony that you are a child of God. They enlighten the depths of your soul, and so your own soul becomes a witness." [29]

---

[29]Johann Tauler, O.P., Spiritual Conferences, TAN Books, Rockford, (1978) pg 142, 145.

Who Is God?

A deacon once asked, *"Who is God, and what does He deserve, in terms of worship, respect, love and justice from His creation?"*

God is our creator, our savior, and our teacher of truth. He is love (1 Jn 4:8), and He is the Spirit of Truth (Jn 16:13). Without Him we could not love. All genuine love that we have comes from Him, and is His gift to us. He is the source of all the good we are, for only He is good (Lk 18:19). He is ever faithful, constant in His love for us, and mindful always of His role as our father, brother, teacher and sanctifier. He is the Way, the Truth and the Life. (Jn 14:6) He is the one who comes to us in each of His persons to teach us how to relate to Him, to help us know Him better, and to help us love Him more. He is our love, our hope and our judge. He will reward us, or pass judgment when we condemn ourselves by our failure to live in accordance with His will. He is the one upon whose act of will we depend for our very existence. Should He not will us to be, we would simply cease to exist and would never have existed, for He exists and operates outside of time.

He deserves everything we can give Him because He is God. He deserves our continual worship, both public and private, through prayer and through liturgy. He deserves our homage, our recognition of who He is, and our subservience to Him. He also deserves our recognition of Him as our loving father, our savior, and our teacher. He deserves all the love we have, for all the love we have comes from Him. He deserves our respect and obedience, because he is God and so that He might avoid having to exercise His justice upon us. Our respect and obedience should come from our love, not our fear. He deserves our truth, so that we do not insult Him, for He is all-knowing. He deserves our love for each other, and our recognition of His presence in each other. He deserves our love for each other for He loves all of us. He deserves our hatred of evil, and all that comes from alliance with evil. He deserves our commitment to Him, our fiat. He deserves our fear in the sense that we should fear to be so weak as to serve self instead of Him, and in so doing disobey and offend the almighty God who loves us infinitely. If we truly love Him, we will do all in our power to avoid doing anything unloving toward Him, and our greatest fear will be to offend Him who loves so much.

We might ask, *"What do we deserve from God, as His creatures? Not what does He venture to give us, but rather what is it we deserve from God?"*

This is another interesting question from the same deacon who posed the previous question. On our own merit, we deserve nothing. Our dignity as a human being comes solely from the fact that God loves us and has made us His children through Baptism, not from anything we can do because of the use of our talents. Everything meritorious we have is a gratuitous gift from God. The products of those gifts should be offerings of thanks to Him. His gifts should always be used by us for His greater glory. As children of God, because He made us His children through the sacrifice of Jesus and through our cooperation with His will and the acceptance of His sanctifying grace, we become entitled to whatever He has prepared for us; nothing more - nothing less, for anything else we demanded would insult Him, for what He has prepared for is that which is most perfect for us.

He asks us to know Him, to love Him, to worship Him, to serve Him, to live in such a way that we can be in union with Him while we are here, and then be together with Him for all eternity. He asks us to be part of His family, to be His adopted children, to share in the inheritance gained for us by His only-begotten Son, Jesus. He asks us to love one another as we love ourselves. He asks us to trust Him, and to trust in His will for us. He asks us to accept Him and His love for us.

Let us now consider the question *Who is God for me?* as a central issue in our relationship with God. God has a distinctly unique relationship with each of us. He also has three Persons, each of Whom relates to us, and we to Them. The first part of the answer might be to consider which Person you most think of when the word God comes to your mind. Is it God the Father, God the Son and Redeemer, or God the Holy Spirit? Within each of these Persons there are roles and activities that make our relationship with the one God both unique and meaningful for each of us. Some folks never get beyond the all-encompassing God because they don't devote the time it takes to find Him in His Persons. He remains that "entity" they claim to worship on Sunday. Others begin to relate to God in terms of His roles in our lives, such as creator, savior, healer, judge, forgiver, etc. Still others relate to God in terms of the individual Persons of the Trinity, thus bringing the relationship to a more personal, one-on-one level. You can then take great delight in getting to know the Person, with all His attributes and aspects that are important to you at your place in life, Who loves you more than anyone else ever could. You can immerse yourself in your love for that Person and His for you. You can pray in a very personal and intimate way to and with the Father, Jesus or the Holy Spirit. You can engage in this conversation most freely, for there is nothing you can tell Him that He does not already know, and He is always the answer to every problem you have. The Person of the Trinity to Whom you relate strongly today may be different from the Person to whom you relate strongly in two years, but all are Persons of God, so you are not slighting or ignoring God by doing this. You are only discovering more of His infinite depth and dimension, and more of what He wants to share of Himself with you.

It is important to understand this, for God is love, and one of the principal driving forces in any relationship of true love is giving, outpouring, of self to the other. Love is always sharing of yourself with the object of your love. God does this by not only sharing knowledge about Himself with you, but by sharing His very Self with you, all because of His unconditional love for you. He does this through Holy Scripture and through the sacraments, especially Holy Eucharist. He does this by giving you the opportunity to participate enough in His nature to become His adopted child (Jn 1:12).

Is 'Who is God for me' different from "Who is God'?

As you meditate on your own relationships with the three Persons of the Trinity, you may also begin to meditate on the relationships between the Persons and use that to enter into more intimate relationships with all three Persons. As you pray and relate to the Person of Jesus, meditate also on the relationship between Jesus and His Father, and between Jesus and the Holy Spirit. What do the gospels tell you about these relationships? This will open doorways for a relationship with all three Persons that you might not have previously explored, or even considered. Ask Jesus to introduce you to the Holy Spirit or to the One Who is both His Father and your Father. It is an intriguing and moving thing to do, especially since we can never fully comprehend God, but can only know Him by contemplating His attributes. The possibilities for exploration of the God-you relationship are infinite.

And so, the question *Who is God for me?* has a developmental aspect, one which asks you to consider the Persons of the Trinity, the attributes of the Person most present to you right now, the relationships between the three Persons, what that means to you, and how you can grow over time in your relationship with all three Persons. It is a way of helping your relationship with God become very personal, and very unique. It also leads to discovering who God is in Himself. It leads to the question *Who Am I for God?*, and is also the best way to get to know yourself.

The question is very different from the question *What is God to me?*, because when we use the word "what", we are focusing on characteristics more than attributes. When we ask "who", we are focusing on a Person, and therefore on a *relationship*, a relationship in terms of attributes, and on making the relationship personal. Once it becomes personal, once we really care about the relationship, it evokes more commitment from us, and ultimately it is our personal and individual loving and total commitment to Him that God seeks from each of us. It is through the relationship that we come to love God, and it is because of our love for God that we desire to do His will.

What does God mean to me; what should He mean to me?

This is a slightly different perspective on the question of Who Is God. We can each ask, "What is God saying to me? How is He saying or asking it? How do I respond? Why do I want to respond? In what way is He forming the basis for our individual relationship?" Does God seem demanding, challenging, or perhaps a 'warm fuzzy' to us? What does it mean to you that He is uncompromising and absolute truth?

When you explore these questions, you are able to come to some understanding of not just Who He is, but Who He is for you at this moment in your relationship. This will change though. Expect change. Do not ever expect a static relationship with God. Because of His love for you, He is always calling you to come closer to Him, always encouraging you to discover more of Him, always eagerly wanting to share more of Himself with you. But to share Himself, He must know that you care, that you are open to Him, at least a little. He has so much to offer, but you must desire at least some of what He is willing to offer. You may never know all He is willing to share of Himself, for He can never be outdone in generosity. The more intimately you know Him, the more intimately you relate to Him, the more you grow in love for Him, the more of Himself He will share.

I would suggest you read any one of the gospel accounts where Jesus told the apostles to do something, such as the account where He told them to go out in pairs and take nothing with them. Ask yourself how He appeared to them. If you were one of them, how would you have responded if your relationship with Him would have been what it is right now? Was He considerate, kind, encouraging, teaching, etc.? Think of your relationship with Jesus. When you sense He is speaking to your heart, do you see any of those same characteristics in His relationship with you? In what way?

Is the following something you might say right now? *"It has been a long time since I pondered God the Father. Last night I came to terms with the fact that I always prayed to Jesus or Mary. I considered the Holy Spirit as a part of all the Trinity. I can't put my finger on it, but if I am to be honest I must admit that I don't have a good feel for God the Father, and I don't know why. I love to meditate especially at bed time, but I can't seem to meditate on God the Father very well. I discern that although they are all God, perhaps a healthy loving relationship with all the members of the Trinity may be necessary to have a balanced spirituality. I would appreciate any input you may have that can help me get a picture of who God the Father is, and how to have a more loving relationship with Him."*

I think if you meditate on the Father through Jesus, concentrating on the relationship between the two of Them, seeking the Father through His Son, you may come to where you desire to be, for you, too, are His child. Read through the gospels and meditate on each passage where Jesus refers to

His Father, and where His Father speaks of Him, such as at the Transfiguration (Mt 17:3-5). The final thing Jesus said before He died was "Into Your hands I commend My Spirit."(Lk 23:46; also see Ps 31:6) When Jesus prayed, it was to the Father. Read very slowly and meditate especially on Jesus' last prayer to the Father in Jn 17. This is a very powerful thing to do. Imagine yourself speaking to the Father this way, so filled with confidence and intimacy and love.

Remember that in coming to you in the Eucharist, Jesus wants to make a little Jesus of you, and thus He wants to make of you someone with the same relationship to the Father that He has, for the Father is also your Father. Note with particularity the passage in Jn 17 where Jesus acknowledges to His Father that the Father loves us as much as He loves Jesus. Make this your meditation objective; to truly love your Father in Heaven and to contemplate how He loves you as much as He loves Jesus (Jn 17:22-23), and what that means to you.

Who Do You Say That I Am?

In Mt 16:15-17, Jesus asked His disciples, "Who do you say that I am?" The question was addressed to them as a group and answered on behalf of the group by Peter. Peter replied, "Thou art the Messiah, the Son of God." Peter's response in faith led Jesus to thereupon proclaim He would establish His church on Peter, give Peter the keys to the kingdom, and give the apostles the Divine power to forgive sin. Quite a reward for a right answer.

Jesus addresses this same question to each of us and looks for an answer in faith, just as He received from Peter. We must give our answers in prayer, in ways which truly express what is in our heart. It makes no sense to try to "fool" Jesus, or to "pull the wool over His eyes." He knows us better than we will ever know ourselves. We need to articulate the answer for our own good, not His. We need to come face to face with who God is for us. In doing so, we come face to face with who we are and where we are in the relationship described by Jesus when He said, "...you are in Me and I in you." (Jn 14:20). He is not in some distant place called heaven, far removed from us. He is within us, in the depths of our souls.

In meditating on this relationship, we gain some insight into how much we have been open to the Holy Spirit so He may share Himself with us. We soon realize that the Holy Spirit cannot do much with us if we are so filled with "self" that there is no room in our "inn" for Him; so filled with "noise" that He cannot be heard. He speaks very quietly. We must turn off the noise of the world for a while in order to hear Him.

Jesus will not ask us the question, "Who do you say that I am?" only once, as He did with Peter. Throughout our lives He will keep asking and keep urging us to an ever deeper understanding and a more intimate relationship so that He can share more and more of Himself. Each time He shares more of Himself with us, we should again try to answer the question, for our answer should be different every time. It is one of the ways we can sense our spiritual growth.

When we discuss this with others who are also making the journey, we find what has been disclosed to them about God, and in so doing we begin to see the infinite variety of ways God reaches out to us. He reaches out to us very powerfully in the gospels. One absolutely invaluable lesson He teaches us is found in the account of the marriage feast at Cana. After the discovery is made that the wine is all gone, and after Mary tells Jesus, and He acts somewhat aloof and says, "My hour has not yet come," she turns to the servers and simply says, "Do whatever He tells you." (Jn 2:5) The importance of this simple statement, beyond teaching us the intercessory role of Mary and how it relates to us, is seldom grasped. She knows that if Jesus performs this first public miracle, it will be the beginning of His public ministry that will end on the cross. This act opens the gate to that public path. She will also be removing from its scabbard the sword that will pierce her heart (Lk 2:35). She knows choosing the time has to be His decision. She does not make the decision for Him, but simply tells the servants, "Do whatever He tells you."(Jn 2:5)

If we were always conscious of everything Jesus told us to do in the gospels, we would have His blueprint for our lives, and for our sainthood. All we have to do is what He tells us. We do not have to guess. It is there in black and white. An interesting thing for you to do, as you read the gospels, is to write down everything He tells us to do; not everything He said, just everything He told us to do.

The answers to the questions we have been discussing about our relationship with God form the essence of the spiritual journey. We never receive a complete answer for it is an ever-evolving relationship, and yet everything of meaning that we do, and are, is a result of our attempt to answer these questions. If we share our insights of faith with each other, we both are enriched and our faith is broadened by a deeper awareness of the truth of Who God is.

If someone were to ask you, "What can I do so that in my heart I can truthfully answer the question Jesus asked His disciples, "Who do you say that I am?"", how would you answer them?

This is actually a very profound question. I would consider doing three different things. Consider each one prayerfully and approach each as you feel the Holy Spirit is calling you to do.

1. Read chapter 1 of the gospel of John, slowly. Meditate on it as you read. Write down what comes to mind about each word or phrase that reaches out to you.

2. Spend a little time each day reading the four gospels. Write down each thing, and only those things, Jesus tells us to do, and note the reference. For example, in Jn 15:12, Jesus says "Love one another as I have loved you." When you are finished, what does this collective set of instructions tell you about Jesus? What does it tell you about your relationship with Jesus, given that these are His instructions for your interior life?

3. Read the rest of the gospel of John, and then the other three gospels, the same way you did for the first chapter of John. Do not try to do this in one sitting. Do a little each day. Try to mentally place yourself there with Him, listening to Him speak. As you do, ask who Jesus, the Person, is for you. Note subtle things like verb tenses, such as when He uses "is" instead of "was" or "will be". For example, in the Beatitudes given during the Sermon on the

Mount, Jesus says, "Blessed are the poor in spirit, for theirs is the kingdom of heaven."(Mt 5:3), and "Blessed are the meek for they will inherit the earth." (Mt 5:5). One is present tense, one future. Try to sense how your knowledge of and closeness to Jesus is changing as you read scripture. Sense how He is becoming more alive and vibrant to you in your soul, someone you want to have a real and loving relationship with here and now, and every day.

What is Prayer?

There are many ways to define prayer:

Prayer is the vehicle of courtship with Christ. It deepens over time, culminates in the consummation of transforming union, and continues, through mutual exploration and intimacy, for eternity.

Prayer is a sustained process of attention to the source of freedom and love into whose Sacred Heart we surrender, day by day, until we breathe our last, and with Christ say, "Into your hands I commend my spirit." You do not do that by making room on your calendar or by an entry into your Rolodex.

St. Teresa of Avila, in The Book of Her Life, Part 8, Section 5, said, "For mental prayer in my opinion is nothing else than an intimate sharing between friends; it means taking time frequently to be alone with Him who we know loves us. In order that love be true and the friendship endure, the wills of the friends must be in accord."[30]

Prayer as a journey of discovery

Prayer is many things. It is our means to discover God. It is the best way to approach the solutions to everyday problems, the way to find the solution to every problem for which there appears to be no solution. Jesus is always our answer, and we go to Him in prayer. It is the way to find peace of heart, to discover love, to discover more about yourself. It is the way to find direction for your life, to

---

[30] The Collected Works of St. Teresa of Avila, Vol. One, Tr. Kieran Kavanaugh, O.C.D. and Otilio Rodriguez, O.C.D., ICS Publications, Washington DC, 1987, p 96.

discern your vocation. It is our most powerful weapon to fight Satan and his temptations. It is the way we encounter God in our lives on a regular basis. It is the door through which we go to acquire virtue to displace vices. It is the key to the interior life. These are just some of the ways in which God enters our lives through prayer and helps us discover Him, love Him, discover His love for us, and respond to His will for us. Prayer is the means by which He leads us on the road to sainthood.

Types of prayer

The key to growth in prayer is to get beyond purely vocal prayer and deepen our prayer life so it includes at least meditative prayer. With God's help, we can also progress to contemplative prayer. To practice even meditative prayer, we must give time each day to prayer, preferably alone. This was Jesus' advice to us in Mt 6:5-7, and He well understood the need for solitude in prayer. Before every major event, He prayed in solitude. He began His public ministry by praying for forty days in the desert (Mt 4).

Liturgical prayer is purposefully communal, but we all need to set aside time each day for solitary prayer. It is in this quiet time, when there is no one there but you, God, and your angel, that you can speak from your heart and listen with your heart to His voice. Before every period of prayer, you should always ask the Holy Spirit for guidance so that you will receive what God intends for you in this prayer session. In each period of prayer, God has an objective in mind for us. We need to train our hearts and minds to listen to what He is telling us. Often this means we remain quiet and let Him speak to our heart. It is hard to hear His voice if our own mouth is going non-stop.

Meditative prayer is that silent prayer which is done using the intellect, and should be involved in all vocal prayer. The mind focuses on God and thinks about the subject of the prayer. One can engage in meditative prayer while saying a typical vocal prayer, such as the rosary. While the ten Hail Mary prayers are said for each decade, you meditate on the mystery associated with that particular decade. This kind of prayer should not be rushed. There is nothing wrong with taking several minutes to say one decade so that you can meditate as long as you feel called to do so. When I pray a five decade rosary alone, it usually takes about forty-five minutes to an hour. Meditative prayer can also be mental discourse which is spontaneous dialogue with God and does not use any formula prayers. It is sometimes called discursive meditation.

Contemplative prayer is very different. It is seated in the heart, originates in God, and is usually not expressed in words. It is a response to grace in which we pour out ourselves to God Who is the object of our love. Contemplative prayer uses the language of love, the language of the heart. It is sometimes called the prayer of love, or prayer of the heart. One aspect of contemplative prayer has been called the Prayer of Quiet. When you are with someone you love very much, perhaps your spouse or the person to whom you are engaged to be married, you do not have to constantly talk. Sometimes just being present to each other is enough, perhaps holding hands or walking together. You are communicating with your hearts, not with your lips. You can do the same with God in meditation.

Discovering our relationship with God through prayer

It is in prayer that we discover God's love, and express our love for Him. It is in prayer that we encounter Him, discover Him, and explore our relationship with Him. It is in prayer that He shares Himself with us. It is in prayer that we learn how to love God above all else, and love others as well as ourselves. It is often in prayer that we learn how to love ourselves properly because He loves us and we love what He loves. It is in prayer that we learn humility. It is in prayer that we learn how to forgive. It is in prayer that we learn how to see Jesus in others. It is in prayer that we learn how to call upon the saints for help. It is in prayer that we learn how to give ourselves, and our will, to God, consecrating all that we are and all that we have to Him. It is in prayer that we learn to pray in and through Jesus.

When we read scripture, we should always first pray to the Holy Spirit for enlightenment. This is particularly important as we read scripture in our quest to discover God; to discover as much as we can about Him from His inspired word.

When we pray from the heart we should always have joy. No matter the circumstances, if we pray from the heart we will have an encounter with God. He loves us. When you experience the love of God, you experience His joy and peace. You may not always experience it consciously because you may go through a period of aridity in prayer, but it will be there nonetheless. Even amid the trials and tragedies of life you must pray for joy and peace to experience a small taste of what He desires to share with you for eternity. When you have time available for prayer, do not waste it. Take advantage of this gift He offers. If your heart is not focused on God in prayer, you are depriving yourself of untold graces, and of the experience of union with God Himself.

Just do it

There are many things we could say about prayer. Volumes have been written about the value of prayer, how we can use prayer in our discovery of God, and how we can use prayer to build up our trust in God and His love for us. But after all the reading, it still has to be actually done and experienced by you, for ultimately the effect of your prayer is a matter strictly between you and the God you are discovering within.

Prayer and spiritual warfare

In Jn 14:30, Jesus says "...the Prince of this world is at hand. He has no hold on Me...." In the Douay-Reims English translation of the Latin Vulgate version of Genesis 3:15, God tells us that the woman shall be the downfall of Satan on earth; victory is to be His through Her. God will not lower Himself to do direct battle with Satan for that would accord to Satan a dignity he does not have. But the greatest humiliation God can impose on Satan in response to his sin of pride is to bring about the defeat of Satan through the instrument of His purely human mother. "I will put enmity between you and the woman, and between your offspring and hers; she will strike at your head, while you strike at her heel." God refers to "the" woman, not women. She will be, through the grace of God, the singular initiator of the eventual destruction of Satan, the single woman who will change the course of human history by her acceptance of her role as Mother of God. The opening of the gospel of John tells us that Jesus, the incarnate Word, came to give us the power to become children of God.

In Jn 19:26-27, Jesus gives us His mother as our mother when He addresses Mary and John from the Cross, giving each to the other. Those who claim Mary was not a perpetual virgin and had other sons do not understand the implications of this statement of Jesus from the Cross. If Mary had other sons besides Jesus, Jesus would have been breaking Jewish law by giving her to John, and insulting Mary in the process, something Jesus would never have done. It also made no sense to give John to her to be her son, since John's biological mother was standing there at the Cross a little ways removed from Mary the mother of Jesus(Mt 27:55-56). John represented all of us, all of her children. In giving her to us as our adopted mother, Christ made Himself our brother. He thus brought to fruition the full meaning of how Jesus taught us to pray in Mt 6:9-14. He told us to address the Father as Our Father. His Father and our Father are the same Person. Jesus also tells us in Jn 17 that the Father loves each of us with the same love with which He loves Jesus. This relationship of love we have with Jesus, with the Father, and with Blessed Mother, requires that our prayer be something more than mere vocal prayer, more than prayer with the lips. Prayer which is a true and loving encounter with God comes from the heart and is the key to a life in God.

Revelation, chapters four and five describe the victory over Satan in Heaven. In Chapter 12, the battle moves to earth (Rev 12:7-9). The battle is Satan's attack against Mary, the woman clothed with the sun (Rev 12:1), and against the Church which she represents. Satan cannot attack Mary directly, so he attacks her through his attack on the Church, his attack on "the rest of her offspring, on those who keep God's Commandments and give witness to Jesus" (Rev 12:17). Like any good Mother, she comes to our rescue. The battleground is here, the prize is our soul. Satan is going to lose. We know that. The only question is how many of us he can take with him as he is cast down to the deepest recesses of the pit of hell (Is 14:12-15). Our greatest weapons are prayer and the sacraments, especially the Eucharist. When Satan is defeated, and the reign of God comes to earth, there is no place for Satan and the condemned angels to go other than to hell.

The spiritual war has been going on much longer than most of us ever realize. We do not see it, and so we are not always conscious of the players or the stakes. Sometimes we see the more evident signs of evil among us, like the pornographic industry, the abortion industry, or the evil that could lead terrorists in the middle east to behead innocent captives and display their atrocity on television.

God created Lucifer, and in him He created a magnificent being who shared in the freedom and power of God. His name meant Light Bearer. It is said that God told

Lucifer of His plan for the Incarnation, and Lucifer rebelled. It meant Lucifer would have to serve the Son of Man, what he saw as a mere human, and that he would be lower than Mary, who was to be his queen. His pride could not take that. "I will not serve", he and his angels shouted. "I will set up my throne above the stars of God; I will be like the Most High." (Is 14:12-15)

Guidance in prayer

Mary wants to share the value, the fruits, of her sinlessness with us. She wants to work with us to help make us "holy and immaculate, without stain ..."(Eph 5:27). She wants us free of sin because we are her children and sin is the only thing that separates us from God, and serious sin is the only thing that keeps us in the kingdom of Satan. She wants to help our hearts to become like hers, and we can only do that through prayer. Christ has told us through various visionaries to be aware of Satan and his works, but to avoid giving mental time and energy to Satan; rather, through the grace of God and with Mary's help, we should focus on Jesus, the Holy Spirit and the Father. By focusing on Satan, we give him mental time instead of giving mental time to God. If our minds and hearts are always on God, there is no door for Satan to enter. The great saints all did this, and we should, too. Are we obligated to seek Mary's help? No, we are not. But her desire for us is to become perfect in Christ, and she will help us get there via the best and shortest route.

God has sent special help to us to teach us about prayer. Every place the Blessed Mother has appeared she has told us to pray. She is allegedly appearing at Medjugorje, a small town in Bosnia. The Church has not ruled on the authenticity of this apparition yet, and we are always subject to determinative ruling of the Church in such matters, but several bishops have been there and have spoken of it favorably. If we read what she has reportedly said, she primarily came to Medjugorje to teach us to pray. The call to prayer is the predominant theme of what are said to be her messages. Ever since the messages reportedly began in 1981, Blessed Mother is said to have taught us more about prayer than about anything else, especially prayer of the heart. Over these years they say she has taught us that prayer is an encounter with God, that through prayer we discover God, that through prayer of the heart we can find the answer to problems which have no apparent solution, that we cannot love if we do not pray, that prayer should be an integral part of our daily life, and it is through prayer that we can live our lives in cooperation with the Holy Spirit.

She has also allegedly given us many lessons on prayer. She has taught us how prayer should be incorporated into both the joys and struggles of our daily life. It is not just finding time for praying, but learning to incorporate prayer into the fabric of our daily life. Even if the Church should ultimately rule there is nothing supernatural about the purported apparitions at Medjugorje, what has been reported is still consistent with the teachings of the Church and the saints. She has reportedly given us the following guidance on bringing ourselves to a state of effective prayer, and has taught why this is necessary if we are to live in accordance with God's plan for our life.

- Always pray before you work and end your work with prayer
- Always begin and end each day with prayer
- Let your morning begin with morning prayer and the evening end with thanksgiving.
- Pray for the grace to experience victory in the temptations of Satan
- Through prayer you can totally disarm him [Satan] and ensure your happiness

- Only by prayer are you able to overcome every influence of Satan in your place.

- Only through prayer can you defeat evil.

- Through prayer you will destroy evil in people and uncover Satan's deceptions

- In prayer you will come to know the way out of every situation that has no way out.

- Now is the time for prayer. Now, nothing else is important, only God.

- Let your every day be filled with prayer of gratitude to God for life and all you have.

- Pray that you may comprehend the beauty and greatness of the gift of life.

As we meditate on this guidance, we can see how active real prayer life is. It is not the passive, static, even boring, stop-to-say-a-quick-prayer kind of activity to which so many of us may have grown accustomed. God is creative life, activity at the highest level, so we should not expect our prayer life to be any different. Our prayer should be filled with life, filled with love, filled with a continual life-expanding encounter with God. Prayer should be our main defense against Satan. If we are in prayer, if we are engaged in an encounter with God, when our mind and heart are united with God, we are clothed in our greatest defense against Satan.

Satan is the antithesis of all this, and, through deception, must dispose us toward himself to make progress. He has to make himself, or at least what he offers, appear to be a good in order to move us in his direction. He is consumed with hatred for God, and of us because God loves us. He has no loving encounter with God, or anyone else. He has no capacity at all for love of any kind, not even for himself. He is the epitome of spiritual death. Therefore, prayer is also a weapon, our chief weapon against Satan. It is through prayer that we defeat evil, for through prayer we are in union with God, who is love. Love is our principal armor against Satan, the one thing with which he cannot co-exist. The Blessed Mother is insistent on this. She tells us that it is only through prayer that we can defeat evil, only through prayer that we can overcome every influence of Satan. That is a strong statement. It is also a true statement.

Prayer and spiritual growth

To many, spiritual growth is a mystery. We don't always understand how it happens, or even understand how to recognize the growth. We don't know what the food is that we need for spiritual growth. Do we pray because we have grown spiritually, or do we grow spiritually because we have prayed? Blessed Mother has reportedly given us the answer to these questions in her messages from Medjugorje. She has said:

- If you knew the graces God was giving you, you would pray without ceasing.

- Pray to the Holy Spirit for enlightenment

- I would like to call you to persistent prayer and penance

- Without prayer there is no peace

- At all times fill your heart even with the smallest prayers

- Let prayer be your daily food

In this guidance, we have very important advice. "Let prayer be your daily food." She also said we should have persistent prayer and penance, and tells us something of the mystery of the graces communicated through prayer. By doing as she allegedly suggests, we are constantly feeding our soul with that which causes it to grow, with that which leads us to ever deeper levels of prayer. We do this by praying for enlightenment from the Holy Spirit and then responding to His inspirations.

Peace through prayer

One effect of prayer is God's peace, the gift He gave us before He ascended to the Father. We must make prayer such an ever-present part of our life that it is important to keep our heart filled even with the smallest prayers. These are those small prayers often referred to as ejaculations, things like "Jesus, love me," or "Jesus, Mary, I love you, save souls," and "My Lord and my God." We can say these small prayers at any time, even while in a conversation or waiting for a bus. If they come from the heart, they are our own prayers, our own words, our own expression of love. If we keep our heart filed with these prayers, we are keeping God always in our consciousness. St. Maximillian Kolbe offered a spiritual communion every quarter hour of the day.

Family prayer

One thing very important is family prayer. Family prayer is not just focused on the family. Like personal prayer, family prayer is focused on all God's children. The difference is that when we pray as a family the family is brought more closely together, with each other and with God. The family members grow closer to God individually and as a family. It is like the family of God. We pray individually, but we pray with and for each other when we come together to offer family prayer, whether in our homes or in church. What are we told family prayer should be like?

- Let all prayer in your home be for conversion of sinners.

- Let prayer take first place in your families.

- Encourage the very young to pray and go to Mass.

- I am calling you to more attentive prayer, and more participation in the Mass.
- Every family should be active in prayer.
- A family cannot say that it is in peace if it does not pray.
- Today I invite you again to put prayer in the first place in your families.

The guidance is very interesting. These exhortations show us not only what we should do when we pray as a family, but what should be the objective of family prayer. Prayer should be the top priority in the family, and therefore prayer is that which should bind the family together. Family unity should be centered in prayer. Family prayer includes going to Mass together as a family. We also should strive for prayer of the heart, beginning with giving attention to what we do during liturgical prayer.

Of particular importance is the relationship between family prayer and family peace. We live in an age where dysfunctional families are entirely too commonplace. We can see families at the highest levels of society and at the lowest who are dysfunctional. But this is because they have not made God a central part of their lives. Everything else has taken precedence. What we are called to do is model our families after the Holy Family, and to make family prayer the means by which we can enjoy family peace.

When we make family prayer a priority, we are putting our family in union with the Holy Family. When we pray as a family, we should be praying for conversions. When we do this, our family prayer unites us not only with the Holy Family, but with the entire family of God which is the Mystical Body of Christ. Family prayer, then, takes us through several levels of encounter with God and participation in His life. It leads us to prayer for self, prayer for our family members, and prayer for the Mystical Body of Christ, the entire family of God.

Begin the discovery with scripture

When we seek God, when we try to discover Him, we begin with scripture. To make our search for God in scripture effective, we must do more than just read. We read scripture effectively when we do so in prayer. There is a method of reading scripture as prayer known as *lectio divina*, a favorite method of St. Teresa of Avila. You can explore the *lectio divina* method on your own, but the important point now is that although we discover God in scripture, we do so effectively only when we explore scripture through prayer. Blessed Mother has allegedly told us in her messages from Medjugorje:

- You can recognize and discover God only in prayer.

- Come to prayer consciously and in prayer you will know the majesty of God.

- I am inviting you so that your prayer may be a joyful encounter with the Lord.

- Pray so that in prayer you have an encounter with God.

- I am calling you to prayer of the heart so every prayer can be an encounter with God.

- In prayer of the heart you shall encounter God.

- Consecrate a time in the day only for an encounter with God.

- Set a time each day when you can pray in peace.

- Decide seriously to dedicate time to God.

- I invite you to decide to give time patiently for prayer.

- I invite you to draw still closer to God through prayer.

- Pray for truth to prevail in every heart.

- Pray that you may comprehend God's gift of holiness more and more.

- Pray so you may be open to everything God does through you.

- Prayer is joy. Prayer is what the human heart desires.

- There is no peace, little children, where there is no prayer.

This series of message segments tells us many things about our discovery of God, principal among them being that prayer is essential. When we discover God, we discover the gifts of God, principal of which is the gift of Himself. The gifts of God include His peace as well as our discovery of Him and His role in our lives. Joy is one of the gifts we receive when we discover God. In these messages we see many of the same things Jesus told us in different words about prayer, such as to go to our room, close the door, and pray in private.

When you speak with someone who has a close relationship with God you sense interior joy as well as inner peace, both given by the Holy Spirit. They may have many problems, but the joy and peace of being in union with God dominates their life. They are not focused on the things of this world, but on the will of God. When we are told to pray for truth to prevail in our heart, we are being asked to give the Holy Spirit reign over our heart. The Holy Spirit's title is the Spirit of Truth (Jn 15:26). If we pray to be consecrated in truth (Jn 17:17), for the Holy Spirit to prevail in our own heart, we must also pray that He prevails in the heart of every person. If the Holy Spirit prevails in the hearts of all, then the rule of Satan on earth will truly have been completely destroyed.

Discovering God's love through prayer

When you discover God in prayer, you discover His love for He is love. One of the precious benefits of discovering God, of coming to know God, is to be immersed in His love. So many of us live a life unconscious of God's love, unaware of the intensity of His love for us. We may know about God, but we do not know God. Knowing about God does not create the relationship with God. We do that through prayer. Sometimes we remain so focused on the world that we never see the value of the greatest treasure we can ever have, which is His love. The only way we can come to know not only God but also His love is through prayer.

- I wish that in prayer you come to know my love and the love of God.

- Pray without ceasing that God reveals His love to you.

- In prayer each one of you will be able to achieve complete love.

- Pray that from your heart would flow a fountain of love for every person born, even to the one who hates you and to the one who despises you.

- Pray, and through prayer you will discover love.

- May your life become prayer in fullness. Without love, you cannot pray.

- Pray to be able to understand the love and goodness of God.

- In prayer you will come to know the greatest joy.

- Pray that prayer prevails in your heart in every moment - prayer will be your happiness and your rest.

– Let prayer be your daily food.

Meditating on this guidance, the gospel once again comes alive. Jesus tells us we should love our enemies. Blessed Mother is reportedly telling us that it is through prayer that we can come to love the way Jesus called us to love. She shows us the critical relationship between love, as God asks it of us, and prayer. She teaches us that without love, we cannot pray, and that we find love through prayer. This sounds like a chicken and egg kind of dilemma, but it is not. We grow in prayer, and we grow in love. An increase in one leads to an increase in the other. This happens as we grow in our knowledge and love for God.

When we pray from the heart, we find that we can do so because we have loved. Once we can pray from the heart, once we love enough, we find that we can love even those who hate and despise us. Jesus told us not to fear those who can only hurt our body. We are able to recognize their hatred as a threat to their own salvation, not as a threat to us. This leads us to pray for them, and, by the grace of God, our prayer and the prayer of many others may very well be the thing that keeps that person from going to hell. This is one of the marvelous mysteries of the Mystical Body of Christ. Christ allows us, through prayer and sacrifice, to be an instrument of His saving love for the unfortunate sinners who otherwise face damnation. The lives of the saints have proved this to us so many times, like the example of St. Monica and St. Maria Goretti, and countless others. It is love which will defeat Satan, and we discover love through prayer.

Discovering God's will through prayer

As we embark on our discovery of God, we discover His love and we also discover His will. Just as we can discover God's love through prayer, we also discover His will for us through prayer. It would be difficult for us to say we have found God, but in the discovery have somehow not been able to find His love and His will. If this is your situation or that of someone you know, then more digging is required, for you are probably not praying from the heart and probably have not really found God. In the spiritual world, this 'digging' means at least meditative prayer. Prayer is our principal means of exploration of God.

- Pray and seek the will of God in your everyday life.

- Pray in order that all that God wills through you may be realized.

- Let your prayer be a sign of your surrender to God.

- Start transforming yourselves through prayer, and you will know what you have to do.

- Forget your desires, dear children. Pray for what God desires.

- Open yourselves to God by means of prayer so the Holy Spirit may work miracles in you and through you.

- Pray, pray, pray, and do that which the Holy Spirit inspires you.

- Today I invite you to prayer. Let prayer be light for you.

In these teachings, we see that our discernment of God's will involves several things. It involves surrender of our will to that of God, and also involves a personal transformation. When we surrender to the will of God, we put Him first in our life. This is how we should all live. In prayer we try to discern God's plan for our life. The problems of the world would all be solved if we all put God first and made our will subservient to His.

All we need do is look around to see how much our lives are focused on self, on the world, and how often God is worshiped more out of obligation than of love. We must be open to the Holy Spirit, and this can only happen through prayer. We must be transformed in Jesus to be the person who puts Him first in our life. We cannot do this without prayer. Through His operation on our hearts, we must be transformed by Him from being a self-centered person into a God-centered person. This takes a great deal of prayer, and learning to respond to the inspirations of the Holy Spirit. It means developing a sensitive ear to hear the quiet voice of the Holy Spirit. We must learn to stop saying to ourselves, "I want" and begin to ask, "What does God want?" When we allow God to transform us, when we respond to and cooperate with the Holy Spirit, He will work miracles in us and through us. Are you ready for a miracle in your life?

Dimensions of prayer

Prayer has five basic dimensions. These include adoration, thanksgiving, contrition, intercession, and petition. In the prayer of petition, we ask for blessings from God for ourselves. When we pray for others, it is called intercessory prayer. When we petition the saints for their help, we ask them to offer intercessory prayer on our behalf. We have a spiritual obligation, as members of the Mystical Body of Christ, to pray for others. Blessed Mother has reportedly taught us:

- Pray every day for the souls in purgatory.

- Pray that you might help yourself and those whom prayer gives you.

Meditating on these two teachings, we realize that when we pray for the souls in purgatory, we are acting as their intercessor, and when they get to heaven sooner because of our prayer, they will in turn intercede for us. One of the exciting things about our introduction to heaven will be meeting for the first time all the souls we prayed for, and who prayed for us. We don't have to worry about what to ask for. God knows best what they need. All we have to do is pray for what God knows they need. What the souls in purgatory need is the grace to be perfected enough to enter heaven, however that must happen for each of them.

Praying for those on earth can be harder than praying for the souls in purgatory. This is especially true if we are called to pray for someone we don't like. But just like the souls in purgatory, we don't have to ask for specific things, even though we often do. It is sufficient to ask God for what He knows that person needs most. For those who are steeped in evil, we need to pray that they experience God's love, for that will put them on the path of conversion.

We can also pray for people we do not know. We can pray for people who are suffering from natural and man-made disasters in the world. We can also pray for the conversion of all people of the world. Praying for the conversion of all people who are in most need of conversion, which means they are in most need of God's mercy, should be our daily prayer, regardless of what else we pray for.

As we pray, we may sometimes be inspired to pray for someone else, perhaps someone we do not know, and may not know why we are called to prayer. We just do, and we pray for whatever God knows that person needs at the moment. For example, I am inherently optimistic, but one day I suddenly felt deep depression while I was home alone washing dishes while my wife was out. I had nothing to be depressed about, so I sat down and prayed for whoever God was calling me to pray for. After a few minutes, the depression had gone and I was my usual self again. I am sure God was calling me to pray for someone who was deeply depressed. I have never felt that again, and I've washed many dishes since.

Conversion supported through prayer

We should also pray for ourselves and our own conversion, for conversion is a daily process. We should never consider ourselves converted, but only as going through conversion, for conversion is a transformation in Christ and we can always become more and more transformed every day of our life. Like loving, being transformed is something that can always be improved. We can always love more, love better, and likewise be more completely transformed.

Once we realize conversion is not a one-time event, but is an on-going process, we can appreciate the need to pray for our own daily conversion as well as the conversion of others. Conversion is also a purification and perfecting process because it is God working in us. Blessed Mother has allegedly given us several teachings on conversion in her messages from Medjugorje.

- Pray with your whole heart and change your life day by day.
- Pray daily and change your life in order that you may be holy.
- Only in prayer will you be able to abandon your heart to the Lord so He can purify it.
- Only in prayer will you be able to recognize the evil that dwells in you and abandon it to the Lord so He may purify your hearts.
- Let prayer be the life of each one of you.
- Let prayer be life to you.
- Start transforming yourselves through prayer, and you will know what you have to do.
- The only one you have to turn to is in heaven.

- God can give you peace only if you convert and pray.

- Reflect and pray and God will be born in your heart and your heart will be joyous.

As you reflect on these teachings the one thing that is very evident is the close relationship between conversion and prayer. Conversion is, except in the case of miraculous events like that which happened to St. Paul, dependent on prayer. When we pray, we are showing God we desire to know Him better. Conversion and prayer are inseparable.

Examine your own prayer life. Try to describe it as clearly as possible. Consider how often you pray, what the prayer periods are like, where your mind is while you pray, whether you feel you have an encounter with God (not necessarily a physical feeling, but more of a sense of moral conviction that there has been an encounter with God), and whether you see a direction taking shape in your life as a result of your prayer life.

Take the first line of the Our Father: "Our Father Who art in heaven." Meditate on this one line, and then write down everything that this line means to you personally. Do this any way you like, whether as a paragraph, a list of bullet items, whatever. Don't rush. Take the time to do it thoughtfully. Take as long as you need. Then examine this product, and try to discern what it tells you about your present relationship with God the Father through prayer. Is it the relationship Jesus wants you to have?

Who is prayer for?

Finally we have to ask, "Who is prayer for? One day during noon Mass at the chapel at Ft. Belvoir in Virginia, Fr. Bill Hartgen was giving a homily on Mt 6:7-15. He said, "Prayer is not valued by God because it represents human achievement. God knows what we need. He does not need to be begged in order to give it. ... We pray because Christ, who lives in communion with God, commands us to pray. ... Prayer is not a numbers game, like we can wear God down. It is not an assault by word. ... Since God does not need our prayer - and we do, then perhaps we ought to pray as if it were for us. We might even benefit from it. We might discover that good prayer brings true blessings."

Fr. Hartgen expressed some ideas in this homily, one principally, which deserve further reflection. Prayer is not for God, but for us. It is to God, but for us. We owe God prayer of adoration, but it does not change God. Hopefully, it will change us and help us realize just how much we do owe to God. Prayer is our way of showing our dependence on God. Liturgical prayer is our way of outwardly, publically expressing our participation in the Mystical Body. It is how we publicly and privately give expression to our love for God. It is our way to publicly and privately lay our petitions before God, and our way to privately and obediently accept His will no matter how He chooses to communicate His will.

Prayer, whether private or public, must be conscious. If it is unconscious, rote, mouthing of words, it has no effect, no merit. This is one of the dangers we must guard against in liturgical prayer, or group prayer when people say the rosary or some other devotion. I say "say the rosary" rather than "pray" the rosary, for if one listens to a group doing this, one sometimes hears people racing to see how fast they can say each prayer, or they each pray at a different pace, thus rendering the experience anything but group prayer said as a collective call of the Mystical Body of Christ.

God does not need our prayer for Himself. He accepts our prayer and uses what He sees in our heart to determine His response to our prayer. How often have we realized that our prayer is most sincerely expressed in our heart when our need, or our fear, is the greatest. How wonderful it would be if we could pray on a regular basis and find the same degree of encounter with God, not because of need or fear, but because of the love we have for Him, our Divine Father. Perhaps if we spent more time thinking about why we, on a personal level, should love God, and ways we could show we love Him with our whole heart, our regular prayer would be ever so much more effective. Perhaps that is why God gives us examples like Mother Teresa and Blessed Margaret of Castello. Most of you know who Mother Teresa is. If you have not read the life of Blessed Margaret of Castello, consider putting it on your "to do" reading list.

Knowing Yourself Through Prayer

St. Teresa of Avila tells us that no matter how far we progress in prayer, we must continually seek to grow in self-knowledge and humility, and we progress in these by increasing our knowledge of God. Do you follow this advice, and if so, how? What works for you? What are your lessons learned?

Who am I? This question is something you can ponder alone, or discuss together with someone you are close to, such as your spouse. You can help each other explore this question, or you can discuss yourself with yourself and God in the privacy of your own prayer (and you should periodically go to this 'desert' to think and pray and discover). Ask the Blessed Mother to help you do this.

When I first began my spiritual journal, I had, on page 3, a series of questions:

Do I need to know myself, face myself, as God knows me?

Can I reach God without reaching myself?

Can I find God within me without knowing who it is that God is in?

How well do I have to know myself?

Can I consecrate myself to God without knowing who it is I am consecrating?

Does it even matter, since I am rejecting my will in favor of conforming myself to God's will?

What does it mean for me to consider, to experience, the power and the providence and the love of God, all of which are always present for me to find and accept, and in which I can always have complete trust?

Within the next eight months, I began to discover the answers. I read Arintero, who says, "The Son of God came into the world to incorporate us into Himself and to make us live by Him as He Himself lives by the Father."[31] Nothing like starting off with a bang. This is the issue I was wrestling with in my questions. It goes to the concept of the deification of man. He says that dogmas of the Catholic faith are not so much established for finding intellectual satisfaction as for motivating us to seek the gift of God. This means that we are led *into* Christ through His deification of our souls. Arintero says that "the supernatural does not come to us as an exterior and violent imposition, oppressing us and depriving us of our nature, but as an increase of life, freely accepted, liberating and ennobling us. It does not destroy our humanity; it makes us sons of God by participation in His divinity."[32]

I also read St. Teresa of Avila's *Interior Castle*.[33] She teaches us that when we begin our life of prayer, we must go through the "rooms" of humility and self-knowledge before we can go any farther, and we must periodically return to these two rooms no matter how far we progress in prayer. Therefore, the answer to my questions is "yes." We must come to know ourselves to some reasonable extent before we can know God and love God and have an intimate relationship with God, for we must have an understanding of who is involved in the relationship before we can understand the importance of God to us and what He wants from His relationship with us. We must know ourselves - not what we are but who we are, well enough to know what in us needs to be improved.

---

[31]Fr. John Arintero, O.P., The Mystical Evolution, Vol 1 of 2, TAN Books and Publ, Rockford, 1978, pg 1.

[32]Ibid, pg 1.

[33]The Collected Works of St. Teresa of Avila, Vol. 2, The Interior Castle, ICS Publications, Institute of Carmelite Studies, Washington DC, 1980, pg 281.

Our self-discovery progresses along with our discovery of God, and so St. Teresa tells us we must keep coming back to discover more about ourselves, and continue to grow in humility, if we would progress in our relationship with God, a relationship that is dependent on the quality and depth of our prayer, especially that prayer which leads us to greater humility. By knowing God, we know ourselves, and find ourselves in Him.

God must permeate our being in order for us to make progress. If we strip away the layers of the false external self we show to the world, and begin to see our real selves, we will find God with us, always trying to perfect us. When we see Him, we will see ourselves for who we are in His eyes. We will see the world, and ourselves, through His eyes. We are, we exist, through Him, with Him, and in Him. The only "place" it makes any sense for us to be is in Him. Jesus Himself told us this. In John 15, He says: "Abide in Me and I in you." "He that abides in Me and I in him will bear much fruit." "If you abide in Me, and My words abide in you, you shall ask whatever you will, and it shall be done unto you." "If you keep My commandments, you shall abide in My love." We can only begin to live this true and eternal reality if we are in the world but not of the world. We must be of Him and in Him; and He must be in us.

We begin to meet God in the "place", the true sanctuary, where we find our dependence on His love, for without His love, we cease to be. That place where we encounter His love is our common meeting place. He is love, and His love for us not only gives meaning to our life, it is the very principle and cause of our being; it is the one thing that gives us dignity as a human. We are held in being by our Creator's love for us.

We can only enter into Him if we can experience truth and leave behind that false, worldly, external self. In so doing we find that God was always there waiting for us. He has to be the one who takes us across the infinite chasm separating natural man from supernatural God. By serving as our bridge to the supernatural, He allows us to share in His divine nature. That is how we cross the bridge. It is how He carries us across the bridge. To do this He needs us to consent, out of love and not fear, to His will for us, to His love and mercy offered to us.

In contemplation we come to know God, not necessarily in a way by which we can describe Him in so many words, but by experiencing His reality in the depth of our being, in our soul. We come to know God by contemplating His attributes.[34] This necessarily makes it a very individual knowing, a knowing which, from some perspectives, may not be relevant to anyone except you and God.

We know God is unique. There is one, and only one, God. You are also unique because He made you that way. Your knowing God, your experiencing Him in the depths of your soul, must be the fruit of that unique relationship between you; a relationship meaningful within the context of that uniqueness. This is different from that general, often liturgically based, relationship He has with all of His children as members of His Mystical Body.

We eventually realize that we only understand ourselves enough, and honestly, by experiencing God within us, by seeing ourselves in relation to Him. By experiencing Christ in us and us in Him, we experience the true essence of who and what we are in His eyes. We should be a living fulfillment of God's love, and therefore inexorably bound to Him in love for all eternity. We must always keep asking if we have accepted His love deep within us. *When we sin, we should also ask how accepting of His love we have been, and*

---

[34]St. Faustina Kowalska, Divine Mercy in My Soul, Marian Press, Stockbridge (1987) par 301.

how much we have returned His love, for the measure of sin in our life is the inverse of the measure of our love for God.

Our true essence, lived as God wills, is to be an embodiment and temple of God's infinite love. We live conscious of our role as a member of the Mystical Body, through which we receive the life of Christ within us, nourished by the Bread of Life (Jn 6:22, et seq.).

On earth, we endure the inner struggle between the external "I" on one hand, seeking to dominate our existence - seeking to be satisfied by the immediately available temporal treasures of the world, and, one the other hand, the desire to die to ourselves so God can fill us with His being. It is a struggle to live His life so He can be the primary reason for all we do. This life in God is impossible until we love Him more than those other attractions which pull at us constantly. God must become our treasure (Mt 6:21). It is a struggle that lasts a lifetime for most of us.

As we examine these external attractions in our lives, we should measure their real value. What experiences, powers, honors, or what knowledge or love, to which we are attracted, or which we seek, or which we have found, can bring us closer to God? Which help us to give more of our selves to Him?

When you visit your "room" of self-knowledge, consider how you think of yourself. Is it your titles, job, honors, trophies, that you think of? If you were asked to describe, or better, define, who you are, what would you say?

Your success in figuring out who you are begins when you stop thinking about yourself as a person separated from God, and think specifically of yourself as a child of God and in terms of Christ in you and you in Him; when you understand and *experience* the realization that without Him you are nothing and can do nothing (Jn 15:5). Your life only has meaning when it is lived in and through Him. Your dignity as a person comes entirely from the fact that He loves you and has given you the power to be His child (Jn 1:12).

This "nothing" that we can do must be understood in the spiritual sense. It begins when you realize that His one desire for you is that you desire Him, love Him, and accept His love for you; that you be all He calls you to be so you can share in all He desires to give you. Only you can prevent Him from giving you all He has planned for you.

Your life really begins when you abide in His love. It begins when you love Him enough to have the humility to accept His sacrament of reconciliation and confess your sin to Him through His chosen representative, the priest (Mt 16:18-19; Jn 20:22-23). When you do, you accept His loving forgiveness and His great joy in your being there.

As a way to approach this, you might try the following:

1. On a sheet of paper, describe yourself. Try to state who you are. Write down in list form whatever makes up your identity as you see yourself. Then, next to each item put the word who or what, depending on how you perceive yourself. What does this picture tell you about how you see yourself? Now, when you think of "me", do you think of yourself in terms of **who** or **what**?

2. Jesus told us that we live in Him and He lives in us. What does this mean to you? Write down your thoughts. Come back to this periodically as you progress through the rest of this book; add to your thoughts as appropriate.

I believe self-knowledge is important, as is self-denial. They go hand in hand, both embodiments of the virtue of humility. I do not think the kind of self-knowledge one seeks is the kind that you find in a personality assessment. I think rather, it is the kind that allows you to see yourself in a spiritual mirror more clearly than you have before. It is like looking at a mirror that is still all fogged up in the bathroom because of the steam from the bath or shower. At first, we might think the shape seems OK, the outline looks OK. But as the fog begins to evaporate we see a few blemishes, a roll of fat here or there, and other imperfections. As the spiritual "evaporation" continues we see ourselves more and more clearly, the good as well as the not so good, for we are looking at ourselves through the eyes of God.

Self-knowledge is the sister of humility, and humility gives us the grace to seek and accept further self-knowledge. But this self-knowledge is always in comparison to God, for Jesus told us to imitate Him (Mt 11:29), and to be perfect as the Father is perfect (Mt 5:48). The spiritual exercises of St. Ignatius Loyola are an excellent vehicle for this kind of self-examination. They help you understand the condition of your soul.

As we grow in self-knowledge, we see how true we are to God in the depths of our soul. We stop fooling ourselves. We recognize how much we seek God for His own sake and how much for our own self-interest. Humility allows us to see ourselves in proper balance. Self-denial allows us to purge our souls of the self-interest and attachments that distance us from God. It helps us seek and love God for Himself alone. This is our life-long spiritual goal. It is seldom achieved perfectly because the process is life long, and it is progress in the process that is important.

The closer we come to loving and seeking God for Himself alone, because He deserves it from us, on His terms and not our terms, the more closely we are united to Him. To the extent we do not do this, we are the proximate cause of our own dis-union with God, for union with God is the ardent desire of God for each of us.

As mentioned previously, when we consider who we are, there is a strong tendency to think of ourselves in terms of what we do, or what education or certifications we have, not who we are. We may tend to say "I am an accountant," or perhaps president of the company, an assembly line worker, janitor, or some other job connected identification. But does that define who you are? If you were to change your profession tomorrow, would that change who you are or just what you are and do?

The answer depends on whether the "what" is also your vocation. Your vocation is that life to which God calls you, whether priest, married, single, or consecrated religious. If you are a husband, that is what you are and also who you are. You will be judged by God on how good a husband you are, not on how good an accountant you are. Sometimes a person may have two vocations. For example, a married man may also be called to serve as a permanent deacon. Teaching or working in the medical field can be both a profession and a vocation, depending on how you approach those activities.

Whatever your secular job, that is what you are, not who you are. If you are a priest, what you are and who you are become one, for priesthood is your vocation. What you do for a living, or as a hobby, may be how you support your ability to live your vocation, but it is usually not the thing that defines who you are.

Another way to look at self-knowledge and vocation is to imagine you have just died, and you now stand naked before God in judgment. What about you will be your witness and what will carry no weight at all? Your education, your possessions, your art collection, the bridges you built, the homes you constructed, all will mean very little. How you did these things could make a difference, depending on how you treated others you worked with, but that is addressing a different issue.

Look at how you have lived your life. Perhaps you spent eighteen hours a day at the office, and one hour a week with your wife and children. Perhaps you had some misplaced priorities. Was your primary motivation to make money well or to love well? If you are a priest, how much time did you devote to building the parish coffers or infrastructure as opposed to ministering to the spiritual needs of your parishioners? Did you teach your parishioners how to pray and how to love God? How will you be remembered by those who knew you well? How important to you was "self"?

There is a poignant story, by an unknown author, which illustrates this. I wish I knew who wrote it so I could give him or her proper credit.

DADDY

"Daddy, how much do you make an hour?" With a timid voice and idolizing eyes, the little boy greeted his father as he returned from work.

Greatly surprised, but giving his boy a glaring look, the father said: "Look, not even your mother knows that. Don't bother me now, I'm tired."

"But, Daddy, just tell me please! How much do you make an hour?" the boy insisted.

The father, finally giving up, replied: "Twenty dollars an hour."

"Okay, Daddy. Could you loan me ten dollars?" the boy asked.

Showing his disturbance at this invasion of privacy, the father responded: "So that was the reason you asked how much I earn, right? Go to sleep and don't bother me any more!"

It was already dark and the father was thinking about what the boy had said and was feeling guilty. Finally, trying to ease his conscience, the father went to his son's room.

"Are you asleep?" asked the father.

"No, Daddy. Why?" Replied the boy, partially asleep.

"Here's the money you asked for earlier," the father said.

"Thanks, Daddy!" rejoiced the son, while putting his hand under his pillow and removing some money. "Now I have enough! Now I have twenty dollars!" the boy said to his father. "Daddy, could you please sell me one hour of your time?"

The are many ways we can go about assessing our job, vocation and spiritual life. Two things we might consider doing are:

1. Make a list of your professional activities, your hobbies, your recreation, all those things, other than commuting time, to which you devote at least 2 hours a week. Next to each thing on the list, estimate the average number of hours you devote to that thing in a typical week. Now write down what you believe is your vocation, or vocations (spouse, parent, teacher, etc.). Next to each write down the average number of hours you devote to your vocation(s) in a typical week. What does this picture tell you?

2. Sometimes a vocation involves others. If you are married, it involves a spouse. If you are a priest, it may involve your pastor or associate pastor. Ask that other to look at the list you came up with. Do they agree?

Living in Truth

What is a lie? This is an interesting question. In one of His appearances to St. Teresa of Avila, Jesus told her:

"Alas, daughter, how few there are who truthfully love Me! For if they loved Me, I would reveal to them My secrets. Do you know what it is to love Me truthfully? It is to understand that everything that is displeasing to Me is a lie. By the beneficial effects this understanding will cause in your soul you shall see clearly what you now do not understand."[35]

In the gospel of John, Jesus gives the Holy Spirit the title of Spirit of Truth (Jn 14:16-17). Being the Spirit of God, that means God is truth, just as He is love. Love cannot be separated from truth. If He is truth, and if we live in Him and He in us (Jn 14:23), we must do so in truth, for God and untruth do not co-exist. Thus, the extent to which we live in truth determines how fully we live in God and how fully we keep His word. He also said that if we love Him, we will keep His word. We can only love Him properly when we love Him with all our mind, heart and soul. We demonstrate our love for Him by how fully we keep His word.

If we love Jesus properly, we are in union with Him and no part of us is separated from Him. Sin is an act of non-love, by definition. It is also a lie for it comes from Satan who is the father of lies. In our lives, there is no in-between in our relationship with God. Jesus told us we are with Him or we are against Him (Mk 9:40). Any part of us that is not with Him, not in Him, is not part of Him, and therefore not

---

[35]The Collected Works of St. Teresa of Avila, Vol 1, The Book of Her Life, Chapter 40, ICS Publ, Washington DC, Kavanaugh and Rodriguez trans., 1987, pg 354.

part of truth. To the extent we are not part of truth, we live a lie. It is this non-truth part of us that has to be purified before we can stand before the Beatific Vision, and if it does not happen here then it will have to happen in Purgatory. Any part of us not fully part of truth would be in agony standing before the Beatific Vision of God.

I think the question of what a lie is goes far beyond whether or not we tell a falsehood, or even what we call a white lie. I think it is much more fundamental and deep-rooted than that, for it goes to the very core of our being and what motivates every breath we take. We breathe His Spirit, we drink His life-giving waters, we consume Him in the Eucharist, we become united in His Divine nature; or we do not.

When Jesus says "everything that displeases Me," He means just that - everything; every thought, word, deed, desire, every movement of our soul. Anything else is not part of Him, not part of the reality which is God, and is therefore a lie. He wants all we do to be done in Him, with Him, and through Him. He wants us to be one with Him as He is one with the Father. We should be so united to Him that nothing we can do, on any plane, is contrary to Him. When we reach this point, we live the fullness of truth. Anything else displeases Him. Anything else is a lie.

Loving God

If any man loves Me, he will keep My word, and the Father will love him, and We will come to him and make Our abode in him.

John 14:23

The Responsibility of Love

Jesus said we must work for food that gives Eternal Life, not for food that perishes (Jn 6:27). For many, the practical reality of what Jesus said is just too much; too much to grasp, too much to take responsibility for, requiring that too much be given up if one is to live the reality of this promise. We can only come to Jesus if the Father draws us to Him (Jn 6:44) through operation of grace, and this requires a responsibility on our part to live a life which is not antagonistic toward God. We must learn to listen to the Father as He teaches us and calls us (Jn 6:45). We must eat the Flesh of Jesus and drink His Blood as a condition of eternal life (Jn 6:51; 6:53 - 58). We must turn away from the world and live a life centered on the Spirit of God (Jn 6:63).

It is hard to turn away from all that is around us in the world and seek the love of God, seek a life centered in love of God, to live a life obedient to His will instead of our own will. Many object, unwilling to accept this responsibility of love. It is reminiscent of the disciples complaint in Jn 6:60, "This saying is hard. Who can accept it?"

For one who does respond to the call of the Father and who genuinely seeks God, the longing is something that never subsides. It is a consuming desire. Many seek God in all sorts of places, through all sorts of prayer styles and methods, but if we just believe what Jesus told us in Jn 14:23, we need look no farther than the depths of our own soul. If we truly love Jesus, our prayer will be what it should be, and we need not seek out exotic methods of prayer for our prayer to be effective. These sometimes strange methods do not make prayer effective. What does make prayer effective is the love we have for God.

110

Jesus also told us what we must do to have this relationship with Him. Jesus told Peter, during the washing of the feet, "If I do not wash you, you will have no part in Me." (Jn 13:8) He was washing feet, but He was speaking of washing souls. As He said, He is the living water that refreshes our soul (Jn 4:10-14). Water can refresh when we drink it and it becomes part of us. It can also refresh when we use it to clean our bodies, and the dirtier we are the more refreshing it is. It cleans the outside and refreshes the inside. Jesus refreshes by cleaning our soul through forgiveness of sin in the sacrament of Reconciliation, and refreshes our soul by His living presence within as our souls are divinized through the action of the Holy Spirit, the Sanctifier. He slakes our thirst, satisfying our longing for Him, as we slake His thirst for souls by seeking Him and helping others find Him. This thirst of His for souls led him to cry out, " I thirst," (Jn 19:28) from the Cross. He comes and dwells within and radiates His Light within us. The more purified we are, the more completely His Light permeates all of our soul. But He and the Father are one, and where They are will also be the Holy Spirit, the Paraclete, the Spirit of Truth. If Jesus is within, the Trinity is within.

To receive the indwelling Trinity, our soul must be cleansed by the Holy Spirit, the Sanctifier. He does this through sanctifying grace. We must accept the responsibility to cooperate with that grace. The purer we are, the more evident will be His presence and the more complete the divinization of our soul. As Paul tells us, He lives His life in us. It is how He satisfies our inner longing for Him. Jesus told us, "seek and you will find." (Lk 11:9; Mt 7:7) It was Himself of which He spoke.

Our God, dwelling within, desiring to permeate our entire soul to overflowing with His Being, is sometimes held in check by our foolhardiness. We fail to accept the responsibility to respond to His prompting of grace. We cling to worldly things, are fearful of turning control over to

111

Him, and we are not open to Him. He asks us to trust Him, and we trust ourselves more. He asks us to love Him, and we love only His consolations. But eventually, if we persevere, we turn inward enough to begin appreciating the treasure within, the infinite value of the loving relationship He so very much wants with each of us. We are then responding to the call of His grace. We are accepting the responsibility required of those who love Him.

Have you ever loved someone very much, but that love was not returned? Do you remember the hurt when your offer of love was rejected? Imagine how it is with Jesus, who loves each of us with an infinite love, when we turn away from His offer of love because we fear the relationship, fear what it will cost us. Is there anything worth more to you than an intimate relationship with God?

We can find all this activity within the depths of our own soul. When we do, we realize we did not find this through logic, through reason, through anything over which we had direct control. We found it through detachment from the world and abandonment to God's will and acceptance of our responsibility of love. We found this by allowing the Holy Spirit to work in us unimpeded. We detach enough, and submit sufficiently, that God then takes charge and brings us to where He desires and in the manner He desires, and this is unique for each of us. It is also the best possible state of being for us, for His plan for us is always perfect.

We each arrive at a decidedly unique relationship with God dwelling within, and in the depths of our soul we communicate with Him directly, intimately, and continuously. When we do encounter God within, God communicates Himself directly to us, and in ways we cannot fathom with reason or the senses. He communicates as much of Himself as is needed for us to fulfill His desire for us, limited only by our preparedness, and can do so in an instant. He communicates as much of Himself as we are disposed to receive. We finally accept the responsibility of love, and receive the gift of God Himself in return. The more mature our spiritual life, the greater the responsibility of love we accept, the more of Himself He will share with us. This responsibility is simply to live our entire life in accordance with His will for us, not our own will. Who, other than He, could possibly know what is best for us?

The Many Aspects of Love

Many will tell you that we cannot really define love. That is not true. Love is God, because God is love. All love has its origin in Him. The key is to understand what this means. Love is recognized when it is manifested through its attributes. We find what this means when we ponder the command of Jesus, "Love others as I have loved you." (Jn 13:34) If we ask how Jesus loved us, the answer is simple. He loved us completely, giving Himself totally for us and for our salvation. Let us consider what this means for us in our relationships with God and with each other.

Real love originates from within and goes out to the object of our love. It is generated within, and goes out. It is not self-focused and reactive to what we receive. It is something we give, and our hope is that it is returned by the one we love. It is not merely reflective of what we receive. It is like the difference between the sun and the moon. The sun generates light from the fire within and that light goes out from itself in all directions. The light comes from within and comes from the essence of the sun itself, regardless of whether any is returned. The moon receives the light from the sun and reflects it toward earth. The light from the moon is cold and does not come from the moon itself. Moonlight is a misnomer, for the moon gives nothing of itself when it shines. It only reflects a part of the sunlight it has received.

God is perfect love, and His love is eternal and infinite. He does not merely reflect what He receives from us. God offers us His kingdom as our inheritance. He asks us to be His child and participate in His nature. He gave His only begotten Son to us as a sacrifice for our sin so we can be redeemed and share in His divine life of Love. He gives Himself to us in the Eucharist. In doing so, He made Himself completely vulnerable to us, subjecting Himself to us completely. The Creator subjected Himself to the created, all because of His perfect love.

With this love of Jesus as our model, what is human love and how should we love? Love is a giving of self, but more. It is making ourselves completely accessible to the other. I truly love my spouse, and this means I make myself completely accessible to her, holding nothing back. No hidden secrets, no part of me unrevealed. I grant her unfettered access to my heart, my mind, my soul, my body. There is nothing of me that I do not willingly share with her. In doing so, I make myself completely vulnerable to her. She has access to all of me; my strengths, my weaknesses, my joys, my sorrows, my fears. I trust in her not to abuse this gift, but she is free to do so. She has free will and that is her right. My hope, and my expectation, is that she will be as accessible to me as I am to her, for then our mutual sharing of self is completely reciprocal. If this sharing is reciprocal, we have become as one, as Jesus said we should be. We become one by mutual giving, not mutual taking. In making myself completely accessible to her, I assume a commitment to her that I would not otherwise have. In not holding anything back, I have committed to give everything I have for her good, including my life. This is love.

God, who is Love, is both simple and complex. Infinite in His being, complex in His Trinitarian nature, and simple in His relationship with each of us as individuals. Simple because He principally asks of us things that are quite ordinary. He asks us to love Him and to obey Him because He is God and because we love Him (Jn 14:23), to love others as He loved us (Jn 13:34), and to be perfect as the Father is perfect (Mt 5:48). Literally everything we do that is contrary to love is contrary to the will of God. Jesus told St. Teresa of Avila that everything displeasing to Him is a lie, and we know who is the father of lies (Jn 8:44).

Love is a natural inclination of the soul of every person, and each of us seeks good and seeks to do good. Because love is a natural inclination of the soul, the soul naturally seeks God as its objective, as the natural object of its love. Love seeks Love. Love always has an object, the being to whom love is offered. God's love for us is perfect, and infinite. Because of our fallen nature, our love is imperfect, and can only be perfected by God as we cooperate with Him (Mt 5:48). The love we give to God is love which came from God to begin with, for God made man in His own image and likeness and impressed love in our soul as part of the nature of the soul. Our being must therefore be a likeness, however imperfect, of God who is pure Love.

When we do something evil, we can only do so when what we do is somehow perceived by us as a good, however warped our logic may be in coming to that conclusion. Satan has to convince us that evil is a good when he tempts us to act contrary to the will of God.

Love has many aspects and dimensions, so let us consider some of them and then see how they resonate within as we reflect on our relationship with God.

Loving God

Loving God is not something we do on our terms. We love God on His terms, with His love, and in accord with the two great commandments Jesus gave us. We cannot make God conform to our imperfect idea of love. God is love and all the love we have comes from Him. There is only one real way for you to love God, and that is with everything in you. Your constant prayer should be that He gives the love you need to love Him perfectly, and that you respond to this grace by loving Him as much as He wants to be loved by you. We can never love Him too much.

If we love God in accordance with the two great commandments of Jesus, we must put God first in our lives. Any person or thing more important to us than God becomes an impediment to loving Him, and to our receiving the grace of His love. He will not force Himself on us, but will lead us in love if we cooperate with Him. This means we must say, with St. John the Baptist, "I must decrease and He must increase."(Jn 3:30)

What does it mean to decrease? Do we go into the desert and eat honey and locusts like St John? No, we decrease by placing God first, always. We never put ourselves first, never put our desires ahead of what God wants. We place God far enough in first place that we will do nothing contrary to His will, even if it means giving up our life for Him.

We cannot have this kind of love for God on the first day of our search. We grow in love for God as He leads us, just as we grown in love for our spouse. Even if you believe you loved your spouse at first sight, you know that your love for each other grew and matured. We cannot grow in love for God, or hear His voice expressing His love for us, if the noise and distractions of the world and our own self-interest drown Him out. We must recognize His will as it is expressed ever so quietly in our life. He will speak to us in many ways. He will speak through strangers He sends into our life, through events, and through the joys and trials we experience. He will speak to us more clearly, or at least it will seem to be more clearly, when we look and listen for His voice in all the things we encounter, when we finally realize that there is no such thing as coincidence. We look for the hand of God in everything. Once we learn to recognize His voice, and conform our will to His, we can begin to approach the depth of love for Him that He desires.

This love relationship with God cannot be static. We cannot sit passively before God and expect Him to do all the work. God's infinite love for us is so powerful, so focused, so personal, that He cannot endure passivity on our part. Jesus said we must love God with our whole heart, soul, mind and will. Everything in us must desire Him above all else. He, who loves us so much, must lead us gently into His infinite love, or He would overwhelm our free will. There is no greater gift we can give ourselves than to remain in His love. He has already given us all of Himself. We must freely give Him as much as we can of ourselves; all of ourselves when possible.

Loving Others

Self discovery is a requisite for loving others as we should, for Jesus told us we must love others as ourselves. How do we love ourselves? How do we know we love ourselves properly? How can we love others the same way? These are not always easy questions to answer. St. Teresa of Avila told us we must continually discover ourselves, and grow in humility, no matter how far we progress in our prayer. We can always learn more about ourselves, and always grow in humility, no matter what else may be true about our spiritual life. We must therefore establish a love relationship with others that is relative; relative to the way we love ourselves. If we cannot love ourselves, we cannot love others properly. The more we love ourselves, the more we can love others.

This brings us to an interesting question. We can love ourselves as perfectly as we know ourselves. But we do not know many of the others we are supposed to love. We are also called to love others we do not like; perhaps even those who hate us. How do we do this? We do this by knowing ourselves not only as the person we are as an isolated individual, but who we are in relationship to God, as part of the family of God. Just as our love for others is relative to how we love ourselves, our knowledge of ourselves grows in comparison to our knowledge of God. When we learn to know and love ourselves this way, we are knowing and loving ourselves as a child of God. Jesus called us to be perfect as the Father is perfect, and thus we are called to know and love ourselves in terms of the growth in perfection we attain as a child of God. Once we have learned to love this way, we love as God loves, not as the world loves. We finally learn what real love is.

Love in the sense in which we are discussing it is never self-focused, but it is self-generated. Love comes from within, from God dwelling within, and goes out to the other. We do not love by seeking what we can get from the relationship, but from what we can give to the relationship. Our capacity to love grows in proportion to how much love we give. God loves infinitely. We who are finite must grow in our capacity to love, so we love by giving love, not by seeking to receive love. Scriptures tells us to lend without expecting repayment. So much more is this true with regard to love. Jesus loved even those who crucified Him. Self-interest is what motivates Satan, not children of God. We saw this admirably demonstrated in the life of Mother Teresa.

We are motivated, called by God, to love others because they, too, are God's children and He loves them. It has nothing to do with how good a person or how clean a person or how nice a person they are. It has everything to do with the fact that God loves them. We cannot hate those whom God loves and also say we love God. How do we love them? By praying for them. That is the principal means whereby we develop our relationship with God, and how we express our love for Him and others. We pray for their salvation, their spiritual growth, their conversion and their sainthood. Without prayer of the heart, we cannot love.

Where Will We Go?

One of the most powerful lessons of love Jesus taught us is one seldom discussed. In the gospel of Matthew, Jesus gives a discourse on the final judgment of the nations. During this discourse, He says, "Inherit the kingdom prepared for you from the foundation of the world" (Mt 25:34). A little later in this same discourse He says, "Depart from Me, you accursed, into the eternal fire prepared for the devil and his angels" (Mt 25:41). If we step back from the main purpose of the discourse and simply meditate on these two teachings of Jesus, we realize none of us is intended to go anywhere but heaven. Not even one. God did not stamp a number on our soul at conception determining that this many of us would go to heaven and that many would go to hell. Our intended place in the kingdom of heaven was prepared by God, for each and every one of us individually, from the foundation of the world, from the beginning of creation. It is the express will of God that we each claim our prepared place and spend eternity with Him.

The only way we can avoid heaven is by deliberately living a life contrary to the will of God. God did not prepare a place of punishment for us. The only ones for whom hell was prepared are "the devil and his angels." We must choose to go to hell. We must turn our backs on the gifts offered to us by God, reject the home He prepared for us, and deliberately choose to spend eternity with the devil. Since it is God's will that we not make this choice, He will give us all necessary means to avoid this calamity. If we end up there, we have no excuse. We have no one to blame but ourselves. God gives us the opportunity to be His child, and this is not just a figure of speech. He will share His nature with us to a degree commensurate with our acceptance of His sanctifying grace, and will give us the means to avoid the enticements of the devil to lead us on the path toward hell. He even took away the confusion factor, and gave us only one light to follow to heaven; Himself.

This whole sanctifying process only works, it only means something, when love is the predominant motive for what we do. We must do whatever we can to live a life in Truth, to avoid living a lie, and to live the two commandments of Jesus to love God and love our neighbor as our self. Our life should be other-focused, not self-focused. We must grow in knowledge and love for God and others, and that means we must have an active prayer life. Prayer is the key to the heart of God and we must use that key frequently.

God actively wants us with Him. He does not sit back and wait for us to come. He is always sending us help, always calling, always drawing us to Himself (Jn 12:32), always sending us different opportunities for grace to lead us to Him. He wants us to behave as the hunter, while He treats us as His prey. The bait He uses to draw us to Him is love. We must never forget what Jesus said in the parable of the lost sheep. At the end of the parable, He said, "In just the same way, it is not the will of your heavenly Father that one of these little ones be lost."(Mt 18:14) Not even one.

The Three Big Choices of Life

One of the things we must do as we grow in knowledge and love for God is recognize the things that separate us from Him and His love. We must learn what to avoid as well as what to do. The more we pray from the heart the easier it is to live the life of love we should.

We make choices all during our life. Proper choices always lead to love and come from love. St. Paul tells us that the virtue of love is the only thing that survives death. When we make choices we choose either virtue, truth and life, or their opposites - sin, falsehood (lie), and death. Virtue, truth and life are the three things which lead us to God. If we live a virtuous life, live in truth, and seek eternal life, and persevere in this way of living, we will eventually reach heaven. If we choose their opposites and live a life of sin, if we lie in the sense that everything displeasing to God is a lie, and if we seek spiritual death instead of sanctifying grace, and if we do not recognize that conversion is an ongoing process, we will eventually reach hell. We must walk one of these two paths every time we act, every time we make a choice. It is in making our decisions in favor of one set of three over the other set that we determine whether we have eternal life with God. What will we choose? Will we choose virtue, truth and life, or will we choose sin, lies and death?

If we are just beginning our journey, we are sometimes unsure how to know when we are making a wrong choice. This is a legitimate question, for the enticements of Satan are often very subtle. How do we recognize "subtle" sin? How do we increase our sensitivity to the border between harmless and sinful? How does love play a part in that recognition process?

Begin by paying attention to what Jesus told us in Chapter 15 of the gospel of Matthew. He said, "But the things that come out of the mouth come from the heart, and they defile. For from the heart come evil thoughts, murder, adultery, unchastity, theft, false witness, blasphemy. These are what defile a person, but to eat with unwashed hands does not defile." (Mt 15:18-20)

So, we begin by paying more attention to how we talk to others, what we say about others, the tone in which we speak, and the content of what we say. At the end of every day, we should look back and examine our behavior, especially our speech. Did we lie? Did we speak ill of another? Did we gossip? Did we use God's name in vain? Did we encourage, condone, or offer adultery? Did we condone other unchastity? Did we speak by our silence, giving silent acquiescence to what we knew was wrong?

122

We can also increase our sensitivity by deliberately living in the presence of God throughout the day. Before we speak or act, recognize that God is with us, that nothing is hidden from Him, and that we should do all that we do in concert with Him. We ask ourselves, "What would Jesus say about this action or speech?" If we are not sure, we should go back to the gospels and read more. The answer is usually there. If we love Jesus, we have the incentive to seek this guidance because any choice for the wrong three - sin, lie or death, is one which rejects Jesus and His love. To make such a choice is to hurt the One we love. If we do not love Him, we will not care. What we say and do tells everyone, including God, how much we love Him. We must always remember what St. John of the Cross taught us; "... for love effects a likeness between the lover and the loved."[36] The more, and more deeply, we love the more like God we become. Consider the implications of the opposite.

The Joy of Love

When we love we should always experience joy. Joy and love should be inseparable. In some instances, love hurts. The one we love does not love us in return. The one we love decides to abuse us or take advantage of us. We give, they take. We express our love truthfully, and they lie. Sometimes the one we love, and who loves us in return, dies. These experiences can make us afraid of love, even make us wish we had never loved.

No one can love us the way God does. His love is completely giving, infinite, and unconditional. No matter what happens in our life, no matter what we do or how we are treated by others, we are always receiving infinite and unconditional love from the one who is the source of all

---

[36]The Collected Works of St. John of the Cross, trans by Kavanaugh and Rodriguez, The Ascent of Mount Carmel, Book One, Chapter 4, ICS Publications, Washington DC, 1991, Pg 124

love. Once we understand this and understand He loves each of us this way, we begin to understand we are always immersed in His love, and always will be. Any other experience of love should teach us more about His love. When we love ourselves, when we love others, when we love God, we are learning more and more about His love for us.

There are no boundaries or limits to God's love or the love He desires to share with us and communicate to our soul. Part of our job as we grow in grace is to increase in receptivity to His love. We do this by imitating in our own self the way He loves us. We learn to love others without requiring recompense. We learn to generate love, to let our own heart become a furnace of love, first for God and then for self and then others. This furnace of love within us has its origin in His fathomless Sacred Heart. When we love with His love, we love in union with Him. If we love others and they do not respond or reciprocate, the circle of love is not completed with that person, but that does not invalidate the love we have given. The validity of our love comes from God's love for that person, and we love Jesus who is in them. We understand what Jesus taught when He said that whatever we do to these we do to Him. By loving them we love Him in another way. When we have faith in Jesus and love Him, our joy is boundless, for the love we have for Him opens the door to eternal life for us. Our name is written in the Book of Life by our love. Our love leads us into eternal life and away from sin, lies and death.

If we understand this, our joy is boundless and perpetual because our love runs deep and sustains us. Our love supports virtue, confirms faith, and gives life to hope. Knowing that living a life of love means we live a life in God cannot help but cause us to live joyously regardless of external circumstances. We begin to live our heaven here on earth by living a life of love in Christ, through Christ and with Christ. The more we live this life the more we die to self so Christ may live in us. This joy of love is the secret of the saints. It is living Christ's life here on earth.

Four Levels of Love

A friend of mine, Mary Ellen Lucas, gave a talk at our parish one evening in which she spoke of four levels of love. These four levels of love are an expression of the growth of love in us, and the growth of God in us. She said:

The first level is love of self. This is not self-centered love, but is the love of self that Jesus teaches, a love of self which is raised up in us because we have become a temple of God. St. Paul exclaims, "Do you not know that you are the temple of God?" (1 Cor 3:16) When we pray the joyful mysteries of the rosary, as we meditate on the fifth mystery, we should meditate on whether the Blessed Mother finds her Son in us, in this temple of God. Are we conscious enough of Jesus in us that we do not do anything to hurt our body either physically or spiritually? Do we respect His presence in us that much and recognize our preciousness to Him? When we see Him working in us, in this temple that He uses to reach out to others, do we also see Him in others because they, too, are temples?

The second level of love is our love for our loving God. In this unique love, we have both an expression and a need. We express our love for God by how we act and pray, but we cannot love God unless He first loves us. God made us so that the natural inclination of our soul is toward Him. Our soul, our being, turns to God as its natural object. We love Him because we trust Him and rely on Him.

The third level of love is loving God simply for being God. We love God for all the things He is in Himself. We love Him because He is omnipotent, omniscient, and all-loving. We love Him for being all-present and for being the natural goal of everything in our life, even the purpose of our relationships with each other. We love Him because of His pervasive presence in all of us and all we do. We love Him for being our God and our Father, for being forgiving and compassionate, for being mysterious and for His desire to share that awesome mystery of Himself with us.

The fourth level of love is loving God so much that we love our neighbor for love of God. This is the love Jesus calls us to, the love He showed us, the love He had for us that led Him to give up His life on the cross so we might live and live more abundantly. He gave everything of Himself so that we might posses everything; that we might possess God Himself. This is the love that we have for God that would call us to lay down our own life for another, for any other. We saw this in the martyrdom of St. Maximilian Kolbe. Because we love God, we realize how precious His gift of life is, and because we love God we give up our own identity and take on His identity; we, as St. Paul says, "put on Christ." (Gal 3:27) Jesus gives us this new identity by giving us Himself in the Eucharist. When we partake of Him we receive His identity through this substantial way. Recognizing the worth of this Gift, we conform ourselves to His image, and, to the extent He works in us, to His likeness.

Love In The Trinity

We cannot pretend to understand the Trinity. The Trinity is a mystery we shall contemplate for all eternity. Through the ages, we have come to understand some things about the Trinity, and our discovery of the Trinity always leads to a discovery of Love. Love in the Trinity is the source of all love there is, ever has been and ever will be.

Part of our exploration of the Trinity helps us see how God loves. The first level of love within the Trinity is the love God has for Himself. God, being infinite, loves Himself infinitely. This infinite love God has for Himself must have an object, for all genuine love comes from within and goes out to another. The object of the love God has for Himself is Himself, and the word of love God speaks to Himself is personified as the Logos, the Word, the Second Person of the Trinity. God's love for Himself is continual and generative. It never ceases. Therefore, because of the continual infinite love of God for Himself, the Second Person of the Trinity is continually being generated, and will be continually generated for all eternity. The Word of God also loves infinitely, and also loves God with an infinite love. The mutual love between God and the Word is also generative, and is personified as the Holy Spirit. Because of what St. John teaches in his gospel about the indwelling Trinity (Jn 14:23), we know the Second Person of the Trinity is continually being generated within our very soul.

The second level of love within the Trinity is the love of the Logos, incarnated as Jesus Christ. Jesus told us that He loves the Father, and that He came to do the will of the Father. In His final hours on earth, He said "not My will be done, but Yours." (Mt 26:39)

The third level of love within the Trinity is the infinite mutual love given Father to Son and Son to Father, without end. They are each the object of the love from the other. This mutual and infinite Love proceeding from the love shared between the Father and Son is personified as the Holy Spirit, the Spirit of love within the Trinity and, as Jesus told us, the Spirit of truth to us. He proceeds from the Father and the Son, is the truth of God, the truth of the Trinity, and is the truth of Trinitarian love. Real love and truth are inseparable.

The fourth level of love within the Trinity is the love of the Trinity for man. God, from the beginning, had the role of Savior. God does not change. Therefore He is, and always was, our Savior. God's infinite love for man determined from all eternity that He would be our Savior. We are not always aware of this infinite, salvific love, even though Jesus told us, in John 17, that the Father loves us with the same infinite love with which He loves Jesus. This infinite love is continuously being poured out in us because of the Trinity dwelling within. The eternal generation of the Son by the Father, and the eternal procession of the Holy Spirit from the Father and the Son, is taking place continuously within our human soul. This infinite, Divine love being generated within us is the most powerful force there is, the force which will destroy the evil of Satan in the world, and is the force always available to us. When Jesus said to seek so that we will find, it is this infinite love within us that we are to seek.

The Infinite Love of God For Man

"In the beginning was the Word, and the Word was with God, and the Word was God. He was in the beginning with God. All things were made by Him; and without Him was made nothing that was made. All things were made by Him; and without Him was made nothing that was made. In Him was life, and the life was the light of men. And the light shineth in the darkness, and the darkness did not comprehend it. ...

That was the true light, which enlighteneth every man that cometh into this world. He was in the world, and the world was made by Him, and the world knew Him not. He came unto His own, and His own received Him not. But as many as received Him, He gave them the power to be made the sons of God, to them that believe in His name. ...

And the Word was made flesh, and dwelt among us, and we saw His glory, the glory as it were of the only begotten of the Father, full of grace and truth. ... And of His fullness we have all received, and grace for grace." Jn 1:1-16

Reading this opening of the gospel of John, we should feel a sense of awe and wonder at how John is introducing us, not just to the mystery of the incarnation, but to the infinite love of God for man. If we read this passage several times over, we get a sense of the awesome reality of what the patristic fathers tried to explain to us. St. Gregory of Nyssa, in his treatise <u>On the Soul and The Resurrection</u>[37], tells us

"Moreover, as every being is capable of attracting its like, and humanity is, in a way, like God, as being within itself some resemblances to its Prototype, the soul is by a strict necessity attracted to its kindred Deity. In fact what belongs to God must by all means and at all cost be preserved for Him. ...Such, I think, is the plight of the soul as well when the Divine force, for God's very love of man, drags that which belongs to Him from the ruins of the irrational and material. Not in hatred or revenge for a wicked life, to my thinking, does God bring upon sinners the painful dispensations; He is only claiming and drawing to Himself, whatever, to please Him, came into existence."

In just the first two sentences of this passage, St. Gregory has said so very much. He confirms that we must share in the Divine nature so that like can attract like, so that God can attract us to Himself because of His gift to us of participative sharing in His nature. He tells us that we belong to God and we must be preserved for Him, at all cost and by all means. Taking the gospel of John together with this, we see that we are not just possessed by God as some kind of property, but we share a kinship with Him, and through that kinship we have been given the power to be made, truly, children of God. Gregory is also teaching us the full meaning of what Jesus told us in the gospel as to why He came among us[38].

---

[37]St. Gregory of Nyssa, On The Soul And The Resurrection, trans. By Rev. William Moore, M.A., EWTN on-line library, Http://www.ewtn.com, accessed July 22, 2004.

[38]For God so loved the world, as to give His only begotten Son; that whosoever believeth in Him may not perish, but may have life

We thus begin to see a glimmer of the meaning of God's infinite love for man. We know that God cannot change, and that He has always had from all eternity everything that He is. He is I AM. We also know He is Love. What can we infer from what John and Gregory are telling us?

As we continue to explore God's infinite love for man, we recognize God is love, infinite love, and has been love from all eternity. His love has never changed. But all love has an object. True love for another comes from within ourselves, from the love which resides in our soul, and goes out from us to the object of our love. We must ask what is the object of God's infinite love, and what change happens in the object of His love when God loves infinitely? We have already explored the four levels of love within the Trinity. The Father loves man, His creation made in His image and likeness, and He loves man infinitely. Thus, the Word, the Logos, is not just a personification of the Father's love for Himself, but also of the Father's love, His infinite love, for man. The Word, the Second Person of the Trinity, is the personification of the Father's infinite love for Himself and for man, a love so immense, powerful, and incomprehensible that He must communicate that Love to us in a way we could never have comprehended on our own, a way which had to be revealed to us in the person of the incarnate Word, Jesus Christ. He loves us so much, and His infinite love reaches out to us with such inconceivable power, that He literally empties Himself for us, He gives us His all, He offers us His entire, His infinite, self; He gives us all of His only-begotten Son.

Knowing from all eternity the condition in which man would find himself because of the sin of Adam, part of the Father's essence, that which makes Him what and who

---

everlasting. For God sent not His Son into the world to judge the world, but that the world may be saved by Him. Jn 3:16-17

He is, an essence which includes His love for mankind, is that of being our Savior. His love for us is so powerful, so consuming, He could not allow mankind to live in darkness and die eternally separated from Him. This part of His essence, this identity as Savior, constituted a fundamental aspect of the nature of the Incarnate Word, Jesus, for everything the Father is, Jesus is also. He and the Father are one. Jesus emptied Himself, He gave Himself to us completely; first as a helpless child through the fiat of Mary, and then on the cross as He emptied Himself of His blood and His life, giving everything He could possibly give, for our redemption. Only He could do this, for the affronts of man against God could only be atoned for by a sacrifice fitting for God. No man, and no number of men, could ever qualify. In the process of emptying Himself, He gave to each and every one of us the ultimate gift of grace, the incredible gift of the power to become a child of God. His complete emptying of self was the fulfillment of His burning need, not just desire, to rescue us. Even the language he uses in the gospel shows this. He speaks of the longing, the desire He had to celebrate the last supper with the apostles, to share Himself with them as He instituted the Eucharist and made them His priests. He could not do otherwise, for the Father loves us with the same infinite love with which He loves Himself, and the same love with which He loves Jesus.

God's infinite love is never static. It is always active, always flowing out from Himself to the object of His love, and the more we are willing to accept Him, the more of His love He will be able to give to us. In chapter 17 of the gospel of St. John, the evangelist gives us a hint as to what this means in part of his rendition of Jesus' prayer to the Father just before His crucifixion.

"Sanctify them in Truth. Thy word is Truth. And for them do I sanctify Myself, that they also may be sanctified in Truth. And not for them only do I pray, but for them also who through their word shall believe in me; That they may all be one, as Thou, Father, in Me, and I in Thee; that they may be made one in Us; that the world may believe that thou hast sent Me. ... I in them, and thou in Me; that they may be made perfect in one; and the world may know that Thou hast sent Me, and hast loved them, as Thou hast also loved Me." [39]

Thus we see that the Father loves us infinitely, and desires to make us one in Him, as He and Jesus are one. "... and the world may know that Thou hast loved them, as Thou hast also loved Me." What a profound statement! Implied in this is also the need on our part to accept and respond to this love. This takes an act of the will, for love is an act of the will. We must love God, and accept His love for us. Without this acceptance and return of love from us to Him, if we reject His love and fail to love Him in return, He cannot communicate His love to our souls, cannot sanctify our souls through grace, and cannot allow us to share His nature and His kingdom as His children, for non-love cannot co-exist with the infinite love of God.

The power we have to become children of God rests in our free will to love Him above all else. We are the only ones who can prevent God's love from entering our hearts. We can become co-heirs by becoming one with Jesus through the operation of sanctifying grace, or we can reject this love and give our love to things of this world, things with which we replace God in our lives.

We cannot conceive of how this rejection of infinite love is responded to by God, for, as Gregory says, our soul "must by all means and at all cost be preserved for Him."[40] But to accomplish His will He had to also give us the gift of free will. This gift, if used to accept Him and love Him with our whole heart and mind, is the key which unlocks His love

---

[39]Jn, 17:17-23

[40]St. Gregory of Nyssa, On The Soul And The Resurrection, trans. By Rev. William Moore, M.A., EWTN on-line library, Http://www.ewtn.com, accessed July 22, 2004.

and allows it to flow freely into our soul, sanctifying our soul and, as John told us, giving us "the power to become children of God." (Jn 1:12) We might ask why God had to do this, why He had to give us this power to become His adopted children, the power to gain, by participation, what Jesus has by nature?

As we ponder the question of why God had to give us the opportunity to be His children, we can understand the answer by examining what must happen if we decide to adopt a child and give that child all rights to be our heir, just as if the child had been born to us. We must find a child we wish to adopt, and then go through the process of formal adoption. If the child is capable of making a rational decision, the child must also accept us, want to be our child, and agree to the adoption. We can do this because there are many beings which share our nature, our human nature. We cannot adopt a dog. We can make a dog a beneficiary of our estate, managed by a trustee, but we cannot adopt a dog. He who is adopted must share sufficiently in the nature of he who is the adopting party. In the case of God, there is only one God; He is completely unique. There are no other beings which have the nature of God. Thus, to adopt us, He has to communicate to us at least some minimal sufficiency of His nature.

The more of God's nature we receive, the more He communicates Himself to us. He does this through the operation of sanctifying grace, a grace communicated through the sacraments. The effect of sanctifying grace is to communicate God's divine nature to our soul, to Divinize our soul. Each time we receive a sacrament, we gain more sanctifying grace, and participate more fully in the Divine life of God. He does this most fully through His gift of the Eucharist. This is an effect we will never be able to fully appreciate until we reside with God in His kingdom.

Thus we see that Jesus, in emptying Himself for us completely on the cross, fulfilling the will of the Father, has given us the power to receive Him within us every time we receive the Eucharist. Not just His body, but His living body and blood, soul and divinity. No wonder He has spoken of the Eucharist, to many of the saints through the ages, like St. Margaret Mary and St. Faustina Kowalska, as the sacrament of His love. This sacrament is the principal means whereby we participate in the culmination of the will of the Father for mankind, the principal means whereby we become His adopted children, and the principal means through which we consummate the final covenant. When we understand this, we see the tremendous advantage of fully participating at Mass and receiving the Eucharist as often as we can, daily if possible. By doing so worthily, in a state of grace, we are fulfilling the will of the Father for us.

The interplay of God's love for us and our free will choosing God, responding to His love and accepting the offer of participation in the Divine life, is one of the sublime mysteries of life. We do this by choosing Him above all else, by choosing Him above every created thing, every thing this world has to offer. He desires to make us His children who may live in this world, but are of God, not of this world. He offers us eternal Life with Him.

St. Gregory of Nyssa explains the love relationship between God and man in terms of virtue:

"It follows, then, that as everything that is free will be united with its like, and as virtue is a thing that has no master, that is, is free, everything that is free will be united with virtue. But, further, the Divine Being is the fountain of all virtue. Therefore, those who have parted with evil will be united with Him; and so, as the Apostle says, God will be 'all in all'"[41]

Here Gregory again tries to explain the operation of Divine love, drawing us through virtue, through freedom from evil, into that state of sanctifying grace whereby we can participate in the Divine life and accept God's offer to be, for us, all in all, we in Him and He in us. As we have seen, love, by its nature, is never self-focused and cries out to be shared with the object of that love. Love is always communicated, even if not received and accepted. It is unnatural for love to arise within and not be offered. It is a gift offered from one soul to another. God's infinite love for man compels Him to share His infinite love with man. But God is love, and thus when He shares His infinite love with man, He is necessarily sharing Himself, and, in communicating Himself to man, He is communicating His nature and His very essence. Thus, we can say with justification and with humility, that He offers man all that He is, and will give to each man all that grace disposes him to receive. The more sanctifying grace possessed by any person, the more God's Divine life is communicated. To the extent we turn our backs on God, on His love, we reject perfect love, perfect goodness, and have chosen sin and evil as our God. Jesus said we are either with Him or against Him. There is no middle ground. Thus Gregory continues his lesson, teaching us[42]

"If, then, love of man be a special characteristic of the Divine nature, here is the reason for which you are in search, here is the cause of the presence of God among men. Our diseased nature needed a healer."

---

[41]St. Gregory of Nyssa, On The Soul And The Resurrection, trans. By Rev. William Moore, M.A., EWTN on-line library, Http://www.ewtn.com, accessed July 22, 2004.

[42]St. Gregory of Nyssa, The Great Catechism, Chapter XV, EWTN on-line library.

Later, when we reflect on the introduction to the gospel of John, we should notice the emphasis on light and life in reference to the Word. Considering the love God has for man, and His plan to both heal and save us, we can begin to comprehend the meaning behind Jesus' words when He said he had not come to save the just man but rather the sinner, for a healthy man does not require a physician. His healing power of love is given to us to heal us from the effects of evil, the state of darkness which imparts death to the soul, that state in which so many souls find themselves. Jesus must find a way to break through that darkness while not interfering with the operation of free will.

In considering the respect Jesus has for our free will, while recognizing His salvific mission, St. Gregory of Nyssa tells us,

"Now it is the peculiar effect of light to make darkness vanish, and of life to destroy death. Since, then, we have been led astray from the right path, and diverted from that life which was ours at the beginning, and brought under the sway of death, what is there improbable in the lesson we are taught by the Gospel mystery, if it be this; that cleansing reaches those who are befouled with sin, and life the dead, and guidance the wanderers, in order that defilement may be cleansed, error corrected, and what was dead restored to life."[43]

In this discussion, Gregory is emphasizing the need for healing as a primary element of the salvific mission. As both God and Savior, Jesus must provide the most efficacious, most perfect, means to rescue His people from the darkness and death of sin in the soul. This most perfect means is, literally, Himself. Thus, he tells us, and John so eloquently confirms, that Jesus is the light which came into the world to drive out the darkness of sin. A soul fouled by

---

[43]St. Gregory of Nyssa, The Great Catechism, Chapter XXIV. EWTN on-line library.

sin, which is the death of the soul, must be healed of mortal sin before the person dies, for otherwise only hell awaits. A soul constricted by venial sin also needs healing, for the purgation suffering the soul must endure in Purgatory is a measure of how steeped in non-mortal sin the soul finds itself. The light, Jesus, thus comes to shine among men and drive away the darkness of sin to heal the rupture in the relationship between man and God. Only God can do this. He comes as the light, and the life, of the soul. He is both healer and sanctifier; and so He gives us both the sacrament of reconciliation and the sacrament of Eucharist. All of mankind is the object of God's infinite love, and He chose to take upon His shoulders the sins of the world for all time and disperse them into the nether regions by His forgiveness, just as He drove the evil spirits, which plagued the tormented man in the cemetery, into the swine, which then cast themselves to death in the ravine, unclean into unclean. As He hung on the Cross for us, the perfect embodiment of the Father's infinite love for man, He brought with Him on that cross all the sins of mankind. When He died and was taken down, He left our sins on the cross, ready to forgive and forget for all eternity. All He ever asks is that we love Him; love returned for love given. It is only we, in our weakness and self-centeredness, who insist on climbing up on that cross to recover those sins, to embrace them as a long lost friend, an embrace of death.

As Jesus watches us climb back on that cross to recover these 'treasures', how He must lament for our souls, how it must hurt to see what He did for us being discarded so easily by those He still loves infinitely. He is ready to forgive us anything, anything, so that the merits of what He has done can be communicated to the soul, but so very many souls still insist on putting walls between themselves and Him, blocking by an act of their free will all the merits and grace He longs to impart to the soul.

137

Those who love God, and desire to be His above all else, also know that one day we must each face the thought that can send a chill down the back of the strongest among us; the thought of God's perfect justice. We speak of Jesus' return to judge us, but isn't it true that we will actually judge ourselves? Will we not judge ourselves by our own deeds and thoughts? The sentence His justice must mete out will stand for eternity, and there is no appeal. The sentence He must pronounce is that which we have already inflicted upon ourselves.

Some tend to question how infinite love and eternal damnation can be reconciled. Just think of the soul steeped in mortal sin, rejecting God's love, a soul void of love. In hell it exists with its like. As Gregory told us, like attracts like. How could a soul void of love possibly exist in heaven, possibly exist in the eternal presence of infinite love? Would not such a soul, void of love, be even more tortured existing for eternity surrounded by, but never participating in, infinite love? Hell itself, for man, is a creation of both mercy and justice.

If we look at how mankind has sinned through the ages, we might ask why, in His infinite mercy and love, did Jesus not come among us much earlier? Why did He not come, for example, right after Cain's act of fratricide? Gregory of Nyssa explains it as follows:

"When once, then the disease of evil had fixed itself in the nature of mankind, He, the universal Healer, waited for the time when no form of wickedness was left still hidden in that nature. For this reason it was that He did not produce His healing for man's disease immediately on Cain's hatred and murder of his brother; for the wickedness of those who were destroyed in the days of Noah had not yet burst into flame, nor had that terrible disease of Sodomite lawlessness been displayed, nor the Egyptians' war against God, nor the pride of Assyria, nor the Jews' bloody persecution of God's saints, nor Herod's cruel murder of the children, nor whatever else is recorded, or if unrecorded was done in the generations that followed, the root of evil budding forth in divers manners in the willful purposes of man."[44]

If we think about it, all sins since the time of Christ are the same sins, or extensions of the same, found at the time of Christ. There was theft, blasphemy, murder, fornication, adultery, paganism, atheism, fratricide, infanticide, abortion, active homosexuality, untruthfulness, lukewarmness toward God (Rev 3:16), lack of charity toward self and others, torture of the innocent, child molestation, and the rest; the only difference possibly being in the degree of baseness between now and then, such as the Jewish holocaust of WWII and partial-birth abortion. And so Jesus came to cleanse us, heal us, of our sin. He showed us that the infinite love of the Father for mankind, personified in the Word and incarnated in Jesus, is the perfect antidote for the threatening death of sin.

Although we still see sin, it is, as Gregory tells us, like a serpent. You can strike it a mortal blow, but it will still twitch and move for some time after. Jesus struck the mortal blow when He defeated Satan in the desert at the beginning of His public ministry, and when He died for us at Calvary. All sin since then is the twitching of the serpent's tail. Satan is a serpent whose power is limited and waning, a serpent who is mortally wounded, whose head will be crushed beneath the Blessed Mother's heel. His only goal now is not life, but to take as many souls as possible away with Him when He descends to the kingdom of eternal death; and it is we who have to give our consent to him to do this to us.

As we consider the love of God for man, we might still ask why Jesus had to suffer and die the way He did. Why did He have to go through His passion, and not just

---

[44]Gregory of Nyssa, The Great Catechism, Section XXIX, EWTN on-line library.

teach and then die peacefully in the presence of His loved ones? The answer seems to be, again, because of His infinite love for man. Jesus could have come, given us the sacraments, taught us, and not done anything else. Had He done so, we would have had to undergo a cleansing suffering we cannot imagine in order to be sufficiently purified of our sins to be able to stand before the beatific vision. But in His infinite love for man, He suffered for us, and took upon His own Divine self the bulk of the suffering we would have to otherwise endure, and having done so, now offers us the opportunity, because of His infinite love, to join any sufferings we endure to His suffering, giving it Divine merit by its participation with His. He thereby offers us the privilege to participate in His redemptive suffering for mankind. We know this because Jesus suffered for only one purpose, the redemption of man, and therefore any suffering we join to His must also acquire that character by participation. Thus, God, because of His infinite love for man, allows our own suffering to become part of the act of His Divine love for all men. However, we must again freely elect to do so. We must make an act of our will and offer our suffering to Him. Without that, it remains merely our suffering and has no spiritual merit. His Love for us drives Him to desire to participate in all we do, and to allow us to participate in what He does; we in Him and He in us.

From all this, we see that the infinite love of God for man, the love which the Father has for man, is personified in Jesus, and through the merits of Jesus and His suffering on the cross, we are given the power to be children of God and coheirs with Jesus to the kingdom of heaven; given the privilege to participate with Jesus in His redemptive suffering for all mankind. All because of our Father's infinite love for man.

"... that they may be made perfect in one; and
the world may know that Thou hast sent Me,

and hast loved them, as Thou hast also loved Me."

Jn 17:23

Finding the Outlet: Plugging in to God's Love

When we contemplate the loving Trinity within, we are often struck by how unaware most people are of this divine presence within us. For so many, the soul lies in darkness, unaware of God's closeness. It is as if the soul is a large, dark crystal, with a network of electric wires running throughout. We see the wires, but don't know what they are, what they are for. We stumble over them and often wish they were not there. We don't know it, but these wires, purposely put in our path, are surging with the infinite love God is eager to share with us. We must find a way to access it, but to do so we must be aware it is accessible.

One day we find the spiritual outlet. This outlet is grace and the sacraments. Through the inspiration of the Holy Spirit, we also discover our personal plug. Our plug is prayer. We begin to grow in prayer, and through that prayer our soul suddenly connects to God's outlet and begins to light up. We recognize God and begin to see what we look like to God. At first we are excited, for we can now recognize Him amidst the clutter in our lives. We see shapes and outlines, even if only dimly. We are experiencing the dawn of our spiritual life.

As we progress the light gets brighter and we notice that some things are kind of dusty, or even dirty and filled with cobwebs. Signs of spiritual neglect are all around. Through prayer we begin to clean house. As we progress, we learn more about God and love Him more. This call to prayer is how God beckons to us, how He transmits His love into our hearts. It is in prayer that we eventually come to the crossroad, the place St. Teresa of Avila calls the Fourth Mansions in her book Interior Castle. This is a pivotal point in spiritual development for it is here that we choose to commit to God without reservation. It is here that we take the step leading to sainthood, that step which we are all called to take but which many choose not to take. This step, this level of commitment, is dependent on the degree to which we have responded to the grace of transformation in Christ. Ultimately, we respond to the love of God by allowing Him to transform us in Christ. By trusting in God to do this, by Taking His Hand without reservation, by loving Him enough, He draws us into Himself, into His life, into His love. We comprehend that if we are made for God, then we are made for love. If we are made for God, then all that He provides us must in one way or another lead to love.

From this point on, the impediments to the flow of God's love diminish and the increasing light of His love causes our soul to shine like a brilliant jewel. We now know that this light which has awakened us to a whole new world is the love of God within us, and has always been there ready to be tapped.

Eventually, this light of love, originating from the deepest part of our soul, permeates our soul completely, turning what was a dark, world-focused existence into a brilliant beacon of the infinite love of God, a love so powerful it pours out from our soul toward all those we encounter. We become a beacon for those who are searching for the love of God.

Recognizing What Is Not Love

There is a difference between loving and unloving. Loving leads us to God. Unloving acts, of any degree, are a failure to love. This does not mean they are evil, just not loving. Unloving acts are those that are non-participation in the life of God because all love comes from God, and God cannot permit Himself to co-exist with non-love. All that lives in God must be founded in love.

If we are to embrace a disposition toward loving, we must do so through prayer. As we progress in prayer, our prayer life moves from vocal prayer, including meditative prayer, to contemplative prayer. Our objective in contemplative prayer is to attain a loving union with God, the Divine source of all love.

Contemplative prayer directed by Christ is by its nature the opposite of unloving. It originates in the very core of our being, that place deep within where the Trinity dwells. Through contemplative prayer we become fundamentally loving persons. It strengthens us, and that strength originates in God. By pursuing a path toward contemplative prayer, we find the means to rid ourselves of the habit of unloving acts. By seeking loving union with God, we attack sin and the causes of sin at their foundation. Contemplative prayer, which is rooted in love, is the most effective way to root out sin. Because we have a divine command to love others, we become intermediaries between the love of God and those God sends into our lives, and we become united, through love, not only to God, but also to all those God loves.

Contemplative prayer, and in particular infused contemplation, is a gift of God, but we can only embark on the path toward contemplative prayer and become present to God by an act of our will. We build our capacity for deepening our relationship with God through our contemplative prayer and we give our consent to progress in prayer as we cross each new threshold. Each new threshold of prayer changes our relationship with God and with everyone else we encounter. God is truth, and in our contemplative prayer we come face to face with the truth of God, the truth of ourselves, and the truth in all we encounter.

Growth in prayer means corresponding growth in virtue. Of all the virtues, the highest virtues are the three theological virtues of faith, hope and charity. It is through these theological virtues that we live most completely in the life of God. It is through these three that the other virtues acquire augmented, transfigured life in us. To live a virtuous life does not mean always walking around with our hands folded, wearing a silly grin, with our eyes looking up toward the sky. It is something lived in the core of our soul, a way of being which is founded in love of God and love of others, a way of being which has God at the center of all we do. We cannot grow in virtue without prayer, and we cannot have a living prayer life without virtue. Life in God is a way of composite living. It is a comprehensive sense of who we are as a covenant being, of who God is, and how we exist as His divinely loved children. It involves a fundamental awareness of being called, individually, by name, by God Himself because our infinite, omnipotent, omniscient, all-loving God loves us individually.

The Gospel of Love -The Gospel of John

When we desire to make a retreat, we often seek something specific on which we can focus over a relatively few number of days. Perhaps we are struggling with a vocation issue, or a change of career, an important decision, of perhaps we are looking for a way to grow closer to God.

One excellent way to make a retreat is to take one book of the Bible and use that as your retreat material. You first pray for guidance from the Holy Spirit, and then read it slowly and reflectively. Stop whenever you come to a passage which seems to call for your attention. I previously suggested you begin reading the gospel of John meditatively. As we continue our exploration in loving God, let us do this together. The Gospel of John is often referred to as the gospel of love. Throughout this book we have often reflected on passages of John in support of one concept or another, but now we will focus on the complete gospel.

"In the beginning was the Word, and the Word was with God, and the Word was God. He was in the beginning with God.

All things came to be through him, and without him nothing came to be. What came to be through him was life, and this life was the light of the human race;"

The Word of God has always been, is eternal, has been with God and is God. The Word of God became Incarnate, which began His human existence, but His divine existence did not begin then, for He is the eternal God. Without the Word, who is God, nothing else that exists or has ever existed came into being. Yet what came to be through Him that is of supreme importance to us, made in the image and likeness of God, is life, and the life of which

John speaks is the Divine life of Christ, displayed to us through the activity of His human life among us. It is this Divine life that is the source of our own immortal life. Without Him, we have no immortal life. His life is the source of all good which comes to us. It is our beacon, the light of our soul, that which gives direction and purpose and value to all we do that is good. It is the Divine life of Christ within us that is the light for our own soul, and, through us collectively, the light to all souls of the world who have not yet found Jesus. We are His beacons, just as He is our interior beacon leading us to the Father, leading us to union with Himself in the Trinity. He is the eternal light, the light of all mankind, the light which seeks to illuminate all souls and make them children of God. He is the light which guides us and leads us away from darkness, the darkness of sin and separation from God. Darkness can never overcome light, and evil can never prevail over His light in our soul without our consent. If we choose Him, we choose light, we reject darkness, we reject sin, we embrace life. By choosing His light, we choose His life, and we become one with Him. Through Him, we become a light to the world, a lighthouse leading souls away from destruction, because He shines in us. We are drawn to light, we are drawn to life, we are drawn to that light and life which is Jesus Christ.

"But to those who did accept Him, He gave the power to become children of God, to those who believe in His name, who were born not by natural generation nor by human choice nor by a man's decision, but of God." (Jn 1:12-13)

Who are those who accept Him? They are those who believe in His name and who were born of God. They are those who were born of God, not by human choice and not by a man's decision. We are re-born when we accept Him - for ourselves or our infant children for whom we are responsible - believe in His name, and accept Baptism. When we make the choice to accept Him, we are responding to His

146

grace, cooperating with the call of the Father, and we place control over our actual spiritual birth in His hands, for it is God acting in us. Our choice ends when we make ourselves receptive to His grace, when we ask for and respond to His grace. When we stand before the priest or deacon at our baptism or that of our child, the minister of the sacrament asks the question, "What do you seek?" We answer for ourselves or on behalf of the infant, "I seek Baptism." We ask for this grace, we do not demand it. We do not approach God and tell Him what to do. We recognize Him, learn about Him, understand what we can about Him, learn to love Him, desire to be with Him for eternity, and accept Him as our God. When we do, and submit ourselves to His sacramental action, He pours the Holy Spirit into our soul as the priest or deacon pours the water on our head. The pouring of water is the outward sign of the inpouring of grace. The Father calls us, we respond, and we are then filled with grace by God, as He wills. We are re-born of water and Spirit. (Jn 3:5)

In accepting God, He gives us the power to be His child. This adoption is conditional, for to maintain this filial bond with God we must remain in the state of grace. This underscores the importance of grace to our soul. It is not just something nice to have; it is absolutely essential to our eternal survival. When God communicates His sanctifying grace, He is communicating Himself. That is the action of sanctifying grace; to sanctify us, to make us holy. Jesus told us that only the Father is holy, and to be perfect as the Father is perfect. To be holy is to be possessed of Divine nature, the supreme gift of God. We cannot be a child of God unless we share in His Divine nature, and this means the pendulum has swung back again. The ball is initially in our court, on our behalf or that of our infant. We have to seek God. When we do, the emphasis shifts to God. Once God accepts us and conveys sanctifying grace to us, He makes us His child. Now the responsibility is shifted back to us, and remains with us for the rest of our life. We must maintain that state of grace, that filial relationship. God will always help us because He loves us, but we have the responsibility. We must recognize when we fall, and we must seek His forgiveness in confession so we can be restored to grace. His love for us and His patience toward us is infinite, as is His mercy. He will always come to our aid if we seek Him, but we must seek Him and His grace. We cannot sit back, kick up our heels, and say, "OK God, do it to me." All of the virtues come to play in this maintenance of grace, including humility and obedience.

"He first found his own brother Simon and told him,"We have found the Messiah" (which is translated Anointed). Then he brought him to Jesus. Jesus looked at him and said, "You are Simon the son of John; you will be called Kephas" (which is translated Peter)." (Jn 1:41,42)

When Andrew followed Jesus and stayed with Him that evening, the revelation of who Jesus was came over Andrew and he knew. This was the promised one of God. This was the one for whom they had been waiting. God was once again taking action among His people, revealing more of Himself as salvation history continues to unfold. The unfolding revelation from Noah and Abraham and Moses continues, and here He is. Jesus had called and offered Andrew the chance to be an important part of the greatest thing that ever happened to mankind, and Andrew accepted.

Andrew's choice of words is interesting. "We have found the Messiah". Yet if we read the prior passage we see that it was John the Baptist who said, in effect, "There He is", and it was Jesus who invited Andrew to "Come and you will see." In that one evening spent with Jesus, Andrew has recognized, or found, the Messianic identity in Jesus. Jesus is not just the carpenter from Nazareth, not just the son of Joseph and Mary, but the Son of God, the Anointed One of God, the Savior, Emmanuel - God with us.

We can only sit in wonder as to what transpired that evening. To contemplate what their conversation must have been like, to contemplate the wondrous grace that must have flowed into the two apostles, is enough to bring one to tears. How awesome it must have been for those two apostles to seek out a man, to sit down with Him, only so they could find out what John the Baptist was excited about, and in the process discover God Himself. They were not only told, but so infused with grace that any and all doubt was erased. He says, "We have found the Messiah."

This certitude of faith is what we must all seek. This absolute certitude is, in and of itself, evidence of the Holy Spirit working in us. Jesus will identify the Holy Spirit later in John's gospel as the Spirit of Truth. When we know God within, when we know with certainty we have encountered God, we have encountered truth, we have encountered the "Splendor of Truth". It is this truth that sets us free, for it is in this truth that our faith and our confidence in Jesus is confirmed.

When Jesus meets Simon He immediately changes his name to Peter. We recall that in Lk 7:24, Jesus asks the crowd with regard to John the Baptist, "What did you go out to the desert to see - a reed swayed by the wind?" Fr. Andrew Fisher once explained to us that Simon means reed. Jesus did not want to found His church on a reed which would be swayed by passing opinion and political correctness. He needed a rock on which to found His church, and Peter means rock. It intrigues me that in their initial meeting the first thing Jesus tells Simon is that He is changing Simon's name, and Simon offers no objection and raises no question. How wold you respond if someone you met for the first time said they were changing your name? Peter seems to understand that Jesus has the right to do this. How much infused grace did it take for this to happen? How wonderful it must have been to encounter Jesus then, to be called by God without yet understanding why, and still have such certitude.

The next day He decided to go to Galilee, and He found Philip. And Jesus said to him, "Follow Me." ... Philip found Nathaniel and told him, "We have found the one about whom Moses wrote in the law, and also the prophets, Jesus son of Joseph, from Nazareth." (Jn 1:43-45)

The experience of Andrew was repeated with Philip, but with an interesting difference. When Andrew approached Jesus, he did so with a question, "Where are you staying?", and Jesus answered with an enticement, "Come and you will see." Andrew responded and found that Jesus was staying, always, in the Father and the Father in Him. Andrew was invited into the life of the Trinity and he accepted. With Philip, John tells us that "Jesus found Philip." Jesus sought him out, and when He found Philip He simply said, "Follow Me." Philip's response was the same as Andrew's. The outpouring of grace into both men was the same, and the result was the same. They both came away saying they had found the Messiah, the promised one. Andrew sought Jesus, curious because of the herald proclaiming His arrival. Jesus sought Philip, and called him. Both had equal status as apostles.

These two men seem to represent many of us today, sort of precursors of how we approach Jesus. Some hear about Jesus, feel a desire to know more, and out of curiosity they inquire. Seek and you will find. With open hearts, they receive Him through cooperation with grace. Others hear the call, and come to Jesus in many different ways, each according to his or her station in life. Some through a sacramental marriage, some responding to the priesthood or religious life, and others seeking Him while remaining single. Each is responding to grace, each is finding Jesus in their own way. All of them come away with the experience expressed by the two apostles, "I have found Him."

Once you have found Him, your life is never the same. There is line in a song from a Rogers and Hammerstein Broadway play, South Pacific, which says "Once you have found him, never let him go." This should always be our response to Christ. No matter how we find Him, whether through curiosity or through response to His call, we experience the same Christ, partake in the same Mystery and share the same discovery.

All around us we see people, young and old, seeking to "get high" on all manner of substances, ruining their bodies in the process, and becoming in many ways less human. If only they could have an Andrew or a Philip experience! There is no "high" that can ever compare with the high of personally encountering God.

In the beginning of Chapter 3 of the gospel of John, we find the discourse between Jesus and Nicodemus. In this dialogue, Jesus tells Nicodemus that "no one can enter the kingdom of God without being born of water and the spirit. What is born of flesh is flesh and what is born of spirit is spirit." (Jn 3:5-6) This is Jesus' confirmation of what John says in the prologue to this gospel (Jn 1:12); we must be born of God to be saved. John continues, telling us that because God loves us He sent His only Son so that "everyone who believes in Him might not perish but might have eternal life." (Jn 3:16) This also relates back to Jn 1:12.

These two central themes, of belief followed by rebirth, grouped together in the opening chapter and again in chapter 3, teach us the foundation for all else that happens to us spiritually. We can make no gain without these. Belief, faith, is the key that opens the door and rebirth is the action that initiates us into a life as part of the family of God. It is only through our life in God that we can gain eternal life. Through our faith, we are introduced to the truth that is God, and through our rebirth in baptism we are able to share in the Divine life of God and inherit the kingdom as His child.

Just as we grow physically after we are born, we grow spiritually once we are reborn in Him. How much we grow is a condition of how much we love Him and keep His word. Once we are reborn we must begin our journey of love by first knowing Him as best we can, for our love for Him will come first through our knowing Him.

This belief and rebirth involves a commitment on our part. We cannot say we really believe if we do not act as if we believe. True belief demands action for otherwise we are lying to ourselves; we are interiorly inconsistent. Belief in God, belief in Christ, is not a passing kind of thing. It initiates a relationship which is dynamic, demands attention, demands growth, and requires recognition of the mutual commitment. It is a covenant relationship. It cannot survive if it is not fed with love. It cannot remain static. No love relationship can remain static. It grows or it begins to die. This is even more true when we encounter infinite love. Anyone whose heart is cold enough to respond with lukewarmness to infinite love cannot claim they know God, cannot claim they love God (Rev 3:16). Even in periods of aridity where we do not feel any sign of God's love directly, we must thank Him for the love expressed in His gifts and ask Him for the love we need to be faithful to Him.

It is questionable whether anyone can truly believe in God and remain indifferent to His love. Belief is a precondition to genuine rebirth, and without rebirth we cannot live a life in God, cannot truly experience loving God.

John then makes an unexpected statement. Here, early in this gospel, he gives a verdict. It is not an opinion, or an exhortation, but a verdict. One must ask against whom or for whom this verdict is rendered.

John says "this is the verdict." (Jn 3:19) The light (Christ) came into the world, but the people of the world preferred darkness. They preferred not to have God among them. They had this preference because their works were evil. John says that those who do evil do not want their evil to be seen by others. They hate the light because under the light their works will be exposed. John then tells us that "whoever lives the truth comes to the light, so that his works may be clearly seen as done in God." (Jn 3:21)

Jesus told us that He is the Light, and that the Holy Spirit is the Spirit of Truth. (Jn 15:26) Those whose lives are in God do works which are done in and through God, and are done in truth. No one who operates from a platform of truth has any concern with examination of his works. He is never ashamed of what he does, and is never fearful of others seeing what he does. How many mothers tell their little children, when teaching them how to behave even when alone, "God sees you." These mothers try to instill in their children the understanding that they never work in secret, and that they should never do anything they will be ashamed of if that work becomes known by others.

On which side of this verdict scale are we? How many of the works we do each day are works we would prefer others not see? How many of our works are we indifferent to with regard to examination by others? These are not questions of privacy but questions of ethics. When we consider our works at our place of employment, at home, in our recreation, on which side of the verdict scale will they be placed? Do we act in a way that hurts others at work so that we might advance? Do we take credit for the work of others? Do we treat our spouse and children with respect and love? Do we treat our parents with love? Do we cheat on the ball field? Do we deliberately try to hurt players on an opposing team so that they will not be able to continue? Do we cheat, or encourage others to cheat, at school? Do we shoplift at the grocery, perhaps by eating a product before we get to the checkout counter? Do we take office supplies, or other company property, for our own use at home? Is there anything you do, in any context, that you would be ashamed of if it came to public light? Is there anything that you should be ashamed of and are not? If you live in truth, live in God, you will not be afraid of these questions. The next time you examine your conscience before confession, ask yourself if you live in truth. Ask if you meet the test of John's verdict.

Chapter 4 of John opens with the account of Jesus meeting the Samaritan woman at Jacob's well. Jesus is responding to her question when He says,

"If you knew the gift of God and who is saying to you 'Give me a drink,' you would have asked Him and He would have given you living water." (Jn 4:10) Then He says, "Everyone who drinks this water will be thirsty again; but whoever drinks the water I shall give will never thirst; the water I shall give will become in him a spring of water welling up to eternal life." (Jn 4:13-14. He will use this analogy again in Jn 7:37-38)

The gift of God: The gift of God is Jesus, who brings the gift of salvation and eternal life. When we know Jesus, we know God, and we know why Jesus came. We know He is the Messiah and gives us eternal life. We ask for salvation and we ask for life. The life He gives us is His own Divine life, and we have our life in Him. In verse 22, He tells the woman that her people worship what they do not understand, but the Jews worship what they do understand, and salvation is from the Jews. Without the understanding, the worship is empty, conveys no relationship, and has no merit. To emphasize the need for understanding, this woman is the first person in the gospel of John, other than the apostles, to whom Jesus explicitly identifies Himself as the Messiah (Jn 4:26).

"If you knew, ... you would have asked ..., and He would have given..." John gives us a conditional, similar to that found in Jn 14:23. This requires a relationship and a desire. He does not say "If you knew, you *might*, or *perhaps* you would, or *perhaps* He would." Jesus is telling us, first, to get to know Him and understand what He offers. Second, He tells us that if we know the gift of God - Jesus, salvation, eternal life, divine filial relationship - then we cannot help but ask for His living water, this life giving water. If we know the gift of God and ask, Jesus will grant our request. Once we know the gift, we cannot turn our back on life. If we do ask, He will give us the gift of God - He will give us Himself, Eucharist, eternal life - for His mission is to save us, to redeem us, to share with us His eternal life.

Thirst implies both a lack and a desire. It implies a recognition of the deficiency. We know what we lack and so we thirst, we desire this gift of God. The better we know the gift of God, the more we desire, and the greater is our thirst. Only God can satisfy this thirst. We thirst for God, we desire to possess Him and possess eternal life. We may not fully understand, but we recognize our need and thirst for the gift of God and know we cannot have life without it.

Living water can impart life. Regular water cannot. Regular water may support physical life, but it cannot create life or give life. It cannot give what it does not have. Living water imparts life from the Holy Spirit in Baptism when we are washed clean and receive the gift and grace of spiritual life, sanctifying life, eternal life. If we understand and appreciate this gift of divine life, we nurture it in us through prayer and the sacraments. We encourage it to grow in us so that it wells up, pouring eternal life throughout all the faculties of our soul and spilling over to those we encounter, helping them develop their own desire and thirst for the gift of God.

In Jn 4:39-42, we have a most important, lesson. We know the Samaritans and the Jews hated each other. In setting the scene, the Evangelist tells us that the Jews and Samaritans used nothing in common (verse 9), and His

155

disciples were shocked He was even talking to the woman at the well (verse 27). This whole account of the Samaritan woman at the well is setting us up for two great lessons. The first is the need to know the gift of God, which requires a relationship and takes action on our part in order to receive the gift. The second is that God came among, and for, all people. These sworn enemies of the Jews were deliberately approached by Jesus Himself. He did this for one purpose, unity; to teach us that He was bringing salvation even to those who were not Jews, to all who would believe in Him, and that salvation is from the Jews. We can see here a clear relationship to Jn 1:10-12. It is particularly important to recognize that Jesus used as His instrument a woman who would have been considered an outcast in Jewish society because of her immoral life. He made this sinful woman His instrument to reach the whole community in which she lived.

After speaking with this woman, Jesus sends her out as His messenger into her village. When the villagers meet Him, their reaction is the same as hers; "we know that this is truly the Savior of the world." (Jn 4:42) It is a reaction so similar to that of Andrew and Philip.

We have no further account of these villagers in the gospel other than that Jesus stayed two days with them (Jn 4:43), an experience again similar to that of Andrew who stayed with Him and came away changed forever. We, too, must "stay with Him," retreat with Him, to stay for a time only with Him so that we may be changed through the encounter. We seek Him out, we stay with Him, and are changed forever if we open our hearts to Him, as did the Samaritan woman at the well. Early Christian records tell us the woman is the martyr Photina. In the Russian Orthodox Church they have a beautiful icon titled "The Holy Martyr Photina, the Samaritan Woman." In the icon she is standing, holding a scroll which reads, "O Lord, give me this water that I may not thirst."

After the Resurrection, the Apostles returned to this village (Acts 8:5-25) and brought the message of resurrection and salvation to these people who so readily accepted Jesus. What happened to these people in the meantime? How was their faith, which glowed so brightly when they had Jesus with them, maintained without Him? We can be sure the means were provided them for this to happen, for Jesus never did anything without effect. What the means were we do not know. Trusting in His love we can be certain He did claim them as His own. It would be interesting to see how this encounter affected the village. How much was the village changed? How were their hearts changed? What did Jesus give them to sustain them until His apostles and disciples could come to them to announce the resurrection? Perhaps one day we will find out. Until then, each of us can have our own personal experience staying with Him in the Eucharist. If we stay with Him, we, too, will change.

As we continue our journey through the gospel of John, we look for signs of God's chosen people understanding who Jesus is and asking Him for the gift of God. We saw the recognition and understanding in the accounts of Andrew and Philip becoming apostles. But in Jn 5:41-47, Jesus castigates the scribes and pharisees for their lack of recognition and belief. He refuses to accept their praise because they do not recognize the source of the works He does. He chides them for accepting human praise, but not seeking honor from God. They have not recognized the gift of God, they have not felt the thirst for God and His gift of eternal life, they do not have the love of God in them and they do not believe. The reason is that they have not sought the honor of God. They have not fulfilled their obligation to love God and have instead sought their salvation in scriptures. They failed to see that words do not save, but love for God does. They relied on the words of scripture because that gave them, as the interpreters of the law, power over the people. When we love one another as God calls us to do, we do not seek power; we seek to share. Our power is in God and His love, and the more we share His love the more it increases in us. There is no greater power in the universe than the love of God.

Chapter 6 of John opens with the account of the multiplication of the loaves and fish. Two things impressed me in this story. One was the care with which the fragments were collected after the people had eaten. The gifts of God should never be wasted, and should be shared. Twelve baskets were filled. Nothing is said about what is done with the baskets of leftover food. Knowing Jesus, could anything other than distributing them to the poor have been done? This meal was a gift from God, and many recognized it as miraculous. But in their ignorance, they wanted to make Jesus a king instead of giving thanks to God. How frustrating this must have been for Jesus we can only surmise.

The other thing that I found interesting was that it was a child who provided the loaves and fish. The apostle Andrew tells Jesus that a boy has five loaves and two fish. Nothing says that the boy was asked to share them, or that he gave them to Jesus. It just says that Jesus took the food, gave thanks, and distributed it to those reclining. Nor does it say whether the boy got any of the leftovers to bring home to his family. What it conveyed to me is an unspoken trust and faith in Jesus on the part of the child. He trusted in Jesus, and was willing to give Jesus the only food he had. Jesus accepted the food and used it to perform a miracle. Jesus told us that we must have the faith of a child to enter the kingdom and asked that children be allowed to come to Him. We don't know what words passed between Jesus and the boy. We can be sure that great graces were given the boy and, probably, through him to his family. The boy's generosity was there before he arrived in the crowd. He was with others seeking to know Jesus, to know the gift of God. That says something about his mother and father.

This event was a preview of the Eucharist and its distribution at Mass. At Mass the priest receives the gifts brought up at the offertory, and after giving thanks he blesses and consecrates the gifts. When the gifts are consecrated, they become the greatest gift God has given to mankind. When we receive this gift of the Eucharist with understanding, we are interiorly disposed as Jesus told us we should be when He spoke with the woman at the well. When we receive this way, we can ask for the living water. If we do not receive with understanding, we insult God and we receive, in effect, an empty basket instead of the blessed gift of God. I do not mean that the Eucharist itself is changed at all or in any way affected by our disposition, but rather that the benefit we receive from the Eucharist is diminished. Our openness to grace is lacking. We inhibit God working in us because we have not loved and trusted and understood and thirsted enough to accept His most precious gift for what it truly is.

Immediately following the multiplication of the loaves and fish in Jn 6, the Evangelist introduces us to rapidly expanding public manifestations of the divine power of Jesus. We first have the account of Jesus walking on water. In the other gospel accounts of this event, the emphasis is on Peter jumping on the water, then losing courage and beginning to sink, crying out to Jesus to save him. John does not even mention Peter. John has something of greater significance to teach us. The only thing John records Jesus saying is, "It is I. Do not be afraid." (Jn 6:20) When we have Jesus, we have everything. It is becoming more and more apparent that the Last Supper and the Passion are on John's mind as he enters this phase of the gospel. He begins laying out the fundamental doctrines, theological principles, and Church authority that will govern and guide the Church through the ages, all coming directly from Jesus Himself.

John's focus here is on the divinity of Jesus, and His dominion over everything, including space and time. The boat is about two or three miles off shore. Once Jesus has instructed them not to fear, He instantly brings the boat to shore, beyond the limitations of space and time. (Jn 6:21)

Almost everything which follows in the gospel is leading to Calvary. John tells us the sea was stirring due to a strong wind, but not enough to keep them from rowing the boat. It was not the wind that disturbed them, but the sight of Jesus walking on the water. They had already seen Jesus perform miracles, but most were things like curing the sick, healing the afflicted, and the multiplication of the loaves and fish. Here, Jesus was controlling nature itself, as well as space and time. His authority was clear. His omnipotence was evident. Soon, they would have to trust and believe in His infinite power, a power even over death itself. He who is all-powerful is with them and is telling them that as long as He is with them, they need fear nothing.

Later, Jesus will tell them He will be with them always. (Jn 14:16; Mt 28:20) This is true for us today. And yet they did fear, as do we. When Jesus was arrested, the apostles scattered. We scatter in our own way, lacking in courage by reacting in fear to those who can only hurt the body, and often ignorantly ignoring those who can hurt the soul through social policies, loose morals, explicit media presentations, bad example, refusal to demand or give accountability for wrong actions, the demands for compromise on almost every issue, the suppression of any reference to God or religion in the public schools or public buildings, and the inordinate emphasis placed on the acquisition of worldly goods.

We must ask what Jesus' command to us, "It is I. Be not afraid.", means in our lives today. How close to Him do we stay? How do we assess our confidence level in Him? We know we can be fearless as long as He is with us. Are we?

What is there about our lives that tells us He is with us, that we are conscious of His presence? How confident are we that we live the Commandments, live His commands to love God and neighbor? To what extent is the virtue of courage exemplified in our life, especially the courage to stand for truth and the word of God in the face of worldly opposition? On what are our own personal convictions based? What are we willing to risk for the sake of upholding truth? How do we follow in the footsteps of Christ?

After the account of Jesus walking on the water, John moves into the bread of life discourse. The same crowd which had gathered together the day before and fed on the loaves and fishes was here for this teaching. Isn't it amazing that Jesus speaks to these large crowds, such as the 5,000 men here plus women and children, and the other large crowds such as when He gave the Sermon on the Mount (Mt 5), and, without the use of any kind of sound system, it never says those present could not hear Him.

This bread of life discourse is so central to the whole theology of Christ, and yet is brushed over by so many. Jesus was not just a savior on a white horse who charged into the camp of Satan and rescued us and then, like the Lone Ranger, rode off into the sunset. He established Himself among us in a completely different sense and for all time. We must never lose the sense of Jesus desiring and pursuing us. It tends to go against our sense of balance, our sense of who we are in comparison to God, that He should desire and pursue us, but that is what He does. Gaining this awareness is one of the major outcomes of the Spiritual Exercises of St. Ignatius. Jesus came among us to redeem us, to be our Savior. He also came to sustain us, and to sustain us with Himself. He came to make Himself, in His entirety, the direct source of our spiritual life and the reason for our very life.

The people find Jesus and are focused on discovering how He got where He was, for they did not see Him cross over on any boat. It was as if they were asking a magician, "How did you do that?" But Jesus does not answer their question. Instead, He tells them what He knows they need to hear. He knew they were looking for more of the loaves and fish He had given them the previous day. He tells them to change their focus. He tells them to work for the food that gives eternal life, the food that endures and does not perish, just as He had told the woman at the well to ask for living water.

And as He had told the woman at the well, Jesus also tells these people that He is the one who has to give them this enduring food. He proclaims He has the Father's seal, the seal of God (Jn 6:27). The seal signifies the full authority of the one from whom the seal came. You can almost hear their minds begin to churn. What is He telling us? Is He telling us He is the Messiah, that He is Emmanuel, God among us? These common folks are not His enemies, so they ask for a sign. They, who just yesterday were so impressed with the sign He gave them that they wanted to make Him a king, now ask for a sign. Jesus tells them that "... the bread of God is that which comes down from heaven and gives life to the world." (Jn 6:32-33) Mere ordinary bread which is not living obviously cannot do this. But they have never seen living bread, just as the woman at the well had never heard of living water. Then He explains. He is the living bread. "I am the bread of life." (Jn 6:34; 48) Abruptly, but only for a moment, Jesus moves away from the discussion of Himself as the bread of life and explains how the Father calls us, gives us to Jesus, that Jesus does not reject anyone given Him by the Father, and that He will not lose any of those given to Him by the Father. (Jn 6:36-40) This harkens back to the image of the good shepherd gathering in and protecting His sheep, even the lost sheep. To be part of this fold, we must have true belief in Him, and that requires we keep His word.

The people hear, but are fixated on Him saying He is the bread which came down from heaven (Jn 6:32; 41-42). But what is this bread of life? Is it only an image, a simile? How can a man be bread? What kind of bread? Why does Jesus compare Himself with bread? At the well, He said He would give us living water. He did not say He is living water. Why is He here identifying Himself as the bread of life?

After explaining His relationship with the Father (Jn 6:36-40), that the Father sends us to Jesus, the crowd cannot grasp what He says. Confusion sets in. Satan is trying to generate unbelief, to draw them away from Jesus. Jesus tells them He comes from God, but they think only about what they know of His earthly origin. They cannot reconcile the two concepts. Jesus continues, and tells them again that the Father teaches them and sends them to Him (Jn 6:44-45). He will repeat this again at a later time (Jn 14:7-14).

It is critical to recognize that in this discourse, Jesus is not teaching them in parable form. What He is saying is central to the whole theology of the Son of Man. He is giving it to them straight. They struggle to absorb what He says, but He does not back away, does not explain it as imagery. In fact, He continues and takes them to the next level. Seven times, in different ways, He will explain to them the doctrine of the Eucharist. (1) "I am the bread of life ... that comes down from heaven; whoever eats this bread will live forever; and the bread that I will give is my flesh for the life of the world." (Jn 6:49-51)

He really has them going. They think He is telling them to be cannibals, but more important to them, He is telling them to violate the law of Moses, which prevents them from even touching a corpse. He continues, (2)"Amen, amen, I say to you, unless you eat the flesh of the son of man and drink His blood, you do not have life within you."(Jn 6:53) Now He has really done it. The law says they will be condemned if they drink blood, they are the chosen people, the covenant people, and He is saying if they do not eat His flesh and drink His blood, they will have no spiritual life in them. They will be spiritually dead. Critical to these Jews is that Jesus is telling them to violate the law of prohibition against consuming blood recorded in Leviticus 3:16-17, and 17:10-12. They missed the essence of what He said. Leviticus says the blood gives life and belongs to God alone. Only God can tell them to do what He is telling them to do. He goes even farther. (3)"Whoever eats my flesh and drinks My blood has eternal life, and I will raise him on the last day.(Jn 6:54) (4)For My flesh is true food, and My blood is true drink.(Jn 6:55) (5)Whoever eats My flesh and drinks My blood remains in Me and I in him.(Jn 6:56) ... (6)the one who feeds on Me will have life because of Me.(Jn 6:57) (7)This is the bread that came down from heaven. ... whoever eats this bread will live forever."(Jn 6:58) Over and over He emphasizes the same thing, every way He can. He repeats it seven times, the number which to them signifies fulness or perfection. The significance of repeating this seven times is not lost on them. He leaves them no wiggle-room. There is no middle ground. They must choose, they must decide.

In the minds of those present He is telling them to do what they believe is forbidden. They do not understand He is fulfillment, that the wait is over, for He is here. What He is telling them to do only God has the right to tell them. Everything He has just told them is another way of saying, "I am God, and to Me you owe obedience." Their minds are reeling. But He does not back off. He does not explain what He means in some other terms, for He has not spoken in a parable. He has not merely given them imagery or simile. He has been very explicit. He emphatically repeats His statement seven times. It is unmistakable to them. In the original texts, the word Jesus uses fo eat is their word which means chew or masticate. There is no doubt left as to His meaning.

Jesus is the perfect teacher. The time of His passion approaches. He does not have time to play games with them. No good teacher deliberately confuses his students and leaves them confused. Any good teacher would try another example, another image if there was another way to make the point. But Jesus does not, for He is not using imagery and the crowd knows it. He has explained it perfectly. Their minds have grasped the meaning but not the implications of what He said. They are focused on the method, the how. How will they accomplish eating human dead flesh, and drinking the blood of a dead person. There is only so much of Him to go around. Even if they do as He says, what do they do when He is all gone? What about those who did not get to partake? Will they not have life in them? Jesus is speaking of eternal life. Can dead flesh and drained blood be the source of life, the source of eternal life? Can they accept His word and still be Jews, still faithful to the law of God, still be the chosen people of God? Jesus was not hiding in some obscure place when He taught this, but in the house of God itself. "These things He said while teaching in the synagogue in Capernaum."(Jn 6:59)

The Eucharistic discourse on which we have been reflecting continues, with all the questions still hanging in the minds of the majority in the crowd. The disciples finally respond, "This saying is hard; who can accept it?" (Jn 6:60) Not one person asks how Jesus will do this, how what He asks will give them life, why they cannot have life without it, or why He is giving them this new means to gain eternal life - a means that seems so contrary to the law of Moses, instead of what they are already familiar with as God's chosen people. "Why change?", they probably asked themselves. "How can we do this? Is He going to multiply Himself like He did the bread and fish?" Perhaps they never got that far in their thinking. They may have been too shocked by being told to do what the Law said is prohibited. Once again Jesus does not back off, but continues with full recognition of their concern as He says, "Does this shock you? What if you were

165

to see the son of man ascending to where He was before?" (Jn 6:61-62) Now He really has them in a quandary. Even if they accept what He says, how can they do as He asks if He leaves and ascends to heaven? He is telling them He came from God, where no man has yet been, and therefore He must be God, but they do not comprehend this. They are still focused on how they will do as He said, for they cannot go to heaven to eat His flesh and drink His blood. Nothing is making sense for them through human reasoning.

Jesus continues, "It is the spirit that gives life, while the flesh is of no avail. The words I have spoken are spirit and life." (Jn 6:63) Even today, some people look at this passage and miss the point. They think Jesus was finally explaining that He was speaking symbolically and that when He said "The words I have spoken are spirit and life" all the prior Eucharistic discourse was really referring to His word, to scripture, and was not meant to be taken on face value. But none of the people present at the time misunderstood what He had said, or thought He was speaking symbolically. No one even suggested such an interpretation. To accept this "symbolic" explanation, one has to also explain why Jesus would give a teaching that is so confusing and not explain what He meant, if He meant something else, and if the explanation is as simple as "What I mean is scripture, the living Word of God." That would have made everything so easy. They would have understood that. To accept this explanation one also has to explain why He would use spirit in this metaphorical sense. No place else in all of scripture is spirit used metaphorically. Why would He do so here, and in this way? He also, in the Eucharistic discourse, always spoke of "My" flesh. Here, He says "the" flesh is of no avail. Clearly, He is not referring to the same thing. Nothing about Jesus is ever of "no avail." Jesus would never be so inconsistent and especially not in so important a teaching. Nor could He have been referring to scripture. We would not have the New Testament until about the year 398. The Hebrew scriptures have nothing remotely like the Eucharistic discourse, so He could not have been referring to any scripture any of those present would be familiar with.

Jesus did not retract any of what He said, and "As a result of this, many of His disciples returned to their former way of life and no longer accompanied Him." (Jn 6:66) He did not call them back and explain it differently. If He had only been teaching in metaphors He would have made His point another way, with another metaphor. But He meant exactly what He said, and they knew it.

Jesus then asks Peter if he is also going to leave, and Peter, responding on behalf of all the apostles, says, "Master, to whom shall we go? You have the words of eternal life. We have come to believe and are convinced that you are the Holy One of God." (Jn 6:68-69) The apostles probably had many of the same questions as the others who left, but they also believed, loved and trusted in Jesus and knew that eventually, as always, their questions would be answered. None of them will understand until the last supper, passion and resurrection. Then it will come together for them.

In Jn 7, we find Jesus teaching in the temple area. None of us today find this odd, but the people of His time found it very odd. In His time, children learned to read and write using the scriptures. It is not this kind of learning that amazed the people. He was teaching as a scholar, as a rabbi. This broke with their tradition. Before one taught, before one became a rabbi, one studied under other rabbis. It was a discipline which involved a long apprenticeship. Equally important, to give credibility to what is taught, the one teaching would regularly quote his mentor rabbi, one teacher quoting a prior teacher, and so on. The succession of truth, the tradition of the people handed down through the ages one to another, is preserved. This is how God established that His people be taught.

Now Jesus comes among them, in the area near the temple, and teaches as a rabbi. The people are amazed. They are also confused. He has not been an apprentice and does not quote a mentor, does not quote a teacher whose name they recognize. This is what they meant when the posed the question, "How does He know scripture without having studied?" (Jn7:15) Given this tradition, Jesus' answer had to shock them. He replies, "My teaching is not my own, but is from the one who sent Me. Whoever chooses to do His will shall know whether My teaching is from God or whether I speak on my own. Whoever speaks on his own seeks his own glory, but whoever seeks the glory of the one who sent him is truthful, and there is no wrong in him. Did not Moses give you the law? Why are you trying to kill me?" (Jn 7:16-19) And after chastising them, He says, "You know Me and also know where I am from. Yet I did not come on My own, but the one who sent Me, whom you do not know, is true. I know Him, because I am from Him, and He sent Me." (Jn 7:28-29)

The wealth of what He has just said shocked some of them, amazed others. Most understood the implications, but few had the faith to accept Him. He had just told them He had the right to teach because He was sent by God who is truth, and if they live in accord with God's plan they will recognize the truth in what He says. They also understood He was fulfilling the prophesy which said that they will all be taught by God. Here was the one sent by God, the Messiah, and He was in their midst teaching them.

For those who understood and accepted, you can only imagine what must have gone through them. You can almost see the tears streaming down their faces. The awe was overwhelming. John tells us at 7:31, "But many in the crowd began to believe in Him... ." So few in number. The majority responded as some disciples had not long before, refusing to accept His truth. These men rejected Him, wanted to kill Him, so He had to leave. The seed was planted in the few. It would be up to the apostles to make it grow. How well does His seed grow in us? Do we accept, or do we doubt and reject? How would we have responded if we had been there on that wonderful day and had heard God teaching in our midst?

It has always intrigued me to contemplate how God uses fluid motion to convey life. A fluid is a liquid or a gas. Jesus used the Jordan River for His baptism, not a still water pond. God uses flowing air to bring us the life-giving oxygen which fills our lungs. Stagnant air is not healthy. Stagnant water is not healthy. He uses flowing blood to give physical life as the nutrients are carried to all of the various parts of our bodies. He uses the moving waters of the ocean to give life to the creatures of the sea and to fill the air with life giving oxygen. If you put a fish in still water it will soon die. When blood stops flowing in the body, it signifies death. Hospitals, anticipating the need for an organ transplant, sometimes keep bodies artificially alive by maintaining the blood flow.

The term "living waters" means flowing water, not stagnation. Jesus told the Samaritan woman at the well that He would give her living waters, and if she received this water she would never be thirsty again. Now, in Jn 7:37-38, Jesus says, "Let anyone who thirsts come to Me and drink. Whoever believes in Me, as scripture says: 'Rivers of living water will flow from within him.'" And at Jn 7:39, "He said this in reference to the Spirit that those who came to believe in Him were to receive. There was, of course, no Spirit yet, because Jesus had not yet been glorified." John does not mean the Holy Spirit did not yet exist, but that He had not yet come to guide the Church.

This teaching of Jesus is profound. He reveals to us that not only is He the one source for receiving the Spirit, but that the Spirit will flow into us and give us eternal life, transform us in Him, and that the Spirit, having filled us, will also flow from within us to others who thirst. We not only become the recipients of God's saving and transforming grace, but the instrument of His grace for others. That living water which flows in us is able to flow from us into others. We become a wellspring of grace, not because of our own merit or power, but because of the power of the Spirit working in us. Because the Spirit is infinite, the source and power of this living water is infinite, and we can never experience a loss by sharing this living water with others. The more we share, the faster it flows, and the more life is conveyed.

Many of you have seen the movie, Gospa, about Fr. Jozo. Fr. Jozo said, in one of his talks in 1998, that prayer flows. He said it flows to God and is never the same from moment to moment. Each prayer has a life of its own. When we think about this, we cannot help but appreciate it as part of the mystery of the rosary. The prayers of the rosary are not repeating the same thing over and over, but rather are a series of prayers flowing from our heart to the hearts of Jesus and Mary, each one different, each one alive, each one like a little water jug carrying something from us to them. That infinite Spirit within us, that living water which flows within us, is united with each prayer we say. It "wets" each bead of the rosary, so to speak, giving each prayer life and merit in the eyes of God, sending it into the heart of God as the beads pass through our fingers.

In the beginning of Jn 8, we find the famous story of the woman caught in adultery. The leaders challenge Jesus with the law of Moses which decrees that the woman be stoned. Many people through the ages have wondered what Jesus wrote on the ground (Jn 8:6). They have speculated that He wrote the sins of the people in the crowd who demanded the death of this woman. What He actually wrote, we may never know until we get to heaven. It is not important that we know.

What is important is that the crowd felt the need to challenge Jesus once again with the law. The law ruled their lives. What is also important is that once again Jesus does not argue with the law or the crowd. He never argues, never debates. To argue is to acknowledge the opponent may be your equal. He just answers with truth, for He is truth. He is our example to follow. The leaders raise a question designed to initiate a debate regarding whether the law should be followed. The question is a trap into which Jesus does not fall. They cannot trap Him with His own law. He simply answers, "Let the one among you who is without sin be the first to throw a stone at her." (Jn 8:7) You can almost see their hearts stop for a moment. Each one is afraid to step up, each one afraid that if they do He will challenge their self-righteousness by making public their sin. Each is afraid Jesus might really know their private sin. Each is afraid He really is who He says He is.

Then Jesus teaches us two good lessons about the sacrament of Confession. He teaches us that we should confess our sins in the privacy of the confessional not publicly to the crowds. It is not in their power to forgive sin. That power belongs to God. A person can forgive a transgression against himself, but he cannot forgive sin. Sin is a transgression against God, and therefore only God can forgive sin. Later, Jesus will tell us how we should go about this when He gives the divine power to forgive sin to His apostles and their successors in office, who stand in the person of Jesus for all time. We do not have to know why Jesus did this. It is sufficient to know that He instituted this sacrament as His preferred means for granting forgiveness of sin, as the only means instituted by Him for doing so.

He also taught us another valuable lesson. Merely expressing contrition is not enough. The jails are filled with contrite criminals. Mostly they are sorry they were caught. What really counts is resolve to do better. At the end of this account, Jesus turns to the woman who had been caught red-handed committing a capital offense, and tells her, "Go, and from now on do not sin any more." (Jn 8:11) We know nothing more about this woman. We do not know if she was married and cheating on her husband, or if she was single and sinning with a married man. We do not know if she had a husband who would have to find a way to forgive her, or if she had children who would have to deal with the public exposure of her crime. All we do know is that God forgave her sin, a capital offense, and told her to resolve to sin no more, not to take being forgiven lightly, as if it meant nothing or as if it was her right. It is a gift of God. A precious gift. He is again teaching us not to waste the gifts of God.

After having taught us, through the woman caught in adultery, the importance of resolving to change our sinful lives, Jesus then begins to teach us how to change, how to make good on the resolutions to which He calls us. He will be our example, He will lead the way, He will be our light. "I am the light of the world."(Jn 8:12)

Jesus also begins to teach us about Himself and how He works in us and with us. Those who follow Him do not just follow a path, do not just follow His light, but share His gift of life. "Whoever follows Me will not walk in darkness, but will have the light of life." (Jn 8:12) Jesus desires so much to share His most precious gift, the gift of His divine life, with us. Our only alternative to accepting His life is to seek death, the death of sin and separation from God. We follow His light or we follow the artificial and false lights of the world. One light is real, substantial and gives life. The other is false, has nothing of substance to offer, and has no life to give. One is truth, one is deception. We can only tell the difference by following Jesus, by doing what He tells us to do because we love and trust Him.

The way of Jesus is not easy. We need His light to follow. We would otherwise get lost and distracted along the way. The false glitter of the world is bright, surface deep and cold. The light of Jesus burns brightly within, deep in the depths of our soul, burning with the fire of His divine love. Our free will is like the key to turn on this divine furnace, for it takes an act of our will to decide for Him, to follow Him. He will never force Himself on us, but if we chose Him, if we follow Him and accept all He sends us, our reward is to share His divine life. The world offers instant gratification that can end at any time. Jesus offers His will for us. It can be anything He knows we need for our spiritual growth and to fulfill His purpose for our life. Yes, He has a purpose for your life, for every life, which is His plan for your sanctification. He chose our life, our family, our country, our language, our talents and capabilities, and our personality. He has a plan for how we should use all of these gifts, and we will fulfill that plan if we follow Him. We will not fulfill that plan if we do not follow His light. It is along the way of His path, following His light for us, that we find the purpose of our life. It is in accepting His light into our soul that we realize the purpose of our life. His interior beacon guides us through the darkness of this world, the darkness of sin, and shows us by the light of truth the path we should take. He knows we will stray off the path from time to time, but He keeps calling us back, back to follow His light. He never gives up, never stops loving us, never stops shining His light for us to see. But we have to make the choice. We have to take the steps in His direction. He will lead, but we have to follow the light.

After teaching the people that He is the light of the world, the one who will lead men out of the darkness, Jesus moves away from images and tells them in the most direct way He can that He is God, that He is the one God, and that He is their God, the God of Abraham. He does this in the one perfect way that will be so clear none of them could possibly miss the point. He says, "For if you do not believe that I AM, you will die in your sins." (Jn 8:24) I AM is the name God gave Himself, recorded in the scripture they were all so very familiar with; the name used in Exodus 3:13-14: "I AM who AM", "Tell them I AM sent you."

Imagine yourself there among the crowd as He say this. You hear the gasps of realization and the growl of disbelief. You see two fundamental responses in the eyes and mood of the people. One group, the one with open hearts, will be startled, excited, and eager. They talk softly and excitedly together, everyone speaking at once, eyes continually moving from neighbor to Jesus, back and forth. Eyes well with tears, hearts reach out to the long awaited Messiah, eager to hear His next words. The other group, those with closed hearts, who are focused only on themselves and their position in society, react with fear, anger and hostility. They challenge Him, silently accuse Him of blasphemy, and He repeats His claim. "When you lift up the son of man, then you will realize that I AM, ..." (Jn 8:28) They will finally realize it when He is no longer here to teach them. He then hammers the message home when He tells them, "Amen, amen, I say to you, before Abraham came to be, I AM." (Jn 8:58) Some want to stone Him for blasphemy. They may never accept Him, never realize the meaning of the covenant He came to give them, never participate in the consummation of the relationship between man and God. Their self-centeredness is their downfall. They are not focused on their relationship with God. Rather, they are focused on self and the prescripts of the law. Jesus will one day chide them about their futile efforts to find salvation in the law instead of in God, but not today. Today He is determined to identify Himself without any question. It will then be up to them to make their choice to walk with Him or away from Him. They must make a choice. They must choose conversion of heart. There is no ambiguity. He says "I AM", and that puts them on the spot to accept Him or reject Him. There is no middle ground, no political compromise, no hedging their bets. Yes or no, accept or reject; these are the only choices.

How many times in our lives do we also face this choice. We must choose to have a relationship with Him. We must make choices in our behavior, our thoughts, our desires. We must desire Him or reject Him. He will not tolerate a lukewarm position. To Him, lukewarmness in the face of the furnace of His infinite Love is the same as rejection. The book of Revelation tells us that if we are lukewarm He will vomit us out of His mouth. (Rev 3:16) Each of us must ask ourselves, "What must I do to make sure this does not happen to me?", and then take any action we must to decide wholeheartedly, without any reservation, for Him. We must embrace Him and His truth.

John continues the description of how Jesus revealed Himself. He moves through the cure of the man born blind in Chapter 9 and proceeds directly into the teaching on the good shepherd in Chapter 10. He has just told us He is God, that He is I AM, the God of Abraham. He had told us He is the light of the world. Now He tells us He is the good shepherd who will not just be our beacon but will lead us and protect us. Not all of us can be part of His flock. He has conditions.

"...the sheep hear his voice, as he calls his own sheep by name and leads them out. When he has driven out all his own, he walks ahead of them, and the sheep follow him, because they recognize his voice. But they will not follow a stranger." (Jn 10:1-5) Jesus then explains His words, for they did not understand Him. "Amen, amen I say to you, I am the gate for the sheep. ... I am the gate. Whoever enters through Me will be saved, ..." "I am the Good Shepherd, and I know mine and mine know Me, just as the Father knows Me and I know the Father; and I will lay down My life for the sheep." (Jn 10:7-15)

Those who want to be part of His flock must know Him, not just know of Him. They must do more than just cry out, "Lord, Lord." He knows them. They must know Him as

He and the Father know each other. The implication is that they must love Him. No one can know Jesus and not love Him. That is what conversion is all about; knowing Him well enough to love Him. We must know His voice, and know it well enough to follow that call. We all hear the call, but we do not all recognize the call. We cannot follow Jesus and follow the world. The world is the thief, the son of Satan, who climbs in over the wall to steal the sheep. Those who do not know Jesus, who do not know His call, will follow any voice because they do not have a shepherd to follow. One voice is as good as another. But when you belong to Jesus, you only follow one voice.

When Jesus calls the sheep, what does He want? He wants to lead them to Heaven, into the family of God. He wants to go beyond the confines of Israel. "I have other sheep, and they do not belong to this fold. These also I must lead and they will hear My voice, and there will be one flock, one shepherd. ... I give them eternal life, and they shall never perish. No one can take them out of My hand. My Father, who has given them to Me, is greater than all, and no one can take them out of the Father's hand. The Father and I are one." (Jn 10:16-30)

Once we are part of His flock, once we belong to Him, no one can take us away. We are safe. But we have free will and can walk away. We can turn our back on His leadership and protection. We can follow the stranger, we can follow ourselves. We can only enter the sheepfold of heaven by following Him. Peter said, "Master, to whom shall we go? You have the words of eternal life." (Jn 6:68). What will we say? Any other voice we follow leads us away from heaven. There is only one voice that leads us to eternal life. If we want to follow that voice we must know Jesus and love Him. That is how we recognize His voice. That is the condition for entry to heaven.

After teaching us that Jesus is the Good Shepherd who will led us to eternal life, John moves directly to Chapter 11 and the raising of Lazarus from the dead. Jesus taught us He has the power to give us eternal life and now He is going to show us in a dramatic way He has the power to conquer death. In the process, He also teaches us that we who love Him enough have great influence with Him.

Jesus was good friends with Mary, Martha and Lazarus, three siblings who lived in the town of Bethany in Judea. Like St. Joseph, we have no recorded words from Lazarus. All we know is that Jesus loved them all very much. Mary and Martha send word to Jesus, "Master, the one you love is ill." (Jn 11:3) Most of us would rush to the side of our friend whom we love, and that is what they expected from Jesus. Jesus remains where He is. Jesus never hurries, He never rushes at any time in any of the four gospels. He is always in control. But this situation is different from those the apostles have previously seem Him handle. Jesus deliberately remains where He is for two more days. He told the disciples that this illness possessing Lazarus shall not end in death, but is for the greater glory of God. We don't know for certain if the disciples understood what He told them, but probably not. Then He explains to them, ""Lazarus is dead, and I am glad for you that I was not there, that you may believe. Let us go to him." (Jn 11:15) Here Jesus is still conducting His seminary training. He tells the disciples that He waited, He let Lazarus, whom He loves, die, and He did so for their sake. That had to puzzle them. You can just hear the questions. "For us? Why did He let Lazarus die for us? What does it profit us if Lazarus dies? Clearly it did not profit Lazarus. He loves Lazarus, so why did He do this?" The disciples were also concerned about the danger in Judea, and Thomas even suggests, "Let us also go to die with him." (Jn 11:16) It sounds like Thomas is suggesting a martyrdom party. They will soon understand.

177

Jesus then teaches one of His most important lessons. When they arrive in Bethany, Martha comes out to meet Jesus and cries out, "Lord, if you had been here, my brother would not have died. But even now I know that whatever you ask of God, God will give you." (Jn 11:21-22) Lazarus has been dead for four days, with no refrigeration, and the stench would give no doubt as to his condition (Jn 11:39). Yet Jesus tells Martha her brother will rise, though she does not understand. (Jn 11:24-26) After the dialogue between them in which He tells her "I am the resurrection and the life; whoever believes in Me, even if he dies, will live," Jesus waited while Martha went to get Mary. "When Mary came to where Jesus was and saw him, she fell at his feet and, repeating Martha's words, said to him, "Lord, if you had been here, my brother would not have died." (Jn 11:32) Both women knew He had the power to have kept Lazarus alive. When Jesus saw her weeping ... he became perturbed and deeply troubled, and said, "Where have you laid him?"" (Jn 11:34) The grief of those who loved Him so much touched His heart. They took Jesus to the cave where Lazarus was buried, one much like His own would be. Jesus wept, then called out to Lazarus, one of His sheep, and said, "Lazarus, come out." (Jn 11:43) Lazarus, who knows His shepherd's voice, emerges from the cave, still wrapped in the fetters of death. Jesus said to them, "Untie him and let him go." (Jn 11:44) Lazarus is released, restored, and given back to His sisters. It is almost impossible for us, today, to understand the range of emotions experienced by all those involved. Jesus, seeing this resurrection as a forecast of His own Resurrection in the not too distant future, was moved because of His love for Mary, Martha and Lazarus, but also knowing what He had to do to conform to the Father's will; Lazarus, restored from death, once again being in the embrace of his sisters, having been raised from the dead by God Himself, just as Jesus would be raised from the dead not long thereafter; Mary and Martha, and the awe they must have felt for Jesus as He gave them back their brother; the friends and neighbors, who see Jesus raise a man after four days in the tomb.

Now it is time to return to the seminary. The final lesson Jesus taught the disciples here was one of the power of love. Both sisters had said, "If you had been there, my brother would not have died." These women knew Jesus and the power of their love for Him. They had no doubt of the truth of their statements. Jesus could not have denied their loving plea. He would have had to cure Lazarus because of their great love for Him. But He had a greater need to glorify His Father, and a greater need to teach the apostles the power of love and the power of prayer. So, He waited until Lazarus died before going to them. After Pentecost, the apostles, too, would raise people from the dead through the power of prayer. Do we love Jesus enough for our love to have the kind of influence with Him enjoyed by Martha and Mary?

The cure of Lazarus got the attention of a lot of people, and set in motion the events which would lead to Jesus' passion. The pace now picks up in the gospel and we seem to be almost running toward Calvary. Six days prior to the final Passover Jesus would celebrate, He is the guest of honor at a dinner given by His good friends Mary, Martha and Lazarus. It is a celebration of Lazarus' resurrection, a kind of preview of Easter, and Lazarus reclines at table with Jesus. Mary anoints the feet of Jesus with costly aromatic oil, and dries them with her hair. Judas Iscariot is furious. He is angry at her for what he sees is a waste of the expensive oil. John tells us the real reason Judas is angry. It is because he is a thief. (Jn 12:1-6)

Shortly thereafter Jesus enters Jerusalem for the last time, having already told the disciples that it is impossible a prophet should die outside Jerusalem (Lk 13:33-34), the crowds cheering and laying palm branches down (Jn 12:13) so He would not be covered in dust stirred up by the crowd. Prophesies are being rapidly fulfilled. The cure of Lazarus

179

had been so dramatic and so public that the leaders of the Jews were furious. Many Jews were becoming disciples of Jesus and the Pharisees were losing their hold on the people. Somehow, Jesus had to be stopped, and soon. They also wanted to kill Lazarus, the walking proof of Jesus' power and love. (Jn 12:10-11) Even Greeks who had come to worship were asking Andrew and Philip if they could see Jesus. (Jn 12:21) Jesus tells Andrew and Philip, "The hour has come for the son of man to be glorified. ... Whoever serves Me must follow Me, and where I am, there also will my servant be. The Father will honor whoever serves Me." (Jn 12:23-26)

What now happens seems to be taking place in a shadow land between Heaven and earth. Jesus, seeming to be more in communion with the Father now than before, begins His final lessons for the disciples. "I am troubled now. Yet what should I say? 'Father, save Me from this hour?' But it was for this purpose that I came to this hour." He immediately shifts attention to the Father, and prays, "Father, glorify your name." Just as at Jesus' baptism and at the transfiguration, a voice comes from heaven which says, "I have glorified it and I will glorify it again." (Jn 12:27-28) The crowd hears this voice, and Jesus tells them the voice was for their benefit, not His. They will need all the strength and assurance they can muster in the days ahead. Still gathering His flock even in this late hour, Jesus tells them, "And when I am lifted up from the earth, I will draw everyone to Myself." (Jn 12:32)

As you listen to His words, you can almost see Jesus' spirit rise up and cover the earth, ready to gather in His scattered sheep. It seems as if He is not even conscious of the place where He is, but has transcended the world and is looking down on what He must save. He will glorify the Father and Himself. And yet, at the same time, we see His human consciousness riveted on what is soon to take place. His purpose, His mission, is coming to fulfillment. The

Savior is about to complete His salvific act, about to establish His priesthood, about to establish His Eucharist, about to form His Church. Everything we will need for the rest of time He is giving us now, including Himself. He is ready to offer Himself as the ultimate consummating sacrifice for our salvation, and is offering all this to the Father for us. He is doing this willingly, under his own power, and for one reason. He loves each of us with an infinite love, the real extent of which we may never fully understand while on earth.

Jesus only has a short time left. He is teaching the apostles their final lessons one after another. The crowds keep challenging Him, but, absorbed by what He is about to do, His answers sound almost as if He is ignoring them, as if He is in a different conversation altogether. They ask, "We have heard from the law that the Messiah remains forever. Then how can you say that the son of man must be lifted up?" (Jn 12:34) He knows the Apostles will later teach them the meaning of the Eucharist, through which He will remain forever with them, and that the Holy Spirit will be with them until the end of time, so He just says, "The light will be among you only a little while. Walk while you have the light, so that darkness may not overcome you. Whoever walks in the dark does not know where he is going. While you have the light, believe in the light, so that you may become children of the Light." (Jn 12:35-36)

Jesus had already taught them He is the light of the world, so His disciples understand He is speaking of Himself. He is also teaching that through Him they can become children of God. As children of light, they will have the light within them, and they will therefore have an interior beacon to guide them. Many now believe Him, but they remain in the closet, afraid of the Pharisees. Their light is as if under a bushel. They lack courage and are afraid to be cast out from the synagogue by those whose eyes and hearts are still closed. (Jn 12:42)

181

Jesus continues, "I came into the world as light, so that everyone who believes in Me might not remain in darkness." (Jn 12:46) He teaches that those who reject Him and His word condemn themselves by their own action, because those who believe in Him also believe in the One who sent Him. He is closing the gap, in the minds of the people, that they perceive between Him and the Father. He is teaching them that there is no real gap; "... whoever sees Me sees the One who sent Me." (Jn 12:45) He and the Father are one. They must make a choice for Him or against Him. The political compromise of the middle ground is gone.

Jesus challenges us, today, with this teaching. He challenges us to accept Him as the light of our life and not to rely on ourselves or others who do not walk with Him. He is the true source of enlightenment, we are not. By ourselves, we are like the cold, reflected light of the moon. He is like the intense and continuous light of the sun. He wants us to become His lanterns, to be His lights to the world. He wants His light to burn within us, leading us to eternal life, leading us into the bosom of God, leading others to Him by what He does through us. That is our challenge today, just as it was then. Do we accept Him as our light, or do we act as the officials did and secretly say we believe, but behave as if we do not? Do we have our own Pharisees we are afraid of, our own Pharisees whose approval we value more than the approval of God? Do we live in light and truth? Do we love Him as we ought? Are we true to ourselves and to Him? How vulnerable to Him have we made ourselves? What access to our complete being have we given Him to do His work in us?

It is now the time of preparation for the Passover meal, time to have the Last Supper. In the synoptic gospels, much detail is given about the events of the Last Supper itself. In the gospel of John, we see an emphasis on the final teachings of Jesus to His apostles. The details of the Last Supper events are assumed known.

Jesus first washes the feet of the apostles, a ceremony re-enacted to this day at the Mass said on Holy Thursday. Jesus humbled Himself before them and washed and dried their feet. This embarrassed them, and Peter, who had already proclaimed Jesus was the son of God, cries out, "You will never wash my feet." But Jesus tells Peter, "Unless I wash you, you will have no inheritance with Me." (Jn 13:8) Even though he probably did not understand what Jesus meant, Peter knew he wanted to be with Jesus forever, so he replies, "Master, then not only my feet, but my hands and head as well." (Jn 13:9) Then Jesus says, "Whoever has bathed has no need except to have his feet washed, for he is clean all over; so you are clean, but not all." Judas, under the influence of the devil (Jn 13:2), was not clean.

This lesson is as important for us as it was for Peter and the others that night. When we have been purified by God through the sacrament of confession and have been cleansed all over, we will still pick up some impurities just by walking around in the unclean world. It is these small impurities that we pick up, almost by association, that need a final cleansing before we are ready to stand with Jesus before the throne of God. He is also teaching us the importance of acknowledging even venial sin in confession so we can receive Him in the Eucharist in the purest state of preparation possible. Jesus has taken it upon Himself to cleanse these apostles symbolically by the washing of feet, and will cleanse them actually, spiritually, as they receive His Body in the Eucharist. Only one of them will not be cleansed. Judas cannot benefit from the "foot washing". He must be cleansed all over, he must be bathed, for his sin is betrayal of God, rejection of God's love. Having chosen not to be reconciled with God, he sealed his fate for all eternity. Jesus then teaches the apostles that those whom He sends to do His work must accept a life of service to others. Their job is to bring souls to God, to serve the laity by helping them become children of God. They are to serve, not be served (Jn 13:16-18).

Once again, Jesus confirms for them who He is, using terminology they cannot mistake. He opens up to them the mystery of the Trinity. "From now on I am telling you before it happens, so that when it happens you may believe that I AM. Amen, amen I say to you, whoever receives the one I send receives Me, and whoever receives Me receives the one who sent Me." (Jn 13:19-20) Jesus is not only opening the mystery of the Trinity, He is opening the door to their participation in the Trinitarian life. He is merging their identities with His own to such an extent that if anyone receives His ordained representative, they receive Him just as surely as if Jesus Himself stood before them. And if we receive Jesus, we receive the Father. These first priests, and their successors in office for the rest of time, stand in the place of Jesus for us, truly and not just symbolically, by Divine decree. When we receive them in recognition of their role and position, and accept their priestly service, we receive all the grace which comes with that encounter, a grace that communicates to our soul the presence of God Himself.

Judas Iscariot is given every opportunity for conversion. Jesus even predicts His betrayal openly to let Judas know he was not operating in secret. "And while they were eating, he said, "Amen, I say to you, one of you will betray me." (Jn 13:21) Deeply distressed at this, they began to say to him one after another, "Surely it is not I, Lord?" He said in reply, "It is the one to whom I hand the morsel after I have dipped it."(Jn 13:26). Perhaps, also, Jesus was trying to bring the mind of Judas back to the scriptures, "Even my friend who had my trust and partook of my bread, has raised his heel against me." (Ps 41:10). Jesus sends Judas off to do his evil work. "What you are going to do, do quickly." (Jn 13:27) Anticipation of what is to come is heavy on Jesus' shoulders. He wants it over, His mission as man among men is completed. Judas went out into the night, to hide in darkness to do his foul deed. After telling the apostles that His hour of glory has now come, Jesus calls the apostles His children for the first time. "My children, I will be with you only a little while longer" (Jn 13:33).

The final commandment Jesus gives the apostles is one whose implications they do not yet realize. "I give you a new commandment: love one another. As I have loved you, so you also should love one another. This is how all will know that you are my disciples, if you have love for one another." (Jn 13:34-35) In just a short time they will learn the meaning of this love. They will learn how vulnerable their God has made Himself for the sake of His children. They know He is God, they are seeing the Trinity unfold, and soon they will understand to some measure the depths of Divine love. He is giving them the model they, and we, are all expected to follow. Life in the Trinity is a life of love and sacrifice for others.

Then Peter - big, loveable, outspoken Peter - declares his unfailing loyalty to Jesus. "I will lay down my life for you." (Jn 13:37) You can almost feel Jesus' love reach out and hug this big fisherman. So much will depend on him, so much is being laid on his shoulders. But first he has to be tested. Jesus does not thank Peter for his loyalty, but instead says, "Will you lay down your life for Me? Amen, amen I say to you, the cock will not crow before you deny Me three times." (Jn 13:38) How it must have hurt Peter to hear this about Himself. Did he doubt his own love for Jesus? That is not likely. He probably probed the depths of his courage looking for an answer. Chances are that if the soldiers had charged in that moment, Peter would have fought to his death. But what he had to face takes a different kind of courage, a kind of courage he still had to find within himself, for he will need it years later in Rome when he is martyred. He will have to experience the Third Person of the Trinity before he receives this new courage. He will have to undergo his own final conversion.

John now moves into Chapter 14 which introduces us to the Last Supper discourses. In the opening discourse, Jesus seems to be almost pounding into their heads that He is God and that they must, if they are to survive what is to come, place their faith entirely in Him. He Himself, not someone else, is preparing a place for them in the kingdom. He will also come back for them to take them to the kingdom with Him. Trust, trust, and more trust. First Thomas gets confused, even after three years of seminary training, and wants to know where it is they are supposed to go if Jesus will not be with them. Jesus tells them they are going to the Father. "I am the way and the truth and the life. No one comes to the Father except through Me." (Jn 14:6) Then Jesus says a rather of strange thing. "If you know Me, then you will also know My Father. From now on you do know Him and have seen Him." (Jn 14:7) What is Jesus doing to these special men, these apostles? He said, "From now on." Did they not know the Father before? Is Jesus infusing them with Divine grace, sharing His divinity, making them one with the Father and Him? We shall see a glimpse of the answer in Jesus' prayer to the Father in John 17.

Philip wants some concrete confirmation and says, "Master, show us the Father and that will be enough for us." (Jn 14:8) Jesus' frustration is evident in His response to Philip, but He continues teaching, "Whoever has seen Me has seen the Father." (Jn 14:9) But what has actually changed for the apostles? Jesus said, "From now on...." Jesus is getting the same question, first from Thomas, and now Philip. What is Jesus doing with them that is different from before? From now on, the apostles know the Father and have seen the Father; they have seen the invisible God of Israel face to face. Their God-encounter has gone to a new level. They are being infused with grace to receive this new understanding of the Holy Trinity; Three in One. It is a very new thing for these ordinary Jews, because centuries of revelation has taught them that no one has seen God, no one can see God face to face and live. Now, Jesus is telling them that they see the Father if they see Jesus and they know the Father if they know Jesus, yet He does not call Himself the Father.

The very next lesson (Jn 14:10-14) is subtle, but important. Jesus is in the Father and the Father is in Him. It is an apparent contradiction, but the apostles are given the grace to see it spiritually, and accept it. The Father is in Jesus and does His works, so Jesus does the works of the Father who dwells within. Then Jesus extends this relationship to the apostles. If they have Jesus within them, they will do the works of God. And just as the Father cannot refuse Jesus anything, Jesus tells them, "And whatever you ask in my name, I will do, so that the Father may be glorified in the Son. If you ask anything of me in my name, I will do it." (Jn 14: 13-14)

The unity of works and love, love proved through works of love, God working from within His church through His chosen apostles and their successor priests, is all being made known and infused through grace and because of faith. The life of the Church He will found on Peter is the divine life of God Himself acting within and through His priests. They will not work alone. They will not work as mere men. "Amen, amen I say to you, whoever believes in Me will do the works that I do, and will do greater ones than these, because I am going to the Father. And whatever you ask in my name, I will do, so that the Father may be glorified in the Son. If you ask anything of Me in My name, I will do it." (Jn 14:12-14)

It is now time for Jesus to introduce them to the Holy Spirit. Jesus tells the apostles that after He is gone the Father will send them "the Spirit of truth, which the world cannot accept, because it neither sees nor knows it. But you know it, because it remains with you, and will be in you. I will not leave you orphans; I will come to you." (Jn 14:17) This is another way Jesus confirms he is God, for it recalls to mind the scriptures, "The Father of orphans and the defender of widows is God in His holy dwelling"(Ps 68:6). Children of God are never orphans, and Jesus is telling them it is He who will not leave them orphans. The Spirit of Truth, the advocate, the Holy Spirit, who is unknown to the world, will come to them, overshadow and remain with them, and will reside in them. They are now experiencing the Holy Spirit within as Mary did many years ago. They are now bearers of Divine truth as she was bearer of the Son. Jesus is the Way, the Truth and the Life. The Spirit of Truth is the Holy Spirit. Jesus is answering the question raised by the crowd in Jn 12:34. They are just beginning to see how the Messiah will remain forever.

Jesus continues: "In a little while the world will no longer see Me, but you will see Me, because I live and you will live. On that day you will realize that I am in My Father and you are in Me and I in you." (Jn 14:19-20) What the world will not see, the apostles will see because of the gift of faith. They, and we, will see and experience Jesus in the Eucharist, which the world will not recognize as Him, until the end of time. The apostles will receive Him, and in doing so will receive the inseparable Trinity.

The lessons are coming quickly, one behind the other, in an expanding revelation of the Triune God, the God who will guide His Church until the end of time. In Jn 14:23, Jesus teaches His apostles, "Whoever loves Me will keep My word, and My Father will love him, and We will come to him and make Our dwelling in him. Whoever does not love Me does not keep My word." Jesus is also teaching the conditions of separation from God. It is not enough to merely say you believe. You must keep His word because you love Him; faith in action. Faith demands witness, sometimes through words, but always through action. Faith unspoken and not lived in witness is like the light put under the bushel basket. We are not saved by works alone. We are saved by faith, but faith never confirmed in deeds is empty and lacks grounding. It is like the house built on sand. When we stand on the rock, on Peter and His successors, as Jesus told us, we stand on Him. As He just said, He will be in us and He will accomplish His works through us. Jesus continues, "The advocate, the Holy Spirit that the Father will send in My name - He will teach you everything and remind you of all that I told you." (Jn 14:26) John later reminds us that they have recorded in the gospels only what is necessary for you to believe. The rest of the knowledge, the rest of the foundations of faith, are part of the "everything" that the Holy Spirit will teach the apostles and of which He will remind them. This is the tradition, the body of knowledge, of the early Christian Church, revelation which continued until the death of the last apostle. It is why Catholic doctrine is founded on both scripture and tradition. It was not until almost 400 A.D. that we had the New Testament, so this tradition was essential to the life of the young church. It was not invalidated, but rather was confirmed, when the New Testament was canonized.

Jesus now moves into the lesson on our relationship with Him, and, through Him, with each other. He teaches how intertwined our spiritual life is with His and with each others. He is the Vine and we are the branches. (Jn 15:5) If we do not bear fruit by our work, the Father will take away every non-bearing branch. Our life comes from Jesus, and our resulting work is His work done through us. He confirms this when He says, "... because without Me you can do nothing." (Jn 15:5) Then follows the hard lesson. "Anyone who does not remain in Me will be thrown out like a branch and wither; people will gather them and throw them into a fire and they will be burned." (Jn 15:6) Our salvation depends on remaining in Him. It is not enough to have once been in Him. We must persevere. We cannot just declare Jesus is our Lord and Savior and think we have done everything necessary for salvation, and nothing else we do after that matters. We must have courage and declare our fidelity to Him by word and deed, and to ourselves as well as others, for He reads our heart better than we do.

Our courage is, sometimes, for our own benefit, to confirm what we hope is true about ourselves. This life He gives us is His divine life of love, coursing through the vine and into each of us. We can no more separate ourselves from one another than we can separate from Jesus, for separating from Him is our only means to separate from one another. If I want to reject you, and you are part of the vine, I can only do so by separating from the vine, for the life blood of the vine is the same for each of us, and comes from the same source. We are united in and through Jesus.

Jesus repeats what He previously said, "If you remain in Me and My words remain in you, ask for whatever you want and it will be done for you." (Jn 15:7; See also Jn 14:14) To do as Jesus says requires superhuman love. He gives us this love, for He is the source of all love. Does He hold back? "As the Father loves Me, so I also love you." (Jn 15:9) He is teaching the apostles how we can not only love each other, but also share in the Divine love of the Trinity. Jesus loves us with the same love with which the Father loves Him. God loves infinitely, and cannot love any other way for that would be contrary to His nature. It is this infinite love with which He loves us. It will overwhelm us completely, taking away any chance to exercise our free will, unless He hides His love from us to some extent behind the veil of free will. He must put up veils behind which He waits so that we can make our free choice for Him. When we stand before Him, He will remove the veil and show us the spiritual treasures His love has in store for us.

For the disciples, it is a time of loving intensity, a final grounding to prepare them for tribulation. Jesus repeats His command of love, "This is My commandment: love one another as I love you. No one has greater love than this, to lay down one's life for one's friends." (Jn 15:12) Jesus then reminds them that He chose them, they did not choose Him. He called, He offered, and they responded. (Jn 15:16)

For the rest of Chapter 15, Jesus tells them of the adversity they will face, and how they must respond. Then, in the opening line of Chapter 16, Jesus says, "I have told you this so you may not fall away." (Jn 16:1) He also tells them they will even be expelled from the synagogue, thus confirming for them the need to have established His Church, for otherwise they will have no place to worship. Everything else in the world at that time was idolatrous. (Jn 16:2)

Jesus repeats several other lessons for them, confirming the apostles in His truth. He stresses that what they ask for in His name will be granted (Jn 15:16, Jn 16:23, Jn 16:26), and He tells them again that the Holy Spirit will guide them to all truth (Jn 16:13). He confirms that they will go through much tribulation (Jn 16:33), but He will come for them and when He comes again their joy will be complete and no one will be able to take their joy away from them (Jn 16:22-24). He repeats that the Father loves them because they love Jesus (Jn 16:27). Everything must be grounded in Jesus; everything. Having done all this, it is now Jesus' turn. It is now His time to be alone with His Father.

In Jn 17 we have one of the most beautiful passages in all of scripture. Jesus prays to His Father, one on one, exposing more of their intimate relationship to us, presenting to the Father the gift of the work of His life as the Son of Man, the only begotten Son of God. Soon He will have to offer His very life to the Father in sacrifice on our behalf, and Jesus knows it. But first He offers His work, the fruits of His labor, and petitions the Father on our behalf. He also presents to the Father His apostles. Very little time remains. It is like the offertory at Mass when the gifts are offered preceding the consecration. Jesus' prayer is a prayer of love. Jesus acknowledges to the Father what He has previously taught His apostles in Jn 6:44-46. Now Jesus asks the Father to glorify Him so that Jesus "may give eternal life to all You gave Him." (Jn 17:2) It is the ones whom the Father has given Him who now occupy Jesus' mind and prayer. He affirms the source of eternal life, which is that we know Jesus and know the Father (Jn 17:3). It is not enough to just know about Them. Rather, we must know Them. Jesus glorified the Father by doing the Father's work given to Him. Following His example, we must strive to glorify Jesus and the Father by doing their will for us, by putting faith into action. Jesus then petitions the Father to receive the glory He had with the Father before the world began (Jn 17:5). There is still a gate He must go through to take His place of glory, another bridge He must cross.

Now Jesus lays before the Father the fruit of what He has done (Jn 17:6-8). He has revealed the Father to the apostles and the others whom the Father gave Him. Jesus then says something we seldom hear discussed. He declares, "They belonged to you, and you gave them to me, and they have kept your word." (Jn 17:6) Jesus does not discuss those who did not belong to the Father.

Were the disciples, who walked away (Jn 6:66) from Jesus and no longer accompanied Him, among those who belonged to the Father but turned away in an exercise of free will, or did they not belong to the Father to begin with? Could there be any person who did not belong to the Father? Are those who belonged to the Father those who truly believed in Him and loved Him and were disposed to receive the revelations Jesus gave? Are they those who recognized this chief shepherd's voice and responded to His call instead of to the cacophony of the world? Does the Father call all, and does He desire that all respond? How many must have turned away from this call since the time of Adam and Eve. Should we say pursuit instead of call?

This must be very important, for Jesus reiterates the same point in Jn 17:9-10. He does not pray for the world, but prays for those the Father has given Him because they are His. It raises the question, did Jesus come for all or only for those the Father gave Him? What is the relationship between the call of the Father and Jesus' work of salvation? Is there a difference between those He came for and those He is praying for?

Jesus continues His prayer. All those who belong to the Father also belong to Him, and not only these men, but everything the Father and Jesus each have belongs to the other. Because the apostles and disciples have accepted His word and have understood that Jesus came from the Father and was sent to them by Him, Jesus has been glorified in them. They are His work, just as He is the Father's work, and His work has been accomplished successfully.

Jesus' prayer in Jn 17 continues, now moving into a prayer of petition for the apostles and then for all of us down through the ages. He will soon be leaving the world (Jn 17:11) and prays for His apostles and their descendants in faith. Jesus asks for the Father's protection for them, and we know the Father can never refuse His request. Jesus is our advocate, our mediator, before the Father. Unity is the goal, and Jesus asks that they be kept in the name the Father gave Him so they may be one just as He and the Father are one. With this, we understand a bit more the importance of being a Christian, for it is not just what we are, it is also who we are. It signifies and defines the relationship between us and God. To be one in the Body of Christ - that is the desire of almighty God for us. That is His will for us. Everything else is discord and division, and that is never the will of God. In Him we are one; one flock, one shepherd, one Mystical Body.

Jesus says, "...I protected them in your name that you gave Me..." (Jn 17:12) The apostles needed His protection, and so do we. Jesus asks the Father to protect them now, because He is coming to be with the Father. Jesus is filled with joy in anticipation of this reunion; a reunion, a unity, the depths of which we cannot fathom. He wants the apostles to share in His joy, so He prays this prayer so they can hear Him and share in His joy. He has already told them He will return for them and then their joy, too, shall never be taken from them. He is telling them that no matter what they witness over the next few hours, He is facing the events with joy because He knows He is going to the Father. Jesus prays that the Father not take them out of the world, but that He protect them from evil while they are in the world - just as He had taught the apostles to pray when He gave them the Our Father.

Jesus then confirms that these apostles do not belong to the world any more than Jesus belongs to the world. They belonged to the Father and the Father gave them to Jesus. Now Jesus returns them to the Father's protection. Jesus also asks the Father to consecrate them in truth because He sends them into the world to be guided by the Spirit of Truth, to defend Truth against the work of the father of lies. "Consecrate them in truth. Your word is truth." (Jn 17:17) Jesus is the Word of God, the incarnate Word (Jn 1:1), and He is the Truth (Jn 14:6).

Jesus ends by praying for all of us who believe in Him because of what the apostles teach us. He calls us all to unity with the Trinity and the apostles. (Jn 17:20-21) The love this unity requires is something most of us do not contemplate sufficiently or frequently enough. Over and over Jesus prays for the unity of mankind with the Trinity so that all may share in the Trinitarian life. This, too, we must spend more time contemplating, for the result of this unity is that "..so that they may all be one, as We are one, I in them and You in Me, that they may be brought to perfection as one, that the world may know that You sent Me, and that You loved them even as You loved Me." (Jn 17:23) What a profound statement! We are called to unity with the Trinity, called to perfection as one - not only as individuals, so that all may know the Father loves us with the same love with which He loves Jesus. We are the Father's gift to Jesus, and Jesus wants us to be wherever He is. Jesus finishes His prayer by asking that "the love with which you loved Me may be in them and I in them." (Jn 17:26)

We must spend a lot of time alone with this prayer of Jesus, and in discussion of this prayer with others. It is so important that we grasp its full meaning. Every line of Chapter 17 is rich in content and meaning.

John opens Chapter 18 telling us Jesus went to pray in a place very familiar to the apostles, a place He had often taken them to meet with them and teach them. Judas would know where to find Him. John's focus here is not on the details, already reported by the other evangelists, or of His agony in the garden, but rather on the divinity of Jesus. John does not even tell how Jesus was betrayed by a kiss. Throughout the gospel, especially from Chapter 6 on, John has had his focus on the Divinity of Jesus. Writing this gospel when he was an old man, John has a different mission from that of the other evangelists. John is not just recounting the story of Jesus. He is also combating early heresies which had already begun to surface.

In his description of Jesus' capture, John weaves together two important themes. Jesus is the God of Israel, and Jesus is giving Himself up to them voluntarily. He is the all-powerful God of creation and giving Himself for them to fulfill the will of His Father. John makes these two points in the dialogue between the soldiers and Jesus. Jesus identifies Himself as I AM, the name of God familiar to the Jews. (Jn 18:5-6) As He does so, the power of God casts the soldiers to the ground. It is as if Jesus is saying to these pagan Roman soldiers and the people who accompanied them, "Understand who I really am; know what you are doing, what I am allowing you to do." It is only after they recover that He allows them to take Him.

Jesus also protects the apostles, as He had said He would in John 17, asking the soldiers to let them go. Big, impulsive Simon comes to the rescue, cutting off the ear of the slave Malchus. But Jesus turns to Peter and tells Him to avoid violence, that the Father's will must be fulfilled. (Jn 18:10-11) He is gentle with Peter this time, knowing the trial Peter is about to face. Peter is willing to face the sword, but can he face his inner fear? Is it himself or God who is the source of his courage? Perhaps Peter was trying to show Jesus, and himself, that Jesus' prediction of his denial of Christ was not going to happen.

In spite of his courage with the sword, Peter denies Jesus three times. John does not dwell on this, does not show Peter's agony as his eyes meet those of Jesus. Peter has dealt with this story many times before John writes this gospel, and has already been martyred. John keeps his focus on Jesus. John shows the truth of Jesus. Jesus is the way and the light. He could not remain hidden. In the face of accusation by Annas, Jesus says, "I have spoken publicly to the world. I have always taught in a synagogue or in the temple area where all the Jews gather, and in secret I have said nothing. Why ask Me? Ask those who heard Me what I said to them. They know what I said." (Jn 18:20-21) Jesus is going to force them to accuse Him and convict Him with something other than truth. They must convict Him with lies, spawn of the father of lies. They can never convict Him with truth for He is Truth. Jesus is then brought to Caiaphas, and from Caiaphas to Pilate. Jesus' dialogue with Pilate, in which Pilate asks if Jesus is really the king of the Jews, ends with Pilate asking, "What is truth?" (Jn 18:38) How often have we asked this same question? Have we progressed enough in our life in Christ to answer the question? Do we accept that Jesus Himself is truth (Jn 14:6) and we only live in truth when we live in Him because we keep His word (Jn 14:23), all of His word? Finding no guilt in Jesus, Pilate makes the people choose between evil - Barabbas, and truth - Jesus. The people choose evil. (Jn 18:40)

John opens Chapter 19 with the final confrontation between Pilate and the crowd. Pilate almost seems like Jesus' defense attorney, but the crowd has one final, and decisive, argument. "If you release Him, you are not a friend of Caesar." (Jn 19:12) Pilate finally hands Jesus over to be crucified.

John mentions the crucifixion almost casually. Perhaps he is deferring to the accounts of the other evangelists. As he writes this gospel, the crucifixion is decades in the past, but John probably remembers it like it was yesterday. Perhaps it is still too painful an event to discuss for this one apostle who stood there at the cross with Mary, the apostle known as the one whom Jesus loved.

John recounts how the inscription nailed to the Cross came to be there. (Jn 19:19-22) Years later, when St. Helena found the true cross, that inscription was still affixed. It is one of the ways she was able to identify the true cross. The remains of this inscription, and what remains of the true cross, can be venerated today in one of the churches of Rome in a special chapel established for this purpose. One wonders why Pilate had the inscription written in three different languages. Was it a way to get back at the Jews for forcing him to crucify an innocent man? Was it his way of trying to cleanse his soul of guilt by testifying to truth? Had Pilate been given the grace of an answer to his own question? Did this public testimony save his soul? The apparent reason was because Jerusalem was a commerce center and many people were reading the inscription, both residents and visitors.

John describes the soldiers dividing the garments of Jesus by casing lots, so that scripture would be fulfilled. (Jn

19:23-24) Jesus wore a seamless robe, possibly made by His mother before He embarked on His public ministry. Artifacts from that time do not indicate that such a seamless robe was typical of the garments of the time. The nature of the garment was what led the soldiers to cast lots for it. This was necessary for scripture to be fulfilled, and this has led to the suggestion that the Blessed Mother wove this garment.

From the cross, Jesus gave His mother to us as our mother, and us to her as her children (Jn 19:26-27). Many who claim Mary, the mother of Jesus, had other sons and daughters do not understand the implications of what Jesus said, for if she had other children Jesus would have been breaking Jewish law, something He would never have done. Under Jewish law, when the eldest son of a widow died, the next eldest child in line had the responsibility to care for the mother. Giving Mary to John as his mother would make sense only if Jesus was her only child. John cared for Mary for the rest of her life on earth.

The Church has always interpreted this mutual giving of Mary to John and John to Mary in this context, especially since John's biological mother was there with them (Mt 27:56). It made no sense to give John to Mary if John's mother was there. How much the Blessed Mother influenced how John wrote this gospel by sharing with him all that Jesus had taught her over the years, we can only speculate. I do not see how this immaculate soul could not have influenced the apostle whom Jesus loved. They both had such great love for Jesus, and Jesus taught her for thirty years before beginning His three year public ministry.

Before describing how Jesus was buried, John describes how the soldier thrust his spear into the dead body of Jesus, causing blood and water to flow out. (Jn 19:34) The last drops of Jesus' blood, which had pooled in His heart, were released by, and probably onto, this young soldier. His name was Longinus. He later converted and died a martyr. I often wonder how many others who participated in the Passion of Jesus converted. Could anyone that intimately involved with this crowning event in salvation history walk away unchanged?

In Chapter 20 John begins with the account of the discovery of the empty tomb. First Mary Magdalen and then Peter and John. Following this discovery, Peter and John return to the apostles, but Mary remains behind and is sitting weeping near the tomb. The two angels ask her, "Woman, why are you weeping?" (Jn 20:13) She then turned and saw Jesus and He asked her the same question, (Jn 20:15) and then He asks whom she is looking for. Mary explains, and then Jesus says her name and she recognizes Him and is amazed. Why did she not recognize Him at first? It was not because He was glorious or dazzling, as at the transfiguration, for she thought He was the gardener.

Mary embraced Jesus but He told her not to hold Him for He had not yet ascended. (Jn 20:17) Jesus entrusts Mary with the responsibility to tell the apostles He is going ahead of them to His Father and their Father. Later on, in the upper room, Jesus directs the apostle Thomas to touch Him (Jn 20:27), telling him to place his finger in the wounds of Jesus' hands, and his hand into Jesus' side. Why would Jesus tell Mary Magdalen not to touch Him because He had not gone to the Father, and yet direct Thomas to touch Him, although Jesus had still not gone to the Father? Perhaps it was because Thomas was now an ordained priest with the divine powers to confect the Eucharist and forgive sin. Thomas had the power to offer the sacrifice of the Mass, and in doing so hold Jesus Christ, Body and Blood, Soul and Divinity, in his hands. Mary did not have the power. There was nothing else essential that separated Mary the disciple from Thomas the apostle. They both loved Jesus, and both were in a state of grace. Only one was a priest.

Jesus appeared in the midst of the apostles with a now familiar refrain; "Peace be with you." Jesus then says, "As the Father has sent Me, so I send you. And when he had said this, He breathed on them and said to them, 'Receive the Holy Spirit.' Whose sins you forgive are forgiven them, and whose sins you retain are retained." (Jn 20:21-23) The prior promise to Peter and recorded in Matthew 16:18-19 is fulfilled. They are now, in every possible sense, standing *in persona Christi*, in the person of Christ. They have been given the divine power to confect the Eucharist and they have been given the divine power to forgive sin. These are the two essential characters of priesthood. No person on earth other than an ordained priest has these gifts, these powers. It is the most precious gift there is this side of heaven. Except for the account of the creation of man where God breathed on man and gave him life (Gen 2:7), this is the only place in scripture where God breathes on man and changes him. In this case, He is giving them new infused divine life, the life of the Trinity, and with it the divine power to forgive sin. This power invested in His Church is the only means Jesus provides in the gospels for the forgiveness of sin, aside from holy martyrdom. (Jn 15:13)

Following the famous encounter with Thomas (Jn 20:24-28), John tells us that many things were done which have not been recorded, and then says, "But these are written that you may come to believe that Jesus is the Messiah, the Son of God, and that through this belief you may have life in His name." (Jn 20:30-31) Once again John emphasizes that true life comes only through Jesus, and that to gain access to His life we must believe in Him as the Messiah and Son of God. God came among man, God became man, to save man from the tragedy of sin. God came to man so that man may become one with God.

In the epilogue to the gospel, John recounts two important lessons. The first is the dialogue with Peter in which Jesus asks Peter three times if Peter loves Him. One time for each time Peter denied Jesus during the passion. It was a painful, but strengthening reminder. Making that declaration was important for Peter and it is no less important for us as we face that same choice every day. Every day, probably several times each day, we must choose between God and the world.

It also gives a possible clue why Jesus chose Peter as the one on whom to build His Church. Jesus does not only ask if Peter loves Him. All of the apostles loved Him. The first of Jesus' three questions is, "Do you love Me more than these?" (Jn 21:15) It was Peter's greater love for Jesus that merited for him the place of primacy among the apostles and the responsibility of being the Rock on which His Church was built.

Jesus then tells Peter to be prepared for the day when by his martyrdom he would glorify God. Peter's martyrdom, like all martyrdom, means we choose God above all else and in doing so give up control of how and why we die. Once we chose God without reserve, we give up control of the chain of events, turning that control over to God.

The other lesson is that we should not be concerned about what God has planned for others. Your task is to love God and do His will for you. His will for you is for you, not for someone else. It does not matter what He asks of another, when He calls them, how He calls them, or what He asks of them. That is between God and them. What is of concern to us is what is between God and each one of us as we are called to do His will.

Loving God Above All Else

As we journey to God, and study the writing of the great mystical doctors of the Church, like St. John of the Cross and St. Teresa of Avila, we see that the objective of the search for God is our transforming union in Him. The impetus for the search, the driving energy which quells our worldly appetites and which propels us, is our love for God. It is therefore appropriate to examine further our love for God, and His for us. Once we move out on the journey, it is our love for God and our desire for Him that becomes the paramount motive for our very life, for all we do. If we lose this desire for Him, we will not have the strength to continue on toward Him. Expressed in football terms, we lose sight of what and where the end zone is.

Without a deep love for God, the motivation for the search is missing, and the reason needed to focus on union with God and quieting of the appetites is not formed. But many ask, "How can I love God? How can I, a mere human, love the infinite?"

Pope Paul VI, speaking at St. Peter's in Rome as he addressed the Congress on the Apostolate of the Laity on October 15, 1967, and desiring to express what, for him, constituted lay spirituality, gave us an incredibly important teaching. He said, "It will suffice to tell you in a word: only your personal and profound union with Christ will assure the fruitfulness of your apostolate, whatever it may be."

St. John the Apostle tells us that God loved us first so that we might love Him (1 Jn 4:10). God, being love, forges the love in our hearts by which we may love Him in return, and in so doing imparts to our heart some of His divine essence, for He is love. This love of God for mankind is the underlying explanation, the reason, for everything Christ did which affects His people. It is the impetus behind creation, the incarnation, His suffering and death on Calvary, His resurrection, the formation of His Church, His institution of the sacraments, and especially His giving us the sacraments of Reconciliation and Eucharist. His love for us, and His desire for our love, is why He has gone so far to make His infinite self so reachable and accessible to us, who are so limited.

St. Therese, the Little Flower, spoke of the love we should have for God as being confident love.[45] In the realization of the confident love we should have for God, we rediscover the beating heart of the Gospel, the beating heart of His love for us and the kind of love we should have for Him. God's love is what makes the gospel come alive. It is why the gospel still has relevance for us 2000 years after the events described. God created the universe out of love for us so He could fill us with His love and His mercy. It is because of His love that we exist, for His will, by which we exist, is bound to His nature, which is love itself.

It was clearly not out of necessity that He created us, nor out of justice, for He does not owe us anything. It is only because of His love for us that we exist. When we turn our backs on God, we are turning our backs on His love, which is both the most powerful force and the most precious treasure in the universe. The apostle John has tried to reveal the secret of this love in his letter when he says simply, "God is love."(1 Jn 4:8). God loves us so much that He sacrificed His only-begotten Son, and His only-Begotten Son willingly complied with this will of the Father, because They love each other, and us, so much.

We recognize our weakness, or at least we should. We even ask, "How could Jesus do what He did on the cross for me? I am so weak and miserable." We must realize that it

---

[45]St. Therese of Lisieux, Story Of A Soul, ICS Publ, Washington DC, 2nd ed, 1976, pg 72

is because of our misery that He loves us, for it is His love that causes Him to want so much to share His nature with us, transforming us in Himself, thus making us so much more than we are or ever could be on our own.

Jesus gave us the greatest treasure we could ever have, the gift of Himself, purchased with His life. He gives us Himself in the Eucharist, He gives us Himself by sharing His nature with us and thus making us the adopted children of the Father. He gives us the gift of the transforming union with Himself through which He communicates Himself, His love, to us in a way we can experience but not explain, for it is beyond explanation. He gives us the grace to contemplate Him; His love and His mercy, as well as His justice. He gives us the gift to love Him enough to accept His love and His mercy so that we do not have to experience His justice.

All these things are mysteries of love, mysteries of contradictions. The omnipotent God, creator of the universe, became a vulnerable child in a bed of hay in a chilly stable in Bethlehem. He lived for three decades in common circumstances and simple obedience to His human mother and adopted father. He took upon Himself in Gethsemane the weight of all our sins, your individual sins and mine. He covered our sins with His blood at Calvary to wash them away, thus obtaining for you and me the right to stand before the Father who will forget our sins and accept us as His children. He took our sins on Himself and offers us the merits of His sacrifice. He does all this because He loves us so much, and, in so reaching out to us, allows us to touch Him, to reach the infinite God.

As we contemplate His love, we also must understand the underlying value of sacramental confession. Jesus took our sins on Himself, He urges us to give them to Him in confession as our gift to Him, and He transforms us with the sanctification of His Blood as He forgives us. He can only do this if we accept this offer, if we are willing, if we are humble enough, to acknowledge and hold out to Him our sins and ask Him to accept them. No matter what they are, He desires to do this. He gave His life so this can happen. He can accept all our sins, from all of us, and does so gladly, giving us the protection of His Blood in return, but we must be willing to admit our sins and give them to Him in confession. He begs us to give Him our sins. No sin is too great or too shameful for Him to accept. His capacity for mercy is as infinite as His love, for it is a manifestation of His infinite love.

God, in asking us, begging us, to give our sins to Him is also satisfying His own need. Although completely self-sufficient in Himself, He needs our cooperation in order to fulfill His role as our merciful savior. It is through our rejection of sin that He is able to slake the thirst for souls which drove Him to cry from the cross, "I thirst." This gift to Him of our sins, a gift most of us find hard to give because we do not perceive it as a gift, can only be accomplished through an act of our will, an act where we deliberately and consciously identify our sins to the priest and ask Jesus, through the priest, to remove them from our shoulders, after which we resolve to go forth and sin no more. Jesus does this gladly and lovingly.

These aspects of God's love and mercy would never have been experienced by us if Adam had not sinned. God turns all things for His greater glory, and because of the sin of Adam He had the opportunity to reveal much more of Himself than He would have had to reveal had things been otherwise. As we saw previously, Jesus told St. Faustina that His greatest attribute is His mercy. Because of this revealed love and mercy, we can have the confident love to give our sins to God and ask for the price of His Blood, His merits, which is our salvation. Instead of trying to amass things of this earth, we must try to change our lives and turn away from the world and come, finally, before God with empty hands and a full heart, so that with St. Therese we can say, "... for having nothing I shall receive everything from God."

The Everyday Struggle to Love God

Suppose someone came to you, as they did to me, and said:

My PEACE is at its all time WEAKest! I can look at other people's lives and problems and say, trust in God, he knows what he is doing, all things work to good, but this past week I have had a heck of a time trying to apply it to my own life. They say that the bible comforts the afflicted and afflicts the comfortable and this week it is painfully true for me. I kind of got my focus back thru scripture and prayer--from focusing on God's presence and praying to desire only Him. Now I feel like I can hardly pray at all, to even make the one tiny prayer. I think, my life is not flourishing--just about choked off--, maybe I am not "fearing the Lord" right. Maybe I am doing something wrong that I need to straighten out and I just don't see it. I don't know how much longer he (God) thinks I can hold on.

How would you respond to this cry? Here is what I told this person:

What you are experiencing is not uncommon for one God is drawing close. A priest friend of mine said he thought God was giving us all, somehow and to some degree, what He gave to Job so He can test our faith; but more than that, to give us the chance now to prove to ourselves how strong our faith really is because before too long we will need to rely on it more than ever.

Jesus told us in scripture that we can do nothing without Him. We cannot just pray; He has to allow us to pray, or pray with us. The times He wants to be our conscious prayer partner is when we need Him the most. Right now you need, more than almost anything, not just to pray to Him, but to ask Him and the Blessed Mother to pray with you to the Father. Have you been trying to do it all, all by yourself? Ask yourself this question, for the answer might be enlightening to you. In all you do, including prayer, you need a prayer partner and a constant anchor. That is the Lord. You cannot do it by yourself. The fact that you can pray at all means He is there with you and is allowing it. He has not abandoned you. Ask Him to pray with you and to give you His yoke and His burden, and to help you shed the ones you may have created for yourself. His are a lot better.

Don't fall into the traps Satan sets for you. God gives His gifts without condition, as He wills. That is why they are gifts and not loans. He desires you to act as He wants at all times, whether He is giving you gifts or not. Maybe that is what He is asking right now. He asks two things: love God and love your neighbor. He expects you to share what you receive. Don't waste or horde His gifts. When He fed the multitudes, He said, "Gather the fragments left over, so that nothing will be wasted." (Jn 6:12) They were more than what He started with. I suspect He had the disciples distribute them among the poor. What are the fragments of His gifts to you that you can share? One thing about His gifts; they never diminish if you share them - they just increase, for both you and the ones with whom you share. Have you ever done a spiritual gift self-inventory? It is an interesting thing to do. Do you keep a journal and jot down when spiritual gifts or trials come your way? It often helps us to keep things in balance when we read it over periodically. Perhaps your spiritual root system is getting deeper and stronger, and when the winds of the spiritual desert blow, and others whose faith was only surface deep are blown away, you will be steadfast.

Another time I received the following:

"I have a dear friend who was hoping in the Lord concerning the impending abortion of her grandchild. We've

207

been praying, tons of people been praying for us (we're talking whole seminaries praying for the children involved). We have been making every effort to put it all in God's hands. For both of us, our relationship to God has been strong and sturdy, up until now. Well I am still waiting, but my friend's grandchild was aborted (forced by the girl's parents) and that whole family is so devastated. I really know all of those philosophical responses about why bad things happen to good people or how God makes good from everything. But somehow it does not seem to be helping me cope. Despite all, I really do love God and if he needs us to go through all this stuff for some obscure Godly reason, I want to. I do not trust, in the least, that God will not give me more than I can handle, because he already has given me more than I can handle. I feel like a hypocrite because I can find encouraging words for others, but don't seem to be able to follow them myself. Sorry to be so negative.... 'How long, Oh Lord? How Long?'"

I responded: God has not abandoned you, He never does. But it sometimes seems that way. You are going through a really difficult period, and part of the disappointment related to the abortion, at least for your friend, was a disappointment that God did not interfere with someone's free will. But that free will was His gift to them, as it is to you, and He doesn't take His gifts back. He will no doubt turn that somehow to a spiritual good, somewhere, for someone, and you or your friend may never know. That is where the trust really comes in.

We have to love God no matter what, and trust that His love will always eventually prevail. Sometimes this love and trust it is a lot harder than other times, and He knows that. That's why He gave us the story of Job. No matter what He did to Job, Job never stopped loving Him, for God was worth it and He deserved it. Sometimes, that is the only motivation He has left us with, and we should rejoice, for that is His way of telling us that our faith is so strong He knows we can do this. Jesus told us to have faith that would persist, that would endure until the end (Mt 24:13), and if we do we will have our reward. That's trust! He thinks you're up to it. Trust His judgment of you.

I suggest He has not given you more than you can handle, for you are still here, and you can still say to God that you love Him. If you can do that, you haven't lost faith. All you have lost is God's consolations in your life. Maybe He thinks it's time to focus a little more on Him and a little less on the consolations. Love the God of consolations, not the consolations of God. Don't focus so much on peace in your life as on peace in your soul. What is happening to you is happening for a reason, His reason, and He wants you to trust Him enough to accept it will be for your spiritual good, regardless of the external effects.

As to why it is happening, don't even try to think about the why. If God wants you to know why, He'll find a way to tell you. In the meantime, just trust. Abandon yourself to Him as much as you possibly can. Give God, at the beginning of each day, all your trials for that day, and at the end of the day thank Him for the opportunity to do His will that day. It is an opportunity to come to grips more than ever with your dependence on Him and His Love for you.

Accepting Christ's Love

How do you accept God's love? How do you prepare yourself to receive His love? What does it mean to you to receive His love?

One of the things we already know is that God is love. All the love we have and give to others comes from God. The apostle John tells us this in the fourth gospel and in his letters, and we find it in the writings of the other apostles. Love of the kind God has for us and the kind He wants us to have for Him is supernatural. It seems apparent, therefore, that to love God we must first accept His love for us. But many have a problem with this and are not sure what it means or what to do. If you were to have a conversation with God in which you asked Him how to advance in love for Him, He might say something like,

If you could accept in your heart that I, your God, creator of the universe, love you, personally, with a love that is infinite; that I will never hurt you spiritually; that I am powerful enough to do literally anything for you; that I want to do everything for you that is good for your soul; that I will do anything to have you spend eternity with Me because I love you, but will never interfere with My gift to you of free will; if you could accept all this, then you would be able to accept My love, and would love Me in return as you should. You would then always strive to do My will by abandoning yourself to my will. Meditate on My Son's passion to gain this grace.

Look at Christ's Suffering With Eyes of Love

Sooner or later, we must come face to face with the fact of Christ's passion as His act of unlimited love for each

210

of us individually, and from which we are to learn how to love both Him and each other. Many people have a problem meditating on Christ's passion as they should. They look on the passion in a somewhat detached way, as a historical fact, something that happened 2000 years ago. They are also aware of His resurrection. The worldly, human tendency is to think:

He suffered for us all, and very much, and my sins are somehow included, even hidden, in that large mass of all the sins, of all humanity, for all time, for which He suffered and died. But then He rose from the dead and is now king and master of heaven and the universe, is infinite and omnipotent. He will be the judge of all mankind. How do I respond to the Passion, now, today, 2000 years later, after the Resurrection?

Taking all this together, and rationalizing away our own individual responsibilities and participation in that for which He died, it is hard for many to respond to His passion and death as we should in order to understand His love for us and accept that love in light of that understanding.

We tend to focus on the outcome, the end result, the resurrection, and not on why the passion had to happen in the first place and what it means to us for God Himself to have gone through that for us. It is not the *result* of the passion we need to focus on, but why the passion had to happen in the first place, and why it happened to the extent it did, beyond merely understanding the need to fulfill prophesy.

We need to recognize that our sins against God were and are an affront to Divinity and are not redeemable by any suffering, however great, undergone by any one or more members of humanity. Our suffering offered to God in recompense for our sins, on its own, means nothing to God in a redemptive sense; no more than the suffering of a worm means to us. In order for our suffering to have any supernatural value, it must acquire a character we do not have the power to give it.

Therefore, as part of God's plan, Christ had to be our redeemer. An affront against Divinity can only be recompensed by something which has actual value to the one against whom the affront has been committed. Our sins required a recompense to Divinity by Divinity.

Christ Suffered for Me

It was necessary for God Himself to suffer so that we might have life. By becoming man and suffering for us, and calling us to imitate Him, He enabled us to join our suffering to His and have His suffering impart to our suffering the Divine character necessary for it to have reparative meaning to the Father.

It was purely a result of God's love for us that this salvific act of Christ took place. God is completely sufficient without us. He could have dismissed us. But because of His infinite love for us, because of His role as both savior and sanctifier of our soul, we receive the benefit of that love through the incarnation, the passion, and the death of Christ.

It is Christ's suffering which changes the character of our suffering, making it worthy for Him to offer to our Father. Just as He unites us to Himself when we receive the Eucharist and thereby imparts divine life to our soul, He joins our suffering to His and imparts to our suffering the same character as His own. He suffered for one purpose, so if He joins our suffering to His, our suffering assumes that same purpose and character. But this can only happen when we offer our suffering to Christ and ask Him to unite it to His. By joining our suffering to His, He imparts to it the same reparative purpose as His own, thus giving our suffering, however slight or great, true reparative value. He did not have to do this. He does it out of love for us when He brings us into His Mystical Body and allows us to participate in His divine life. If we do not join our suffering to that of Christ, our suffering remains ours instead of becoming His; it remains mere human suffering and has no spiritual value.

Understanding Why Christ Suffered

In looking at Christ's suffering, we know that any suffering, no matter how insignificant, undertaken by Christ for us would have been enough because He is enough. He is God. But He is also our teacher, and because of His love for us He never asks us to do anything out of love for Him which He was not willing to do, and more, out of love for us. His suffering was a recompense for the sins of all men for all time, including every sin each of us individually has ever committed or will ever commit, regardless of how serious. He knows intimately each of our individual sins, including the reasons, excuses, motives, and results. He knew them in the garden and when He hung on the cross, just as He knows them now. He suffered and died for the forgiveness and reparation of each one of our sins. He did not see our sins in some kind of global melting pot. He knew, and suffered for, each individual sin. In spite of that, He still loves each of us with an infinite love.

In the garden, the night before He died, when He saw every sin for which He would die, He suffered most when He saw those souls, individually, who would refuse to accept His gift, turn their backs on His infinite love and life, and choose eternal death instead. They refuse an offer of infinite Love and choose spiritual death, total absence of love in any degree, instead.

But we still have a price to pay. There is still temporal punishment we owe for our sins, even after they are forgiven. If your child breaks a neighbor's window, the neighbor might forgive him, but the child should still pay for the broken window. Given the nature of our affront to God,

213

that temporal punishment should be great beyond all measure, even for those who accept the grace of God's forgiveness. But out of love for us, God thought of that as well. We may have to suffer, but He has mitigated the degree of our suffering by taking on Himself the greater portion of that cleaning suffering we owe to God, and thereby has mitigated even the degree of suffering we will endure if we but give ourselves to Him; if we but love Him. He told us to take up our cross and follow Him, but He also said that His yoke is easy and His burden is light (Mt 11:30). It is easy and light compared to what it would be without Him, without His help. He does not say harness or bridle, but yoke. That is because a yoke is always made for two oxen to pull a single load, and many are configured to fit the particular ox to be used. His yoke is offered to us because He is the other in the yoke with us, pulling our burden with us, taking the larger portion for Himself.

That We Might Suffer Less

Every drop of blood Jesus shed, every bit of physical and emotional injury He suffered, even being betrayed by a disciple with a false act of love - a kiss from a friend, was all accepted for our redemption. He was scourged, beaten, crowned with thorns, mocked, insulted, and made to carry His own cross. He was crucified publicly as an enemy of the people He had come to save. All of this was done to redeem us, but also so that each of us individually might suffer less. All was done to compensate for us, to teach us how to love and suffer with patience, and how our suffering can take on a Divine character by being joined to His.

He taught us our need for His yoke and His help in bearing our suffering when He accepted help from Simon of Cyrene. Most importantly, He underwent His suffering willingly because He loves us, not because He was forced to do so. Prior to His passion, He told us to love others as He loves us. By His passion, He showed us He loves us unconditionally.

Even though He had redeemed us, He could still have allowed us to suffer all the temporal punishment due for our sins, and we would have had no justifiable complaint. Purely out of love for each of us individually, He continues to share our suffering by giving us the grace to rely on and trust in His strength and His love for us. Our response has to be to accept that act of love unconditionally and unite ourselves to Him in every way we can, completely trusting in His love and mercy.

Living Virtuously

Living a virtuous life is difficult, especially in these immoral times, if we are not firmly grounded in the love of Christ and anxious to live according to His will. Many today do not even know what virtues are. The idea of living virtuously makes some people today laugh, and those who do are sometimes called "goody-two-shoes", "teacher's pet", "mamma's boy", "prude", "stuck-up", "pansy", and all sorts of other derogatory terms. But if we read the lives of the saints, we learn that to live a life of virtue is very difficult, and we find that the various virtues usually have to work in concert in order for one to respond to any one virtue. It is worth spending time reflecting on what the virtues are and how we can live virtuously.

The Three Theological Virtues

When we think of the three theological virtues of faith, hope, and charity (love), we may have many conceptions of what they mean and how they interact in our lives, and what is required for living these virtues. If we ask ten people, we will likely get at least nine different answers. We must understand what each theological virtue is, on what each depends, and how we gain the benefits of these virtues.

We begin by recalling the difference between Mary and Lucifer. Lucifer said, "I will not serve." Mary said, "Be it done to me according to your word." Mary was, and is, the epitome of human obedience to the will of God, and this total submission to the will of God is the "secret of the whole spiritual life."[46]

---

[46]Boylan, Dom M. Eugene, This Tremendous Lover, Christian Classics, Inc., Westminster, 1989 reprint, pg 21.

The supernatural virtues are those focused on our union with God. In the life of virtue, these theological virtues are like the first three of the Ten Commandments. The effect of these graces is to raise us to a supernatural mode of being through which we can become children of God. The key for us is understanding what these virtues are and how we gain their benefit.

We must first consider God's unique plan for each of us. But no matter what the details, His plan is always a plan for our sanctification, and "the whole of God's plan for our sanctification consists in making us living partners in the life and death of Christ."[47] Through the operation of grace, we share in what Christ does, we share in what He has done, and we share in what He will do. His Life in us becomes our life in Him. It is only through His Life, as He told us in the gospel, that we have life. It is only through Him that we can come to the Father. But since "sanctification is a supernatural work in the strictest sense of the term, God alone can be its principal cause and agent."[48] Our sanctification is a work done by God in us for His glory. We give glory to God by cooperating with that sanctification process. We deny God the glory due Him when we reject, by sin, the gift of our sanctification He offers us and which we should offer to Him. Now let us explore each of these theological virtues individually.

Christ told us in the gospel that He is the animating principal of the life of our soul, for He is the way, the truth, and the life (Jn 14:6). He gives us this supernatural life through the operation of grace derived from the three theological virtues. If God is the life of our soul, we must share enough of His nature, must be merged in Him and He in us, for this life to take proper effect. He does this for us, and we are sanctified, because of our humble obedience to

---

[47]ibid, p 28.
[48]ibid, pg 28.

His will for us. This humble obedience is how we express our love for God. Christ offers us life, everlasting life, His life, and the more we cooperate in His sanctification of our soul the more of His life He will share with us. There is no limit to this sharing, for His life and His love are infinite, inseparable, and He desires to share as much as we are disposed to accept.

There is no known limit to the capacity of the soul to share in this divine life other than the limit we impose on ourselves by our faith and our cooperation with His will. We are the ones who create the limits of our own capacity for receiving His life. We do this by our sinfulness and our lack of conformance to His will for us; by our lack of humility. When we sin, we reject to some extent, governed by the seriousness of that sin, that real, substantial and supernatural change in nature conferred upon our soul by God through sanctifying grace; we refuse the fullness of grace that makes us beautiful children of God. By refusing that grace we step back away, to some extent, from the Divine adoption process. When we commit mortal sin, we completely reject His life, His nature, His adoption of us, His love, and our participation in all He desires for us. We choose total spiritual darkness. But He loves us enough to allow us to reject Him, and gives us the means to return to that divine love through the operation of the grace of repentance, and the sanctifying grace we can receive through the sacraments of confession and the Eucharist. To maintain our soul in a state of readiness for God's Divine action in us, we can do nothing more important than attend and participate fully in daily Mass. The second most important thing we can do is to become proficient in prayer. Becoming proficient in prayer takes time. In the absence of competing family obligations and limitations on transportation, Daily Mass requires mostly an adjustment of our schedule and a determination to fully participate.

It is important for us to understand the relationship between the Mystical Body, our partnership with Christ, and the theological virtues. We have already considered the Mystical Body from several aspects. We have seen that through the Mystical Body, we can share in the merits of others, and can aid others who need help. Boylan addresses this same issue by posing the question, "How can one man take away another's guilt? How can one man actually render the offender pleasing in the eyes of the offended? How can one man actually merit in the name of another?"[49] This is one of the fundamental mysteries of the Mystical Body. Boylan says that some have tried to use a 'ransom' argument, one that views Christ as buying back our souls from the devil. However, he says, we cannot pursue this reasoning very far or else "we would have God paying a price to the devil for our deliverance, which is unthinkable."[50]

This view is unthinkable because it has the devil in control and able to extract some form of deference to himself from God, and this is impossible. If we will not negotiate with terrorists why would we expect God to negotiate with Satan? Boylan says that the answer lies in our becoming united with Christ, Him in us and we in Him. When we look at the gospel passages of Jn 14:18-23, 15:1-5, and 17:19-26, we see this more fully. In these gospel accounts we see the unity of Christ and the Father, and them with us. We are in them, and they are in us, and this unity with God is the result of our growth in prayer to the point where we really can say in all honesty that we love God and are keeping the word of Christ. We have the opportunity to enter into a mystical union with Christ, and a mystical evolution of our being, as He increases in us. Reaching this unity, to which Jesus must bring us, is accomplished through the sacraments and participation in the Mystical Body of Christ. The mechanism

---

[49]ibid, pg 34.
[50]ibid, pg 34.

for living this life in us is the theological virtue of love. We grow in all of the theological virtues through prayer.

In Jn 15:19-26, we see the concept of unification and perfection. We are "made perfect in one" through the operation of sanctifying grace. Our perfection is not being perfect physically, but rather spiritually. We become perfect spiritually by doing as Christ did; by always, without self-interest, conforming our will to that of the Father because we love Him. When we conform to His will, we become united in Christ's Spirit, we participate in His nature, and we tend toward the everlasting union of ourselves with God through operation of grace.

Because we are all members of the Mystical Body, and all members are united to some extent with Christ, we need to see Christ in others, for His life is the life of their souls as well as ours. How we respond to them is how we are responding to Christ in them. Even if a soul is dead from sin at the present moment, Christ can actually infuse grace to bring the soul to repentance and through that repentance to participation once again in the sanctifying life of Christ through the sacraments of confession and Eucharist. Through the Mystical Body we share in the life of Christ in us, but we also share in the merits of each other through operation of grace and the merits of Christ who is the life of the soul, the life of the Church, and the agent of merit, for all merit comes through union with Him and through conformance with His will.

"Conformity, then, to the will of God, is the fundamental principle of vital union with the Body of Christ, and every act of obedience to God's will is an act of real communion with Christ. There is the secret of the whole Christian philosophy and history."[51] Clearly, those who work for the good of the whole, for the good of the Mystical Body,

---

[51]ibid, pg 42.

work for their own salvation and for the salvation of other members of the Mystical Body. Those who serve the Mystical Body also serve the will of God. This is the activity of a life lived in virtue. It is what it means to be virtuous.

Each of us can say, "The weaker I get, the stronger I become, for God is my strength, and His will is my will." My self-dependence and self-will serve to do nothing other than get in the way of God acting in me. Jesus is my way, my truth, my life. I must diminish myself so He can increase in me, so He can increase as I decrease. When I sin, I spring a leak and let His grace pour out from me as I fill that space with the emptiness of the world and my self-will. I must plug the leak through the sacrament of confession and be replenished with Him through the sacrament of the Eucharist.

So we come to the question of participation in the life of Christ and how it relates to the virtue of faith. Faith is a gift from God. It must grow because God is life, God is act, God is never static. His gifts never result in inaction and static response. Faith grows by sharing it with others and by our abiding trust in God operating in our lives. "Let it be clearly understood that Christ and His Spirit are not present in the soul inactively, merely as a dwelling; their desire is to share and to animate every single action of our lives."[52] In the Eucharist, "He pours Himself into us, intimately unites Himself to us, and mingles His Body with us, so that we may be *unum quid*, one thing, one entity, as a body joined to a head; for this is the very desire and longing of ardent lovers."[53]

St. Paul, in several places, speaks of this unitive participation in and with Christ. He speaks of being baptized **in** Christ, and when we suffer we are crucified and made

---

[52]ibid, pg 49.

[53]ibid, pg 51.

alive **with** Him. The Latin text of Paul's letter uses the prefix *con*, not the word *cum*. Cum means with, in the sense of two separate beings doing something with each other, such as when they walk down the street one with(cum) the other. The prefix *con* signifies a unifying context. Priests *con*celebrate Mass as if they are one being. A married couple is sacramentally *con*joined together as one, and *con*summate their marriage with each other. The priests who concelebrate Mass, and the couple who marries and becomes one spiritually, still retain their individual natures. And so we are joined together with Christ in a unification that must be participative and substantial in order to take effect in us in a way allowing us to truly be children of God and share in the inheritance of Christ. This participative union with Christ is not mere fiction, but takes place in each of us in accordance with the capacity we have to accept in humility the will of God for us. We become changed, we become truly transformed in Christ. We become unified with Christ in a way impossible for us to effect, but which Christ effects in us to the degree that we humbly live in accordance with His will.

All of our exploration of a life of virtue means we have somehow come to know God. To love God is essential, but how do we as rational beings come to know God sufficiently for us to love Him, knowing that as rational beings we cannot love what is not known? "In this world, the only way one can know God supernaturally is by faith. Faith alone can put us in vital contact with Him, for when we believe in God, we share His knowledge, we lean on Him, and draw our strength from Him."[54]

In common parlance, ordinary faith signifies personal opinion, a certain level of conjecture, and all of it wrapped in some form of uncertainty. We say "I believe" that we will win a game, or go to a certain place, or that some event will

---

[54]ibid, pg 60.

occur, or some other such view. In all of these concepts of faith there is an underlying concept of accepting something as true on the basis of some testimony of another. We 'believe', perhaps, it will rain if the weather forecaster tells us it will, and we take action by carrying an umbrella. The less astute among us may 'believe' the outcome of a race will be as a racetrack tout said, and may bet a large sum of money on the belief of the credibility of this prediction. The level of credibility of the one on whose opinion we rely tends to control the level of faith we have in that pronouncement.

When it comes to supernatural faith, to belief in God, the gospel is the revealed word of God Himself, and has infinite credibility. It is the revelation by God to His people that makes the Judeo-Christian body of faith so unique. We did not invent God. He revealed Himself to us. Scriptures are the history of that revelation. He is the one on whose testimony our faith is based. "In supernatural faith, we accept truth on the testimony of God Himself, so that it leads to absolute certainty. ... it is the yielding of the mind to divine testimony."[55] Without the revelation of God, we could not know God and could not have faith. We could not know His many attributes, especially His attribute of mercy. To have faith takes an act of the will, since through free will our intellect is free to reject this truth. When we have faith, we accept the revelation of God. We believe in this truth because of the credibility of the one giving the testimony, and we act accordingly.

Once we have received the grace of faith, and accept the testimony of God through our belief in His word as recorded in the inspired scriptures, we are then prepared for the gift of hope. Pray for the gift of greater faith.

Up to this point, we have examined some aspects of the relationship between the operative effect of the Mystical

---

[55]ibid, pg 61.

Body and the virtue of faith. We saw that the Mystical Body is not just an organization, but is a living mystical organism through which Christ communicates His life to us and allows us to enter into a participative union with Him. We need faith to put this into effect. St. Paul tells us that "Faith is the substance of things to be hoped for, the evidence of things that appear not."[56]

St. Paul is here drawing a relationship between the theological virtue of faith and that of hope. Through faith, we believe in the testimony of God, and have absolute trust and confidence in what God has revealed. We have faith in the goodness and omnipotence of God since He has revealed this about Himself. The virtue of hope, like faith, is based on that knowledge of the goodness and omnipotence of God.

We must examine what hope means for us. Like faith, there are some common street definitions of hope, and alternatively there is the concept of hope as it pertains to our relationship with God. In common parlance, we hope for many things, all of them an uncertainty. We hope for good weather, or that we will win the lottery, or that our children will be virtuous and excel in what they do, or that our child's application to Harvard or Notre Dame is accepted. There is an uncertainty about all this. However, on a theological level, the object of our hope is God Himself. Our hope is the hope of union with God, and we hope in God's goodness and omnipotence and mercy.

Boylan says hope is "possession of Him, and for the means to obtain it. We also hope in God, because it is upon His infinite power that we rely to bring us to Himself, and because it is upon His goodness and mercy that we count to move Him to do so, and not upon our own merit."[57] This

---

[56]Hebrews 11:1

[57] Boylan, Dom M. Eugene, This Tremendous Lover, Christian Classics, inc., Westminster, 1989, pg 63.

really says a lot in just a few words. Instead of hoping for the uncertain, our hope is for salvation and this hope is founded, not on ourselves, but on the revealed goodness, love, will and omnipotence of God. We rely on His mercy, knowing He desires our salvation and has the power to accomplish it in and for us. It is then up to us to accept and use the means He gives us to accomplish this. Quite simply put, we need to have the humility to conform our will to His and to accept the sacraments He has given us, to receive through them His sanctifying grace, His Life.

We know through revelation that we need His help. So the *activity* of hope (the theological virtues are never static and always imply action) is an inner reaching out to God, a stretching out of our hand to His extended hand so that through operation of sanctifying grace He can draw us home with Him, into His embrace where we belong. He is our life, and our life preserver. We know He can do this because of His infinite power and goodness. We know He will do this because He loves us.

One rather unique aspect of hope is that even if we know we have rejected God's grace through commission of mortal sin, we still have hope because of His infinite goodness and power and love, and we hope in His mercy. Our hope is the attainment of the ultimate good, God Himself, and the means He gives us to restore us to that state of grace necessary; the sacrament of Reconciliation. It takes enough desire on our part to want to return to Him. We, as His prodigal children, are able to hope in God and the grace we need to return to Him. We also have to be humble enough to accept His help. This often takes courage, the courage to change. Coming back to God, seeking sacramental forgiveness and turning your life around, often takes courage to change over time. It is very different from deciding to do something that is a one-shot deal, like leaving a live-in lover or quitting a job that requires you to be dishonest with yourself and others, or deciding not to see a pornographic movie. It takes the courage to make a life-changing commitment to God, to re-orient your being toward God. It may affect old friends, familiar activities, and even lifestyle. It take courage and it also takes perseverance. In going through this change we usually find we cannot do it alone. We need God's help, and we also call upon the help of the Mystical Body of Christ, our fellow members who pray for us each day.

Hope, like faith, is tied to the Mystical Body. We, and all members of the Mystical Body Christ, call the infinite merits of Christ our own, and offer them to the Father for all our needs; and that special title to these merits, which is acquired in baptism, endures as long as we are not in mortal sin. If this is so, is there any limit to our hope?[58] Boylan says further that "the foundation of Christian hope is not one's own merits, but the infinite merits of Christ; not one's own goodness and justice, but the infinite goodness and mercy of God."[59]

We know that when we have achieved our goal of being united in heaven with God, faith and hope go away, but the virtue of love remains, for God is love. Possession of God is possession of love. The term charity ordinarily means some form of humanitarian gesture or alms-giving, and for many is primarily an issue of tax exemption. Boylan defines charity as "that virtue by which we love God above all things for His own sake, and by which we love our neighbor for God. It is the essential virtue of a living member of the Mystical Body of Christ."[60] This is another way of saying that charity is living the two great commandments of Christ. Remember how St. Paul says that no matter what else we do, or how good our works may be, if we do not have love we have nothing. It is the one thing in us which survives this life

---

[58]   ibid, pg 65.

[59]   ibid, pg 65.

[60]   ibid, pg 65.

on earth. St. John of the Cross said we will be judged on how well we have loved.

The supernatural virtue of charity is "love of God for His own sake, and is beyond our nature. We need a special virtue infused by God to enable us to love Him as He should be loved."[61] Think of what this is telling us. We cannot love God as we must, in the way demanded of us when we exercise the supernatural virtue of love, unless God has entered our life, for we must receive this supernatural love from God in order to love Him in return.

This presents us with an interesting paradox. To love God as we should requires a supernatural love. This means the love we must give God has to come from Him. The love we need to give God is a participation in the love He has for Himself, the only love proper for God who is infinite. We know that God's love which flows between the Father and the Son is personified as the Holy Spirit. Therefore this love of God for Himself is shared with us and comes into our heart through the power of the Holy Spirit. However, the love we have for God, to have merit, must be *our* love. Our Love for God cannot be only His love, for then we would be Him. It must be our love for Him. God had to impress love into our being when He made us in His likeness, so we can love Him with our love, even though our love comes from Him. We do similar things for our own children. Does not a father give a child some money with which to buy his or her mother a birthday present?

Our Love for God is the result of that unitive participation that exists between us and Christ, whereby we retain our individuality but share in His nature by participation, and through that unification our love for God becomes merged with and transformed by Christ and united to His love for the Father. The love we have for God must be

---

[61]   ibid, pg 66.

our love in order for it to be a proper tribute to God, and yet it must have the supernatural character of God's own love in order for it to be worthy of being offered to Him. This must happen through and in our unification with Christ. Without Him we can do nothing. If through pride we think that what we want for ourselves is more important than what is good for the Mystical Body, then we will be spiritually strangling ourselves, cutting off our life, and making ourselves one of the many branches which produce no fruit and which will be cut off and thrown into the fires, as Christ told us in the gospels.

The love each of us has for God is unique, for His relationship with each of us is unique. It is one of the benefits to us of being loved by an infinite God. This is also an enormous privilege. Mankind is privileged with the gift of intellect and free will, through which we can reject God or love Him, through which we can serve in humility or rebel in pride, and through which we can offer Him a love which is truly ours and which no other creature can give Him, for no other created creature has free will. We put on the love God gives us, we make it ours though participation in grace, and return it to Him as a truly unique unification of our love with His love, a love that is a truly different gift from each one of us.

This is the secret of the gospel parable about the wedding guest who did not come properly dressed and was treated harshly by the host. In Christ's time, the bridegroom provided the garment for the guests. It was the gift of the bridegroom, and became the guest's garment, and the guest honored the host by wearing it and in a sense offering it back to him that way. To not wear the garment was an insult to the bridegroom, and so the bridegroom acted accordingly. Christ is telling us how God gives us His love so we can put it on and honor Him properly by making it our own love. We pray for the grace to accept His love in humility and honor Him properly with our love.

Love is so important that without it we are nothing. Boylan says, speaking of our works and quoting an earlier writer, that "whatever be its motive, unless it be derived from the love of God, it profiteth nothing."[62] This is a most profound statement. Nothing we do, nothing at all, has any merit whatever in the eyes of God unless it is based in the love of God. Whatever we do for God, for others, and for ourselves must be done out of love for God if it is to have spiritual merit. This does not mean that good deeds cannot otherwise be done at all, since some good can be done even by an atheist. The issue is spiritual merit, not earthly satisfaction. Many people make philanthropic gifts and contributions for their own sake, motivated by pride or a tax advantage. We do things for the love of God when we accept His will for us and are obedient to that will. That may be doing our job the best we can, accepting our station in life, accepting our gifts and thanking God for them, or accepting our crosses and thanking God for them. It does not mean we have to constantly and at all times have God foremost on our minds, but rather doing things, living our lives the best we can, because that is God's will for us. It is avoiding those things and people we know are sources of evil or temptation. We try to live our lives according to God's will because we love Him. It is that simple; and that hard. "... for a healthy Christian life, all a man's work must be done with God, for God, and in God; the love of God is at once its source, its end, and its principal value."[63]

Mother Angelica had an interesting view of love on her show September 20, 1994. She said that love is like the cross. We need to have in our lives a personal relationship with God, which is like the vertical beam of the cross. We also need to have a love relationship with others, and that is like the horizontal beam of the cross. The horizontal beam cannot stand, cannot remain in place, unless it is supported

---

[62] ibid, pg 71.

[63] ibid, pg 71

by the vertical beam. It is our love of God that supports and makes it possible for us to love each other with the kind of love of which Christ speaks in the gospel.

And thus we see that faith, hope and charity have a special nature. "They represent a power to perform an action which directly tends to God, and this power itself can be rightly described as a participation of God's own power. This threefold power is the first effect of our incorporation in Christ and consequent divinization of our souls by grace. ... yet this action depends also upon our own free will - so that we are truly authors of these acts, and cannot lose these powers except by our own deliberate choice."[64]

The Joy of Faith

Jesus gave us many examples of God's response to faith. When He chides the apostles, one of the most common complaints He expresses is, "O you of little faith!"

When He cures the afflicted, He often says something like, "Your faith has saved you. Be healed." He extols the faith of the centurion whose servant He was asked to cure. (Mt 8:5-8) In our reflections on the gospel of John, we saw the faith of Mary and Martha when Jesus raised Lazarus. But we seldom see the pure joy which comes from faith lived. Jesus wants us to be joyful, not glum. He wants our love for Him and our faith in Him to bring joy to our hearts.

One example of this joy of faith is seen in Chapter 10 of the gospel of Luke. Jesus had already sent the twelve out to proclaim the kingdom, giving them the power and authority to cast out demons and cure the sick (Lk 9), and Jesus had already experienced the transfiguration. He is nearing the end of His time to walk among men on earth. Now, at the beginning of Chapter 10, Jesus sends the

---

[64] ibid, pg 67.

seventy-two disciples out, two by two, to every town and place He intended to visit. He was preparing the souls for His seed of faith. He told them to cure the sick in every town in which they were welcomed. He sent them out as His personal representatives. "Whoever listens to you listens to Me. Whoever rejects you rejects Me. And whoever rejects Me rejects the one who sent Me."(Lk 10:16)

The disciples did as Jesus asked, and then they returned rejoicing (Lk 10:17-20). Put yourself in their presence and listen as they describe with joy the fruits of their faith in Jesus. They "returned rejoicing." Not just happy, but rejoicing. They cry out with joy to Jesus, "Lord, even the demons are subject to us because of your name." (Lk 10:17) They have never been so excited. "You should have seen what was happening!", they seem to exclaim. It is hard to contain their excitement, and Jesus loves it. They are on a spiritual high and Jesus is right there with them. His own joy at their news is great. You can see the huge grin on His face, His head tilted back in laughter, as He embraces them and exclaims, "I have observed Satan fall like lightening from the sky." (Lk 10:18) He then confirms the source of their power lest they forget. "Behold, I have given you the power 'to tread upon serpents' and scorpions and upon the full force of the enemy and nothing will harm you. Nevertheless, do not rejoice because the spirits are subject to you, but rejoice because your names are written in heaven." (Lk 10:19-20) Wow!

What a marvelous lesson He teaches in so few words. He confirms He is the source of their power, has conferred upon them the power to defeat the devil, and has rendered the devil powerless against them. And yet, in spite of all this, and as much a source of joy as it is, Jesus tells them that their real source of joy should be that their names are already in the book of life. They are already written in the scroll of the saints. Satan has lost, and they have won, because of their faith in Jesus. Their faith has given them joy, not only now, but for eternity.

The Virtue of Courage

I believe it was Cervantes who said, "He who loses wealth, loses much; he who loses a friend, loses more; he who loses courage, loses all." Courage, also called fortitude, could almost be called the lost virtue in our self-focused society. It stands as one of the cardinal virtues, but is seldom seen as the motivator of people. Courage is that prudent point somewhere between recklessness and cowardice that inspires the motivation for our actions. Most importantly, it is that supernatural virtue which is most needed when one is called to uphold truth, to confirm our faith. Courage requires informed conviction just as surely as truth requires an informed conscience. We cannot wallow in ignorance and also espouse either truth or courage. Courage is needed by everyone. Without courage, we cannot properly deal with fear. We need courage to trust in God's love for us, and to do what we know is His will. "So for one who knows the right thing to do and does not do it, it is a sin." (James 4:17). And Paul, addressing the same concept, teaches, "Although they know the just decree of God that all who practice such things deserve death, they not only do them but give approval to those who practice them." (Rom 1:32). Is not this last statement from Paul a perfect definition of mortal sin?

When we act with courage, we do what we know is right in the eyes of God even where there is a likelihood of consequent suffering such as physical harm, social scorn, loss of position, or loss of property or companionship. The martyrs are our primary examples of this.

Jesus told us that if we follow Him, we will need courage. That is why fortitude is one of the gifts of the Holy Spirit. Jesus told us not to fear those who can only harm the body, but to fear greatly those who can cause the death of our soul. Lack of courage causes us to reverse that priority. The instances of people lacking courage are all around us; in school, at work, at play, in politics, and in many of our leaders. We even saw it in some bishops as the clerical abuse scandal unfolded. It is said that some of these bishops have apostolic authority but lack apostolic courage.

Most lack of courage is based in fear and the absence of a true relationship with God. We see students cheat because they fear getting a bad grade. Some people at work, to aid their own advancement, do things which deliberately harm others. In sports we see unsportsmanlike conduct, which is often a lack of courage and another form of cheating. In politics, many men and women compromise so often and on so many issues that they eventually compromise their own integrity and easily support a position they know is wrong rather than stand for truth or for what is right. We see this especially among so-called Catholic politicians who support abortion rights and many other things condemned by the Church. Perhaps they should take to heed what we quoted from Paul in the Book of Romans, just above.

Our civic and religious leaders in dioceses, business, in the legislature, in the courts, and even in law enforcement, who lack courage cause the most harm. Lack of courage allows companies to buy products from sweatshops, prevents legislators from opposing what is clearly evil - like abortion, particularly late term abortion, and permits those in the executive branch to champion policies encouraged by unethical lobbyists. It is lack of courage which drives companies to focus entirely on profit instead of on people, proving to employees that money is more important than they are.

Courage and morality are often seen as twins. It is hard to have one without the other. Morality usually provides the foundation on which courage stands. Morality gives us the anchor we need to be courageous, and helps us rely on something besides ourselves in the face of challenge. Most of all, we need to be grounded in Jesus Christ. We must live our lives in Him and through Him, and take to heart His advice given over and over - "Be not afraid!" We must do what is right, always, and with conviction. Evil is never conquered by cowardice and compromise. Evil is conquered by love and courage. We tell our children in school to "Just Say No" to drugs. How often do we say "No" to ourselves when tempted to do what is wrong? Acting in accordance with truth is courageous, and never wrong. The opposite is always wrong, for in doing so we act contrary to Christ, Who is truth.

If courage is the virtue needed to do what we know is right, morality is the base that provides the certitude. We have no excuse for being morally ignorant. We have an obligation to ourselves to have an informed conscience, and the help we need is readily available. The teaching magisterium of the Church is our primary source of information. Prayer, real prayer, is our other equally important source. Both are ways Jesus teaches us, and therefore what we learn from each will never conflict. Anytime we hear someone say they "prayed on it" and decided the official teaching magisterium of the Church is wrong, we should be very skeptical. It is most likely a case of a self-informed or Satan-inspired conscience instead of a truly informed conscience. In the face of such ignorance, we need the courage to stand with the Church. We may face scorn, but we know we are standing with the Church which Jesus told us is His, and which He said would stand until the end of time. It takes special courage to stand with the Church when even a cleric may go against the Church. It takes courage to do what is right without fighting or getting angry. It takes courage to pray for those who scorn you. It takes courage to forgive.

It takes courage for a young person to refuse the trap of illicit drugs, to risk being called "chicken" by their peers.

It takes courage to have the self-discipline to embrace abstinence before marriage when you are called all sorts of names by your peers and the pressures to engage in premarital sex are all around you. In society today, sex is often a requisite for popularity among youth.

In business it takes courage to do what is right in dealing with customers, especially in retail sales. The pressure is to make the sale, not whether the customer needs or would be helped by the product, or can afford the product. The pressures of the commission or bonus are strong. It takes courage for a doctor to refuse to perform a procedure he or she knows is immoral, especially when the patient lacks morality.

At every level, within and without the Church, the opportunities to act with courage are everywhere. Whether we do or not is indicative of the strength of our relationship with Christ.

The Virtue of Justice

Justice has many faces, depending on who the players are. Sometimes people confuse justice with revenge or punishment. The virtue of justice, in its most fundamental sense, is that infused gift of the Holy Spirit which inspires or inclines us to give to each what belongs to him. Justice is one of the four cardinal virtues: prudence, justice, fortitude (courage) and temperance. Together with the three theological virtues, they form the seven supernatural virtues.

Justice is the underlying theme of many of Jesus' teachings. He told us to render to Caesar what belongs to Caesar, and to God what belongs to God. Through the gift of justice, we give to every other, God and man, that which is due. To act with Justice toward God, we must pray, give obedience to His will, and offer Him our love. He told us to do unto others what we would like done to us. He told us that he who is without sin should be the one to throw the first stone at someone else. He taught us to ask the Father for forgiveness to the same extent we forgive others. He told us to love others as we love ourselves. He told us to live in Him, to abide in Him (Jn 15:1-7). He told us that He is our way, truth and life (Jn 14:6). Therefore, what belongs to or is due to another, and what we give them or allow them to retain if we act justly, is not just property, but also forgiveness and love and truth and life, and support in their journey following Christ. We cannot destroy life, born or unborn, and act justly unless we are acting in self-defense and have no other alternative. When we take an unborn life, we act unjustly to both mother and child, as well as to God Himself, who is the author of life.

Virtues give us access to the grace we need to combat vice. Each virtue has a vice against which it operates. The Holy Spirit assists us in exercising the virtue of justice through His gift of piety. Piety is the gift which moves us to worship God, and to treat others well because of our reverence for God who is the Father of all. If we act with greed or avarice, we are not acting justly. When a young person assaults another to steal a jacket or a pair of shoes - an all too common occurrence today, they act unjustly on several levels. They are taking that person's dignity, property, peace, and physical integrity, and are creating in them the vice of anger, and possibly vengeance. When they kill that other for the same material objective, the injustice is compounded.

Being a supernatural virtue, justice is infused into the soul with sanctifying grace, communicated through the sacraments. When we lose sanctifying grace through serious sin, we lose access to the virtue of justice and must rely on actual grace for the strength needed to escape from spiritual death and return to a state of spiritual life. During this time, we are subject to the onslaught of Satan to drive us farther away from God and lead us into activity that is self-focused and lacking in justice toward others, especially toward God. It is only by responding to God's justice toward us that we are able to return to His love and to His forgiving, sanctifying, life giving, grace.

The Virtue of Temperance

Without the supernatural virtue of temperance, we are subject to a high degree of self-focus and self-indulgence. Temperance is that supernatural virtue that communicates to our soul the grace we need to moderate our inclination toward worldly and sensory pleasures and keeps these inclinations within proper limits. This is not to say we should have no sensory pleasure or worldly desires, but that the inclinations toward them should be kept within the limits of reason as inspired by grace. We must eat, and there is nothing wrong with enjoying what we eat. There is nothing wrong with wanting to stay warm during the winter. It is the virtue of temperance which keeps these inclinations within limits and allows us to give proper focus to God and our responsibilities to Him and our neighbor. Without the virtue of temperance, we would not have the self-control we need to live a proper life. It is a virtue essential our spiritual life.

Temperance is the sister virtue of courage. Courage gives strength, and temperance gives moderation. Together they help us live a properly balanced life. The gift of fear of the Lord is the highest expression of the virtue of temperance. We fear offending the God who loves us and upon whom we are dependent. Temperance conveys to our soul the grace we need to counter the sister vices of gluttony and lust. Temperance helps us remain God-centered.

Temperance and trust are also closely allied. With temperance, we abstain from the temptation to hoard goods such as food, clothes, and other necessities and luxuries. We trust in God and so we do all things in moderation. Through the operation of the virtue of temperance, we are able to avoid excess in eating, drinking, entertainment and other legitimate sensory pleasures. It even includes avoiding excesses in companionship. With temperance we remain God-centered and all else takes second place. God is always first. Temperance is the virtue which allows us to seek the will of God ahead of our own will.

Temperance is the virtue which allows us to abstain from illegal drugs, avoid excessive consumption of alcohol, and avoid excessive speed on the highway. It helps us maintain interior balance whether we are alone or with others. It gives us the grace to resist the peer pressures that lead us to engage in conduct we know is improper. It gives us the grace we need to avoid promiscuous conduct. Temperance, with courage, gives us the grace we need to avoid the people or situations we know may lead us to sin. It gives us the grace to avoid doing those reckless and stupid things so many do just to showoff, or to be daring. It helps us avoid gossiping, which is always self-focused.

Temperance helps us remain interiorly calm. It helps us maintain our trust in God and His love for us. It helps us achieve the virtue of patience. In the gospels, Jesus never runs. The Father is always with Him. Jesus is always with us. It is up to us to trust in that truth, and live the truth of His continual presence.

The Virtue of Prudence

Prudence is the fourth cardinal virtue. Prudence is the guardian of our moral decisions. It is the virtue which helps us make the correct moral choice among the many tempting, possibly immoral, alternatives always available.

In 1970 my son was five years old and he needed open heart surgery. The condition was very serious, called Tetralogy of Fallot, and at that time only two surgeons in the country could perform the operation. There were no adults who had had the surgery, so the long term prognosis was uncertain. Our cardiologist in Denver said he had a sixty percent chance of making it through the surgery. He also said that I could choose not to have the surgery, in which case my son would live until he was twelve or thirteen, but would get weaker each year until then. I loved my son very much and wanted him with me as long as possible. Prudence demanded I make the right moral decision. Fortitude and justice, working with prudence, demanded I make the right choice to give my son what was rightly his, the chance to grow as a child of God.

Prudence and justice also demanded I get the best care I could afford for him. My decision had to be focused on his best interest, not my desire to hold onto him. The only virtuous alternative was to have the surgery.

The surgery was done at Mayo Clinic. I did not realize it until I got there, but Mayo Clinic was actually a group of specialized hospitals. All of the heart work was done at St. Mary's Hospital. There was a beautiful bronze figure of St. Francis of Assisi in the hospital courtyard. All the doctors, but most importantly the surgeon, expressed confidence. The surgeon was fairly young, but very skilled. He estimated success at ninety-five percent. My son came through the surgery in excellent condition, and in May of 1999 he was ordained a priest, and his two young brothers were the altar boys at his first Mass.

Two or three years after my son's operation, I was working in Pennsylvania. I read an article in the paper about a young girl, also five years old, who had an operation at a local hospital. She had only one of the four problems my son had, but it was serious nonetheless. Her parents also made the same prudent decision, and elected to have the surgery. That little five year old girl did not make it through surgery. Her parents went home without her. Both decisions were correct, but only one outcome from the two surgeries was the one desired by the parents. Because we act virtuously does not mean we always receive an outcome consistent with our own desires or goals. Nor can we question God's decision to bring that little girl home to be with Him.

Why do these things happen? We do not know. Perhaps God knew she would grow up to lose her soul if the surgery was successful. Perhaps He knew something would later cause her parents to divorce unless this loss brought them close once again. The possibilities are countless. We don't know why, nor is it our business. We follow God's will, we do not question His will. That is part of the strength which comes with making virtuous decisions. We trust that the result of prudent decisions and actions will be in accord with God's will, and His will is always in accord with His infinite love for us. If we cannot trust His infinite love, we cannot trust anything.

The Virtue of Patience

There are many virtues important to our spiritual growth. St. Teresa of Avila tells us that humility and self-knowledge are absolutely essential virtues. As we look at the different virtues, it is important to recognize them as a set of graces given to support correct and God-centered behavior. We must understand them in terms of what each is, but we must look upon them as the set of essential elements of the blueprint of our spiritual life. Each is important. Although one virtue or the other may be the subject of our focus at different times as we try to improve, we should not think any virtue is unimportant to us.

Patience is a virtue that we must all practice. Part of the difficulty in practicing patience is the tendency to react quickly, often without thinking. We are conditioned to respond by many things in our lives, from school classrooms to sports events. In some cultures, when a question is asked, the average time until the beginning of the response is seven seconds. In America, we get anxious after only two seconds. Read the gospels and see how Jesus responds in tense situations. When the people were going to stone the woman caught in adultery, Jesus bent down and wrote in the ground for a while before responding to the question put to Him. When He was asked about taxes, He asked for a coin and then asked some questions before He answered. He did not give a knee-jerk answer. He also never ran anywhere. You never read any account of Jesus hurrying to some destination, not even when a person was ill or dying. He is our model. We must learn to think before we speak, consider before we act, and act deliberately.

"You cannot unring a bell," said the judge to a lawyer after the client said something without thinking and the lawyer tried to take it back or have the judge disregard it. You have to stand by what you say. How often have you said something and wished you had not? You may spend a lot more time, and have a lot more anguish, asking forgiveness than you ever would have waiting a few moments to think first before you speak. On the football field, think before you hit someone the wrong way. Think before you gossip. I must accept the fact that people are not perfect, including me. If I do not want people speaking ill of me, I should treat them the same way, regardless of whether they had the courage and patience to curb their own behavior.

Patience is especially hard when you are tired. After a long day at work you are worn out, and the children or your spouse put demands your attention, sometimes insistently. Do not lash out, thinking only of yourself. Think of how much you love them, and how much they love you. When the children run up to you demanding your attention, and your instinct is to scold them for making noise and bothering you, reach out instead and hug them for a few moments and think about their perspective and how soon they will be grown and on their own. They are full of energy, may not have seen you all day, want your love and attention, and deserve it. Look at it as an opportunity to love and teach.

Sometimes something bad happens. You lose your job or someone you love dies. The last thing you want to do is answer a lot of questions from the children. Instead of sending your children away, hug them. Ask them to sit with you and just be quiet with you for a while. Tell them you need a little quiet time and ask them to share it with you. Then after a little while, do something with them to show you love them.

When we practice the virtue of patience, we must make it a continual part of life, and it helps a lot to make humor a part of your practice of patience. One day my brother-in-law came home from a long shift at the hospital. My sister watched through the kitchen window as their golden retriever ran up to him, wagging her tail, obviously showing great pleasure as he spent a few minutes to give her his attention. As he came into the kitchen, he gave my sister a peck on the cheek and sat down at the kitchen table to read the paper. My sister could have responded differently, but she smiled and said, "I noticed that you gave the dog more attention when you came home than you gave me." My brother-in-law, without missing a beat, responded, "If you came running up to the car with no clothes on, wagging your tail at me, I'd give you a lot of attention, too." They both got a big laugh out of that and turned the situation into one which actually brought them closer.

Part of patience is not taking those we love for granted. It is not allowing ourselves to let love become commonplace. Love should be an adventure, and that is not possible without patience. Sometimes we forget how much we love our spouse. We get too accustomed to their love for us and our love for them. Sit down and talk from time to time about nothing else but what you mean to each other. Get out the old pictures and look at them together. Reminisce about the things you have encountered together. The more conscious you each are of the other's love, and your love for them, the more patience you will have with each other.

At work, patience is demanded of you at all times. Others will push you to the limit. Impossible deadlines are routine. The ambitious try to climb the corporate ladder on your back, others take credit for your work. The opportunities for grace are endless. The prospect of worldly treasure is a powerful lure for many. Keep your focus on the right kind of treasure. Store up treasures in heaven. Focus on what has real worth. Let patience guide all your actions. Live in grace.

The Deadliest Sin

When considering virtue, we must also be aware of the opposite of virtue, for we must know what is trying to draw us away from a life of virtue. The seven deadly sins are pride, envy, gluttony, lust, anger, covetousness and sloth. There is an opposing virtue to each of these sins that provides the grace to overcome these sins. Pride is opposed by humility, envy is opposed by love, and so on. The saints have told us that when we try to overcome sin, rather than attack the sin we are plagued with we should instead try to increase the opposing virtue. Think of the soul as a glass filled with a clear, lightweight liquid. This clear liquid represents sin. The soul is filled to capacity with sin. Through grace, we are moved to conversion and desire to fight against our habitual sin. Now think of virtue as a heavy liquid which is a beautiful blue color. As God pours the blue fluid into our soul, it settles to the bottom, each drop displacing an equivalent drop of clear liquid. By bringing more virtue into our soul, we displace the evil of sin that was there since they cannot co-exist in the same space.

The deadliest sin may not be on the list of the seven deadly sins. I am not speaking of the "unforgivable sin" mentioned in the gospel, for there is much debate as to what that sin really is. I am speaking of vainglory. Vainglory is a sin which has no opposing virtue with which to fight it. Vainglory is doing good things, but doing them to win honor for yourself, without regard to the praise of God and the good of one's neighbor. It is insidious in that this impure motive may not be initially recognized. A person may begin doing good with right reasons, and then continue because of the praise and glory heaped upon them, and then do even more good to gain more praise. It is the one vice generated through performing good works.

Padre Pio was asked, by his spiritual director, Padre Agostino, for an assessment regarding two people who were working hard for the Church. Padre Pio, an exemplar of humility, replied,

"I recommended the matter a number of times to Our Lord and it seems to me that he wants me to speak of vainglory so as to put them on their guard against such a powerful enemy. This is an enemy that assails those who have consecrated themselves to the Lord and embraced the spiritual life. ... The saints refer to it as the wormwood of holiness. ... This vice is all the more to be feared by reason of the fact that there is no contrary virtue by which it can be fought. ... It seeps into the holiest acts and even in humility itself, if one is not watchful, it sets up its tent. ... Every evil is born from evil; only vainglory proceeds from good and therefore it is not extinguished by good but on the contrary is increased. ... All the other vices hold sway only over those who allow themselves to be vanquished and mastered by them, but vainglory raises its head against those very persons who combat and defeat it. ... It is an enemy that is never wearied, an enemy that enters into all our actions to wage war on us, and if we are not on our guard we fall a victim to it. ... it follows virtue everywhere. It would be useless for the body to try to escape from its shadow... . The same thing happens to anyone who is striving for virtue, for perfection:

the more he flees from vainglory the more he is beset by it. Dear Father, let us all fear this great enemy of ours. Those two souls should fear it still more, for there is something impregnable about this enemy. They must be always on the alert and not allow this formidable enemy to invade their minds and hearts, because once it gets in it mars every virtue, corrodes all holiness and corrupts everything that is beautiful and good. Let them open wide their hearts to trust in God, always bearing in mind that all that is good in them is a pure gift of the heavenly Bridegroom's supreme bounty. The devil is always on the watch; he is the most envious of all and he seeks to seize at once this treasure consisting of the virtues as soon as he recognizes it. This he does by having us attacked by this powerful enemy which is vainglory. If the enemy attacks them ... let them shout in his face, 'my holiness is not an effect of my own spirit, but it is the Spirit of God who sanctifies me.' Let them invariably direct their actions to the pure glory of God... ."[65]

We must always live virtuously and recognize that all we have is a gift from God which we use to glorify Him, not ourselves. Any time we see ourselves basking in, or even looking for, praise because of the good we do, we should be watchful, and, at least interiorly, divert all praise to God for whom we do this work. If we receive a compliment, receive it on behalf of God, not just yourself, and thank God for using you as His instrument of good.

---

[65] Padre Pio, Letters I, Number 142, pg 445, Our Lady of Grace Cap. Friary, Italy, 1984.

The Supporting Nature of Virtues

In the gospels, Jesus was always chiding the Pharisees and Sadducees, men who believed they were virtuous, above reproach, but who were in reality anything but virtuous. They set themselves up as the standard, the model to which the people of their time should aspire. They knew what should be done, but never did it themselves. They considered themselves above the burdens of the law they placed on others, similar to the way our own Congress exempts its members from the laws they pass to govern the rest of society. Jesus told the people to do as these hypocrites say, but not as they do. He said they were like sepulchers, whitewashed tombs, virtuous in public appearance but spiritually dead inside.

Consider the incident recorded in chapter seven of the gospel of Luke, when Jesus was invited to supper as the guest of honor at the home of Simon, the Pharisee. It is worth noting the different virtues, and lack of virtue, evident in the various participants. Consider the two principle players other than Jesus. One is Simon the Pharisee, a religious leader of the people, and the other is an unnamed woman of the streets, a sinner. Many believe she was Mary Magdalen, but in Luke she is not identified. Which one of the two behaves virtuously?

First consider Simon. Common courtesy in those times dictated that an invited guest was given water to wash his feet and perform the ceremonial washing before eating, and that his head is anointed with oil. The host also gives the guest the customary kiss of greeting. Simon did none of these for Jesus. Why would Simon omit all these customary courtesies, things almost automatic, for an invited guest? Evidently Simon had also invited other Pharisees, for in verse 39 Luke tells us "Now when the Pharisee who had invited him saw it, he said to himself, "If this man were a prophet, he would have known who and what sort of woman this is who is touching him, for she is a sinner." If Simon were the only Pharisee there, Luke could simply have used the man's name. But Luke is also giving us a clue to Simon's behavior. Jesus has been taking the Pharisees to task publicly. Simon is more concerned about the opinion of his counterparts than he is about showing courtesy to this wandering teacher who challenges their position and authority; the one the people call a prophet. Simon is putting Jesus on display before his fellow leaders, not inviting Jesus to supper out of a desire to learn. His motive, fed by pride, is to satisfy the curiosity of the Pharisees, and if they are fortunate, to answer in the negative the question in the minds of them all, "Is this man really a prophet as so many claim?" Simon would love to embarrass Jesus and expose Him as a fraud in front of his Pharisee friends, making himself a local hero and taking the people's hero away from them. Jesus, rather than acting insulted, which He had been, simply took His place, reclining at table. He knew what was about to happen. They did not.

Now let's look at the woman of the streets. She has been among the people following Jesus and has heard many of His teachings, perhaps from a corner of the crowd so she would not be noticed. What He said touched her heart. She experienced a complete conversion. Jesus taught in the day and she is a woman of the night, a streetwalker, unwelcome among the ordinary people of the community. She may also have seen some of the miraculous things Jesus did, but the one thing which apparently made an enormous impression on her is His frequent forgiveness of sins. This is something she craves in the deepest recesses of her being. She cannot live His teachings until she knows she is forgiven. She cannot receive His life within her until she is forgiven. This has become her burning desire. To come before Jesus will take great humility and determination, not to mention courage. She has been given the virtue of faith, great faith.

For her, seeking Jesus is everything, the number one desire of her life right now, and nothing is going to deter her. She is motivated by love, faith, courage and humility, in contrast to the pride and self-love of Simon. Virtue in the heart of the despised playing against vice in the heart of the most respected. The drama begins to unfold.

The woman, hearing Jesus was at the house of Simon, maybe even having followed Him there, approaches the door. Aware there is no way she could ever have received an invitation to attend this supper because of the life she has led, and her sole objective being to reach Jesus, she enters the house. She does not care what the various honored guests might think of her, or of her boldness at crashing the dinner party. She knows they consider her unclean, and unworthy to enter this house. Nothing she can say or do would change their opinion. She does not ask permission, does not go to Simon and beg entry into his house. She boldly enters the house and goes straight to Jesus. As is the custom, Jesus is reclining at table, legs fully extended, for they did not use chairs in those days.

She is too ashamed of her sin to come face to face with Jesus, or even speak to Him. She speaks only with her heart. Standing behind Him, she weeps and her tears wash over His feet. Seeing what she has done, she wipes the tears from His feet with her hair. She then anoints His feet with the costly ointment she brought with her. Still, she says nothing, trusting in Jesus to see the agony of repentance which fills her heart.

Simon, on the other hand, is quick to judge both the woman and Jesus. He sees an opportunity for victory very early in the evening. Simon recognizes her as a woman of the street, a sinner. Is it her dress that gives her away? Or perhaps Simon knows from first hand experience. In any case, he judges her and in doing so also judges Jesus, for he says to himself, "If this man were a prophet, he would have known who and what sort of woman this is who is touching him, for she is a sinner." Simon immediately concludes Jesus consorts with streetwalkers and therefore could not possibly be a prophet. Tasting victory, and filled with pride, he prepares for the kill. Perhaps his heart even skips a beat from the excitement of his discovery. No man of honor and respect would ever allow a sinful woman like this to be in his presence, at least not publicly, nor would he allow her to touch him. Doing so at table, in the presence of important guests in the house of a Pharisee, is unthinkable. He would have scolded her, maybe even beaten her, and sent her away, back into the night where she obviously belonged. God, this Pharisee knows, would not allow one of His prophets to associate publicly with such a woman as this, to be touched in this way by a public sinner.

At last, Jesus will be exposed for the fraud He is. Simon will be a hero to his fellow Pharisees. He could almost hear the conversations tomorrow morning. His guests will all be telling the others in the Temple area or in the Sanhedrin, "My friends, last night in the house of our worthy companion Simon, Jesus the Nazorean was finally exposed for the fraud he is. You should have seen it. ..." Perhaps a smile crossed Simon's face as he fantasized about the conversation.

Then Jesus spoke. Knowing Simon's thoughts, Jesus calmly says, "Simon, I have something to say to you." Certain that Jesus could do nothing but dig the hole He was in even deeper, and hopeful Jesus will say something to prove his case even more certainly in front of his guests, Simon replies, "What is it, Teacher?" Was Simon just mocking Jesus by calling Him Teacher? Probably, for at this point Simon does not feel Jesus has anything to teach him, a Pharisee, a religious leader of the community. It is Simon who will clearly be giving the lesson this night. He is also, perhaps, just trying to give Jesus more rope with which to hang Himself in front of all those present. After all, no one could later say Simon had been discourteous to Jesus.

In much the same way Nathan led King David to condemn himself by telling David a story and asking him to judge the outcome (2 Sam 12:1-7), Jesus says, "A certain creditor had two debtors; one owed five hundred denarii, and the other fifty. When they could not pay, he forgave them both. Now which of them will love him more?" Simon, clearly wishing to show his wisdom before the guests, answered, "The one, I suppose, to whom he forgave more." Like David before him, Simon answered correctly, but soon wished he had not. Jesus, confirming His role as the real teacher, said to him, "You have judged rightly." At this point Simon may have been wondering to himself, "Now what is Jesus going to do; what trick is He up to?" Perhaps now Simon's smile was being slowly replaced by a frown. Jesus will not disappoint him. Turning toward the woman, but not speaking to her, Jesus said to Simon, "Do you see this woman?" This seems an odd question, for surely Simon could see her. Jesus was actually making the point that Simon could see the outside, but could not see her soul, could not see the love in her heart motivating everything she did. Then, forcing Simon to judge himself, Jesus compares the lack of common courtesy with which He had been treated by Simon, even though He was an invited guest, with the love with which He had been treated by the woman Simon considered an unclean sinner unfit to enter his house. Jesus said, "I entered your house, you gave me no water for my feet, but she has wet my feet with her tears and wiped them with her hair. You gave me no kiss, but from the time I came in she has not ceased to kiss my feet. You did not anoint my head with oil, but she has anointed my feet with ointment. Therefore I tell you, her sins, which are many, are forgiven, for she loved much; but he who is forgiven little, loves little." Simon is made to see himself clearly, in front of all his household and guests. Simon, whose self-love forces him to lead a life lacking in virtue, is told he cannot expect to be forgiven by God. This was more of a shock than Simon anticipated, being a religious leader of the people. How could God possibly not forgive him? Had he, indeed, actually done anything needing forgiveness? Didn't he always follow the law? Then Jesus ices the cake, so to speak. He said to the woman, "Your sins are forgiven." He said no such thing to Simon or the other guests. Everything Simon wanted to happen was going down the tubes very quickly. Everything he wanted to avoid was happening. He was rapidly losing face with his fellow Pharisees who began to question among themselves, "Who is this, who even forgives sins?" And then, placing the cherry on top of the icing, Jesus said to the woman, "Your faith has saved you; go in peace." Jesus has once again claimed the divine power to forgive sin and asserted His role as Savior, and right in Simon's house in front of his guests. Simon, no doubt, was furious.

Simon got much more than he bargained for. Instead of embarrassing Jesus, he only embarrassed himself. His pride led him down a path to public humiliation. I wonder who left Simon's house first, Jesus or the other guests? Simon probably once again imagined the conversations of his fellow Pharisees as they walked home. "What did Simon think he was doing, embarrassing us like this? This Jesus not only chides us in public, he comes into our homes and does so. How could Simon do such a thing? How will we explain this to the others when they ask what happened? That woman, the street walker, will be telling everyone about this, how she was there with us and how Jesus forgave her sin but didn't forgive Simon, or us, because we don't love enough. I bet Simon's wife loved that one. We'll never live it down. How can we explain away that we had supper with a streetwalker? We need to do something about this Jesus, and quickly."

The woman only accepted the generosity and forgiveness of Jesus in response to her love. She never said a word the whole evening. Jesus forgave her, and that was enough. That was her great desire. She understood what Jesus had done for her, and she would be His disciple forever. Simon acted like he didn't have a clue. Perhaps he did not. We can hope, however, that his heart was somehow touched and that eventually he did convert and become a follower of Jesus. Many who encountered Jesus eventually did. It would be interesting to witness the encounter between Simon and the woman of the streets after his conversion. How would she respond? How would he?

Looking back on this event, we can see an interesting play of virtue against vice. Vice operates at the surface, always superficial, as if it can only provide a facade. Virtue runs deep, like living water, always reaching the heart, always providing a firm anchor. We might ask how the virtues in our own life compare to the same virtues seen in this woman who, at least up to the time shortly before her encounter with Jesus, was a woman of the streets. She exemplified the virtues of *faith, love, courage,* and *humility.* Do we? We have access to Jesus in the sacrament of Confession as often as needed. Do we have the love to appreciate this grace, the courage to admit our guilt before Him, a passionate desire to be forgiven? Do we, like Simon, make self-serving assumptions about ourselves and refuse to look into the mirrors of virtue? Does the vice of cowardice cloud our mirror of courage? Do we stand up for what we know is right? Do we defend our faith in the face of ridicule? Do we even admit our faith in response to secular humanism? When we encounter atheism, so rampant among university professors today, do we have the courage to say, "I believe"? Do we instill the courage to believe in our children? Do we have the courage to accept the sacrament of Confession and say, truthfully, "Bless me father, for I have sinned."?

The woman of the streets in Luke taught us an important lesson. She taught us that virtues work in sets and compliment one another. It took four different virtues operating together to help her through that evening. As a result, she went down in history not as someone to be despised but as someone to be admired, and we don't even know her name. She could be any one of us, perhaps with a different kind or mix of sins needing forgiveness. We must look within to see what is truly important to us, to see which virtues are critical to our spiritual success, which sins stand as impediments to progress. Each must ask, "Could I have done what this woman, this public sinner, did? Would finding Jesus and receiving His love have been that important to me? Would I have had the courage?"

Courage:

Each virtue can come in many different hues. Let us consider the virtue of courage. It took great courage for the woman in the gospel of Luke to do what she did. Today, in our society, we find many occasions which call for courage. We often need courage to face others, to face danger, to stand up for our convictions, to face hard situations, to face ourselves.

Courage is a very interesting virtue, for so many of our popular media outlets try to convince us that courage is something we have within ourselves, something that is part of our own makeup. We are told it is rooted in self, not God. Rambo is alive and well in the popular media. Everything we see tells us that strong people have courage and weak people do not. Courage is portrayed as glorious. If you do not display courage, you have little worth. But if courage is a virtue, then God is in this picture someplace. We cannot separate virtue from God. Virtue comes from God, not from self. The exemplification of virtue depends on the relationship we have with God. Everything we do to enter the heart of God, to let Him enter our heart, requires an active relationship, and courage is no different.

How do we know? One great example is St. Peter. One night, sitting before a fire, he was terrified of a young woman, a maidservant, who simply asked him a question, "Aren't you one of His followers?" Peter, afraid to follow the steps of Jesus, lied, "I do not know the man." Then he looked into the eyes of Jesus and wept bitterly. A few days later he was in the Temple preaching about Jesus and three thousand were baptized on that one day. He was on fire, unstoppable. He would continue his public proclamations about Jesus in Jerusalem, then as the first bishop of Antioch, and later as the first bishop of Rome. He would continue until he embraced martyrdom. When Peter was being led to his death, he said he was unworthy to die the way Jesus had died, so they crucified our loveable fisherman upside down.

Sometimes we find this kind of heroic virtue in young children. The relics of St. Philomena indicate she was a young girl when she was martyred. We don't know how she was martyred, but it was during the early days of the Christian persecutions. Her tomb was discovered in the catacombs and we know she was a martyr because in the typical custom of the time a small vial of her blood was buried with her. This was the sign she was a martyr.

In more modern times, we have the example of the Italian teenager, St. Maria Goretti, who accepted martyrdom rather than sacrifice her virginity. As she was being stabbed, she told her attacker, "I forgive you." This so affected him that he converted while in prison, then became a friend of her family, and stood next to Maria's mother at the canonization ceremony of the young saint.

But what about the ordinary people in modern society? Does courage play a part in your everyday life? Absolutely. It takes courage not to continue to live as a battered spouse, whether physical or emotional. It takes courage not to have an abortion when your spouse is threatening to divorce you unless you do. It takes courage not to cheat in school when someone is offering you the answer. It takes courage not to engage in unethical behavior at work, especially if by doing so you would significantly enhance your chance for a promotion. It takes courage not to smoke or take drugs when most of your friends do and call you chicken for refusing. It takes courage not to use foul language in conversations. It takes courage to refuse to listen to popular music with the wrong message or unacceptable lyrics. It takes courage to accept proper correction when you are wrong. It takes courage to admit you did something wrong. It takes courage not to respond with violence in the face of violence. It takes courage to face the onset of Alzheimer's disease. It takes courage to face the onset of Alzheimer's disease in a spouse. It takes courage to give up something valuable for someone else; sometimes even giving up your life, as did St. Maximillian Kolbe in a German concentration camp during World War II. It takes courage to stand up for the Church and its teachings. It takes courage to face a serious illness with acceptance of the outcome as God's will, even where great pain is involved.

Sometimes it takes courage to face the fears generated by the events of ordinary life. There are many different kinds of fears faced by many people each day, fears which go largely unexpressed. Each day may bring on an uncertainty with respect to competition you face at work, or the fear of not being able to stand up to the continuous pressure for more sales and more profit. You may be an attorney who faces the fear of losing a trial, or perhaps the fear of winning a criminal case and putting the criminal back on the street to terrorize someone else, maybe your neighbor. You never used to consider such things, but now you do. You may be a doctor who fears making an error diagnosing a serious illness in an infant. You may face the fear of having to play a role every day that you know is not really you, at least not the you which you have become. Maybe the flashy, joke cracking, back slapping salesman is someone you used to be, but not who you are now, and you don't know how to let go and be who you are. You may fear you will not live up to the expectations of others; the expectations of a boss, co-workers, spouse, children, even self. Perhaps you dread the look of disappointment on the face of your young child because they believe you lack courage. Each breaking day, each time the alarm clock goes off, you have to draw on an inner reserve of courage to get up and do it one more time, to work through the fear, the uncertainty, and come out on the other side as spiritually unscathed as possible. Perhaps you found you can do this when you began to place yourself, your life and your being in the hands and heart of the God who you learned loves you infinitely.

There are innumerable types of situations that call for courage of all kinds. Politicians spend much of their lives compromising. It is the way things get done. In the process they often turn their backs on their convictions and, more importantly, on truth. Consider how many compromise away their integrity over time without even realizing it. How many Catholic politicians have you heard say something like, "I'm personally opposed to abortion, but I can't let that influence my vote." Do you buy this line of reasoning? You should not. Truth is never subject to compromise. Compromising truth is cowardice, not courage. Many try to rationalize their behavior by saying that all truth is relative. That is also cowardice. God's truth is absolute. Compromising truth is compromising Christ (Jn 14:6). John Paul II said you cannot claim to be Catholic and also support abortion because the two are not compatible. They are as incompatible as sin and God. How many similar examples are there? How often do we see a public official take an unpopular stand on an issue that is very emotional, and support their position with truth?

Courage is rare and should be highly valued. One can be courageous in many ways and even the smallest or the physically weakest among us can be courageous. Courage comes from the heart, not from the muscle. Walk through the children's ward at Mayo Clinic or some other top hospital some time and speak to the patients. You will encounter some remarkable examples of genuine courage. And it is not based on ignorance. These children know what is happening and they ask their doctors some very penetrating questions.

I live in Fauquier County, Virginia, which is adjacent to Spotsylvania County. A few years ago our whole area was shocked when two young girls, sisters, were abducted from their front yard. A few days later their bodies were found. Around that same time, another young girl was abducted from her front yard, and her body was also found a few days later. I marvel at the courage the families of these young girls have to enable them to face each day without their daughters. I marvel at the courage and determination of the FBI and other law enforcement officials who continued to pursue this serial killer and refused to give up even though the trail got colder with each passing month, until he was eventually found. In the meantime, every other family in the area had to have courage just to let their young children on the school bus, knowing the serial killer was unidentified and still at large.

Being cowardly is very easy. We see this in the whole system of suicide mentality surrounding the so-called "death with dignity" movement. We are told that if someone is facing anything uncomfortable or painful, they should commit suicide to avoid the pain. That is cowardice, not courage. Eleanor Roosevelt is reported to have said that we gain in strength and courage from every experience in which we have to look fear in the face. By doing so, we can train ourselves to be courageous. We never know when we will have to call upon this reserve of courage.

In 1989, Israel awarded a man named John Damski the Righteous Among Nations Award for Gentile heroes of the Holocaust. He received this award because he, a Polish Catholic, was in a German prison camp during World War II. He escaped, but instead of leaving for safety he risked his own life many times helping the Resistance rescue Jews who were escaping Nazism. During this time, he was arrested three more times and escaped each time to continue his rescue work. He was living what Jesus told us, "Love others as I have loved you." It took enormous courage for Mr. Damski to do this.

If you were married and had children, what would you do if you suddenly found out you had a degenerative terminal illness? Would you have what it takes to leave your children a legacy of courage, encouraging them to ask questions and talk about how they feel about what is happening? Sometimes this is how God asks us to teach courage to our children, and to ourselves. This situation is faced by families every day.

Sometimes we are called to have courage of another kind, such as when an illiterate adult decides to do whatever it takes to learn how to read. Someone who does this has to have the humility and courage to ask for help and the courage to stick to the task until it is done. Courage is not a lack of fear. It is not recklessness. It is a resolve to face fear, to act on truth in a considered and prudent way, always asking for God's help. Prudent does not just mean safe. It means acting in accord with your informed conscience and convictions when you know there is no acceptable alternative. Prudence does not mean staying alive. It may mean saving your soul, even if that means losing your physical life. The three young men who faced the fiery furnace rather than break the command of God (Daniel 3) acted prudently with regard to their eternal salvation.

It takes courage to forgive. It also takes the companion virtue of love. Holding a grudge is easy. Forgiving, especially forgiving unconditionally, is hard. Forgiving someone who hurt you, including those who hurt you emotionally, is very hard. It is usually not possible without God's help. When you fight back, and do not forgive, the evil is perpetuated, regardless of the emotion or reason behind your response. Evil feeds on itself. So does hatred. It is what keeps feuds going. Both are self-consuming. It is the principle way of existence for Satan, for it is all he has to motive him. We cannot call it his life principle, for he has no meaningful life. He is spiritually dead. The way evil grows is to feed off of the hatred it finds in others. It is almost impossible to keep hating someone who always loves you. You have to either remove them from your life or succumb to their love by loving in return. Love is generated from within and self-perpetuating. It comes from God who dwells deep within your soul, and goes out to others without discrimination. When others hate, but find only love in you, their hatred either eventually dissipates or they have to find someone else with whom they can exercise mutual hatred. If love is genuine, that genuineness, that truth, is sensed, and must be responded to. Satan will try to beat it back, beat it down, but it will always prevail because its power comes from within and the source is infinite. Love will always outlast hate. If we respond to hatred with hatred, we help perpetuate it. If we respond to hatred with love, the hatred eventually dies of starvation. Jesus taught us this on the cross.

It also takes courage to respond to the fears that can steal our faith. We are all called by God to believe in things we cannot prove, things we cannot see. The singer Crystal Lewis has a song called Only Fools in which she proclaims that only fools believe in only what they see. How true it is. Courage and faith are both virtues, and it sometimes takes courage to let faith surface. In the materialistic world in which we live, the constant cry is, "Prove it." We are told if we can not prove it with science, it does not exist. Souls do not exist. God does not exist. Even when we accept the truths of God's reality and our soul's existence, and God's love for us, we face other disbelief.

As Catholics, we face disbelief even from other Christians. For example, real Catholics believe in the Real Presence of Jesus Christ in the Eucharist. We accept this on faith. In addition to what Jesus taught us in John 6 and what we have from the early Christian Fathers in the first and second centuries, there have also been many Eucharistic miracles over the centuries to substantiate our faith in the Real Presence of Christ in Eucharist. In Lanciano, Italy, around the year 700, a Host, immediately after being consecrated, became a piece of real human flesh. This flesh is still there today and can be seen by visitors. It was examined a few years ago by a group of doctors and was identified as a slice of human heart. It was as fresh as if it had just been taken from a living heart, even though it is not kept in any kind of refrigeration and is about 1300 years old. This miracle of the Eucharist confirmed that not only is the Eucharist the Real Presence, but it is the Real Presence of the living God, the real, true Bread of Life. This is hard for non-Catholics to believe, for, besides a general ignorance of thing like the Eucharistic miracles, they lack the historical base found in the Catholic Church. But the evidence, even the physical evidence, is there for all to see.

There have been other Eucharistic miracles through the years, some taking place in our own time. In Betania, Venezuela, a consecrated Host bled. It bled from the top of the Host. It was not blood pooling at the bottom of a corpse, but blood being pumped to the top by the heart of the living Christ. In Ogden, Utah, at Holy Family Church, the priest's chalice began to bleed after the consecration. This continued for a few years. It was something witnessed by my wife and me, and our two boys. The blood ran down the outside of the chalice and also got on the corporal. We took pictures, with the permission of the celebrant and pastor, Fr. Sweeney, and put them on our own parish web site. Jesus knows the trials to our faith and so has provided us with everything we need to believe in Him and in His Real Presence in the Eucharist. It is up to us to have sufficient faith and courage to accept the gifts He has given us. These things support our courage. Other people, who call themselves Catholic but who in reality are not, reject the doctrine of the Real Presence either out of ignorance for which they have no excuse, or rebellion against what they cannot prove in a laboratory. Usually, the real reason is more deep seated and self-serving, for it boils down to an excuse not to devote time and attention to God. After all, they reason, if the Eucharist is not real, can't we keep holy the Lord's day at home just as easily as at a church building? For how long will they actually keep this day holy, whatever that means?

Patience:

Consider the virtue of patience. Read a newspaper thoroughly for about one week. Note how often you see stories about babies being shaken to death because they cried, often shaken by the live-in partners of their unmarried mother. Note how often you read about what has been given the name "road rage". A man in our area got into a traffic altercation with another, the cars collided, and the man's young daughter sitting beside him was permanently disabled. Now, every time he looks at her he remembers why she is hurt. Every time she looks at him, she also remembers. Another man was having a similar altercation. He leaned out his window to shake his fist and shout obscenities at the other driver. When he did, he lost control, crashed and was killed. He left behind a wife and two children.

The number of stories about people losing patience to such an extent they become a news item seems to grow with each passing season. What about the instances of lost patience we do not hear about? In your own life, how many times a day do you experience a loss of patience? Perhaps you lose patience with a child or pet, perhaps with a spouse, perhaps with clerk in a store, or on the phone with a telemarketer or your HMO. If you find this happens frequently, and you recognize it for what it is, a lack of virtue, do you use the sacrament of Confession as a source of strength to deal with your struggle? How else do you deal with a loss of patience? Do you even try?

When I began to commute on I-95 in Northern Virginia, an experience, we are told, second to none but Los Angeles freeways, I found myself losing patience frequently. Our pastor calls I-95 Purgatory Alley. I tried listening to the radio, but that did not help much. The fifty six mile trip is a seventy-five minute drive on a good day. My worst morning so far has been a three hour drive. The one bright spot that record setting day was the opportunity to roll down the window and meet the equally encumbered people in the adjacent car. Lucky for me, they did not think I was some sort of nut case because I engaged them in conversation. After all, how often do you get the chance to do this while driving on an interstate highway?

After a few months of frustration and frazzled nerves, dealing with maniac drivers weaving in and out of lanes and driving as fast as they can for whatever distance they can, even in very short bursts, resulting in my letting loose a few choice words of my own on more than one occasion, and finding myself arriving at work tired, up tight, and not mentally ready for the start of a new day in the office, I changed my approach. I decided to pray.

I turned off the radio and began to pray the rosary or the Divine Mercy Chaplet, or both, as I drove to work and again as I drove home. It had a dramatic effect on my own responses and on my mental state when I arrived, regardless of the length of the commute. I no longer lose my patience, or temper, and I am relaxed when I arrive. Nothing on the radio had really helped. Even the traffic reports didn't do much except give me an idea of how long the commute would be, which I could not do anything about. Alternate routes are usually not available, and, if any are, when an incident occurs the traffic on those routes gets so bad so quickly that it does not help to use them. So, now I pray the whole trip. If the commute takes longer, it just means a few extra decades.

Sometimes we need a different kind of patience. My sister, Louise, lives near New Orleans and is a nurse at the hospital where she and I were born. My brother-in-law, Tom, is an anesthetist at the same hospital. My mother lived with my sister's family for the last several years of her life. During the last few years my mother suffered from Alzheimer's. At first it bothered her when she realized she was suffering memory losses. It embarrassed her to some degree, so she would avoid social situations. Later, she became largely unaware, often not recognizing me and other family members, although she remained physically quite capable and could go for long walks. She would ask the same questions repeatedly, so patience was always necessary when responding. Answering repeated questions was fairly easy since the patience needed came from love and understanding. Louise and Tom had to deal with the situation on a daily basis, for I lived too far away to be of much physical help. It took enormous patience to deal with this overall situation, and when you face dealing with this kind of condition there are few, if any, emotional outlets. Dealing with all the little daily frustrations and situations has to be done with great love and patience and with little relief. I often think Louise and Tom won their sainthood caring for Mom. It is very difficult to anticipate everything, every potential safety hazzard, as anyone who has dealt with a very physically able and ambulatory Alzheimer's patient can testify. And when it is over, new and unexpected emotions take over. It takes quite a while to adjust to the conflicting emotions of loss of a loved one and freedom from worry for that person. It takes great patience with self as well as others. Often, it is something that can only be dealt with between you and God.

Truth:

The virtue of truth is an interesting one, for it involves so many aspects. It is like the hub of a wheel having many spokes all reaching out to the same outer circumference. We are all offered the opportunity each day to tell the truth. We also have opportunities each day to live truth. Jesus did not only tell the truth, He is Truth. The themes of love, truth and life run through gospel of John continuously. Jesus identified the Holy Spirit as the Spirit of Truth. When we choose not to tell the truth, we often try to give ourselves the excuse that we are living virtuously because it is somehow necessary to lie to save face, or to avoid offending another, or for some other justified reason. But are these excuses valid? Can we ever do something that is the opposite of virtue and call it virtue? Can opposites be the same thing? When we turn from truth, we turn from Jesus who is truth. If we turn from Jesus, we necessarily turn from virtue.

In John 18:37-38, Pilate asks the question which has echoed through the centuries. "Pilate said to him, "So you are a king?" Jesus answered, "You say that I am a king. For this I was born, and for this I have come into the world, to bear witness to the truth. Every one who is of the truth hears my voice." Pilate said to him, "What is truth?""

Jesus doesn't answer the question because He had already given the answer. He said, "I have come into the world to bear witness to the truth." He had previously taught us (Jn 14:6), "I am the way, and the truth, and the life; no one comes to the Father, but by me." One has to wonder what the pagan Pilate understood to be truth. Did he know Jesus had said, "I am truth"? Could Pilate bring himself to even consider truth as being embodied in a person, as Jesus claimed? Given the multiplicity of gods worshiped by the Romans, and the politics of Rome, it must have been hard for Pilate to determine truth, if he even still tried very hard. One can almost hear this politician asking himself repeatedly, "What truth? Whose truth?" But it does seem the question had a certain attraction for him, something he had considered before and perhaps abandoned after years of failure at finding an acceptable answer, at finding real truth. It is as if Pilate was a real life early version of the character in the novel Dr. Zhivago. As the empire came tumbling down after the Russian Revolution and Zhivago found his whole social order turned topsy-turvey, he seemed to be wandering aimlessly. But it was not aimless. An acquaintance of his says of him that when his social world collapsed, Zhivago spent his time searching for absolutes such as love and truth, so that no matter what ever happened, they could be a constant anchor in his life. Zhivago looked in many places and people, but not for God. Too bad, for in God he would have found everything he sought. Pilate seems to have had a similar desire, at least at some time. This desire awakened again as Pilate spoke with Jesus.

One wonders if the desire for truth is something fundamental to the human soul. It would seem so. God, who created man in His own image and likeness, would surely create in the soul a natural inclination toward Himself, and thus a natural desire for Truth. When one seeks and lives genuine truth, one therefore lives seeking union with God.

The word of God, the word spoken and taught by Jesus, is truth. We must teach our children this truth. One Sunday at Mass, just before the distribution of Communion to the faithful, we said, "Lord, I am not worthy to receive You. Say but the word and my soul will be healed." Our son Daniel, then five years old, leaned over to my wife and said, "Mom, quick, what's the word?"

In many ways adults are less caring than this five year old who had not yet made his first Communion. How many do we see not really paying any attention to these special times during Mass? How often do we see adults and teens engaged in joking and casual conversation during the Mass, even during these precious moments during and after the consecration? What does that say about their faith? What does that say about the courage they would have to stand up for what they claim is their faith? Would they have the faith of that five year old, even as immature as it was? Would they have his interest in Jesus coming to dwell within and heal his soul?

Jesus gave the Church the command to go forth and teach all that He taught us. He promised to leave us a Church which He commanded to teach truth. He did not promise to leave us a book. He did not command His apostles to write. He commanded them to preach His word, His truth, to the whole world, making disciples of all nations (Mk 16:15-18; Mt 28:18-20). The fullness of truth is found in the Church He founded. Her teachings on faith and morals are based on tradition and scripture. They are also kept from error by a promise of Jesus Himself. She is our source of the truth of Jesus, the Mystical Body of Christ. In her teachings she is guided by the Holy Spirit, as promised by Jesus (Jn 14:25-26).

Teaching the truth of Jesus sometimes means teaching the mysteries of God. We are convinced of the truth of the mysteries of God for Jesus has told us they are true, even if we cannot always fully understand them. When we believe only what we can understand, we place ourselves as the judge, or the standard, against which all possible truth of God is tested. It is an attitude of pride, not virtue. As happens so often, we see virtues and vices operating in pairs. Pride, greed or fear is usually the source of lies. Truth is founded in humility and trust. Jesus is the source of all truth, for He is truth and can never deceive us. He is also the epitome of humility.

When we live truth we are guided by our informed conscience. Therefore, to live truth means we must inform our conscience, and that means we do so under the guidance and tutelage of the Church. We seek truth, we do not wait for it to find us. We embrace truth, we do not hold it at a safe distance to examine without commitment. Our objective is to live moral truth, to seek moral truth in all we do. It is not a game of legalistic boundaries, trying to thread a line between what is allowed or not allowed. What is sought is that which is morally right, living moral truth. We live truth because that is the only correct thing we can do, not because it is the law. There are no legal boundaries one can skirt; no legal loopholes or hidden moral tax credits. There is only moral truth or something else. Choosing anything other than moral truth is living someplace other than in the heart of Jesus. If we live outside His heart, we live where there is no life.

We use all sorts of excuses to avoid moral truth. One way we can help ourselves is to avoid making choices based on emotion. This evil generation tells us that if it feels good, do it. That is a sure path to hell. Feeling good has nothing to do with moral truth. Elizabeth of the Trinity tells us, "A soul that debates with its self, that is taken up with its feelings, and pursues useless thoughts and desires, scatters its forces, for it is not wholly directed toward God. Its lyre does not vibrate in unison and when the Master plays it, He cannot draw from it divine harmonies, for it is still too human and discordant."[66]

Our choices should follow a period of reflection. Our decisions should be based on what we know to be moral truth, not based on what would satisfy our personal desires, on what we wish were moral truth. We should reflect sufficiently before choosing a course of action. Elizabeth of the Trinity has also taught us, "It is the same for the soul that has entered into the fortress of holy recollection; the eye of the soul, opened in the light of faith, discovers its God

---

[66]Elizabeth of the Trinity, *The Complete Works, Volume One*, ICS Publications, Washington DC, 1984, pg 142.

present, living within it; in turn it remains so present to Him, in beautiful simplicity, that He guards it with a jealous care."[67]

Sometimes we reflect, but not enough. A woman may reflect on whether to go someplace with a group, or a person, but not reflect on what the group or person may want to do when their destination is reached. A teenager may reflect on whether or not to go to someone's house after school, but may not reflect sufficiently on what that person is likely to want to do once they are inside, or on how successfully they can respond to temptations that may arise.

Conversely, when we deliberately seek moral truth as the basis for all of our actions, we are training our mind and our conscience to live in accord with this truth. The more we seek truth the more sensitive we become to truth, and the more it serves to guide us. If we develop a habit of asking, "What is right, what is truth?" before we take action, our conscience is tuned to respond to Jesus first, above all else.

Often, as we seek truth, we encounter situations where the correct decision may not be clear. In these situations, we should seek out holy and experienced persons and ask their advice. These persons may be holy priests or some other person whose guidance you can trust.

In Jn 1:14-17, we read, "And the Word became flesh and dwelt among us, full of grace and truth; we have beheld his glory, glory as of the only Son from the Father. ... And from his fulness have we all received, grace upon grace. For the law was given through Moses; grace and truth came through Jesus Christ." We have law from Moss, but grace and truth from Jesus. We find His truth in His Church, in His teachings handed down through the apostles, and in His sacraments.

---

[67]Ibid, pg 143

Hope:

Chapter 19 of the gospel of Luke opens with the account of the chief tax collector named Zacchaeus.

"He entered Jericho and was passing through. And there was a man named Zacchaeus; he was a chief tax collector, and rich. And he sought to see who Jesus was, but could not, on account of the crowd, because he was small of stature. So he ran on ahead and climbed up into a sycamore tree to see him, for he was to pass that way. And when Jesus came to the place, he looked up and said to him, "Zacchaeus, make haste and come down; for I must stay at your house today." So he made haste and came down, and received him joyfully. And when they saw it they all murmured, "He has gone in to be the guest of a man who is a sinner." And Zacchaeus stood and said to the Lord, "Behold, Lord, the half of my goods I give to the poor; and if I have defrauded any one of anything, I restore it fourfold." And Jesus said to him, "Today salvation has come to this house, since he also is a son of Abraham. For the Son of man came to seek and to save the lost."

As we read this account of the meeting between Jesus and Zacchaeus, it brings to mind the passage in John (Jn 8:31-47):

"Jesus then said to the Jews who had believed in him, "If you continue in my word, you are truly my disciples, and you will know the truth, and the truth will make you free." They answered him, "We are descendants of Abraham, and have never been in bondage to any one. How is it that you say, 'You will be made free'?"

"Jesus answered them, "Truly, truly, I say to you, every one who commits sin is a slave to sin. The slave does not continue in the house for ever; the son continues for ever. So if the Son makes you free, you will be free indeed. I know that you are descendants of Abraham; yet you seek to kill me, because my word finds no place in you. I speak of what I have seen with my Father, and you do what you have heard from your father."

"They answered him, "Abraham is our father." Jesus said to them, "If you were Abraham's children, you would do what Abraham did, but now you seek to kill me, a man who has told you the truth which I heard from God; this is not what Abraham did. You do what your father did." They said to him, "We were not born of fornication; we have one Father, even God." Jesus said to them, "If God were your Father, you would love me, for I proceeded and came forth from God; I came not of my own accord, but he sent me. Why do you not understand what I say? It is because you cannot bear to hear my word. You are of your father the devil, and your will is to do your father's desires. He was a murderer from the beginning, and has nothing to do with the truth, because there is no truth in him. When he lies, he speaks according to his own nature, for he is a liar and the father of lies. But, because I tell the truth, you do not believe me. Which of you convicts me of sin? If I tell the truth, why do you not believe me? He who is of God hears the words of God; the reason why you do not hear them is that you are not of God."

Having previously told the Pharisees that they are not Abraham's children, nor God's, but are the children of the father of lies, the devil, Jesus has now told them that this little man whom they despise, the chief tax collector, is a son of Abraham and that salvation has come to his house. We can only imagine how this must have grated on the nerves of the Pharisees. Their pride must have been sending them into an internal frenzy, and yet they had to hold their tongue in front of the people.

This encounter is also a beautiful example of hope. Zacchaeus reminds me of the woman who was a sinner, the one who washed the feet of Jesus with her tears at the house of Simon the Pharisee. She was looked down upon by the people, just as was Zacchaeus. She had hope that Jesus would accept her and heal her. Zacchaeus also looked for acceptance. He just wanted a glimpse of Jesus; to reach out and touch Him even if only with his eyes; to be a part in some way of what Jesus was about.

Zacchaeus knew how the people felt about him, so he knew they would never let him move to the front of the crowd even though he was too short to see over their heads. So, he ran ahead and climbed a tree. He had hope that from his elevated vantage point he would see Jesus. We can only imagine how his heart must have raced when Jesus stopped by the tree and then looked up at him. And when Jesus invited him down, he must have been so overjoyed. Of all the people in the crowd, Jesus chose the house of Zacchaeus to enter. He knew Zacchaeus would not refuse. The streams of grace flowing from Jesus to Zacchaeus are so evident they are almost visible.

It was also an interesting social exchange. In those times, one never invited oneself into the home of another for a meal. One had to be invited. Only close acquaintances were invited into the recesses of a man's home for a meal. Yet Jesus, who had never met Zacchaeus, invited himself into his home for a meal. He knew the heart of Zacchaeus and how much Zacchaeus wanted to have Jesus near him. Jesus also needed to use Zacchaeus as His instrument to make a point regarding the Pharisees for the people. Jesus had great compassion for the people because they were like sheep without a shepherd (Mt 9:36; Mk 6:34), and Jesus was there to be their good Shepherd (Jn 10:11-16).

The crowd, the predicable crowd, always agitated by the self-loving Pharisees, was envious and complained. This man was a tax collector, which in their minds was equal to sinner. In truth, this was not generally an inaccurate description, but there are always exceptions and we are judged by God individually, not as a group or class. Zacchaeus, wishing to justify himself to Jesus, tells Jesus how he tries to be honest, and Jesus rewards him, just as he had rewarded the woman at Simon's house. He tells him, and the crowd, that today salvation has come to this man's house. Zacchaeus' hope is fulfilled in Jesus. We don't hear any more about Zacchaeus, but Jesus never does anything ineffective.

Jesus is teaching us that those who hope in Him, those who genuinely seek Him with their heart, are never disappointed. He will not let one who truly seeks Him be lost. His love for us could not let that happen. He tells us, too, that He wishes to come into our house, our soul. We must ask how well we have prepared our house for this special guest. Where could He rest that He will not be soiled? Have we had enough hope in His coming within us to make frequent use of the sacraments? Have we tried to keep our house in order? Is our hope strong enough to believe He will one day ask us, too, if He can stay in our house? Is it bolstered by sufficient faith to believe it will happen, that He will enter, if we but live in expectation of His arrival? Has He perhaps already entered?

Our responsibility is to make sure that when we seek Him we are seeking Him for His own sake, seeking His will in our lives, and not just seeking Him to do our own will, to answer our own worldly dreams. I often wonder how many people pray to win the lottery, but never pray to be freed of their sin.

A Passion For Truth

Let us reflect for a time on the Passion of Christ from a perspective different from a focus on His physical suffering. There were several levels of spirituality all happening at the same time during the Passion of Christ.

Consider Mk 14:53-72. This is Mark's account of the capture and trial of Jesus. It begins "They led Jesus away to the high priest." Remember John's account of this incident wherein he shows us that Jesus was not led away except by His own permission. All He did was speak His identity, I AM, and His alleged captors fell to the ground (Jn 18:6). His power was made clear to them, as was their own lack of real power over Him. After having had this experience of having no power whatsoever, after having been knocked to the ground by the mention of His name, His identity, alone, one can only imagine what went through the minds of the minions who reached out first to take Him. Did they hesitate? Were they afraid to touch Him? When "they led Jesus away," did they really believe they were leading Him? Were they, perhaps, just glad He was not of a mind to do more than knock them down? Or were they so blind that the significance of the event had no effect on them? Were they knocked to the ground because they encountered infinite love for the first time in their lives, an experience so different from that which they had as an unwitting disciple of Satan?

"They led Jesus away to the high priest." The shepherd is being led by those who should be the sheep. The blind sheep led the shepherd who could see all and who knew all; He who could see to the very core of their individual souls. Jesus' strength was in truth. Theirs was in numbers. Jesus spoke His truth in the light, in the temple. These men were executing their deed in the night, hidden from truth, hidden from those crowds who loved Jesus; those whom Jesus had cured, fed, raised from the dead, and whose sins He had forgiven.

It was Jesus' time for glory. In the midst of all He suffered, His truth would shine forth. His truth would confound His accusers. He would suffer His passion to bring truth to the world, or, as He will put it, to testify to the truth. It is important for us to understand the premium Jesus puts on truth, and how truth weaves such an integral thread through the whole experience of His passion.

Mark continues, "The chief priests and the entire Sanhedrin kept trying to obtain testimony against Jesus in order to put Him to death, but they found none."(Mk 14:55) Truth can never testify against Truth. The truth of God is absolute, not relative. These evil men could try as hard as they might, but there was no way for them to obtain truthful testimony against Jesus which would condemn Him before the Jewish law. He was the author of the law.

These men sought His death. He knew they would be successful, but He would not allow them to be successful on the basis of truth. He was going to die for you and me, and He would do so willingly for our salvation and redemption. There was no possibility of Jesus allowing His sacrifice, His condemnation, to be effected because of truth, for He was being condemned as an enemy of God and therefore an enemy of Truth. His condemnation was going to come only because of lies. A lie never stands against truth. His truth will prevail for all time.

Thus we see, "Many gave false witness against Him, but their testimony did not agree." (Mk 14:56) How reminiscent of the account in Chapter 13 of the Book of Daniel where the young Susanna was condemned by false testimony and Daniel saved her with truth, by exposing the lies of her accusers.

People lie to obtain or keep an advantage, and it often backfires. We see it so often, and it always causes hurt. Every relationship worth having is injured when a lie enters between the parties. Spouses lie to each other and the marriage suffers. Children lie to parents and the trust previously placed in them disappears. Lawyers lie in court and if caught they end up disbarred. Employees lie and are fired.

In this case, there was no truth which could condemn Jesus, but likewise there was no lie which could stand against Him and prevail. He would not be condemned by truth, and He would not allow a lie to prevail over truth with regard to Himself. If He was going to be condemned, it would have to be because of the evil in the hearts of His accusers, or their weakness, or both.

His offering of Himself for you and me had to be so pure, so above crass evil, that history would always see it for what it was. There could be no doubt left for those of His time, nor for us, as to why He died. It was important to Him, for our sake, that His sacrifice of love for us is seen for what it is; a sacrifice of pure love, founded in truth, a testament to truth, and offered willingly by the only one who could make the sacrifice. The only words He spoke, the only defense He offered at any point in His trial, was a challenge of truth to those who spoke lies.

Lies often result in frustration. The liar tries to convince, and the more the lie is resisted the more frustrated the liar grows and the greater the lie becomes. The frustration of the accusers is evident. "The high priest rose before the assembly and questioned Jesus, saying, "Have you no answer? What are these men testifying against you?" But He was silent and answered nothing." (Mk 14:60)

Truth is truth. It does not have to justify itself in defense against a lie. It was evident the testimony against

Him was false because the testimonies did not agree. These men were also very familiar with the story of how the young Daniel saved Susannah from condemnation by showing the inconsistencies in the testimonies of the accusers, and the sentence of death given against those accusers for their lies (Dan 13). Would they face a similar fate? They had to push forward and prevail, somehow, for truth was against them. If they continued to lie and bring false witnesses, and it was discovered by the people, they would be digging their own graves. They challenge Jesus to refute the testimony, but He remains silent, allowing truth to shine forth. They did all these things under the cover of night, not publicly before the people (Jn 3:19-20).

John, who may have been the one who went in with Peter, also tells us that when questioned during the encounter with Annas, "Jesus answered him, 'I have spoken publicly to the world. I have always taught in a synagogue or in the temple area where all the Jews gather, and in secret I have said nothing. Why ask Me? Ask those who heard Me what I said to them. They know what I said.'" Then one of the guards struck Him and Jesus replied, "If I have spoken wrongly, testify to the wrong; but if I have spoken rightly, why do you strike Me?" Then Annas sent Him bound to the high priest." (Jn 18:20-24) Jesus continually challenges them with truth, and they have no way to respond in truth. Their only response is frustration.

Jesus finally seals His own fate with truth. "Again the high priest asked Him, and said to Him, "Are you the Messiah, the Son of the Blessed One?" Then Jesus answered, "I Am"." Truth affirming Truth. Jesus continued, "...and you will see the Son of Man seated at the right hand of the power and coming with the clouds of heaven." (Jn 18:15-16) Jesus was also teaching His disciples, at least those two close enough to hear. He was reminding them of what He had recently taught "...and you will see the Son of Man seated at the right hand of the power and coming with the clouds of heaven." (Mk 13:26). One can only wonder if the Book of Psalms came to the mind of His accusers, "Sit at my right hand till I make your enemies your footstool." (Ps 110:1) It was getting dangerous and the chief priest had to move quickly. Were they destined to be Jesus' footstools? What would the Jewish people do if they knew the truth?

They were past the time where testimony could do any good. They had to get past this hearing and have the people believe Jesus had been condemned by truth before the Sanhedrin. That would give these evil men credibility in the minds of the citizens. So, the chief priest took the only action he could. "At that the chief priest tore his garments and said, "What need have we of witnesses? You have heard the blasphemy. What do you think?" (Mk 14:63) They all condemned Him as deserving to die. He would die for telling the truth.

The evil deep in the hearts of Jesus' accusers now takes over. They begin to treat Jesus like a criminal, as if He had already been condemned to die. In their minds, He was as good as dead. They just had to convince the Romans, and time was running out. The Passover was approaching. Time would be on Jesus' side if they did not have Him executed before the Passover feast. The people would have too much time to learn the truth of the conspiracy conducted before the Sanhedrin, too much time to ask questions. Mark continues, "Some began to spit on Him. They blindfolded Him and struck Him and said to Him, 'Prophesy!'. And the guards greeted Him with blows." (Mk 14:65)

These evil men taunted Him to tell them which of them had hit Him. If He had spoken, He would not have bothered to answer their question. What purpose would it serve, for all were guilty. Those who struck Jesus, those who approved, those who taunted, those who stood by in silent acquiescence, all were guilty. So, why did Christ not speak? Could it be that if He had spoken He would not have told them who hit Him, but rather would have told them the conditions of their souls, in detail they could not deny? What would have been their reaction? Would they have been unable to continue with the execution, and thus prevent the sacrificial act known by God to be necessary from the beginning?

Is it not ironic that the one thing Satan might have been able to do to prevent the culminating act of salvation history was to encourage the conversion of these men? Instead, Satan spurred them on toward Calvary, probably hoping they would kill Jesus before He could be crucified so that prophesy would not be fulfilled. But Love prevailed over evil at all levels. The salvation of mankind would be accomplished. The act of supreme Divine love would not be denied.

But the soldiers did not ask Him to tell them the condition of their souls. They were not after truth and virtue, nor were they seeking purity of soul. They were left with the opportunity to convert after the divine sacrifice on Calvary, beginning with the centurion who would confirm Jesus' Divinity at the foot of the cross (Mt 27:54). Many of them did eventually convert, including the soldier, Longinus, who thrust his spear into the side of Jesus. Longinus eventually become a martyr for Christ, playing a major role in salvation history.

The underlying part truth played throughout the Passion of Christ continued, not being confined to the lies of His accusers and torturers. Jesus had already predicted the part truth would play in the actions of Peter, but Peter could not believe what he had heard. Now, Peter must learn that truth will prevail (Mk 14:66-72).

As Jesus' position before the tribunal was solidified and His fate became more evident, fear crept into the heart of Peter. He who would have given His life in the garden of

Gethsemane for love of Jesus was now experiencing fear. He who drew his sword, cut off the ear of the servant (Mk 14:47; Jn 18:10-11), and would have fought to the death for Jesus was now desperately alone. Peter's convictions are threatened, his confidence shaken, and a new kind of fear wormed its way into his heart.

As Peter sat before the fire on this chilly night, surrounded by the enemies of Jesus, he is accused by a woman of being a disciple of Jesus and he denies it. He denies it repeatedly, until finally the cock crowed the requisite number of times. The truth of what Jesus had said, and the truth he had to face about himself, all came down on him at the same time. Mark tells us, "He broke down and wept." (Mk 14:72) In Luke, we get a little better picture of what Peter was dealing with in himself, a better picture of his stark confrontation with truth. Luke tells us, "Just as he was saying this, the cock crowed, and the Lord turned and looked at Peter; and Peter remembered the word of the Lord, how He had said to him, 'Before the cock crows today, you will deny Me three times.' He went out and began to weep bitterly." (Lk 22:60-62)

Luke teaches us a very important lesson. No matter what we do or have done, when we face the truth we can be cleansed, provided we do it in union with Jesus. He is truth, and we cannot properly deal with truth unless we do so with Him. Jesus was there for Peter. Their eyes met. No words were necessary. Love and Truth led Peter to a deeper interior conversion. Peter could no longer sit there silent. He had to leave. He had to let happen the rest of what Jesus had predicted about His own passion, which I am sure was swimming through Peter's head without ceasing. Peter had to be mindful of the rebuke he had recently received from Jesus when he suggested that Jesus should not suffer and die at the hands of the chief priests and scribes (Mk 8:32-33). Peter may not have understood why all this had to happen, at least not fully, but he knew it had to happen and that it was the will of God. So he went out and let it happen, filled with sorrow, knowing it was happening for him as well as for you and me.

The role of truth continued. When Jesus was on trial before Pilate, Pilate was trying to figure out what was going on and who this Jesus was. He did not understand why He was being condemned by His own people. None of the testimony or evidence was supportive of the verdict being sought by them.

Pilate interrogated Jesus privately, trying to get to the bottom of all this. "So Pilate said to Him, 'Then you are a king?' Jesus answered, 'You say I am a king. For this I was born and for this I came into the world, to testify to the truth. Everyone who belongs to the truth listens to My voice.' Pilate said to Him, 'What is truth?'" (Jn 18:37-38)

What a profound dialogue. Jesus will testify to only one thing: truth. Jesus came into the world for only one thing; to testify to the truth. "And the Word became flesh and made his dwelling among us, and we saw his glory, the glory as of the Father's only Son, full of grace and truth." (Jn 1:14) His truth sets man free from the clutches of sin. Truth is the source of our salvation, for Jesus is truth. His truth gives us a deeper knowledge of the Father. His truth shows us the mercy of God as well as the justice of God. His truth shows us the love of God for man. His truth will open the gates of heaven and set us free (Jn :32). His truth will open the way to receive God's forgiveness for our sin. His truth will allow us to become children of God. His truth will allow us to be one with Him, and His truth will provide us the opportunity to participate in the life of God through the indwelling Trinity. Everything He does, and all of His truth, is founded in love. Yet, standing before truth Itself, Pilate can only recognize his own confusion, and asks the question which has echoed through the ages, "What is truth?" He wonders if there is a real truth. "Whose truth?", he wonders.

Is all truth relative? Nothing is making sense. What will he say in his regular governor's report to Caesar? How will he explain this? Can he tell Caesar he condemned an innocent man to death? Is that Roman justice? If he does not do as the crowd asks, will these already angry people revolt? Could he quell a revolt? What should he do? How can he make all this just go away?

Then Pilate, taking Jesus aside, trying to convince Jesus to testify on His own behalf, asks Jesus if He realizes the power he, Pilate, holds over Him; the power of life and death. Jesus calmly responds, "'You would have no power over Me if it had not been given to you from above. For this reason the one who handed Me over to you has the greater sin.' Consequently, Pilate tried to release Him; but the Jews cried out, 'If you release Him, you are no friend of Caesar. Everyone who makes himself a king opposes Caesar.'"(Jn 19:11)

Once again Jesus seals His own fate. He leaves Pilate no choice. If word gets to Caesar, and it would, that the people revolted because Pilate was no friend of Caesar, he would have no way to recover. Lacking the courage of his own convictions, Pilate cannot see any way out other than to do as the mock jury, the mob, has demanded. Jesus is handed over for execution. He is condemned for testifying to the truth. It is why He came among us.

One cannot help wonder whether Pilate subsequently converted. We can only hope every one who heard of Jesus, and every one who saw or touched Jesus during His passion, converted as a result of this encounter.

Jesus was crucified on that cold Spring day after He was scourged, crowned with thorns and had to carry His own cross to His execution. Already weak from loss of blood, He was crucified and raised up at the top of the hill of Calvary, the same hills where Melchizedek encountered Abraham

281

(Gen 14:18), and where Abraham brought Isaac to be sacrificed (Gen 22). Pious tradition says this is the place where Adam was buried. It is called Golgotha, which means skull place (Mt 27:33). The cold wind, not buffered by any shelter, must have been brutal against His naked and torn flesh. His executioners were performing a duty they had probably performed many times before. As they waited for Jesus to die, they cast lots for His clothes. The crowd taunted Him, challenged Him to come down from the cross, and gave Him gall to drink.

Through it all, He forgave the good thief, gave us Mary as our mother, gave us to her as her children, and prayed to His Father. Finally, after three hours of darkness during the middle of the day, accompanied by an earthquake and the tearing of the curtain in the temple, He surrendered His spirit into the hands of His Father.

Something happened during His last moments, something about which we do not have the details. Mark recorded, "When the centurion who stood facing Him saw how He breathed His last he said, 'Truly this man was the Son of God.'" (Mk 15:39) In the midst of all the torn flesh, the blood, the pain and tears and agony which were an essential part of the execution process, this soldier, who had seen and participated in these executions many times before, saw something that changed his life. Mark says that when the centurion "saw how he breathed His last he said, 'Truly this man was the Son of God.'" Jesus was dead, but this centurion was undergoing a major conversion. Truth sprang from Jesus even in death. This centurion, a battle hardened commander of one hundred soldiers, who had seen many men die and who had probably killed many, came face to face with the man he now knew was the Son of God. Mark does not say it was because of what Jesus said, but rather it was because of "how" Jesus breathed His last. We do not know precisely how Jesus died other than the obvious death from crucifixion. That was evidently not what Mark is referring to for that was too commonplace for this centurion. He saw something else. He somehow saw truth in an encounter with God as He looked upon Jesus, and his life was never the same. Given his position, we can only wonder how many others he influenced. Did he come to know the apostles? Did he become one of their disciples? Did he even, perhaps, become a priest? We do not know. What we do know is that truth poured into his heart from the cross during the final moments of Jesus' life, and it was recorded in this gospel to be recounted through the ages. This man, during the last moments as Jesus died, found that he belonged to truth, he belonged to Jesus. He, like Jesus, testified to the truth. Jesus' passion throughout His life among us had been for love and truth. Love and truth can never be separated.

Love's Reward: The Kingdom of Heaven
The Spirituality of Love in Matthew

The Kingdom of Heaven is like...

The gospel of Matthew is filled with Jesus' descriptions of what the kingdom of heaven is like. It is our reward for loving God by doing the will of the Father. Jesus had to tell us, for no man had yet been to heaven. So Jesus opens door after door throughout this gospel to give us an insight into heaven, the joy awaiting us, and what we must do to get there. It is rather intriguing that no one asks Jesus how He knows these things.

Let us look first at how Jesus uses parables to teach us about heaven. He is describing a spiritual world, an eternal kingdom of love, to simple people scratching out a living in a very physically demanding world, people who up to this time only knew they were God's chosen people and had to follow the law. In spite of God's revelations up to that time, many did not know much about the kingdom of God and the place He is preparing there for us. Indeed, one group of Jewish leaders, the Sadducees, did not believe in a resurrection. The common people were like sheep without a shepherd (Mt 9:36; Num 27:17; 2 Chron 16; 1 Kg 22:17).

"Seeing the crowds, he went up on the mountain, and when he sat down his disciples came to him. And he opened his mouth and taught them, saying: "Blessed are the poor in spirit, for theirs is the kingdom of heaven. "Blessed are those who mourn, for they shall be comforted. "Blessed are the meek, for they shall inherit the earth. "Blessed are those who hunger and thirst for righteousness, for they shall be satisfied. "Blessed are the merciful, for they shall obtain mercy. "Blessed are the pure in heart, for they shall see God. "Blessed are the peacemakers, for they shall be called sons of God. "Blessed are those who are persecuted for righteousness' sake, for theirs is the kingdom of heaven". (Mt 5: 1-10)

When Jesus taught these beatitudes, He specifically used different verb tenses for the first and last from that tense used for the others. The first and last use the present tense, and the others use the future tense. In each of the middle beatitudes Jesus says they "shall." In the first two He says, "for theirs is the kingdom of heaven." Those who are poor in spirit, and those who are persecuted for the sake of righteousness, seek and possess the kingdom of heaven now. It is not an issue of being poor in terms of material goods. A rich person can be poor in spirit if he is not focused on his wealth but is focused on God, and his wealth is incidental to his life. Those who are persecuted for the sake of righteousness are following Christ, living in intimate union with Christ, and to follow Christ this way is to live in the kingdom. You may not sense you are walking in the kingdom while you live on earth, so Jesus is telling you that this is what you are doing. It is a way He encourages us to live the life of the kingdom here on earth. It is a call to sanctity, a reward of love.

"Think not that I have come to abolish the law and the prophets; I have come not to abolish them but to fulfill them. For truly, I say to you, till heaven and earth pass away, not an iota, not a dot, will pass from the law until heaven and earth pass away. Whoever then relaxes one of the least of these commandments and teaches men so, shall be called least in the kingdom of heaven; but he who does them and teaches them shall be called great in the kingdom of heaven. For I tell you, unless your righteousness exceeds that of the scribes and Pharisees, you will never enter the kingdom of heaven." (Mt 5:17-20)

The law and the prophets; these are what give life to the Jewish people. Not the Pharisees and Sadducees and scribes. The law was given by God to Moses. The prophets were God's spokesmen. It is just like the Catholic church today, which bases its doctrine and teachings on scripture and tradition. Scripture is equivalent to the law and tradition is equivalent to the prophets. Every dot and iota is important.

Obedience is a great virtue in the eyes of God. He speaks of it often. Here, again, He tells us to obey His law and to teach His law. He also teaches us not to be cafeteria Catholics, but to obey every iota He teaches through His Church. When heaven and earth are recreated, as Jesus tells us in Revelation, then the law shall pass away, for it shall be written on our hearts. Whoever relaxes His commandments and teaches others to do so shall be called the least in the kingdom of heaven. They shall be least in terms of intimacy with God. But those who follow the commandments and teach others to do so shall be called great in the kingdom of heaven. This is a sobering thought for all bishops and priests.

In Mt 13:10, we will see that Jesus explains to the disciples how He is gathering in the little ones, the humble and the poor to give them the secrets of the kingdom, and why others who are proud and lord it over these little ones remain in the dark. A preview of this is seen in the Magnificat prayer (Lk 1:46-55) said by Mary in Luke's account of the visitation. "He has shown might in His arm: He has scattered the proud in the conceit of their heart. He has put down the mighty from their seat, and has exalted the humble. He has filled the hungry with good things, and the rich He has sent away empty."

"Judge not, that you be not judged. For with the judgment you pronounce you will be judged, and the measure you give will be the measure you get. Why do you see the speck that is in your brother's eye, but do not notice the log that is in your own eye? Or how can you say to your brother, 'Let me take the speck out of your eye,' when there is the log in your own eye? You hypocrite, first take the log out of your own eye, and then you will see clearly to take the speck out of your brother's eye. Do not give dogs what is holy; and do not throw your pearls before swine, lest they trample them under foot and turn to attack you." (Mt 7:1-6)

In the early part of the gospel of Matthew, Jesus has a whole series of teachings on a variety of topics. In this particular passage, Jesus is teaching us how to live in the kingdom by living a proper relationship with each other. We cannot expect to live a proper relationship with God if we cannot live a proper relationship with each other. Jesus tells us not to judge others, for if we do we will be judged by God according to our own standard. We have to adopt God's standard of love and forgiveness if we expect to be judged by that divine standard.

Jesus uses the pearl as an analogy of something of great value which must not be denigrated. Swine are forbidden to the Jews and are considered unclean. Jesus tells us to treasure and respect that which has great value; sanctity and virtue. We must work on our own sanctity and not waste time judging the sanctity of others. That is for God, not man.

"Not every one who says to me, 'Lord, Lord,' shall enter the kingdom of heaven, but he who does the will of my Father who is in heaven. On that day many will say to me, 'Lord, Lord, did we not prophesy in your name, and cast out demons in your name, and do many mighty works in your name?' And then will I declare to them, 'I never knew you; depart from me, you evildoers.'" (Mt 7:21-23)

What constitutes a meaningful relationship with God? This is an essential question which derives from the above passage. The people have said "Lord, Lord", they have prophesied in the name of God, they have even cast out demons in the name of God. They have done other mighty deeds in the name of God. What does Jesus call them? He calls them evildoers. However, the most frightening thing

Jesus says is, "I never knew you." How chilling it would be to hear this on judgment day. Doing the will of God is the essential basis for our relationship with God. Without that, nothing else has merit. The only way we can do the will of God is to love. Without love it is impossible.

Jesus is saying He does not recognize anything of God in the soul of this person. It is not what they do, but the motive with which they do it, that is important. If they are not forgiving and motivated by love, nothing they do will have merit. It is not following the letter of the law that is important but living the commandments of God in the depths of their soul, and Jesus will tell us that all of the law and all of the commandments are founded on His two commandments of love. It is love which gives value to what we do. It is love which turns rocks to pearls, water to wine, what was evil into what is good. It was love which knocked Paul down on the road to Damascus and turned him from a persecutor of Christians into a great saint. Paul did not become a great saint because of the law but because of love. It is God's love which gives each person dignity as a human being. It is God's love which has given us the great saints of the church. Love demands change and growth. We should each ask, "How have I changed and grown because of love? How much more does God possess me, and how much more do I possess Him, than was true a year ago?"

"Then the disciples came and said to him, "Why do you speak to them in parables?" And he answered them, "To you it has been given to know the secrets of the kingdom of heaven, but to them it has not been given. For to him who has will more be given, and he will have abundance; but from him who has not, even what he has will be taken away. This is why I speak to them in parables, because seeing they do not see, and hearing they do not hear, nor do they understand. With them indeed is fulfilled the prophecy of Isaiah which says: 'You shall indeed hear but never understand, and you shall indeed see but never perceive. For this people's heart has grown dull, and their ears are heavy of hearing, and their eyes they have closed, lest they should perceive with their eyes, and hear with their ears, and understand with their heart, and turn for me to heal them.' But blessed are your eyes, for they see, and your ears, for they hear. Truly, I say to you, many prophets and righteous men longed to see what you see, and did not see it, and to hear what you hear, and did not hear it." (Mt 13:10-15)

These people are those the Father has sent to Jesus, who come to Him with an open heart. They look for a leader who will help them, not one who just demands their servitude. They seek a savior, not just a king. Jesus is exactly what they seek. He will exalt these humble ones and inflame their hearts with the fire of His love. He is giving them what all the prophets through the ages longed for. Recall old Simeon (Lk 2:29-31) who said, "Now, Lord, you may dismiss your servant in peace, according to your word, for my eyes have seen your salvation which you prepared in sight of all the peoples, a light for revelation to the Gentiles, and glory for your people Israel."

These simple people now know that revelation of the kingdom is a secret shared only with those whom Jesus chooses to share it. The kingdom He is revealing to them is what He wants them to work for. It is hard to convince the rich and famous to put aside what they have and work for something unseen, something they can only have through love.

Jesus uses many similes to explain the kingdom. No living man has seen the kingdom, and none has lived in a spiritual world, so He has to bring knowledge of the kingdom to them in terms with which they can relate. The people of His time were an agrarian society, so they understood farming and they understood dependence on God and weather.

"Hear then the parable of the sower. When any one hears the word of the kingdom and does not understand it, the evil one comes and snatches away what is sown in his heart; this is what was sown along the path. As for what was sown on rocky ground, this is he who hears the word and immediately receives it with joy; yet he has no root in himself, but endures for a while, and when tribulation or persecution arises on account of the word, immediately he falls away. As for what was sown among thorns, this is he who hears the word, but the cares of the world and the delight in riches choke the word, and it proves unfruitful. As for what was sown on good soil, this is he who hears the word and understands it; he indeed bears fruit, and yields, in one case a hundredfold, in another sixty, and in another thirty." (Mt 13:18-23)

Here Jesus explains the responsibility they owe to themselves and others when they hear His word. He would also tell them (Jn 15:22-24), "If I had not come and spoken to them, they would have no sin; but as it is, they have no excuse for their sin. ... If I had not done works among them that no one else ever did, they would not have sin; but as it is, they have seen and hated both Me and My Father." They have to hear with understanding, hold what they hear in their heart, and share this word with others. They understand what He means by getting choked with thorns or yielding fruit because from one seed you grow a vine, and that one vine produces many grapes. One person who receives the word with understanding will multiply that word in the hearts of many others, and they in turn will do likewise. A mathematician would understand it as the geometric progression of the word of God, but Jesus is the perfect teacher and these people need an example they can, in a sense, hold in their hand as well as their heart.

These people also understood the concept of a rich harvest, and wealth as a function of harvest. Thus, they understood what He was saying when He spoke about yield being thirty, sixty or a hundred fold. The yield is dependent on what they do with His word and how well they sow His word in other rich soil. Their spiritual reward in the kingdom is a function of their harvest, just as their reward in life is a function of the bountifulness of the harvest from what they plant.

They understood that the yield of their harvest was a function of the work involved in spreading His word. They could speak at random and hope for the best, or they could plant His word deliberately and yield the maximum harvest. They understood this because in those times, some lazy farmers would tie sacks of grain on a donkey's back, punch a hole in the sacks, and then send the donkey out to wander around, dropping seeds as it did. Other farmers would lay out a field, plan the seeding pattern to get the maximum yield from the land, and then harvest an abundant crop.

We must ask ourselves what we do with His words of love. His word is a treasure and a seed. If we keep it all to ourselves, we do no work for Him. If we spread it in the way we can by using the gifts He has given us, then we are doing His will to increase the harvest of souls.

"Another parable he put before them, saying, "The kingdom of heaven may be compared to a man who sowed good seed in his field; but while men were sleeping, his enemy came and sowed weeds among the wheat, and went away. So when the plants came up and bore grain, then the weeds appeared also. And the servants of the householder came and said to him, 'Sir, did you not sow good seed in your field? How then has it weeds?' He said to them, 'An enemy has done this.' The servants said to him, 'Then do you want us to go and gather them?' But he said, 'No; lest in gathering the weeds you root up the wheat along with them. Let both grow together until the harvest; and at harvest time I will tell the reapers, Gather the weeds first and bind them in bundles to be burned, but gather the wheat into my barn.'" (Mt 13:24-30)

Most of us believe we understand this parable from the New American Bible, but in these modern translations we perhaps miss the full meaning Jesus tried to convey. I imagine nearly everyone who has ever planted a garden of any size at all has had to weed that garden, and sooner or later has uprooted a plant by accident while trying to remove a weed. But what is the real message here, since we can usually tell the difference between a tomato plant and a weed?

In this case Jesus speaks of, we do not just have an act of nature through which weeds might grow. We have an enemy, Satan and his demons, sowing the weeds of confusion, temptation and doubt among the good seed planted in men by God. Sometimes Satan uses people who try to draw us away from the faith into atheism, idolatry, or other faiths having less than the fullness of Truth. Some may be those who denigrate our belief and use every means at their disposal to prevent us from expressing our Faith, even to the extent of making such expression unlawful, as we have seen in India and other places. Others are the heretics who condemn us for believing truth.

So what was Jesus' real point? Why is He speaking specifically about wheat? What has that got to do with weeds? In the earlier translations which are more faithful to the original Greek or Latin, such as the Douay-Reims or The Jerusalem Bible, the weed is specifically named instead of using the generic term weed. The weed is identified as darnel, or tares. Tares are a specific kind of darnel, also called the bearded darnel, only found in the Palestinian area, whose seeds are poison. Tares looks just like wheat when it first begins to grow, so it cannot be distinguished from the real wheat by looking at it. It is only when the wheat begins to bear fruit that the tares can be recognized for the poisonous plants they are. If you pulled one of the plants in this field to early, it might be wheat, not a weed. Therefore, the point Jesus was really making is that there are those in the Mystical Body who, like Judas among the apostles, appear to be good, but are in truth just poisonous elements that try to draw the life from the faithful ones. When their true nature is revealed, these poisonous agents among us will be separated from the true faithful ones and burned. Jesus is speaking of those who outwardly appear to be one of us but who work to destroy our faith and the Church from within, like some insidious professors in so-called Catholic colleges, and the administrators tolerating them, who actually try to poison the minds of the faithful students against the Church and against God. These hidden poisoners are different from those who do not bother to hide and who proclaim their real nature, perhaps by forming or joining groups opposing Church doctrine or the official teaching of the Church, having names like Catholics for Abortion Rights, and so on.

A concern many have, and which every priest should have, arises because many are believers but not apologists. They accept the truth without a desire or apparent need to truly understand or defend the faith. Their ability to spread the faith, to bear more fruit, is thus severely limited. When the "tares" attack their faith, these unprepared ones do not have a sufficient understanding of the underlying basis for the truth, and when they are unable to defend their belief in a systematic manner against attack, it causes them confusion and doubt, and some leave the Church.

Instead of admitting their lack of expertise and referring the challenger to a knowledgeable priest, some of these good people try to defend the faith on their own. Most are not equipped to do so, and should take one of two actions: they should refer the person to a priest, or get educated enough to serve in an apologists role.

We have the promise of Christ that He will be with His Church for all time, and we have the guidance of the Church by the Holy Spirit for 2000 years. All of this is available to us collectively in the deposit of faith communicated by the teaching Magisterium. Jesus' message is simple and straightforward enough so that even the most uneducated person is able to understand what he must to reap the reward of the kingdom. Under no circumstance did Jesus ever suggest that the simple and uneducated will not be able to understand His word and gain the rewards of Heaven; quite the contrary. Jesus seeks the little and the humble. He does not seek out the proud and exalted.

He wants all of us, but requires we exhibit qualities more readily found among the humble. He wants our minds focused on Him and our hearts open to His word. He does not ask us to defend His word, just believe His word, live that belief, and love Him. Our obligation to ourselves is to read scripture each day, listen to and obey the teaching magisterium of the Church, and trust in Jesus' care and love.

"Another parable he put before them, saying, "The kingdom of heaven is like a grain of mustard seed which a man took and sowed in his field; it is the smallest of all seeds, but when it has grown it is the greatest of shrubs and becomes a tree, so that the birds of the air come and make nests in its branches." He told them another parable. "The kingdom of heaven is like leaven which a woman took and hid in three measures of flour, till it was all leavened." (Mt 13:31-33)

These parables are very interesting. What do a mustard seed and yeast have in common? Both are used as a simile for the kingdom of heaven. One begins as a small object and when hidden in the fertile soil grows to something else many times its original size. The seed dies and in doing so sprouts forth the bush, multiplied many times over in size. The seed is transformed and in being transformed becomes something different and majestic in comparison to its former self. The kernel of the seed gives life to its potentiality and it becomes a new being. The seed appeared dead. Its potential had not been obvious. Its life is now evident.

The yeast is hidden in the flour by being mixed in as the loaf is kneaded. It does its work unseen and the potential it has is not evident. But the loaf is transformed from a flat sheet into a beautiful loaf many times its original size. The leaven has worked from within, unseen, but the result is easily discerned by all who examine the transformed loaf.

The kingdom is like this seed and yeast. We die to self, and the word of God which has been planted in us, which is hidden within our heart and soul, begins to work in us and we become transformed in Christ. We decrease and Christ increases in us, as John the Baptist said (Jn 3:30). When He increases, as a seed sprouting, as leaven causing the loaf to rise, the kingdom is increasing within us, for where He is, there is the kingdom. The more the kingdom increases in us, all the more will others encounter the kingdom when they encounter us. They encounter, not us, but Christ who dwells within us. The larger the 'bush', the bigger the 'loaf', the more of Christ they will encounter. We bring the kingdom to others, just as Mary brought the kingdom to Elizabeth, just as Jesus brought the kingdom to those He encountered, just as the apostles brought the kingdom to the Gentiles.

We increase the yield of the harvest for God by cooperating with God and allowing Him to work in and through us. We carry the kingdom within, and we go to the kingdom when we leave this world. This should give us some concept of the extent of the soul. The soul is like the loaf, and Jesus is like the leaven. As He increases in us, our soul's capacity - its growth in grace, to hold Him increases. We must think about the soul without boundaries, without being limited by the space occupied by our physical bodies, and think of the soul as a tabernacle for Christ, which expands to accommodate as much of Christ as He deems shares with us. How much He shares depends on how much we are disposed to receive, and that depends on how much we love and how much sanctifying grace we have received.

"The kingdom of heaven is like treasure hidden in a field, which a man found and covered up; then in his joy he goes and sells all that he has and buys that field. Again, the kingdom of heaven is like a merchant in search of fine pearls, who, on finding one pearl of great value, went and sold all that he had and bought it." (Mt 13:44-46)

This is one of the more intriguing passages of scripture. Jesus continues to describe heaven in terms of the relationship between man and God. He always chooses the perfect words for the lessons He teaches. He never describes heaven as a bounded place, nor does He describe heaven in terms of how it looks. It is always in terms of God's relationship with us. He teaches us that the kingdom of heaven is so valuable that we should sacrifice everything else to achieve it, for when we possess the kingdom within we possess God within. The field is like the Church, which contains the treasures of the deposit of faith and the Holy Eucharist. We buy this field by our fidelity and commitment to Jesus and His word. When we have Him, particularly when we have Him dwelling within, we have the treasure beyond all treasures, a treasure so valuable we cannot describe it, and one which is so wonderful the mind of man has never been able to even imagine it for it is sharing in the life of God. St Paul (1 Cor 2:9), referencing Is 64:3, tells us "What eye has not seen, and ear had not heard, and what has not entered the human heart, what God has prepared for those who love Him."

The reference to the pearl of great value is also interesting. Jesus never refers to any gem in the gospels other than a pearl. It is the only gem made by a living creature. It is also a symbol of the life of our soul. When we begin our life sheltered in the state of grace, it is like a small foreign object sheltered in the oyster of Baptism. The more sheltered we stay through participation in the sacraments, the more grace will grow in our soul, just as the pearl continues to grow, layer upon layer, while it is in the oyster. But if we remove the pearl from the oyster, it ceases to grow. If we place it in vinegar, it begins to dissolve. So it is with the soul when we remove ourselves from the shelter of grace by exposing ourselves to temptation and sin and focusing our life on things of the world. When we sin, it is like vinegar on the pearl, for we lose more and more grace the more we sin. If we sin seriously, we can lose all of our grace. But when we go to confession, it is like putting the pearl back into the oyster. The oyster begins once again to add layer upon layer and the pearl will grow larger and larger and more valuable. The balance is restored. As we grow in grace we grow in perfection and are pleasing in the eyes of God. We are also cooperating with God when we do this because without Him we can do nothing. We grow in grace by letting Him work in us to produce a soul of great spiritual value. It is so amazing that God willingly died to save this soul united to Him. We become a soul clothed in the garments of divine love.

"Again, the kingdom of heaven is like a net which was thrown into the sea and gathered fish of every kind; when it was full, men drew it ashore and sat down and sorted the good into vessels but threw away the bad. So it will be at the close of the age. The angels will come out and separate the evil from the righteous, and throw them into the furnace of fire; there men will weep and gnash their teeth. "Have you understood all this?" They said to him, "Yes." And he said to them, "Therefore every scribe who has been trained for the kingdom of heaven is like a householder who brings out of his treasure what is new and what is old." (Mt 13:47-52)

The kingdom of God is characterized once again by the relationship between man and God. God sends His Word among men to tell us the kingdom of God is at hand. He casts out His word to capture the hearts of men. Some respond and some do not. At the end, just as the weeds were separated from the wheat, the good fish are separated from everything else which comes up in the net. Everyone who has fished understands this, for we have all caught our share of old shoes, shirts, tin cans, sticks, water plants, and other things, including fish which are not good to eat. Just as we must separate the good from the bad from our harvest, whether from land or sea, so God will separate the worthless from the valuable. The sadness is that some of the junk we harvest from the sea has no intrinsic value, but perhaps at one time had value to someone. So, too, the souls who have become junk and are lost did have value at one time because they were loved by God and God died for them. But they have, by their own volition, become a spiritual junk heap sorted by the angels and cast into hell. They do it to themselves.

When asked by Jesus if they understand what He is saying, they answer in the affirmative. Then Jesus says something intriguing. The new scribes who will respond to the word of God bring forth a new treasure from what is old and from what is new. These new scribes, these evangelists, will bring forth and meld into one history and doctrine the Hebrew Testament and the new gospel, one foretelling and one fulfilling. They lay before man, inspired by God, the fullness of revelation from God. With this fullness comes not only joy but also responsibility. We now have a pearl of enormous value and must care for and protect it. We have what all the prophets of old longed for, even Moses. It is critical that we recognize and treasure this gift.

"At that time the disciples came to Jesus, saying, "Who is the greatest in the kingdom of heaven?" And calling to him a child, he put him in the midst of them, and said, "Truly, I say to you, unless you turn and become like children, you will never enter the kingdom of heaven.

Whoever humbles himself like this child, he is the greatest in the kingdom of heaven." (Mt 18:1-4)

The people of Jesus' time were so conscious of a hierarchy of power, so conscious of the rights and power of royalty, so conscious of their status as a conquered people, that they naturally assumed the kingdom of God would have a hierarchy of power and wondered where they might fit in the kingdom of God. Would they be at the bottom of the heap again? Would the Pharisees and Sadducees be the power mongers in the kingdom as they are among God's chosen people on earth? Would there be conquerors there as well? How does one become the greatest in the kingdom of God? How does one get on top of the heap?

Jesus answers their question by showing them a child. How utterly profound! No one among the crowd suspected this would be His answer. Children had no role in decision making, no power and no authority. They were still learning the basics of life. But they are also trusting, and humbly submit to the authority of their parents. They also rely on their parents to provide for their needs.

In the kingdom of God, when we stand before God Himself, when we recognize our position in relation to God, the only way we can approach God is in humility. Pride, to any degree, cannot stand before God. Pride has no place in the kingdom of God. The only thing which can stand before God, the only thing we can give God that is of worth to us and to Him, is love offered with humility. Humbly offered love is not groveling, is not self-denigrating, and is not false. It is always founded in truth, and the truth is that in the kingdom of God we will have been chosen by God to be His child. We have dignity solely because He loves us. He has prepared a place for us, individually, from all eternity, and awaited our coming with great anticipation. He will welcome us into the Kingdom if we have kept His word - if we are humble.

As we have seen, St. Teresa of Avila, in her book Interior Castle, tell us that the two things we must do continuously throughout our period of spiritual growth is to grow in self knowledge and humility. We grow in humility by comparing ourselves with God. As we recognize how much farther we still have to go to reach the perfection to which God calls us, we grow in humility. We can do nothing without God and so we cannot grow in grace without Him. We have Jesus' word on that. Thus, we can never take credit ourselves for the good we do, but must give credit God for doing good through us, for using us as His instrument for good.

"If your brother sins against you, go and tell him his fault, between you and him alone. If he listens to you, you have gained your brother. But if he does not listen, take one or two others along with you, that every word may be confirmed by the evidence of two or three witnesses. If he refuses to listen to them, tell it to the church; and if he refuses to listen even to the church, let him be to you as a Gentile and a tax collector. Truly, I say to you, whatever you bind on earth shall be bound in heaven, and whatever you loose on earth shall be loosed in heaven. Again I say to you, if two of you agree on earth about anything they ask, it will be done for them by my Father in heaven. For where two or three are gathered in my name, there am I in the midst of them." (Mt18:15-20)

Here Jesus is establishing an intimate love and trust relationship between heaven and His chosen people on earth. He is linking decisions to bind and loose made on earth, and acceptance of those decisions in Heaven. God in heaven has chosen to be bound by the decisions of men on earth. We have heard this statement about being bound and loosed so often, and it has become so commonplace, we seldom think of what it really means. But consider that the infinite and perfect God, Creator of the universe, the God who will judge all men, has given imperfect and sinful men the power to bind and lose on earth and God will respect this decision in the kingdom of God. Imagine how intimate the relationship must be that Jesus has created between Himself and His representatives on earth, His priests, who stand in the person of Christ, *in persona Christi*. These acts of men, representing Christ, done in time, have eternal effect from which there is no appeal.

Jesus is also linking our prayer of union with His presence. He is encouraging common prayer, liturgical prayer, prayer groups, praying with the sick, the homeless, and the incarcerated, and other forms of group prayer. In this group prayer He is telling us we should have a common purpose or common petition. When we come together in prayer, we are not to come together to pray as individuals, but as a collective body together with Him, as our head, among us.

This group prayer is different from the kind of prayer in which Jesus tells us to engage at other times, when we are to go to our room and pray in private. Jesus did both. He prayed privately with the Father, and publicly with His people.

The important point in this discourse of Jesus is recognition of the intimacy between what we do and how God responds, even to participating in joint decisions. How much He must love us to desire to do this with us! How awesome, and humbling, it is to even consider God working so intimately with His people to bring about the salvation of as many as possible. He is making us one with Him while we are still here on earth. That He is willing to do this is a true mystery, a mystery of love. He is allowing us to experience Heaven to some degree while we are still here on earth. He is teaching us that Heaven truly is, not so much a place, but man living the life of God, sharing in His divine life.

" Then Peter came up and said to him, "Lord, how often shall my brother sin against me, and I forgive him? As many as seven times?" Jesus said to him, "I do not say to you seven times, but seventy times seven. Therefore the kingdom of heaven may be compared to a king who wished to settle accounts with his servants. When he began the reckoning, one was brought to him who owed him ten thousand talents; and as he could not pay, his lord ordered him to be sold, with his wife and children and all that he had, and payment to be made. So the servant fell on his knees, imploring him, 'Lord, have patience with me, and I will pay you everything.' And out of pity for him the lord of that servant released him and forgave him the debt. But that same servant, as he went out, came upon one of his fellow servants who owed him a hundred denarii; and seizing him by the throat he said, 'Pay what you owe.' So his fellow servant fell down and besought him, 'Have patience with me, and I will pay you.' He refused and went and put him in prison till he should pay the debt. When his fellow servants saw what had taken place, they were greatly distressed, and they went and reported to their lord all that had taken place. Then his lord summoned him and said to him, 'You wicked servant! I forgave you all that debt because you besought me; and should not you have had mercy on your fellow servant, as I had mercy on you?' And in anger his lord delivered him to the jailers, till he should pay all his debt. So also my heavenly Father will do to every one of you, if you do not forgive your brother from your heart." (Mt 18:21-35)

Again we see Jesus equating the kingdom of God with the action of God and our relationship with God. He is showing us how life is lived in the kingdom of God, not describing how it looks or telling us where it is. If He tried to describe its appearance the explanation would probably not have any meaning to us who live in a physical world.

Jesus is calling us to live the life of the kingdom of God now, by asking us to accept the decision criteria of God as our own criteria. God has unlimited love and patience, and is willing to forgive us as long as we ask with the correct spirit of contrition and love. He asks that we approach Him is this spirit of humility.

He also imposes on us a responsibility to treat others as we pray He will treat us. Jesus tells us that we will be judged individually according to our own standard. There is no collective judgment imposed on several; only individual judgment. What an awesome thing to consider. God, being infinite, is aware of how each of us individually responds to others in every instance throughout our life on earth. He is aware of how easily we forgive and how often we forgive; and how we have refused to forgive.

How many times have you heard someone say, "I will never forgive him for what he did.", or read in the paper, "He killed my child, and I want to watch him die." Often we say these things without understanding the consequences. We expect God to forgive us no matter what we have done, and yet are unwilling to forgive others. We hear, "I am saved because I have chosen Jesus as my Lord and Savior.", and often this person speaking refuses to forgive others for what they did to him or her. They fight, sue, and take other antagonistic action, and the net effect is often that their lawyer gets rich and they remain bitter.

We seal our own fate by acting this way. If we want to live in the kingdom of God we must begin to live the life of the kingdom of God now. We must begin to think and act like a child of the kingdom to legitimately say, "The kingdom dwells here within me." Thinking and acting like a child of God does not begin as we walk across the threshold of Heaven. We must act with love always, and we cannot act with love if we are unwilling to forgive.

"The young man said to him, "All these I have observed; what do I still lack?" Jesus said to him, "If you would be perfect, go, sell what you possess and give to the poor, and you will have treasure in heaven; and come, follow me." When the young man heard this he went away sorrowful; for he had great possessions." (Mt 19: 20-22)

In this well known account of the rich young man, Jesus emphasizes once again the relationship between heaven and earth. When we live our life on earth focused on God and His kingdom, we do not allow material riches to take priority in our life. This young man was a good man who tried to live a good life. After the man had confirmed to Jesus that He was doing what is necessary to be saved, Jesus urges him to take the final steps toward perfection. The young man could not take this final step for he had too strong an attachment to his worldly possessions.

The lesson Jesus teaches is a confirmation of His commandment to "love others as yourself." We gain treasures in Heaven by serving others, not by serving self. This is so very important, and we see it in the lives of the saints and people like Mother Teresa of Calcutta. We have many of these other-focused 'angels' all around us, working in homeless shelters, soup kitchens, AIDS clinics, the St. Vincent DePaul stores in parishes, bring the Eucharist to the infirm and elderly, and performing other such services. As Jesus said, we will always have the poor with us. They are our opportunity for sainthood. They are the source of our treasures.

"And Jesus said to his disciples, "Truly, I say to you, it will be hard for a rich man to enter the kingdom of heaven. Again I tell you, it is easier for a camel to go through the eye of a needle than for a rich man to enter the kingdom of God." When the disciples heard this they were greatly astonished, saying, "Who then can be saved?" But Jesus looked at them and said to them, "With men this is impossible, but with God all things are possible." (Mt 19:23-26)

Jesus continues unfolding His revelation that the kingdom of God is the relationship between men and God. Jesus is continuing the lesson given to the rich young man. Men with many possessions and who allow those possessions to gain a strong hold on their life are depriving themselves of participation in the kingdom. But we are all physical beings and depend on a certain level of material possession if we are to fulfill our vocations as, for example, parents and spouses. I cannot properly care for my wife and children if I keep giving away all that I have to the poor. How can I do as Jesus told the rich young man to do and still fulfill my responsibilities?

The implication in the account of the rich young man is that he was single and had no responsibilities except those to himself. He could therefore leave everything and follow Jesus. He was called to a consecrated life of service to Christ, and could not bring himself to answer the call. Jesus also calls us to live our vocations as spouses and parents, and the obligations we thereby incur take priority after our duty to God.

So, the disciples ask how any person can do the things Jesus asks, and He says we cannot do it on our own. We can only do so when we are living the life of the kingdom of God, when we are living in a relationship with God. Jesus says that on our own we cannot do what He asks, but with Him we can do everything. He does not just say that with Him we can learn how not to let material possession govern us. He says that with God all things are possible; all things. Jesus is opening up the boundaries of possibility within the relationship between man and God, and in fact is removing the boundaries. The more intimately we live in God, and the more intimately we participate in the life of God, the farther out the boundaries go which limit what can be done by God through us and by God working in us.

So, do we go to heaven? No, we are brought to heaven by God, brought into union with God to the extent we have prepared our souls through love and forgiveness. All is possible only with God, and this includes our entry into complete union with God.

"Then Peter said in reply, "Lo, we have left everything and followed you. What then shall we have?" Jesus said to them, "Truly, I say to you, in the new world, when the Son of man shall sit on his glorious throne, you who have followed me will also sit on twelve thrones, judging the twelve tribes of Israel. And every one who has left houses or brothers or sisters or father or mother or children or lands, for my name's sake, will receive a hundredfold, and inherit eternal life. But many that are first will be last, and the last first." (Mt 19:27-30)

Peter is being so very human here. Everyone wants something in return for what he or she gives. If we have something of value, and we make an offer, we always expect something in return. So Peter, being very normal, and again speaking on behalf of all the apostles, turns to Jesus and asks what the disciples will be given in return for what they have given up for Jesus. Jesus gives Peter an answer which was totally unexpected. Jesus does not give Peter something of like value. What Jesus offers to Peter and the disciples is better, a throne in heaven, a throne from which Peter and the others would judge the tribes of Israel. On what will Peter and the others judge the tribes of Israel? On their acceptance of Jesus as the Messiah. The tribes of Israel will be judged on what they have given up for Jesus, just as all of us will be so judged. When we do place Jesus first, ahead of both things and people, He promises us eternal life. An overlay of humility covers the relationship.

"As they went away, Jesus began to speak to the crowds concerning John: "What did you go out into the wilderness to behold? A reed shaken by the wind? Why then did you go out? To see a man clothed in soft raiment? Behold, those who wear soft raiment are in kings' houses. Why then did you go out? To see a prophet? Yes, I tell you, and more than a prophet. This is he of whom it is written, 'Behold, I send my messenger before thy face, who shall prepare thy way before thee.' Truly, I say to you, among those born of women there has risen no one greater than John the Baptist; yet he who is least in the kingdom of heaven is greater than he. From the days of John the Baptist until now the kingdom of heaven has suffered violence, and men of violence take it by force. For all the prophets and the law prophesied until John; and if you are willing to accept it, he is Elijah who is to come. He who has ears to hear, let him hear." (Mt 11:7-15)

Now Jesus is teaching the people, not where the kingdom of God is, but what it is like to live in the kingdom. The greatest of all the men born of woman who ever lived, every king or prophet, is not equal to the very least in the kingdom of God. This had to make them perk up. Jesus first tells them that no man born of woman is greater than John, not even Moses or Abraham. Many were wondering, no doubt, how a desert hermit who spent his days living off the land, proclaiming the coming of the kingdom and baptizing with water could be on a par with Moses or Abraham or David. But as great as these men are, the least in the kingdom of God is greater than any of them. Jesus tells them that when we live the life of God, we receive the gift of participation in His divine life that is unlike anything we could possibly imagine.

But what is the violence the kingdom of heaven has suffered? How could the kingdom of heaven suffer violence? Isn't God immune to violence? What Jesus teaches here is the same thing John was preaching. The kingdom of God is at hand, and is now here, brought among men by and with Christ. John announced that Christ had come and he was telling his disciples, "Behold the lamb of God (Jn 1:36)."

307

This was the call to war, the response Christ brought to His followers to answer the violence unleashed by Satan and his demons against the kingdom of God. They could not harm Christ, but they could harm His followers. Jesus later prayed to the Father, "I do not ask that you take them out of the world, but that you keep them from the evil one....Consecrate them in truth. Your word is truth." (Jn 17:15-17)

Satan cannot do violence against Christ, but he can try to do violence against the Church Christ founded and against the followers of Christ. Thus, Christ promised us that hell would not prevail against His Church. We need that assurance to persevere.

"When the disciples reached the other side, they had forgotten to bring any bread. Jesus said to them, "Take heed and beware of the leaven of the Pharisees and Sadducees." And they discussed it among themselves, saying, "We brought no bread." But Jesus, aware of this, said, "O men of little faith, why do you discuss among yourselves the fact that you have no bread? Do you not yet perceive? Do you not remember the five loaves of the five thousand, and how many baskets you gathered? Or the seven loaves of the four thousand, and how many baskets you gathered? How is it that you fail to perceive that I did not speak about bread? Beware of the leaven of the Pharisees and Sadducees." Then they understood that he did not tell them to beware of the leaven of bread, but of the teaching of the Pharisees and Sadducees.

"Now when Jesus came into the district of Caesarea Philippi, he asked his disciples, "Who do men say that the Son of man is?" And they said, "Some say John the Baptist, others say Elijah, and others Jeremiah or one of the prophets." He said to them, "But who do you say that I am?" Simon Peter replied, "You are the Christ, the Son of the living God." And Jesus answered him, "Blessed are you, Simon Bar-Jona! For flesh and blood has not revealed this to you, but my Father who is in heaven. And I tell you, you are Peter, and on this rock I will build my church, and the powers of death shall not prevail against it. I will give you the keys of the kingdom of heaven, and whatever you bind on earth shall be bound in heaven, and whatever you loose on earth shall be loosed in heaven." Then he strictly charged the disciples to tell no one that he was the Christ." (Mt 16: 5-20)

Jesus once again emphasizes the relationship between God and men, this time reminding them of the care God has for them and how He has on at least two other occasions taken care of their bodily needs as He fed them spiritually. He had already taught them that the kingdom of God was like the leaven in a loaf of bread. Now, drawing on that same image, He tells them to beware of the contaminated leaven of the Pharisees and Sadducees. The evil one, in his attempts to contaminate the hearts of men, will try to use the same tactics God uses to purify the hearts of men. Can man do this, can he avoid this contamination? With God all things are possible. The relationship with God is necessary to live the kingdom of God and avoid evil. You do it together with Him, not alone.

Jesus then takes the apostles aside and states He is founding His Church on Peter, is giving Peter the keys to the kingdom of God, and is giving him and the apostles the power to forgive sin, to bind and lose on earth. In doing so Jesus acknowledges the relationship God has already established with Peter because Peter was given the insight to answer as he did when acknowledging the divinity of Christ. Because of this relationship which exists between God and the apostles, not only will Jesus found His church on Peter, but He declares that the power of death will never prevail against it. He is telling them three things here. One is that Satan and the demons will attack His church. Another is that Satan and the demons will not be victorious. There will be attacks and battles, but His Church will survive. The third is that it is His Church, not just some church He is starting. It belongs to Him, now and forever. It is His Mystical Body. How privileged are we who live the life of His church!

"From that time Jesus began to show his disciples that he must go to Jerusalem and suffer many things from the elders and chief priests and scribes, and be killed, and on the third day be raised. And Peter took him and began to rebuke him, saying, "God forbid, Lord! This shall never happen to you." But he turned and said to Peter, "Get behind me, Satan! You are a hindrance to me; for you are not on the side of God, but of men.

"Then Jesus told his disciples, "If any man would come after me, let him deny himself and take up his cross and follow me. For whoever would save his life will lose it, and whoever loses his life for my sake will find it. For what will it profit a man, if he gains the whole world and forfeits his life? Or what shall a man give in return for his life? For the Son of man is to come with his angels in the glory of his Father, and then he will repay every man for what he has done. Truly, I say to you, there are some standing here who will not taste death before they see the Son of man coming in his kingdom." (Mt 16:21-28)

Jesus teaches us how subtle are the attacks of Satan, and how desperately Satan tries to keep us from living in the kingdom of God. He does this by urging us to what is an apparent good. Peter loves Jesus. So Satan urges Peter to defend Jesus and try to dissuade Jesus from what He has predicted about Himself. Jesus sees right through and, knowing what He must do for the salvation of mankind, and knowing how much Peter needs to understand this, He rebukes Peter in front of the other apostles. It is a humbling experience, but a necessary one. He does not take away Peter's position as leader, and does not retract what He had previously told Peter about the relationship Peter enjoys with the Father, but Jesus does give Peter a stern lesson on how easily Satan can influence man, even one so very close to Jesus. Each of the apostles learned from Peter's experience.

Jesus then returns to a previous lesson on the kingdom of God. It is not the life we have on earth that must be preserved, but that in the kingdom of God. We can lose this life in the kingdom by what we do, and it is on the basis of what we do that Jesus will come in glory to repay us, and each case is dealt with individually. Forgiveness for forgiving, love for loving, condemnation for hate and lack of forgiveness. When we love and forgive and keep the word of Jesus, we are already living the kingdom of God.

"For the kingdom of heaven is like a householder who went out early in the morning to hire laborers for his vineyard. After agreeing with the laborers for a denarius a day, he sent them into his vineyard. And going out about the third hour he saw others standing idle in the market place; and to them he said, 'You go into the vineyard too, and whatever is right I will give you.' So they went. Going out again about the sixth hour and the ninth hour, he did the same. And about the eleventh hour he went out and found others standing; and he said to them, 'Why do you stand here idle all day?' They said to him, 'Because no one has hired us.' He said to them, 'You go into the vineyard too.' And when evening came, the owner of the vineyard said to his steward, 'Call the laborers and pay them their wages, beginning with the last, up to the first.' And when those hired about the eleventh hour came, each of them received a denarius. Now when the first came, they thought they would receive more; but each of them also received a denarius. And on receiving it they grumbled at the householder, saying, 'These last worked only one hour, and you have made them equal to us who have borne the burden of the day and the scorching heat.' But he replied to one of them, 'Friend, I am doing you no wrong; did you not agree with me for a denarius? Take what belongs to you, and go; I choose to give to this last as I give to you. Am I not allowed to do what I choose with what belongs to me? Or do you begrudge my generosity?' So the last will be first, and the first last." (Mt 20:1-16)

Jesus is teaching us in this parable that in the kingdom of God the motivation behind all God does is love, and that God is not bound by time or the values of men. Men put a time-based value on what they do. This is very natural since we live in a time governed world. But God looks to the heart, not the hours, in determining whether we should be rewarded with His life and love. Again, it is the relationship of love between God and man that is important, and if we love God we will do His will. It is not a question of for how long we have done His will, but that we desire to do His will always. If time played a pivotal role, death-bed conversion would be impossible and we know God will give us the opportunity to convert up until the moment of death. It is His gift of grace which He bestows, and it is His right to determine upon whom He bestows it. God is not bound by our concepts of justice but by His own understanding of love.

"And again Jesus spoke to them in parables, saying, "The kingdom of heaven may be compared to a king who gave a marriage feast for his son, and sent his servants to call those who were invited to the marriage feast; but they would not come. Again he sent other servants, saying, 'Tell those who are invited, Behold, I have made ready my dinner, my oxen and my fat calves are killed, and everything is ready; come to the marriage feast.' But they made light of it and went off, one to his farm, another to his business, while the rest seized his servants, treated them shamefully, and killed them. The king was angry, and he sent his troops and destroyed those murderers and burned their city. Then he said to his servants, 'The wedding is ready, but those invited were not worthy. Go therefore to the thoroughfares, and invite to the marriage feast as many as you find.' And those servants went out into the streets and gathered all whom they found, both bad and good; so the wedding hall was filled with guests.

"But when the king came in to look at the guests, he saw there a man who had no wedding garment; and he said to him, 'Friend, how did you get in here without a wedding garment?' And he was speechless. Then the king said to the attendants, 'Bind him hand and foot, and cast him into the outer darkness; there men will weep and gnash their teeth.' For many are called, but few are chosen." (Mt 22: 1-14)

There are many layers of spirituality in this parable. In describing Jesus as the bridegroom of our soul, we are taught that our life in the kingdom of God is a life of love. It is a life of intimacy with God, where we become one with God just as we become one with our spouse in a physical marriage. It is a union of spirit. Jesus also teaches us that this union of love with God is open to everyone, regardless of their station on life. Many are accepted, regardless of their circumstance, provided they approach God in humility and with thanks and with love.

He also teaches us that indifference toward God will not be tolerated. God will invite many, but will not tolerate the lukewarm and indifferent (Rev 3:16). We must place Him first in our life. We cannot place other things and people ahead of God and expect God to be content with us. If we reject Him, He will reject us. His justice demands this.

When we come before God and expect to take our place in His kingdom, we must be properly prepared. Our garments are the garments of grace. If we come before God without being prepared, we cannot remain with Him. He cannot allow those who are not properly sanctified to be in His kingdom. We must be purified before we can enter the kingdom.

"Then the kingdom of heaven shall be compared to ten maidens who took their lamps and went to meet the bridegroom. Five of them were foolish, and five were wise. For when the foolish took their lamps, they took no oil with them; but the wise took flasks of oil with their lamps. As the bridegroom was delayed, they all slumbered and slept. But at midnight there was a cry, 'Behold, the bridegroom! Come out to meet him.' Then all those maidens rose and trimmed their lamps. And the foolish said to the wise, 'Give us some of your oil, for our lamps are going out.' But the wise replied, 'Perhaps there will not be enough for us and for you; go rather to the dealers and buy for yourselves.' And while they went to buy, the bridegroom came, and those who were ready went in with him to the marriage feast; and the door was shut. Afterward the other maidens came also, saying, 'Lord, lord, open to us.' But he replied, 'Truly, I say to you, I do not know you.' Watch therefore, for you know neither the day nor the hour." (Mt 25:1-13)

In this parable, Jesus is teaching again the lessons He has taught in other parables. His emphasis on these lessons shows how important they were in His mind, and therefore how important they should be for us.

We must be always prepared for Heaven, always prepared to encounter Christ as the bridegroom of the soul. We must be vigilant, always prepared for the time when we will be called into the banquet of God. We cannot ever count on having more time to get prepared. Preparedness is a never-ending activity. We each have responsibility for our own preparedness. It is very important that we seek the sacraments regularly so that our soul will always be ready to answer the call.

Nor can we get what we need from others who many have only enough for their own needs. We get the 'lamp oil', the grace, we need through prayer and the sacraments. The more sanctifying grace we have the more prepared we are.

We should take advantage of opportunities for confession frequently. Going to confession regularly, at least once a month, is like taking a shower each day instead of once a year. It makes much more sense to keep the soul clean than to wait until it is substantially encumbered with sin before we seek the grace of confession. After all, you may be called on your way to confession instead of when you are coming from confession.

In this parable Jesus also teaches once again the need to do the will of God and place Him first in our life. Otherwise, we will hear that chilling sentence, "I do not know you." Pray each day that you are not removed from the mind of God.

"For it will be as when a man going on a journey called his servants and entrusted to them his property; to one he gave five talents, to another two, to another one, to each according to his ability. Then he went away. He who had received the five talents went at once and traded with them; and he made five talents more. So also, he who had the two talents made two talents more. But he who had received the one talent went and dug in the ground and hid his master's money. Now after a long time the master of those servants came and settled accounts with them. And he who had received the five talents came forward, bringing five talents more, saying, 'Master, you delivered to me five talents; here I have made five talents more.' His master said to him, 'Well done, good and faithful servant; you have been faithful over a little, I will set you over much; enter into the joy of your master.' And he also who had the two talents came forward, saying, 'Master, you delivered to me two talents; here I have made two talents more.' His master said to him, 'Well done, good and faithful servant; you have been faithful over a little, I will set you over much; enter into the joy of your master.' He also who had received the one talent came forward, saying, 'Master, I knew you to be a hard man, reaping where you did not sow, and gathering where you did not winnow;

so I was afraid, and I went and hid your talent in the ground. Here you have what is yours.' But his master answered him, 'You wicked and slothful servant! You knew that I reap where I have not sowed, and gather where I have not winnowed? Then you ought to have invested my money with the bankers, and at my coming I should have received what was my own with interest. So take the talent from him, and give it to him who has the ten talents. For to every one who has will more be given, and he will have abundance; but from him who has not, even what he has will be taken away. And cast the worthless servant into the outer darkness; there men will weep and gnash their teeth.'" (Mt 25:14-30)

God gives us many graces, and many opportunities for grace, each day. He expects us to invest this treasure by reaching out to others through prayer and action. If we do not invest this grace, and hoard it for our self, we will lose what we do have, for our life in God is always a life of love, and love is never self focused but rather other focused. The kingdom of God, the reward of love, is not gained by our failure to share the grace of God with others. The more of His grace we share the greater our store of grace will be. It is increased by sharing it with others, and lost by not sharing. We give of ourselves and in doing so we give to God and we give God. We share His grace, and thus share Him with others. We give this gift to God because He has told us that what we do for others we do also for Him. In this teaching Jesus is once again emphasizing that the kingdom of God we live now is the relationship we have with God. The more intimate the relationship we have by living the will of God for us, the more we share in His divine life.

"When the Son of man comes in his glory, and all the angels with him, then he will sit on his glorious throne. Before him will be gathered all the nations, and he will separate them one from another as a shepherd separates the sheep from the goats, and he will place the sheep at his right hand, but the goats at the left. Then the King will say to those at his right hand, 'Come, O blessed of my Father, inherit the kingdom prepared for you from the foundation of the world; for I was hungry and you gave me food, I was thirsty and you gave me drink, I was a stranger and you welcomed me, I was naked and you clothed me, I was sick and you visited me, I was in prison and you came to me.' Then the righteous will answer him, 'Lord, when did we see thee hungry and feed thee, or thirsty and give thee drink? And when did we see thee a stranger and welcome thee, or naked and clothe thee? And when did we see thee sick or in prison and visit thee?' And the King will answer them, 'Truly, I say to you, as you did it to one of the least of these my brethren, you did it to me.' Then he will say to those at his left hand, 'Depart from me, you cursed, into the eternal fire prepared for the devil and his angels; for I was hungry and you gave me no food, I was thirsty and you gave me no drink, I was a stranger and you did not welcome me, naked and you did not clothe me, sick and in prison and you did not visit me.' Then they also will answer, 'Lord, when did we see thee hungry or thirsty or a stranger or naked or sick or in prison, and did not minister to thee?' Then he will answer them, 'Truly, I say to you, as you did it not to one of the least of these, you did it not to me.' And they will go away into eternal punishment, but the righteous into eternal life." (Mt 25:31-46)

Jesus could not be more clear in this teaching of the kingdom of God. All of our merit in the sight of God is dependent on love, and that is proved by how we treat others. Every good thing we do for another we do for Him. If we live this way, we will not hear Him say, "I do not know you," but rather, "Come, O blessed of My Father, inherit the kingdom prepared for you from the foundation of the world."

Desired Into Life

As we go about our busy lives, we lose sight of the dynamic of the life we have with God. We lose the sense of His presence with us and within us. There are several things we must consider as we ponder our life with God.

St. Teresa of Avila tells us "...little is explained about what the Lord does in a soul, I mean about the supernatural."[68] How often do we pray and in doing so enter a dialogue with our Lord, or beg His favor, or ask His pardon, but all the while think of our soul as unchanged by the experience, as being the same before and after our prayer? Yet in every prayer we should have an encounter with God, and at every prayer time God has an objective - something He wishes to accomplish in our soul. We should never emerge from prayer unchanged, for if we do we have not truly prayed.

God is always drawing us to Himself, always bringing us closer, if we will but cooperate. Imagine how frustrating it is to Him when we think we come to prayer, and then do not give Him our minds and hearts to work with, but send them elsewhere, focused on things of this world. Imagine the spiritual treasures we lose, the graces we could have received but do not. Prayer is an encounter with God. We approach God, and He approaches us. We work within His heart through prayer, and He works in us, sanctifying us, drawing us closer and closer to Him, into His heart. These prayer times are treasures of grace we may never be able to recapture, for God never does the same thing exactly the same way twice. He does each thing perfectly, and once.

---

[68] St. Teresa of Avila, The Collected Works of Teresa of Avila, Vol 2, Interior Castle, First Dwellings, Chapter 2, ICS Publications, Washington DC, 1980, pg 290.

I wondered at one time, as I considered the activity of God in our souls during prayer, if our soul can grow, so to speak, depending on the degree of grace received. As we explore our soul, does each new grace add a new dimension so that more of God may be reflected throughout the soul and in effect allow Him to increase in us as we decrease, as St. John the Baptist said? Do we use prayer and meditation to both enter and navigate through the soul, and in the process increase in grace with each new discovery?

St. Teresa of Avila tells us that we must consider some unconventional thinking in terms of our soul.[69] We habitually think of ourselves in terms of limits. We say we are so tall, so heavy, so white or brown or black or whatever, so bald or hairy, so young or old, always defining differentiating boundaries by which we can be identified. She teaches us that we need to remove such limitations when thinking of the soul. The identification of the soul is most properly done in terms of grace and the degree to which it has been identified with Christ, the degree to which it has been transformed in Him. She places great emphasis on self knowledge as she tells us to roam through the soul to discover ourselves and Christ. There are two places, or what she calls rooms, of central importance in the soul, the rooms of humility and self-knowledge. The room of self-knowledge is an exception among the rooms, an exception not shared by any other, even the room in which our Lord resides, for we must return there often.

St. Teresa shows us that self-knowledge is very important, and she makes a strong connection between humility and self-knowledge. She also makes the point that in self-knowledge we see how base we are and how we are still associates of the things which separate us from God, and that through this ever-increasing recognition we gain humility, especially as we meditate on God and how base we

---

[69]Ibid, pg 291

are in comparison. We never lose the need to revisit this room where humility is gained and maintained.

She also tells us that "In my opinion we shall never completely know ourselves if we don't strive to know God."[70] The emphasis St. Teresa places on self-knowledge is seen in her assessment of how the devil uses so many tricks to keep us from gaining the advantages of humility and self-knowledge. She speaks of fear, and fear coming from our lack of self-understanding.

It may be difficult to grasp the full meaning of what St. Teresa is getting at in her emphasis on self-knowledge unless one has been through the Spiritual Exercises of St. Ignatius Loyola. In the book of her life, St. Teresa says she was greatly impressed and influenced by the writings of Ignatius, and sought out Jesuits as her confessors. Look for a moment at Ignatius' concept of self-knowledge. Self-knowledge is not our activity of trying to understand ourselves. We cannot trust ourselves enough to do that. The dynamic is, through prayer, letting God reveal us to ourselves. It is gaining an understanding of those attachments we have which interfere with God working in us. Thus, to gain self-knowledge, we must encounter God through prayer. We trust that God is acting in us to bring about this personal relationship. God is inviting us into the relational life of the Trinity, not in some kind of sporadic or episodic way, but continually, at every moment of our life. He reveals Himself to us, and reveals us to ourselves through His eyes. Thus, the link between self-knowledge and humility. They are inseparable. God calls us to recognize the religious dimension of all of our earthly experiences, to feel His touch in our lives. In our quest for self-knowledge, we do not need to know everything. We need to know what God wants us to know, so He has to lead us there.

---

[70] Ibid, pg 292

A pivotal point made by Ignatius, in what he calls the principle and foundation, is that since we are made to praise, reverence and serve God, and thus save our soul, all of our experience has this as an objective. We eventually find within us the experience and certitude of knowing we have been desired into existence by God, and because God loves what He desires, we are desirable, not only to other persons, but to God. This is a continuous condition and underlies our entire relationship with God. We live our lives desired by God, desired into earthly life, desired for eternal life, at all times and in all circumstances. It is how we are able to experience the presence of God. In gaining self-knowledge, we work to discard our fears and attachments so that the absolute deepest desire of our being, of our heart, is God Himself, so that in satisfying His desire for us we satisfy our desire for Him. We desire to possess this absolute Mystery who is God, and everything else is approached relative to this desire. Since we do not yet know God well, since He is still the great Mystery, our desire is for "I know not what," a recurrent theme found in the writing of St. John of the Cross.[71]

---

[71]St. John of the Cross Digital Library, Version 1.0, Spiritual Canticle, Stanza 7, ICS Publications, Washington DC.

Responding to the Good Shepherd

God is always serving us as the Good Shepherd. He is always seeking out those of us who are lost or drifting, and is always trying to place us on His broad shoulders to bring us back. Some of us fought hard for a long time, then found that being carried on God's shoulders is so much easier when we cooperate. He finds us when we open our hearts to His love, when we respond to His call. We have learned to recognize His voice (Jn 10:4). He carries us back to safety, to a state of grace, through the sacraments, purifying us with His Blood. In doing so, God shows His confidence in our response to Him as we begin to understand St. Therese's concept of confident love for God.[72]

Who does Christ call? You. He calls us all, especially when we stray (Mt 18:10-14; Lk 15). He showed us this in so many ways. Even at the foot of the cross, who was there? Mary Magdalene, the repentant sinner; St. John, the pure teenager; and Mary, His mother. To whom did He appear first after the resurrection? Mary Magdalene[73]. He shows us through this that we should never let past forgiven sins haunt us and serve as an obstacle between us and Him. Once forgiven, they are no longer a blot on our soul. We have been made righteous (Rom 5:19). It is not Christ, but rather Satan, who tries to put your past forgiven sins between you and Christ. Jesus puts no limits on His mercy and love for us, no limit on what He is willing to forgive, so we must put no limits on our love for Him. We should not be tentative in our love.

---

[72]St. Therese of Lisieux, Story Of A Soul, ICS Publications, 2nd ed, Washington DC, 1976, pg 72

[73]John 20:11-17

We should likewise never fear approaching the good shepherd in confidence, for to say you are afraid to approach Jesus after everything He did for you must be another wound for Him. He willingly died for you. Why would He not want to embrace you? Why would He not rejoice at your return to His fold? Do not the angels rejoice at the return of one sinner (Lk 15:10)? We should give glory to Jesus by accepting His gift of forgiveness, accepting His love and remaining as part of His flock (Jn 10). Once Christ has cast our forgiven sins to the depths of the ocean, do not go diving to try to find them. He took them up on the cross with Him and left them there. Do not climb back up on that cross to take them back. Leave them there where they belong.

Those faults still remaining in us can be used as a source of humility and a source of faith in God's infinite mercy. As these aspects of His love take root in our heart, we will be less inclined to offend Him because we find ourselves loving Him more. In our growing love for Him, we will have less and less inclination to succumb to those faults, to favor those separating appetites that keep us from Him, and we will have an increasing desire to serve Him and reach union with Him. Our appreciation for His mercy becomes more profound.

How much importance does Christ place on our love for Him? One clear indication is what He asked when He founded His Church on Peter after the resurrection. Three times He asked Peter if he loved Him (Jn 21:15-19). Each time Peter responded affirmatively, Christ said to feed His sheep and lambs, and then gave Peter the keys to the Kingdom. Christ will give us missions, and His help, in response to our love for Him and desire to serve Him. From what we read in the letters of St. Paul and in the works of St. John of the Cross, we can conclude that the smallest movement of pure love is worth more to the Church than all other kinds of works put together. St. Therese said the desire of our soul should be, "to become the prey of Your Love."[74] Look at many of the other saints, people like St. Francis, St. Margaret Mary, the many martyrs. What is the one underlying strength of them all? It is unconditional love for God.

God gave us the gift of free will primarily so that we could freely choose to love Him. If we have no free will, we cannot choose love. If we do not have love, we do not have God Who is love. People choose what they love, and this love creates a preference for that which is loved. God wants us to prefer Him to all others. He makes us choose by keeping Himself hidden. He keeps Himself hidden, almost on the level of a creature, for if we perceived Him in His glory, we would not be able to choose another. He hides so that we might choose, and when we choose Him, He rewards us by sharing His nature with us, by making us His adopted children (Jn 1:12), by allowing those who love Him enough to unite with Him in a transformation of our souls otherwise impossible on earth. How close we come, how much of His nature He shares, and whether He will accept our soul as His bride, is dependent on our love for Him.

Just as a husband and wife become one by mutual consent, so God allows us to become united with Him provided we consent through our acts of the will to what He sends us. We are serving our time on earth in exile from our heavenly home. How well we spend this time and what we will find when we go home depends, again, on how much we love Him. Let us spend this time of exile loving God, consecrating ourselves to Him, showing our preference for Him over all others. Through our love for God, we gain the grace of His guidance and His power in our life. As we give Him our hearts, He gives us His life. We should take up our cross gladly, not hesitantly (Lk 9:23). The more we hesitate

---

[74]St. Therese of Lisieux, Story Of A Soul, ICS Publications, Washington DC, 1976, pg 200.

and step back, the less trusting of God we are, and the heavier the cross will be. In doing so, we are saying to the almighty God Who loves us beyond measure that we do not love Him enough, we do not trust Him enough, to do as He asks, to accept what He sends.

Because of His Love, and our love for Him, we do what we do out of love, not mere duty. We respond as His friend and His child, not as His hired servant (Jn 10:12-13) or as His slave (Jn 15:11-17). Our love for God takes the ordinary natural act of duty and makes it supernatural by making it a sacrifice done for love of God.

But what about duty? It is not the opposite of love, but rather can be an expression of some level of love. We change diapers out of duty to our infant child, and if that is our only motivation at the time then it is a minimum level of love. A soldier obeys out of duty, but may also obey as a form of self-sacrificing love of country and family, especially during conflict.

Having received God's love within us, we must spread this love, and this means we must go far beyond mere talk about love. We must know the love of God by discovering God in scripture and in our neighbor. We must be able to find God in our neighbor. We must believe in His love, we must pray to be filled with His love, and we must try at all times to live the life of the love of God. When we are confronted by the hatred we see in the world, we can fight it only with love, and the power of love is the omnipotence of Christ.

Love is self-generated, not reflected. If we love, it comes from within and goes out to the other. The power of this love within us comes from God. This love, His love in us, leads us to humility and obedience, and these are the foundation for the three theological virtues. It all begins with love. Through our love for God, we submit our will to His, mindful of Christ's admonition in the gospel that those who are saved are not those who cry out "Lord, Lord", but "those who do the will of my Father." (Mt 7:21) Because of His love, we can be small in the arms of the Good Shepherd, allowing Him to carry us when He knows we need to be carried, confident of His love, fearless in the face of the wolves who prowl the world seeking to destroy our souls, fearless of anything as long as He is with us. Even, as St. Therese says, "... confident to the point of audacity in the goodness of our Father." In the storm, when Christ asked Peter to walk out on the water to Him, Christ said, "It is I. Do not be afraid." (Mt 14:27-29; see also Jn 6:20). In the midst of the storms of our life, we must always remember this.

We must work to let our love for God supplant our fear, including our fear of God's actions. When we consecrate ourselves to Him, or consider doing so, we often wonder what will He ask of us; what will be required; what will we have to give up; how much will it hurt? If we are afraid of failing, or if we are afraid that by failing we will hurt God, we wound Him. We show a lack of confidence in His love for us. We are afraid of risking what must be risked when we give ourselves to Him completely. But if St. Therese is correct, then it is our fear, our lack of full trust, that hurts Him most, for it is His Love that would never allow Him to do anything that would hurt us spiritually.

Ask yourself: Am I a joy for Jesus? Should not a Father and child be joy for each other? Could our Heavenly Father be any less a joy for us if we would just accept Him as our Father, as our source joy? Am I faithful to my Good Shepherd?

Measuring Love

There is a certain simplicity to the way God loves. He is infinite, and therefore loves us all infinitely. However, when we love, being the finite beings we are, we do not love infinitely. God is the source of all love, so the only way we can love is to love with God's love. But that is something of a catch-22. If God is Love, and God is infinite, and all love comes from God, why isn't my love, and all love, infinite?

We can get a better understanding of how to measure love by first of all understanding more completely the requirements for love. Once again we turn to Lucifer and to Mary as our opposing examples. Lucifer is entirely self-focused and filled with pride. Mary is entirely humble. Lucifer said, 'I will not serve." Mary said, "Be it done to me according to your word." Humility is the key to understanding human love. The more humble we are the greater is our capacity for love. The more prideful we are the less capacity we have for love. God's perfect love is sacrificial in every sense of the word, from His humility in taking human form at the Incarnation, to sacrificing Himself on the Cross for love of man. Love is measured by the sacrifice we are willing to make for others. Love is measured by how much we do for others, how much of ourselves we give to others. It is limited by our humility.

When Mary was told by the angel that she was to be the mother of God, she was also told that Elizabeth was in her sixth month of pregnancy. Mary immediately went to serve her cousin Elizabeth. Most people in her circumstances would have spent the time right after the announcement going over and over in their minds what they should do, how they should explain it to others, what they should say and wear, wondering what others would say about them, worrying about what Joseph would say and do, and so on. Mary only thought of God and of her cousin.

Mother Teresa of Calcutta spent her life as a religious in service not only to others, but to those others who were in greatest need. Her thoughts were always on God first, and then on Jesus whom she saw in all those she met. Her strength came from her love for God and her humble giving of herself to God.

Human love, being an act of the will, is that which comes from ourselves and which we deliberately give to another. Therefore, love is measured by the level of attention given others, not self. There is a deliberateness about it that gives it focus and purpose. Human love is not an automatic emotion to which we respond or react, for we would have little or no control over how or whom we love, and it would require some feedback to which we could react. It would mean human love would function at an animal level. The kind of love of which we speak is different from the emotion we often call love in a dog for its master, or the emotional crush a young person might have on another - often called puppy love. Human love is unique in the universe as we know it. The more willfully we love Jesus, the more of ourselves we place at the feet of others.

Jesus humbled Himself, gave of Himself, all of Himself, and placed Himself at the feet of all humanity that they might be saved. Some accept His gift, and some do not. His act was a deliberate and total giving of Himself for others, even those who hated Him then and hate Him now. He desires our love, but does not condition His gift of love on our response. He will share Himself with those who do respond, for He will give them a share in His divine life, but His offer is to all. We need the humility to accept this love, and our response is how we measure our love.

Our response to love, in particular to God's love, is therefore measured by our willingness to accept His love in recognition of the humility with which it is offered to us mere creatures, and the level of our humility to recognize how unworthy we are, in and of ourselves, to receive His love. We do not earn His love, we receive His love as a gift. He makes us righteous through His love and mercy (Rom 5:19), He does not just declare us righteous as a divine juridic act. We do not deserve His love for nothing we have ever done can demand the infinite love of God as the reward. In fact, we can not even do anything of spiritual value on our own without God, and we have His word on that (Mt 19:26).

It is only pride that stops us from giving to God all possible love in thanks for the gift of His love. Any degree to which we hold back on our love is an indicator of the degree to which we are self-focused.

Everything is centered in love, for when we are centered in love we are centered in Him. We love God by loving all He sends into our lives. We love the consolations and happy things, and, yes, we love the crosses we are called to bear.

It is often difficult to respond with love to the crosses we receive, and it is likewise difficult to love the crosses we see others bearing. It is difficult to see these crosses as gifts, but that is what they are. Some crosses are Jesus' way of allowing us to share in His redemptive suffering, some are to atone for some aspect of our life, and we may never know the difference in this life. It does not really matter which we carry, for whatever the nature of and reason for our cross, it is the best possible cross for us at this time. God could not send us any other kind of cross than that which He knows is the best for us. It is really that simple. We need this gift from God more than we need anything else right now, otherwise He would not send it to us. This simple fact is sometimes the hardest to grasp, probably because it is so simple. The question is, now that we have it, what will we do with it? How will we carry it? If we recognize that we do truly need this right now, then we can carry it properly, even embrace it. It takes great love to do this. How we do this, how we follow in His footsteps, is a way we measure our response to His love. It means we have the eyes of our soul focused on the real purpose of life - to gain the greatest possible union with Christ. We should live our life to know, love and serve God; not to seek as much comfort as possible at the expense of everything and everyone else. We do this by accepting each gift God sends us with equal gratitude, whether cross or consolation.

The Spirituality of the Mass

Being a Congregation

One of the greatest acts of love we can offer God is to fully participate in the holy sacrifice of the Mass. In our need to understand the Mass and its importance, we must understand the importance of preparation for Mass. If we consider a more secular matter, would we go to a senior prom, a formal dance, dressed in a bikini? Would we go to the British Embassy for a personal audience with the Queen of England dressed in shorts, a T-shirt and flip-flops? To do any of these things would be an insult to the dignitaries and to all others involved. How much more important is it for us to come before our Lord, our King, our Savior and our God properly prepared?

Being able to properly participate in the sacrifice of the Mass means we must understand the spirituality of the different things going on. Proper participation goes beyond the mere understanding of what the priest is saying, or being able to see what is happening, or listening to the readings, or reciting the prayers and responses, or understanding the origin of the vestments and other implements of the Mass, all of which are important. Participation means we have an active involvement in what is happening, an involvement which includes spiritual participation. Mass is the highest prayer there is. If we attend Mass with our bodies but our minds and hearts are elsewhere, we are not participants but rather spectators. To understand our role we have to understand what it means to be a congregation, what it means to be a congregation in the church, and the significance of what is taking place, especially at the Eucharistic consecration. We also need to retain our understanding of our role as members of the Mystical Body, for that is central to proper participation in the Mass. This means we cannot really participate in the Mass as we should if we are late, use the time to balance our checkbook, leave our minds elsewhere, use the time to gossip or conduct other conversations with our neighbor, and if we never take the time and effort to learn what the Mass is really about. Have you considered that at Mass you offer yourself to God? If this is so, what is it you are offering if all that participates is your body? How could you offer God your love?

Being a congregation means more than just being part of a group of people who are sitting in church while Mass is being celebrated. It means understanding why we should be focused on what happening. The Mass, and our proper role in the Mass, is clearly important enough for us to be properly prepared. In Medjugorje, the people spend an hour praying the fifteen decade rosary, led by the priest, as their preparation for daily Mass. We generally don't have that luxury, or for whatever reasons don't take that kind of time to prepare even if the time is available. So what are we supposed to be if we are a congregation? A congregation is not simply a group of disconnected people in one place who have varying reasons for being there.[75]

To quote Fr. Guardini, "Congregation is formed only when those individuals are present not only corporally but also spiritually, when they have contacted one another in prayer and step together into the spiritual "space" around them; strictly speaking, when they have first widened and heightened that space by prayer. Then true congregation comes into being, which, along with the building that is the architectural expression, forms the vital church in which the sacred act is accomplished."[76] How many of us are not aware there is a spiritual connectedness between us, a

---

[75]Guardini, Fr. Romano, <u>Meditations Before Mass</u>, Sophia Institute Press, Manchester, 1993, pg 11.

[76]ibid. pg 11.

connectedness intended by God and accomplished by Him as the source of our unity? How many understand that when Jesus told us He would be present among us when two or more are gathered together in His name, He really meant we are to be conscious of being gathered together as one, are to be conscious of being together in His name for a common purpose, and are to participate in prayer together, united in prayer and in Him?

When we enjoy a Mystical Body awareness, when we are contacting each other in prayer and stepping together into that spiritual space around us, we are in every real sense imaginable behaving as members of Christ's Mystical Body. We are truly preparing to participate with Him, through the action of the priest, in the offering of Himself to the Father in the sacrifice of the Mass. When we do, because we are the Mystical Body of Christ, we are also offering ourselves to God. This offer only has meaning when we make it consciously and deliberately, otherwise it is not really an offer. We do this in reparation for our sins and those of all people everywhere. We must join fully in that sacrificial celebration. We must be, and act, like members of the Mystical Body. We must understand the spiritual realm, not just the physical environment, within which the Mass will take place. If a church building is destroyed, the only way we may have to participate in the sacrifice of the Mass is for the congregation itself to be properly formed, to properly create that spiritual connectedness together, and to create an indestructible church to surround the priest who is leading us in offering that sacrifice of the Mass. If we are not a real congregation, we cannot do this. As Fr. Guardini says, we must "learn and practice the art of constructing spiritual cathedrals".[77]

If we are to take the time to connect together in prayer, to construct our spiritual cathedral, we cannot have

---

[77]ibid. pg 12.

our minds and hearts in all sorts of other places. We need to be preparing our minds and hearts for the sacrificial celebration to come. We must develop a sense of anticipation of the enormous mystery about to take place, a mystery wherein God will come down to us and cross that invisible threshold between man and God. He will make Himself available to us so that we might fulfill His gospel directive to be in Him and He in us, for without Him it cannot be done. This Holy Communion, the central mystery of the Catholic Church, is a "... meeting of the soul and the heart with the invisible God. For this reason, the soul and the heart must be ready, must feel the presence that reveals itself simply in the bread and wine. And the soul must listen to the divine silence with which God speaks to us and looks after us."[78]

The Mass is the greatest of mysteries and should never be commonplace. If it is, it is something much less than the awesome mystery it should be. We should not be able to go to Mass and leave unchanged. Some go to Mass all their lives and are not changed much because there has been no preparation, no understanding, no encounter with God. To them, it has been nothing more than fulfilling an obligation. Where there has been no preparation for Mass, the participation is corporal, not spiritual, and therefore there is no interior transformation.

We should come to church sufficiently in advance of the beginning of Mass so that we can spend the right amount of time in silent composure. We need to spend time in prayer and anticipation of what will soon happen at Mass, conscious of our spiritual connectedness with each other in the Mystical Body. We should spend time in thanksgiving to Jesus for what He did sacrificing Himself for us and for what He continues to do for us. We should thank God for His Church, for the guidance of the Holy Spirit, for the grace of

---

[78]Barbaric, Fr. Slavko, Celebrate Mass With Your Heart, Faith Publishing Co., Milford, 1994, pg xvii.

our Blessed Mother, for the saints, and for the sacraments He has made available to us through His Church. We should give thanks for the wisdom and guidance of the Church and our Holy Father, John Paul II. We should spend time reflecting on our lives and how we have responded to Jesus.

As we meditate on our role as part of a congregation, we cannot be composed, and cannot arrive at the interior silence and anticipation of the events about to unfold if we are filled with a spirit of anger at others or of rebellion against the magisterium of the Church. These feelings are inconsistent with the love we must have to offer ourselves to God in the Mass. We need to remember that the first sin, that of Lucifer and his follower angels, was a sin, not of breaking God's command, but one of rebellion; a sin of perverse pride that forever separated them from God's love, and condemned them to an existence void of love. The first sin of man was one of rebellion; a sin of pride which led Adam and Eve to desire to be independent of God, to be free from obedience and subjugation to Him. The consequence was the fall of man. It is only through God's mercy that this condition has a hope of reversal for each of us. But if we live in a state of rebellion against God's commands, against the teachings of the Church inspired by the Holy Spirit, against submission of ourselves and our will to the will of God, if we allow our perverse pride to give preference to ourselves instead of to God, then we are removing ourselves from God just as the fallen angels did. The more pride motivates our lives, the less love motivates our lives. The more love motivates our lives, the closer we are to God. Pride and rebellion against God are incompatible with a life dedicated to accepting God's love, dedication of our lives to God in humility, and acceptance of His will for us. Preference for our own will is the antithesis of preference for God's will in us. Preference for our own will is synonymous with preference for Satan for it takes us farther and farther from God.

This silent composure, this interior attitude, does not just happen; it must be created by us. It takes time, and takes an understanding of what is about to happen on the altar, and to us because of what occurs on the altar. We cannot properly sit, kneel or stand unless we are truly aware of what is occurring. These are not mere body positions; they are positions taken in reverence for God truly present among us. When we make the sign of the cross, we need to understand we are asking the Triune God to bless us and what we do, and therefore we must make the sign of the cross with reverence, not like we are swatting a fly. We enter church blessing ourselves with holy water in the name of the Father, and of the Son, and of the Holy Spirit. We begin our prayer with the same sign, and we conclude the Mass the same way. When we use our eyes, it is to see and fully participate in the Mass; not to check out everyone else around us, making judgments about their posture or behavior or fashion consciousness. When we use our lips, it is to give glory to God; not to gossip or engage in trivial comments. In short, we are focused; mind, heart and soul. We are mystically connected to God and our fellow worshipers. God needs to be the central focus of everything we do in our lives. We need to be committed, dedicated, and attentive children of God. We must also teach our children these things, and not cater to their every whim to play during Mass. It takes time and patience.

The Thresholds of Mass

Fr. Guardini[79], in his book <u>Meditations Before Mass</u>, has introduced some very interesting concepts about various thresholds related to the Mass. When we participate in the Mass it helps considerably if we recognize the thresholds we cross or approach, both physical and spiritual.

---

[79]Guardini, Fr. Romano, <u>Meditations Before Mass</u>, Sophia Institute Press, Manchester, chapters 7, 8,and 9.

First, we recognize what a church is. While it is true that Mass could possibly be celebrated almost anywhere, it is most fittingly celebrated in a church. Virtually anything else has one or more other purposes, and this includes natural settings as well as structures. We have had open air Masses, battlefield Masses said on the hood of a jeep, and Masses in private homes, but none of these places is exclusively dedicated, exclusively consecrated, to the worship of God[80]. A church is consecrated and dedicated to one purpose; the worship of God. In church, we bring people into the community of God through baptism, consecrate them into adulthood through confirmation, consecrate their unity in God through marriage, teach them about God, celebrate their consecration to God in administration of holy orders, and we say farewell to our community members at a funeral Mass. Through all this, we come together daily in church as a congregation for the celebration of Holy Mass.

A church, then, is a holy place where holy activities take place, and where only such activities should take place. We should never trivialize what a church is, and never lose sight of the fact that God, the incarnate wisdom, resides in church and waits for our presence and homage. When we enter a church, we are not merely walking into a building, but are walking into the place of residence of God Himself, a place as sacred and as holy as the Holy of Holies of the Hebrew Testament where God used to reside among His first chosen people. Just a surely as God once was in the temple of the ancient Jews, residing there under the appearance of a cloud, He resides for us today in the tabernacle under the appearance of the consecrated Host. The stark fact that God is there, present to us, makes the church a holy place and demands our undivided attention, demands our coming together as a true congregation. This begins for us as we

---

[80]Code of Canon Law, Canon 1214, Canon Law Society of America, 1983.

cross the first threshold, the physical threshold of the church entryway.

The Mass is the single means chosen by God to come to His people in fulfillment of the directive given by Christ in Chapter 6 of the Gospel of St. John. It is the one and only means provided by God whereby we can receive the living Christ, Body and Blood, Soul and Divinity. The awesome majesty of the Mass should never be trivialized by our behavior or attitude. When we cross the physical threshold of the church, we enter into the sacred chamber of our salvation.

In a sense, our reception of the Eucharist is a form of Passover whereby Jesus passes into His people, blesses them, and offers Himself to them as the Food of Salvation, the Food of Eternal Life to save them from eternal death. The Eucharist marks our soul as a child of God, just as the blood of the lamb marked the doorposts of the Jews to identify them as a chosen people of God to save them from death. Padre Pio said that at the consecration of the Mass, his heart was joined to that of Christ so closely that the Blessed Mother could hear, not two heartbeats, but only one.

All this happens unawares if we are not a congregation, if we do not understand the spirituality of what is happening, if our presence and activity is merely corporal. It is the absent condition of mind which allows people to be present during Mass, to spectate rather than participate, and then leave completely unaffected, bored by the whole thing. They miss the encounter with God.

When Mass is over, the spiritual threshold of the altar is closed, and we cross back over the physical threshold of the church to re-enter the world of mankind. But the fruits of our encounter with God remain in our soul. If there has been no encounter, there are no fruits, and we leave as we entered, unchanged and unaffected.

When we consider how we participate at Mass, when we consider where our hearts and minds are during Mass, we should remember what Fr. Arintero tells us. "Those acts which do not merit [eternal life] are by that very fact evil, because the just man who does not act in conformity with the "new man", ever meriting an increase, works according to the "old man", and falls and loses merit."[81]

Liturgy of the Word

Keeping in mind the concepts of congregation previously discussed, and mindful of the physical and spiritual thresholds, it is time now to look at the conduct of the Mass itself. We will focus not so much on the activity but on the spirituality behind the activity. In doing this, we will focus on two forms of the Mass, both legitimate forms. One is the common vernacular form, known as the Novus Ordo, which we usually experience daily. The other, specifically allowed in accordance with the encyclical Ecclesia Dei issued by Pope John Paul II, is the Mass of Pius V, sometimes called the Tridentine Mass, Indult Mass, the Traditional Latin Mass or the pre-Vatican II Mass. We will make reference to the prayers of whichever of the two Masses will help us to gain a fuller understanding of the spirituality of the particular part of the Mass being discussed.

Realizing what is going to happen during the consecration, our focus and everything we do, during our preparation for Mass and during the conduct of the Mass, should be directed toward that event. The consecration should not be something that sort of sneaks up on us during the Mass or something that is a "one of many" events during the Mass. The consecration is the pinnacle of the Mass, the sublime offering to the Father of the sacrifice of Calvary. We celebrate the sacrifice of the Mass. The sacrifice takes place

---

[81] Arintero OP, Fr. John G., The Mystical Evolution, TAN Books and Publishers, Rockford, 1978, Vol 1, p 293.

on the altar, the place of the spiritual threshold between Divinity and humanity. Therefore, we need somehow to focus on the altar, and relate everything else to that consecration event which is about to take place or which has just taken place.

To begin Mass, the priest celebrating the Novus Ordo Mass bows before the crucifix, ascends the altar, begs for God's grace and peace, and begins the Introit, the introduction of the Mass of the day. This is followed by a recollection of our sins, and then the confiteor, also called the penitential rite, is said by the priest and faithful together. The faithful then say the Misereatur, "May Almighty God have mercy on you, forgive you your sins, and bring you to everlasting life."

The sacrificial preparatory focus is immediately evident in the Tridentine Mass, where the priest comes before the altar, bows, ascends the stairs right foot first, and places the chalice on the altar. He also unfolds and places the corporal in the center of the altar. He does this himself because prior to Vatican II, it was forbidden for anyone whose hands had not been consecrated to touch the sacred vessels (chalice and ciborium) which would hold the precious Body and Blood of our Lord. The priest then returns to the foot of the altar and begins the prayers at the foot of the altar.

The prayers at the foot of the altar of the Tridentine Mass clearly set the spiritual tone and focus for the entire rest of the Mass. The priest makes the sign of the cross, and then begins, "Introibo ad altare Dei, ...", "I will go to the altar of God,...". This prayer is taken from psalm 43 (formerly part 3 of psalm 42); and sets the focus for the Mass. It focuses us on the altar where the sacrifice will be offered, and focuses us on the One to whom the Mass is offered; God the Father. We must always keep in mind that a Mass is a sacrificial offering to the Father. Sometimes we tend to lose sight of this focus, and tend to forget to whom and for what the Mass is offered. This opening prayer at the foot of the altar is:

"I will go to the altar of God, to God who gives joy to my youth. Judge me, O God, and distinguish my cause from an ungodly nation; deliver me from an unjust and deceitful enemy."

There then follows an acknowledgment of God's strength, a petition that He send out His light and His truth for us, followed by a song of praise and hope in God as our salvation. In this prayer we see all the fundamental elements of prayer.

Following this, the priest makes a profound bow and says the confiteor asking for forgiveness for his own sins. This is the prayer which begins "I confess to almighty God, ...". The server, speaking on behalf of the people, responds with the Misereatur, "May Almighty God have mercy on you, forgive you your sins, and bring you to everlasting life." Then the server, with a profound bow, and speaking on behalf of the people, repeats the Confiteor and the priest follows with a repetition of the Misereatur. Thus, the priest has begged forgiveness for his sins, and the people have begged forgiveness for their own sins.

Then the priest, following these prayers at the foot of the altar, prays for merciful pardon, absolution, and remission of sins. This sacrifice, being offered on the altar, is made for the remission of sin. The focus and purpose of the Mass is unambiguously established. Following this petition, he ascends the altar, right foot first, to begin the Liturgy for the remainder of the Mass. As he does, he says the beautiful prayer which begins "Aufer a nobis, ..", "Lord we pray Thee to take away our wickedness from us, so that we may worthily enter into the Holy of Holies with pure minds, through Christ our Lord. Amen."

Let us consider what has happened right from the first, in just these few opening moments of the Mass. Before the priest has even ascended the altar to begin the Liturgy of the Word, there is an acknowledgment of the presence of God with us in the tabernacle as, in the prayer Aufer a Nobis, the priest acknowledges the sanctuary as the Holy of Holies; there is a focus on sacrifice with the attention given to the altar; there is a prayer of petition and praise to God the Father, and there is a confession of our sinfulness. This sinfulness is what Christ was sacrificed for, the reason why the Mass is necessary. The mood has been set. The focus has been established. There is no doubt as to what kind of place we are in or to whom the Mass is directed, nor the place of focus for our attention for the rest of the Mass. An altar has only one basic purpose; sacrifice. If "I go to the altar of God, ...", I am clearly going to offer a sacrifice to God. In this case, the priest is making a sin offering for his sins and the sins of all men. This idea of a sin offering will become extremely important later as we focus on the liturgy of the Eucharist.

In the Tridentine Mass, as soon as the priest reaches the altar, he places his hands to the sides of the corporal (not touching the corporal) and says the Oramus te, ... "We beseech Thee, Lord, by the merits of Thy saints whose relics are here, and of all the saints, graciously to forgive me all my sins. Amen." Here the priest is asking for forgiveness of his own sins before he dares to continue with the sin offering to God the Father, and before he dares to touch the precious Body and Blood of our Lord in the Eucharist.

This harkens back to the prayers of the priest in the Temple in Jerusalem before he dared to venture behind the veil into the Holy of Holies to offer the annual sacrifice for the sins of Israel. This prayer was very important to the Israelites. Roy Schoeman points out in his book, *Salvation is*

From the Jews[82], that before the annual Rosh Hashanah sacrifice was presented to God as the sin offering, a scarlet cord was attached to the outer door of the Temple. If the cord turned white, it was the sign to the people God had accepted the sin offering and their sins had been forgiven. If God did not accept the offering, the cord remained scarlet. It is what the prophet Isaiah was referring to when he said, " Come now, let us set things right, says the LORD: Though your sins be like scarlet, they may become white as snow; Though they be crimson red, they may become white as wool." (Is 1:18) From the time of the crucifixion when the Temple veil was torn in two (Mt 27:51) until the Temple was destroyed in 70 AD, the cord never again turned white.

After all this preparatory prayer has been offered in the Tridentine Mass, the priest begins the introductory prayers, the Introit. At this point the Novus Ordo Mass and the Tridentine Mass are quite similar. After the Introit, there follows the Kyrie (Lord have mercy), the Gloria (Glory to God in the highest,..), and then the readings of the day, terminating with the gospel of the day.

Following the gospel in both the Novus Ordo and the Tridentine Mass, the priest once again focuses on the sin for which the Mass is being offered when he says the Per evangelica dicta, "By the words of the gospel may our sins be blotted out."

Following the gospel, the priest gives the homily. The priest then begins the Creed, which is said by all the faithful. Then follows the general intercessions.

This ends the Mass of the Catechumens, the Liturgy of the Word. In the early church, all those who had not yet been baptized in the faith would leave, and the

---

[82]Roy H. Schoeman, Salvation Is From The Jews, Ignatius Press, San Francisco, 2003, pp 129-132.

communicating baptized faithful would remain for the liturgy of the Eucharist, the fulfillment of that for which they had been prepared.

Liturgy of the Eucharist

All of the previous prayers of the Mass have led us to the point where we are ready to begin the Liturgy of the Eucharist. The priest uncovers the chalice and places the hosts to be consecrated on the corporal. If the hosts are in a ciborium, the ciborium is placed on the corporal. The priest then lifts the paten which holds the large host he will consecrate and says:

Tridentine

"Holy Father, almighty, eternal God, accept this spotless host which I, Thy unworthy servant, offer Thee, my living and true God, for my countless sins, offenses and omissions and for everyone here, as well as for all faithful Christians, living and dead. Accept it for me and for them, that we may be saved and brought to everlasting life. Amen."

The priest then slides the host off the paten onto the corporal, without touching the corporal and slips the paten under the corporal.

Novus Ordo

"Blessed are You Lord, God of all creation. Through Your goodness we have this bread to offer, which earth has given and human hands have made. It will become for us the Bread of Life."

The people respond "Blessed be God forever."

In the Tridentine Mass we see a very strong focus on a sin offering. The gifts are being prepared as an offering in reparation for our sins. There is also a reference to a "spotless host." The priest likewise brings all the Mystical Body, Christians who are living or who have ever lived on earth, into the Mass and the sin offering is for all of them, as an offering to gain their eternal life. The priest asks God to accept this offering. He has established a focus on the gifts themselves, but in a special way. He is asking that this little gift, mere bread, be sufficient to be accepted by God and through it asks that God give us everlasting Life. Clearly, a little piece of bread is not sufficient. Something else must have to happen to this bread for it to have the effect we ask.

In the Novus Ordo Mass the priest is offering the gift to the Father, and indicates that it will become the bread of life. This is a reference to the bread of life discourse in Chapter 6 of the gospel of John, and all the gospel teaches us in that chapter is implied here. We especially note that the priest makes reference to this little piece of bread somehow becoming something much more.

After the preparation of the bread, the priest pours wine and water into the chalice, reminiscent of the Blood and Water which flowed from the side of Jesus when the spear was thrust into His side at the crucifixion. As he does, he says a prayer which acknowledges in the Mass, for the first time, the spiritual effect these offerings will have for us, and makes even more clear that something quite awesome will happen to them in order for this effect to take place.

Tridentine

"O God, who wonderfully created human nature, and even more wonderfully restored it, grant that through the mystery of this water and wine we may partake in the divinity of the One Who deigned to share our humanity: Jesus Christ, Thy Son, our Lord, Who is God, living and reigning with Thee in the unity of the Holy Spirit, for ever and ever. Amen."

"Lord, we offer Thee the chalice of salvation, asking Thy mercy, that our offering may rise with a sweet fragrance in the sight of Thy divine majesty, for our salvation and that of the whole world."

Then the priest says the prayer which originates in the prayer of Azarias to King Nebuchadnezzar: "With a humble spirit and contrite soul, may we be received by Thee, Lord, and may our sacrifice be offered in Thy sight today so that it may please Thee, Lord God. Come, Sanctifier, almighty and eternal God, and bless this sacrifice prepared for Thy holy name."

Novus Ordo

The priest lifts the chalice and says, "By the mystery of this water and wine may we come to share in the divinity of Christ, who humbled Himself to share in our humanity."

"Blessed are You, Lord, God of all creation. Through Your goodness we have this wine to offer, fruit of the vine and work of human hands. It will become our spiritual drink." The people respond "Blessed be God forever."

"Lord God, we ask you to receive us and be pleased with the sacrifice we offer you with humble and contrite hearts."

Why did Christ use bread and wine to institute the Eucharist at the Last Supper? Why not some other part of the Passover meal, such as the lamb, which more closely resembled Christ in physical substance and sacrificial purpose, or bitter herbs? Aside from the practical facts that bread and wine are the fruits of our labor we offer as the gift, and that they will be more readily available to all and more easily handled when being distributed to the people of God, Melchizedek, the first appointed high priest, who was also a king, used bread and wine at his first offering to Abraham (Genesis 14:18). Jesus was careful in following the law, and in Leviticus 21:6, among the requirements for the priests are that "They shall be holy to their God, and shall not profane His name: for they offer the burnt offering of the Lord, and the bread of their God, and therefore they shall be holy." The bread of God will now become the Bread of Life and the basis of the new and everlasting covenant. Christ also referred to Himself as the vine and us as the branches in describing His Mystical Body, and He used wine, the fruit of the Vine, as part of the element of the sacrifice. We are also incorporated into the one Mystical Body from many members, just as the bread and wine are one, made from many grains of wheat or many grapes.

The "spotless host" referred to in the opening offering prayer in the Tridentine Mass is very important to the idea of a sin offering, and goes way back in Hebrew history. There are two essential things we must understand here if we are to appreciate the spirituality of what is happening.

First, a sin offering, offered according to the ritual of sacrifices as described in Leviticus, chapters 1-4, requires that the offering be unblemished. The "spotless host" directly fulfills the requirement of this concept, especially as it will become the unblemished Christ. In the Tridentine Mass, the host is slipped from the paten onto the corporal without touching it. The priest, only after washing his hands in preparation, will touch the host for the first time when he holds it to say the sacred words of consecration.

Second, in Leviticus 3:16-17, and 17:10-12, we see that God, as a perpetual law, has forbidden His people to consume any blood. Anything having blood and which is to be sacrificed to Him must first be bled completely and the blood given to God. Only then can the flesh be offered or consumed. God said in Leviticus that "Since the life of a living body is in its blood, I have made you put it on the altar, so that atonement may thereby be made for your own lives, because it is the blood, as the seat of life, that makes atonement."

God repeats this prohibition again in Leviticus 17:14, where it says: "For the life of all flesh is in the blood: therefore I said to the children of Israel: You shall not eat the blood of any flesh at all, because the life of the flesh is in the blood, and whosoever eats it shall be cut off."

This prohibition played a very important role in the response of the Jews when Jesus gave them the Eucharistic discourse recorded in the gospel of John, Chapter 6, for in their minds He was telling them to violate this law when He told them they must drink His Blood to have eternal life. They were focused on this law, and their thinking never moved forward to understand that only God could tell them to do what Jesus asked. They never asked Him to confirm He was God, Emmanuel, the Messiah.

In contemplating the spirituality of the Mass, we understand that we derive spiritual life from the blood of God, who is the source of all life and who shed His blood in sacrifice for us for our salvation. In the Tridentine Mass, the priest refers to the chalice as "the chalice of salvation", and once again incorporates the Mystical Body into the prayer of offering.

Keeping all this in mind, we look again at the gospel of John. In John 6:53-58, we find: "Jesus said to them, Amen, amen, I say to you, unless you eat the Flesh of the Son of Man and drink His Blood, you do not have Life within you. Whoever eats My Flesh and drinks My Blood has eternal Life, and I will raise him on the last day. For My Flesh is true food, and My Blood is true drink. Whoever eats

My Flesh and drinks My Blood remains in Me and I in him. Just as the living Father sent Me and I have Life because of the Father, so also the one who feeds on Me will have Life because of Me. This is the Bread that came down from Heaven. Unlike your ancestors who ate and still died, whoever eats this Bread will live forever."

Here we approach full realization of the spirituality of what is about to occur. In order for a sacrifice to be pleasing to God, it must not only die, but according to the law as expressed in Leviticus it must also be bled completely. Blood belongs only to God. The living creature to be sacrificed is given to God in separated form; the body separated from the blood which gives it life. Blood is the life of the being, and all life belongs to God. Yet, in John, Christ tells us to eat His Flesh and drink His Blood. To the mind of a Hebrew who did not understand who Christ was, Christ was telling them not only to be a cannibal but also to break the law of God and consume blood. This, many could not accept, and they turned away. If they had only understood Jesus' divine nature they would have understood that He was offering them the opportunity, by partaking of His Flesh and His Blood, to also partake in His divine Life, in His complete nature, man and God, Body and Blood, Soul and Divinity. He is offering the Life of God, His divine Life; offering us the privilege of being true children of God, true heirs of heaven with Christ. If all blood belongs only to God, only God has the right and authority to give it to man. By offering Man His own Body and Blood, Christ was proclaiming His divinity for He is doing what only God has the right to do. It is also the means through which God, our Maker, will effect the complete union with us necessary for God to be our spiritual Husband (Is 54:5).

We have now come to almost complete readiness for offering to the Father the intended sacrifice. The next thing the priest must do is to prepare himself to perform the consecration. He must be clean before he dare offer this gift

349

to the Father. In the time of Christ and before, when the priest entered the Holy of Holies to offer the sacrifice, he had a rope tied around his leg and had bells on his robe. If he approached God in an unclean state, he would be struck dead and the bells would stop ringing. The people, since they were not allowed into the Holy of Holies, would then drag the priest's dead body back out by pulling the rope. The priest at Mass symbolizes this cleansing by the ritual washing of his hands, which is also a memento of Pilate washing his hands before sending Christ off to be sacrificed.

In the Novus Ordo Mass, the priest pours water on his hands and says, "Lord, wash away my iniquity; cleanse me from my sin." This phrase is Psalm 51:4, Psalm 51 being the Miserere, the Prayer of Repentance.

In the Tridentine Mass the priest, as he washes his hands, says a prayer from Psalm 26:6-12. He washes only the thumb and forefinger of each hand since they will be used to hold the consecrated host. Psalm 26:6-12 says, "I will wash my hands among the innocent and go round Thine altar, Lord, that I may listen to the sound of praise and may tell all Thy wonderful works. Lord, I have loved the beauty of Thy house and the place where Thy glory dwells. Do not let my soul be lost with sinners. Save my life from the men of blood whose hands are sinful, whose right hands are full of bribes. But I have walked in innocence; deliver me in Thy mercy. My foot has stood in the right path; I will bless Thee in the churches, O Lord. Glory be to the Father, ..."

Note in this prayer the focus on the altar, recognition that he is in the place where the glory of God dwells, and the petition for deliverance from men whose hands are full of bribes. Then consider the bribe of Judas as he betrayed Christ. We need to ask ourselves in how many ways does man betray Christ even today? What kinds of bribes do we take today? Do we take bribes of convenience, compromise, laziness, allegiance to anything we place above our allegiance to God, all of which leads us into sin and away from Christ?

The priest then returns to the center and begins the final prayers leading up to the consecration.

Having washed his hands, the priest now begins the final preparation for the consecration of the Eucharist, during which time Christ is offered to the Father in atonement for our sins.

Tridentine

"Accept, Holy Trinity, this offering, which we make in memory of the passion, resurrection, and ascension of our Lord Jesus Christ, and in honor of Blessed Mary ever virgin, of Blessed John the Baptist, of the holy apostles Peter and Paul, of {the saint of the church}, and all the saints. May this offering bring them honor and us salvation, and may those whose memory we commemorate on earth intercede for us in heaven. Through the same Christ our Lord. Amen."

"Pray, brethren, that my sacrifice and yours may be acceptable to God, the almighty Father."

Novus Ordo

"Pray, brethren, that our sacrifice may be acceptable to God, the almighty Father."

The people respond, "May the Lord accept the sacrifice at your hands, for the praise and glory of His name, for our good and the good of all His Church."

The priest then says the Preface, which has many forms, but which typically begins, "Father, all powerful and ever living God, we do well always to give You thanks and praise. ....." This concludes with the prayer, "Holy, Holy, Holy, ..."

The priest then says the Te Igitur. This is the prayer where the priest asks the Father to accept the gifts being offered to Him.

Tridentine

"So, most merciful Father, we pray and beg Thee, through Jesus Christ, Thy Son our Lord, to accept and bless these gifts, these offerings, these holy and spotless sacrifices."

Novus Ordo

"We come to You, Father, with praise and thanksgiving, through Jesus Christ, your Son. Through Him do we ask You to bless these gifts we offer You in sacrifice."

The prayers continue wherein the priest asks that the sacrifices be accepted for the holy Catholic Church, asks that the Father watch over and guide His Church; he offers the gifts likewise for the Pope and the Bishop, asks for peace in the world, and says the prayer of remembrance for those for whom we now pray.

We have noticed the frequent reference in the Tridentine Mass to the spotless sacrifice. The priest now begins the Hanc Igitur, the prayer of the priest in which he asks that the Father accept these gifts, make them holy, asks that they be the instrument of our salvation, and asks that they become the Body and Blood of our Lord, Jesus Christ. The spiritual door at the threshold of the altar is now being opened as we prepare for the Holy Spirit to descend among His people to bring us the instrument of our salvation and our sanctification.

Here we have the incomprehensible mystery of the Eucharist. The bread and wine are prepared, and are offered to the Father. They are separated, bread from wine, Body from Blood; the spotless and unblemished victim. This is how Christ gave us the sacrament at the Last Supper. The paschal victim who was to be crucified, because of the type and placement of His wounds, would by that process be bled, in keeping with the law. And so the priest, at the consecration, offers the bread to the Father and asks that it become the Body of Christ. He offers the wine, and asks that it become the Blood of Christ. The priest begins the consecration rite.

Tridentine

"So, most merciful Father, we pray and beg Thee, through Jesus Christ, Thy Son our Lord, to accept and bless these gifts, these offerings, these holy and spotless sacrifices."

Novus Ordo

"We come to You, Father, with praise and thanksgiving, through Jesus Christ, your Son. Through Him do we ask You to bless these gifts we offer You in sacrifice."

Tridentine

The day before He suffered, He took bread in His holy and sacred hands. Lifting up His eyes to Heaven (priest looks upward, then bows his head over the host), to Thee, God, His almighty Father, He gave Thee thanks, blessed the bread, broke it and gave it to His disciples, saying: Take, all of you, and eat this:

Novus Ordo

On the day before He suffered, He took bread into His sacred hands, (priest looks upward) and looking up to Heaven, to you, His almighty Father, He gave you thanks and praise. He broke the bread, gave it to His disciples, and said: Take this, all of you and eat it:

Here the priest bows directly over the Host as he says the words of consecration.

Tridentine

HOC EST ENIM CORPUS MEUM
THIS IS MY BODY.

Novus Ordo

HOC EST ENIM CORPUS MEUM, QUOD PRO VOBIS
TRADETUR.
THIS IS MY BODY, WHICH WILL BE GIVEN UP FOR
YOU.

Note that in the vernacular Mass a phrase has been added to reaffirm the fact that Christ was sacrificed for us. The priest then raises the now consecrated Host for the congregation to venerate, looking silently and reverently at the Host all the while, and keeping it raised directly over the corporal. This is so that if any particle whatever falls from the Host because it is being held, it will fall on the corporal. The priest then lowers the consecrated Host and lays it on the corporal and genuflects. As he genuflects, he keeps his hands always over the corporal so that any particle which may have adhered to his fingers will fall upon the corporal.

Then the priest begins the consecration of the wine, starting with the prayers "In a similar manner, He took the chalice ...". As he pronounces the words of consecration, the priest bows low over the chalice and speaks the words of consecration.

Tridentine

HIC EST ENIM CALIX SANGUINIS MEI, NOVI ET AETERNI TESTAMENTI: MYSTERIUM FIDEI: QUI PRO VOBIS, ET PRO MULTIS EFFUNDETUR IN REMISSIONEM PECCATORUM.

FOR THIS IS THE CHALICE OF MY BLOOD, OF THE NEW AND EVERLASTING COVENANT: THE MYSTERY OF FAITH: IT WILL BE SHED FOR YOU AND FOR MANY UNTO THE REMISSION OF SINS.

Whenever you will do these things, you will do them in memory of Me.

Novus Ordo

HIC EST ENIM CALIX SANGUINIS MEI, NOVI ET AETERNI TESTAMENTI, QUI PRO VOBIS, ET PRO MULTIS EFFUNDETUR IN REMISSIONEM PECCATORUM. HOC FACITE IN MEAM COMMEMORATIONEM.

THIS IS THE CUP OF MY BLOOD, THE BLOOD OF THE NEW AND EVERLASTING COVENANT. IT WILL BE SHED FOR YOU AND FOR ALL SO THAT SINS MAY BE FORGIVEN. DO THIS IN MEMORY OF ME.

After the chalice is consecrated, the priest raises the consecrated Blood of Christ for the faithful to venerate. He looks at the chalice reverently, and then replaces it on the corporal.

My family and I had the privilege of visiting with Fr. Lawrence Sweeney in Ogden, Utah, when, at the consecration of the chalice, the chalice bled both into the chalice bowl and exteriorly onto the corporal. I was able to take pictures of both the chalice and the corporal. There have been other Eucharistic miracles through the ages. These miracles are physical affirmations of the truth of the real presence of Jesus in the Eucharist, and confirmation of what has been Church doctrine since the earliest days of Christianity. Truth affirms truth.

It is very important that we understand the spiritual activity taking place during the consecration. We have to understand that the Eucharist is the real mystery of faith spoken of in the words of the consecration of the chalice in the Tridentine Mass. The priest, standing *in persona Christi*, has pronounced the words of consecration, and the bread and wine have become the Body and Blood of Christ through transubstantiation.

We had offered bread and wine to the Father, and asked that He make them holy. We had asked that He accept the bread and wine and transubstantiate them, through the action of the Holy Spirit, into the Body and Blood of our Lord Jesus Christ who is the perfect, spotless, and unblemished victim; the sacrifice which was offered to Him on Calvary for the remission of our sins. Through the rite of the consecration, done as Jesus had commanded, the Father has done so.

At this point our sin offering, presented by the priest standing *in persona Christi*, has been made and accepted. Christ does not die again, for He can only die once. The priest is offering, re-presenting, to the Father that self same sacrifice offered by Christ on Calvary. But the priest has also petitioned the Father for more than acceptance of our sin offering. The priest has asked that these gifts, this sin offering, become the instrument of our salvation. A dead offering cannot do this for death has no continuing efficacious power in itself. God is the God of the living. Therefore, the Father, at the time of the consecration, brings into effect the full importance of the gospel of Jn 6:53-58, which now becomes clear. We now also understand how God will fulfill the third covenant promise made to Abraham because of his obedience (Genesis 22). It is done because of our obedience to the command of Jesus at the Last Supper. The questions in the minds of the disciples, "This saying is hard; who can accept it?"(Jn 6:60) are now answered. The Mystery of Faith, the Mystery of Sanctifying Life, is accomplished.

We have re-presented to the Father the spotless and unblemished victim, the sacrificed Body and Blood of His Son. The Holy Spirit, the Sanctifier, overshadowed the gifts and transubstantiated each species, both the bread and the wine, into the Body and the Blood of Jesus Christ. The Father accepted these gifts, now made holy, but has done so much more.

The Father has received the Blood of His Son, that Blood which is the divine life of the spotless victim. He now gives this precious Blood back to us as our own source of divine Life. But He does not give it to us as just Blood, since Blood separated from the Body signifies death. He has to give us life; the life of Christ. The Bread of Life, which Jesus identified Himself to be in John cannot be dead, body separated from blood. The Holy Spirit has to give us back the Body and Blood of the living and risen Christ. The Holy Spirit, the Sanctifier, who overshadowed the gifts and transubstantiated them into the Body of Christ and the Blood of Christ, now also reconstitutes them, making *each of them* the true and living Body and Blood, Soul and Divinity of our Lord Jesus Christ. The victim who was sacrificed, the one whose Body and Blood was separated at the crucifixion, has risen and is truly alive, and is now the One who is fully present, Body and Blood, Soul and Divinity, as the instrument of our salvation, the one Who gives us His Life by giving us Himself. It is the living and risen Christ, Body and Blood, Soul and Divinity, which we receive in Communion, *regardless of species*.

The Body and Blood of the Victim, sacrificed once on Calvary and offered here again on the altar, had to be separated to be the proper sin offering, but are reunited by the Holy Spirit and offered to us as the living gift of His Divine Life, the Bread of Life. The gospel of John is fulfilled. Jesus has answered the question of how He can give us His Body and Blood to eat and drink, for all time, in all places, in a form which is acceptable to man and easily consumed. It is also in a form which can be transported by the priest or Eucharistic minister to those in remote areas or who are unable to attend Mass for medical or other good reasons. The Bread of Life, the sanctifying spirit of Divine life, is now with and available to us always and everywhere, giving Life to God's people.

That is why at Fatima, when the Angel appeared to the three children and gave them the Eucharist, He gave the host to Lucia and the chalice of Blood to the other two children. Each then fully received the living Christ in the Eucharist. That is why the consecrated host bled in Betania and in other places in the world, and why I was able to witness the consecrated chalice bleed at the Mass offered by Father Sweeney at Holy Family Church in Ogden, Utah.

Following the consecration, the priest prepares for the distribution of communion to the faithful. The priest asks the Father to recognize that we call to mind the passion, death and resurrection of our Lord, asks the Father to look favorably on the gifts we present and accept them as He accepted the gifts of His just servant Abel and His high priest Melchizedek. He then says the beautiful prayer, Supplices te Rogamus, "Almighty God, we pray that your angel may take this sacrifice to your altar in heaven. Then, as we receive from this altar the sacred Body and Blood of Your Son, let us be filled with every grace and blessing. Through Christ our Lord." The altar in heaven is the altar John tells us about in his vision of heaven recorded in Revelation (Rev 5 and 6). The door at this threshold is wide open.

The priest then says the prayer of remembrance of those who have gone before us, asks for a share in the fellowship of the apostles and all the saints, and then says "Through Him You give us all these gifts. You fill them with life and goodness, You bless them and make them holy."

In the gospel of John, Christ told us that those who receive Him in the Eucharist will be *in Him* and He in us. We also are mindful that it is Christ, as head of the Mystical Body, who leads us, in the person of the priest, in offering this sacrifice to the Father. Therefore, we do this *with Him*. Likewise, those who are to receive Him are in Him and receive the divine life *through Him* as He resides in us, as we receive His life-giving bread of life. This act of Christ, leading His Mystical Body in worship of and homage to the Father, gives the Father glory and honor in the only way acceptable to Him. In recognition of this, the priest then says "Through Him, with Him, and in Him, in the unity of the Holy Spirit, all glory and honor is Yours, almighty Father, for ever and ever. Amen."

The priest then leads the people in the Lord's Prayer. Following this, three prayers are said. The first is the Prayer of Peace. The second is the Agnus Dei, the Lamb of God. The third is the Haec Commixtio, the prayer said as the priest symbolically rejoins the Body and Blood of Christ as he breaks off a small piece of the consecrated Host and drops it in the chalice saying, "May this mingling of the Body and Blood of our Lord Jesus Christ bring eternal Life to us who receive it."

After private preparatory prayer, the priest raises the consecrated Host over the paten and announces to the congregation "This is the Lamb of God, Who takes away the sins of the world. Happy are those who are called to His supper." The people, reminiscent of the words of the centurion (Mt 8:8), respond, "Lord, I am not worthy to receive You, but only say the word and I shall be healed."

Now we have the intended fulfillment of the real mystery of our faith. The Father extends to His faithful members of Christ's Mystical Body the privilege to receive an infusion of Divine Life through reception of the precious living Body and Blood, Soul and Divinity of His Only-Begotten Son, and thereby offers to resurrect us from the death of sin and, through this Bread of Life, offers us the opportunity to accept the gift of developing spiritually as an adopted child of God. Thus, our reception of the Eucharist is not a passive act, not a mere ritual. It is the fulfillment of the most essential element of our Faith, the completion of our mystery of faith, begun at Baptism when we became a child of God.

Recognizing what has just taken place, it is clear that reception of this gift must be done with utmost reverence. The faithful who are in a state of grace and have abstained from food and drink for the prescribed period of time now receive the Holy Eucharist. Asking that the Body and Blood of Christ enter into their hearts, and cleanse and purify their souls, they must be in a state of grace to worthily receive the Eucharist. Receiving the Eucharist while in a state of mortal sin is like throwing the Body and Blood of our Lord on a garbage heap. This is a sacrilege and an outrage which only further removes that person from the state of grace. This is why those who are not in a state of grace must always go to confession before receiving the Eucharist, and should receive the sacrament of reconciliation often to be as pure as possible when receiving the Eucharist.

Following the dispensation of the Eucharist to the faithful, the spiritual threshold at the altar closes as the priest says the closing prayers, gives the final blessing and dismisses the congregation. In the Tridentine Mass, after the priest announces the dismissal, Ite Missa Est (Go, the Mass is ended), he returns to the gospel side of the altar and reads the beginning of the gospel of John, Jn 1:1-14, as a reaffirmation of the mystery of faith which has just taken place. He then kneels at the foot of the altar and says the prayers for the conversion of Russia. Following this, the priest leaves the sanctuary and the faithful depart.

Those who are participating in the Mass should keep all these things in mind and meditate on them before the Mass begins and during the Mass. Many live their faith as mere spectators, not participants, and often, or even habitually, arrive late and leave Mass early, sometimes leaving while our Lord is coming among His people to be received by them. We should remember that the first one who left Mass early was Judas. Let us not be imitators of that betrayer, but rather followers of our Lord. Let us leave Mass as the apostles did, following Christ. Let us participate until He, in the person of His representative the priest, leaves. Let us walk back across that threshold of His Church, His dwelling place, His Holy of Holies, changed and sanctified. Let us also pray for those who have not learned to celebrate Mass with their heart, and for those separated brethren in Christ who receive from their liturgy only the spoken word.

"The Lord of Hosts shall be a shield over them, they shall overcome sling stones and trample them underfoot; They shall drink blood like wine, till they are filled with it like libation bowls, like the corners of the altar. And the Lord, their God, shall save His people, like a flock. For they are the jewels in a crown raised aloft over His land. For what wealth is theirs, and what beauty! Grain that makes the youths flourish, and new wine, the maidens!" Zechariah 9:15-17.

"I come to gather nations of every language; they shall come and see My glory. I will set a sign among them; ... They shall bring all your brethren from all the nations as an offering to the Lord, ... just as the Israelites bring their offering to the house of the Lord in clean vessels. Some of these I will take as priests and Levites, says the Lord." Isaiah 66:18-21.

Finding Christ in Others

Sometimes we have opportunities to respond to others because of our inner freedom, but it may take some initiative. A friend of mine had such an experience. She wrote:

I am writing to share an unexpected grace from God. My neighbor, Lee, had Lou Gehrig's disease. I had only lived in my current home for one year, and had only spoken to Lee twice, both times to say hello as he was getting his mail. He was quiet, kept to himself, lived alone and had no children. The first time I spoke with him, I learned he had retired earlier in the year and was working to fix up his home. He was working in the garage attic when he fell through the ceiling and injured his spinal cord. He was slowly recovering, but he could walk, drive, etc.

When spring rolled around, we noticed his lawn getting higher and higher. His brother said Lee wasn't doing well, and just didn't seem to be recovering. I offered our help, as other neighbors did also, but he said they would take care of it. During the summer, we learned he was dying of Lou Gehrig's disease.

One day, the ambulance took him to the hospital. Lee was having trouble breathing. I knew as a Christian and neighbor, I should be visiting him, but I didn't know what to say or how to handle the situation. I really did not know this man. The two times I had spoken to him had been so brief.

As I headed to the hospital, I asked Jesus to please go with me and help me, for I didn't know what to do. I went into the gift shop and purchased flowers. Entering his room, I saw a very pitiful looking man. His eyes seeming to pop out from their sockets because his muscles had deteriorated so much. I said hello and asked if it was okay to come in. He nodded his head. I placed the flowers on the table. He could no longer speak, but communicated by writing. I could see the pain in his eyes.

Reaching out to hold his hand, I told him God loves him very much. I asked Lee if he minded that I came to visit. He wrote, "This has made my day. Absolutely!" Happiness filled my heart. We discussed the general things of life, where we had gone to school, the neighborhood, etc. I learned his sister was coming in from California that night and he asked me to give her a call. It was a very joyful experience for both of us. I stayed for about 30 minutes, and then left so he could rest. I promised to come back soon. As I left the room, I had such a feeling of joy and peace, not what I had expected. Getting into my car, I realized that I had just been with Jesus on the cross. And I had been Jesus for Lee as he had been Jesus for me. It is an experience I will never forget.

I went back to visit him that Saturday and learned he had developed pneumonia. He died the following Wednesday. My daughters still remember him in their prayers and we pray for his soul. So this man, who I knew for such a brief moment in life, has permanently changed my soul because we shared the love of God during a few brief moments. Thank you God, for this experience. "Take the love of God with you as you go."

The Triumph of Love

St Peter Julian Eymard once said, "Love cannot triumph unless it becomes the one passion of our life. Without such passion we may produce isolated acts of love; but our life is not really won over or consecrated to an ideal. Until we have a passionate love for our Lord in the most Blessed Sacrament we shall accomplish nothing."

There is a huge difference between isolated acts of love and living a life of love. In the gospel Jesus told us that even those who are wicked will do some good things, but He also said that this is of little value (Mt 7:7-11). What He calls us to is the imitation of God. He wants us to respond in love to those who seek our help in their genuine need.

This brings us to the point St. Eymard is making. When we have a passion for love, when love is the overriding influence in our life, love becomes the ideal to which we consecrate our life. If our life is consecrated to love, it is consecrated to God, and we are unfailingly led to a consecration to the most Blessed Sacrament of the Eucharist, the sacrament of love.

St. Eymard is correct in his statement that this must be the passion of our life. If the Eucharist is the passion of our life, everything else in our life comes into balance. When we have a passionate love for the Eucharist, love has triumphed in our life. When love triumphs, love governs, and when love governs we are closer to sanctity than we have ever been. If love governs our life and underlies our motivations, we enter into all the genuine relationships of our life in union with God. It is the means by which we can life a sacramental marriage. It is the means by which we can live the dedicated life of a priest. It is the means by which we live fully as a professed religious. It gives all we do a life it would not have otherwise, a life which comes from God Himself. When love governs our life, God becomes a part of all we do. Everything is done in and through Him. All our prayer, all our actions with respect to others, the way we live our marriage, the way we raise our children, all our motivations, are all done in and through Christ. He becomes the sacramental link to all we do. It is what led De Caussade to the concept of the sacramentality of the present moment. It is the foundation of the philosophy developed by Brother Lawrence of the Resurrection, and given to us in his book, The Practice of the Presence of God[83]. It is what drives us to seek good and avoid evil. It is the basis for sanctity.

---

[83]Brother Lawrence of the Resurrection, Practice of the Presence of God, ICS Publ, Washington, DC, 1997

Expressing What Love Means To You

We often have difficulty expressing what love means to us, especially love for God. To so many of us He is still distant and elusive. Even when we get close, the experience is new and hard to describe. It is interesting to see how those we know are close to God have expressed what it means to them. A few examples from the saints, saints in the making, and the Church, are:

"When you look at the Crucifix, you understand how much Jesus loved you then. When you look at the Sacred Host you understand how much Jesus loves you now."

Mother Teresa of Calcutta.

"It was love that motivated His self-emptying, that led Him to become a little lower than angels, to be subject to parents, to bow His head beneath the Baptist's hands, to endure the weakness of the flesh, and to submit to death even upon the cross."

St. Bernard.

"We adore Thee most holy Lord Jesus Christ, here in all Thy Churches, which are in the whole world, because by Thy holy cross, Thou hast redeemed the world."

St. Francis of Assisi.

"Christ underwent His passion and death freely, because of the sins of men and out of infinite love, in order that all may reach salvation. It is, therefore, the burden of the Church's preaching to proclaim the Cross of Christ as the sign of God's all-embracing love and as the fountain from which every grace flows."

Vatican Council II.

"Each time we accept to bear that cross and be nailed to it, believing against all believing - when it's impossible any longer to believe because of our pain - that's when we defeat him [Satan]. By the Blood of THE LAMB [Jesus in the Most Blessed Sacrament]."

From the novel Fr. Elijah, by Michael O'Brien.

This brings us to another issue we all must face. If we have faith, if we love Jesus, how do we approach others? In Romans (Rom 1:14-15), Paul says, "To Greeks and non-Greeks alike, to the wise and the ignorant, I am under obligation; that is why I am eager to preach the gospel also to you in Rome." Paul has expressed a point here that many shrink from considering. He has the faith, he knows the truth, and he does not see it as a matter of choice whether he shares this gift. He says to you who are ignorant, "I am under obligation." How many of us see the spread of our faith as an obligation? We use many excuses not to step up to the line. We say:

- People already have faith and belong to another religion.

Yet the truth is that many go through the motions and have little grasp of the real truth. They spend a life church hopping, trying to find what they believe is truth. With over 30,000 different denominations in the United States alone, the search for truth can lead one in circles forever, and often deteriorates into looking for what is acceptable, not for truth.

- People have a right to privacy. If they want to know, they will ask.

Yet the truth is that Jesus told us to develop those gifts He has given. Jesus has made an investment in you, and wants you to make that investment grow by investing in others, not just hoarding it. We all have a corresponding obligation to ourselves to learn as much as we can so that what we share is, in fact, the truth.

- I don't have the skills to seek out others. I am too shy.

Yet the truth is that we can share our gift in so many ways. We do not have to go door-to-door as some do. We can teach catechism, or participate in adult discussion groups. We can visit the sick or those in nursing homes. There are many ways to share our faith.

When we share our faith, in grows in us. When our faith grows in us, Jesus grows in us. We each have the opportunity to touch others every day of our lives. God is always sending us opportunities for grace, opportunities to help another, to make a difference in the life of another. These occasions are not always obvious, and sometimes we do not find out about them until later, if ever. There are many instances each day where we affect others lives and do not know.

My wife, Mary Beth, teaches high school. She had a student who was really having problems of all kinds, including drugs. He had a scruffy beard, and was always slovenly in his dress and manners. He hurt himself and spent time on crutches. But she saw something in him, a potential few were willing to recognize and develop, and she tried to help him. She tried and tried to reach him, apparently to no avail. He eventually moved on and she lost contact with him. Several years later Mary Beth was in an auto shop having some work done on her car and a young, well groomed, clean-cut mechanic walked up to her and said, "Aren't you Miss Johnson?" She replied, "I was. I'm married now. Do I know you?" He said, "You probably don't recognize me, but I'm Tom _____, and I just wanted to let you know I turned out OK. I got my act together, I finished high school,

I'm married now and we have a little girl. I just want to say thank you for all you tried to do for me when I was high school."

It is impossible to describe the feelings my wife had from the encounter and what it meant to her to see his desire to let her know that what she had done for him was not in vain. Learning you have positively touched the life of another is one of God's greatest gifts to us. He knew how hard she worked to encourage him to straighten out his life, and her support eventually had an effect.

The bottom line is that God can truly work miracles in the lives of others through us, so never give up on another person. Just remember to pray for them, and always keep in mind that it is not you doing this, but God working through you to do this good work. Give credit where credit is due.

The Vocation of Love

"Love is patient, love is kind. It is not jealous, it is not pompous, it is not inflated, it is not rude, it does not seek its own interests, it is not quick-tempered, it does not brood over injury, it does not rejoice over wrongdoing but rejoices with the truth. Love bears all things, believes all things, hopes all things, endures all things. Love never fails. If there are prophecies, they will be brought to nothing; if tongues, they will cease; if knowledge, it will be brought to nothing. So faith, hope, love remain, these three; but the greatest of these is love." (1 Corinthians 13:4-9,13)

If we accept the challenge of Paul to live life as a vocation to love, we have to look carefully to how we relate to others, for love always has an object outside of self. Look now within yourself and seek answers to the following questions. Perhaps write down the answers. Pay particular attention to the questions where you answer, "I don't know."

1. Do I have encounters or confrontations?

2. Do I speak falsely or live truth?

3. Do I clench my fist at others, or extend an open hand. Do I tighten my jaw, or smile?
4. Do I yield to the proper requests of others, or demand my own way?
5. Do I rejoice in rebellion and fighting the establishment, whatever that may be, or do I rejoice in simple truth?
6. Do I wear a false mask and feign trust, or am I willing to give others the benefit of belief in them?
7. Do I seek gratification of my every desire, or do I control this self for love of Him?

8. Do I get depressed by death and strife, or do I live in hope of eternal life?

9. Do I try to be better than everyone else in all I do, or do I prostrate before God and thank Him for all He has given me?

10. Am I part of the race to achieve worldly goals, or do I seek stillness for my soul?

11. Do I view burdens as a loss, or do I willingly embrace each gift of the cross?

12. Do I serve myself first, or do I now strive to slake His thirst?

13. Do I serve only those I am comfortable with, or do I serve those He sends into my life?

14. Is my heart a cold lump of coal, or does it burn with the fire of His love?

In Story of a Soul, St. Therese of Lisieux teaches, "I understood it was Love alone that made the Church's members act, that if Love ever became extinct, apostles would not preach the Gospel and martyrs would not shed their blood. I understood that LOVE COMPRISED ALL VOCATIONS, THAT LOVE WAS EVERYTHING, THAT IT EMBRACED ALL TIMES AND PLACES....IN A WORD, THAT IT WAS ETERNAL! Then, in the excess of my delirious joy, I cried out: O Jesus, my Love....my vocation, at last I have found it...MY VOCATION IS LOVE!"[84]

---

[84]St. Therese of Lisieux, Story of a Soul, ICS Publications, Washington DC, 2nd ed, 1976, Pg 194

Doing God's Will

Not everyone who says to Me, "Lord, Lord," will enter the kingdom of Heaven, but only the one who does the will of My Father in Heaven.

Matthew 7:21

It seems to me that with Your favor and through Your mercy I can say what St. Paul said, although not with such perfection, that I no longer live but that you, my Creator, live in me. The reason is that for some years now, insofar as I can understand, You have held me by Your hand, and I see in myself desires and resolutions - and in some way have received proof of them through experience with many things during these years - not to do anything against Your will no matter how small.

St. Teresa of Avila, The Book of Her Life, Chapter 6

Responding To The Will Of God

One of the most frequent causes of confusion among those beginning their journey toward God is the apparent wall they encounter when they decide to do God's will instead of their own. Immediately they ask, "What is God's will and how do I determine His will for me?" Often, considerable concern is given to this question and, unable to determine in advance precisely what God's will is for them, they give up in frustration. None of this quandary is necessary. The solution is not in finding what God's will is but in understanding the right question to ask. The real question is, "How do I respond to God's will?"

God does not want us to spend an inordinate amount of time trying to figure out His will, especially His will for us individually. He already told us what His will for all of us is in scripture. He gave us the ten commandments. Jesus gave us the Beatitudes and His two commandments of love. He told us to love others as He loves us. He told us to love Him and keep His word. It is all there in holy scripture. It is not a big mystery.

But God also has a will for each of us individually. It is this to which we also respond. To respond to His individual will for us takes courage, and prayer. It takes courage because it is primarily an act of submission, not an act of discovery. More correctly, as De Caussade[85] tells us, it is a self-abandonment to God's will.

In the beginning of his treatise on self-abandonment, De Caussade makes the very important point that God places before us throughout each day many, many opportunities to

---

[85]Fr. J. P. De Caussade, S.J., <u>Self-Abandonment to Divine Providence</u>, TAN Books and Publishers, Rockford, Il, 1959

live in His will. We make a choice regarding each of these. If we choose the way God wills, we grow in virtue. If we do not, we do not grow in virtue. We don't have to figure out His will because He presents it to us continuously. Each thing we encounter is God acting in our life. He sends us opportunities for patience, for purity, for courage, for all of the different virtues, including the opportunity to love. Our choices are largely choices between virtue and vice. Consider how many opportunities you have each day for truth, and how often you choose truth, or how easily you choose falsehood. Make a point to pick a typical day and note all the opportunities you have that day to make a choice between vice and virtue, even with regard to how you spend leisure or mental time. Make a note of these instances and do an examination of conscience at the end of the day to see how your choices reflect either vice or virtue.

More important, abandoning ourselves to the will of God absolutely, as He wants from us, is a willingness to accept as a grace, without question, whatever God sends us. It is epitomized in the *fiat* of Mary when she said, "Be it done to me according to your word." (Lk 1:38) She did not ask for details, she did not ask to think about it for a time. She said "yes," and in doing so accepted willingly all that came with it. That takes great courage, and great trust in God and love for God. We, as did Mary, must be willing to accept the fact that God will never do anything other than what is best for us. We accept God's will in whatever form it is manifested. In Mary's case, she accepted the glorious role as mother of Jesus, and with that acceptance she also accepted all the joy and sorrow which came with His life on earth. It is what gave her the strength to stand at the foot of the cross and watch her Son being crucified, for she knew this, too, was the will of God. She also knew that each thing we do to accept His will gives Him glory, and giving glory to God is the most important work we do on earth.

God's Loving Will

The one thing we must always keep in mind is the way God moves within our lives. Many people have an impression of God sitting up in heaven, distant, watching, remote, uninvolved in our daily lives. Nothing could be farther from the truth. God made man in His image and likeness, and He loves each of us with an infinite love. It is this infinite love which is the motivation behind everything He does in our lives. He is intimately involved in our daily happenings, even the most minute. He can do this because He is infinite and omnipotent, and He does it because He is a loving Father.

He must do His work with us almost in secret, allowing us to be largely unaware He is there. Many people could not deal with knowing God is this close, continuously, involved in their lives at such a detail level. It would either scare them or cause them to grow in pride, and neither is desired by God. So, as much as He loves us and wants us to accept Him in our lives in this intimate way, for most of us He purposefully remains obscure. It is when we study scripture carefully, and read what the saints have written, that we gain insight into God's loving will and desire to have us live in such intimate union with Him.

There is a clear relationship between our recognition of God's loving will and the trust we have in Him. In Nazareth, Mary had such a deep faith and trust in God and in His will, that she placed everything in His hands. She knew God had given her Joseph to protect her and Jesus, and she trusted completely in her spouse because God sent him to her. When Joseph said he had to take them to Egypt, she went. When Joseph said it was time to return to Israel, she came back. When the angel announced that Elizabeth was with child, Mary went immediately to help her cousin. She accepted her social condition and the other circumstances God determined for her life. She lived every moment in what De Caussade[86] calls the sacrament of the present moment. Each moment, lived in accord with God's will, becomes a sacrament received from God in that by living His will we grow in grace. Thus, we do not spend time worrying about what will happen next week or next year. Rather, we concern ourselves only with responding to what God is sending us now, at this moment.

Do these things God sends into our lives look different? Is there some way to recognize them? Do they have some kind of tag that says 'I am from God' on it? No, they don't. God uses the ordinary to accomplish the extraordinary in us. "Outwardly these events are no different from those which happen to everyone, but the interior invisible element discerned by faith is nothing less than God himself performing great works."[87]

These events are like a little treasure chest which looks very ordinary on the outside, but on the inside is filled with gifts from the treasure storehouse of God. For the most part, we only see the outside. We accept on faith the value of the contents, the reality of which we may not experience until we stand before God in His kingdom.

---

[86]Fr. J. P. De Caussade, S.J., <u>Self-Abandonment to Divine Providence</u>, TAN Books and Publishers, Rockford, Il, 1959

[87]Fr. J. P. De Caussade, S.J., <u>Self-Abandonment to Divine Providence</u>, TAN Books and Publishers, Rockford, Il, 1959, pg 5.

The Secret of Living God's Will

The secret of living in accordance with the will of God and thereby achieve sanctity is that there is no secret. There is no club that the saints belonged to which gave them the secret of God's will as part of an admission ritual. De Caussade tells us, "Do not ask me what is the secret of finding this treasure. There is no secret. This treasure is everywhere. It is offered to us at every moment and in every place. ...Divine activity floods the whole universe; it pervades all creatures; it flows over them. Wherever they are, it is there; it precedes, accompanies and follows them. We have but to allow ourselves to be carried forward on the crest of its waves."[88] Do you see how similar this statement is to the sentiment in what you previously read in Psalm 139? It is not new and mysterious. We have known this, in one way or another, for thousands of years. But have we lived it?

Holiness is the result of our living in accordance with the will of God. It sounds simple, and can be. For many, indeed for most, it does not happen because we do not abandon ourselves to God' will. We respond to His will the same way we respond to the precepts of the Church. We hear about "cafeteria Catholics" who pick and choose what they want to do, or accept, from among the teachings of the Church. This same attitude leads the self-focused person to decide which part or parts of God's will they will choose to live in accordance with. When this happens, they are not living God's will at all. They are living their own will. They are saying to God, in effect, "I will take a look at your will, and I will decide which parts I will conform to in my life. The rest I will ignore." The arrogance and pride underlying such an attitude is usually not recognized by the person so

---

[88] Ibid, pg 7

afflicted in judgment. The eyes of their soul are blinded by arrogant self-love and they walk in abject darkness.

In contrast, the soul who seeks to live God's will, and makes every effort to do so in good and informed conscience, and who, through a mistake in judgment, does not do God's will is not penalized by God. God judges the heart and looks to our intent. He knows our fallibility, fidelity, and sees our love. He will lead us in right ways to correct us and keep us from evil. If we have abandoned ourselves to His will, He will not let us down. He loves us too much.

This means we do not have to always understand God's will to do God's will. We must only do our best to conform to God's will in response to the many opportunities for grace He presents each day. It is developing the habit of asking ourselves how God wants us to respond to each thing we encounter throughout the day. If our response would be contrary to love we can usually sense that, and we know it is not His will. If it is any kind of response that is not in conformance with virtue, we know it is not His will. The more we do this, the more will doing His will become a habit, and thus we develop a habit of living virtuously. The more virtuously we live, the more we grow in sanctity. It is something any person can do, not just the learned. God designed it that way because He wants all of us with Him; all of us.

Getting There From Here

Do we wake up one day and just start doing God's will? Probably not. Jesus was born and, as a child, abandoned Himself to the will of Mary and Joseph. We know this from the gospel account when Jesus was lost in the temple. After He was found, Luke tells us, "He went down with them and came to Nazareth, and was obedient to them; and His mother kept all these things in her heart. And Jesus advanced in wisdom and age and favor before God and man."(Lk 2:51,52)

In this short passage we see many things. Jesus was obedient to them. Even though He had both human and a divine nature, He did not assert His will over and against theirs, but abandoned His will to theirs. Nothing else is known about His private life with them. During this time of His private life He "advanced in wisdom and age and favor before God." Jesus the child, the teenager, the young adult abandoned His will to those whom God had placed in His life to guide Him and teach Him. In doing so, He advanced in grace. He learned the importance of abandoning one's will to the will of God from her whom God had chosen from among all women to be conceived immaculate and to bear the only-begotten Son of God; she whose *fiat* changed the world forever; she who gave her *fiat* without question or condition.

Jesus advanced, or grew. His soul grew in grace as He continually conformed His will to that of God, His Father. By conforming His will to that of Mary and Joseph, He conformed His will to that of His Father. Later, during His public ministry, He said, "I came down from heaven not to do My own will but the will of the One Who sent Me." (Jn 6:38) There was continuous convergence between the will of Mary and Joseph and the will of God; they were not contradictory wills. Those who live in abandonment to the will of God live in His will, always conforming their will to His. The human growth for the Son of Man, Jesus, was one of focus and breadth. He was now assuming the role of Messiah, the role He had always been aware of but which awaited the proper time to assert itself into human history. He was no longer just the Son. His mission of Savior had to be fulfilled.

Jesus also said, "The One Who sent Me is with Me. He has not left Me alone, because I always do what is pleasing to Him." (Jn 8:29) This is the natural consequence of living in abandonment to God's will. Having grown in grace and wisdom in accord with God's will, Jesus, as man and God, is in continual union with God. Jesus tells us the requisite condition for this intimate relationship with God. God never leaves Him alone "because I always do what is pleasing to Him." This is also true for us because Jesus is our model and told us to imitate Him (Mt 11:29). We draw God into our lives and live continuously in His presence when we always do what is pleasing to Him, when we abandon our will to His. As we go through this growth, Jesus grows within us, within our soul (Jn 14:23), leading and guiding our interior life. As John the Baptist said of Jesus, "He must increase; I must decrease." (Jn 3:30) It is through this gradual growth in grace and wisdom gained by abandoning our will to the will of God that we grow in our relationship with God to the point where we live always in His presence. This is the essence of holiness.

The Five Signs

Spiritual progress requires that we get to know ourselves well, but as we progress we should think about ourselves very little. It is an interesting paradox. We must find a way to avoid self-focus and also know we are progressing. This is particularly important for those who are on this journey without the benefit of a spiritual director.

Father Faber[89] tells us that there are five signs to look for, but that we do not have to have all five. The more of them we have the more we are progressing.

The *first sign* is a sense of being called to something. We are not satisfied with the current state of our soul. We want to change. We want to get closer to God. We want to grow spiritually. Fr. Faber tells us this is an excellent sign of God touching our soul, provided it is not motivated by pride and provided it does not cause interior distress or dissatisfaction in our spiritual exercises. Thus, we must know ourselves well enough to recognize what is motivating these feelings. This first sign is like the beginning of the advice Jesus gave us when He said, "Ask and it will be given to you; seek and you will find; knock and the door will be opened to you. For everyone who asks, receives; and the one who seeks, finds; and to the one who knocks, the door will be opened." (Mt 7:7)

When we are discontent with ourselves spiritually, it is time to put this advice of Jesus into practice. Our discontent is God inspiring us to ask for His help to grow, and to help us seek Him on the right path. The right path is, of course, that path God wants us to take. It will be your

---

[89]Fr. Frederick Faber, D.D., Growth In Holiness, TAN Books and Publishers, Inc., Rockford, IL, 1990, pp5-8.

path, not the path of someone else. It will not be my path, your pastor's path, nor your spiritual director's path. It is the path chosen for you by the Holy Spirit and along which He wishes to lead you. Your main task is to cooperate with Him as He leads you along this path.

This is where the importance of abandoning yourself to the will of God really begins to take effect and have very practical meaning in your life. God is going to lead you along the path He has chosen for you, not along the path you may want Him to lead you. It is so crucial that you recognize this, for so many souls begin their search by fighting the will of God because they do not know better. They have a path in mind and are determined to follow it. What they should do is take each day as it comes, looking for God's will in everything and everyone coming into their life that day (Mt 6:34). It does not mean you should not make plans for your life, or invest your resources wisely, or plan for your children's education. It simply means that you look for the possibility of a spiritual reason for each thing happening in your life; there probably is. It means opening yourself to that possibility. It means not getting upset if your own plan or objective has to be changed. There is a reason, and it is a good reason. You may not understand the reason now, and may never understand, but what happens is the best thing for you in the plan God has for you.

The *second sign* Fr. Faber tells us to look for is a surprise to many. He says that we are making progress if we have many "new beginnings and fresh starts." If this happens we should not be discouraged, or think we are going in circles. The key is to look at what this new start is calling you to do. As the Holy Spirit guides you, He will be always calling you, leading you, to a higher state. Therefore, each of these new starts will likely be something that calls for more from you; more commitment to God, greater effort in prayer, greater love for neighbor, and so on. It will generally not be a lessening of spiritual effort on your part, even if it calls for less physical activity. As you get closer to God, it will take some considerable time before things get "easier," for to become what seems easier means you have progressed in prayer to a high state of contemplation and are in a state where you are very passive to God working in you. Before you get there, you have much work to do to place your various appetites under control. St. John of the Cross says we recognize it when our house is stilled. Our house is, of course, our soul, and when we control our appetites instead of them controlling us, our house is stilled. We are then ready to actively search for God Himself. We are no longer content with the signs of God, or the prophets of God. We will have reached a state where only God Himself can satisfy the longing of our soul. Before we get there, we are brought along many pathways, and move continuously to new and higher things. We come to many forks in the road and have to listen to the quiet voice of God to know which branch to take.

If we find ourselves looking for the spiritual easy chair, and think Jesus' yoke is too heavy, even though He told us that His burden is easy and His yoke is light, then our antennae should go up for it probably means Satan is trying to pull us off the road of progress. Another thing we must be sensitive to is the impact of habitual sin on our desire to grow. Our desire for change must be genuine. If it is genuine it will be, as Fr. Faber tells us, motivated principally by an intent to glorify God and will be something which leads to a renewed interior desire for God. Conversely, if we fall back as a result of habitual sin, then our task is to work, through prayer and fasting and sacrifice, for an increase in virtue in whatever area we need strength to combat our interfering habitual sinfulness.

In the case of habitual sin, we will likely experience several falls before the sin is conquered. Perseverance is essential here, and our focus must be on the end result, not on our immediate fall, whichever fall number it may be. We know we will succeed if we persevere because Jesus told us so. Seek and you will find. It takes strength, the kind of strength that comes with vision and focus and grace, to know the value of the end result, and know that the end result is worth infinitely more than anything the result of the habitual sin could possibly give, and to make the choice for God and not allow it to be a choice for repeated sin. We cannot do this on our own. We can succeed only with God's help, for Jesus has told us we can do nothing without Him (Jn 15:5), and that with God all things are possible (Mt 19:26).

The *third sign* of spiritual progress Fr. Faber suggests is to have some specific objective in view. This may seem to contradict the second sign, but it does not. In the second sign, we are looking more at paths which are sections of the overall road. This third sign is more like food which sustains us along the way. By something definite Fr. Faber means some specific current objective, such as to conquer some vice or to grow in some virtue. Ask your family, friends or work mates what to work on. Often they will agree. One of our objectives should always be to strive for habitual virtue instead of habitual sin. However, what we are discussing here in this third sign is focusing on a specific virtue.

This third sign is focused on specifics; a specific virtue, a specific spiritual malady that must be cured, and not on generalities, such as increasing in virtue in general. It may also be learning to learn to accept some particular penance or form of self-denial, such as fasting, to build spiritual strength and virtue.

If we find ourselves being called this way, over an extended period of years it may happen to us several times, each time being focused on some new specific objective we have not previously focused on and conquered. In responding to each new challenge we grow spiritually.

Why would this be a sign of spiritual progress? Beside the obvious gain in virtue and self-control which this sign calls us to, it is also an indication of the validity of our desire for God and the genuineness of our commitment to follow His call. What we are doing is not a "flash in the pan" approach, but a committed journey. We have to decide whether we want to be like the apostles, who responded in a positive way when He said, "Follow Me," or be like the people in the gospel who, when asked to follow, gave excuses of love for family or possessions, duty to care for their herds, or even the need to bury their dead. Everything but "Yes." Something else came before God.

If we desire God above all else, as Jesus said we must, we must be willing to put God first and do what is necessary to progress in our search for Him. This will not happen immediately. We will make many mistakes in our choices before our souls are sufficiently in tune with His that we choose Him almost by instinct. Do not be discouraged by mistakes. Get up and try again. Jesus fell carrying His cross, and the Cyrenian helped Him. These falls help to show us the specific places and things we have to work on to grow in virtue. Jesus will help you with His strength if you ask. To reach Him is everything. There can be no greater prize in all of heaven and earth than to possess God Himself. That is precisely what He wants for us and what He will help us achieve if we but try sincerely. He wants nothing more for us than to share as much of Himself with us as we are disposed to receive. He is the final objective, and that must be perceived by us as worth everything and anything to attain.

The *fourth sign* Fr. Faber suggests alerts us that we are making progress is a sense that God is calling us to some particular mission or task, some specific job He wants us to do for Him. Often this will be in some way related to the gifts and talents He has given us and which He wants us to use for His glory, not our own. It is no accident of fate that we were born in our particular country, that we speak a particular language, that we are of a certain height and color, and that we have the specific talents we do, whether for music or science or writing or anything else. These talents are God's gifts, given to us as we are and where we are. How are we going to use them for Him? If you feel a call, how persistent is it?

I felt a strong call to start our prayer group at church. It had over forty-five people and was growing rapidly when our previous pastor terminated the group and we had to stop meeting in church. When we moved the group to my home, we lost a few people but the group continued to meet every Saturday night. I also felt called to write this book. The call was too strong to ignore. I wrote this book while I was also writing my doctoral dissertation; something almost unheard of. I was also not worried about either. I knew this is what I was being called to do, so I plunged in and did it.

These calls or attractions may be to accomplish a task or they may be a call to work on a particular virtue or fault. Sometimes it may be a call to a particular vocation, such as marriage, the priesthood or the religious life.

Fr. Faber says that such a call to do something may occur several times in a person's life, and other people are called to do one thing for all of their life - such as a call to the priesthood. These calls seldom come out of the blue in a powerful way to one who does not already live an active prayer life. These calls, like so many other things from God, are heard when one has a habit of prayer and has learned to listen during prayer to His voice speaking to the heart. It is often a very quiet voice, even though persistent. Very few people will have a St. Paul experience and get knocked down and blinded, and then enthusiastically lead a life in conformance to the will of God. But it can happen, just as it did to Paul. With God, all things are possible.

Besides prayer, we also must have sufficient self-knowledge to be able to recognize the call as something different, something out of the ordinary. Along with the call, we must also know that the grace needed to accomplish the mission will be supplied by God. When I felt called to write this book, I had no agent and no publisher. I just knew I had to do this. It is very humbling to see how God works in these ways. I took His hand and He led.

The *fifth sign* that Fr. Faber describes is a heightened sense of a desire to be more perfect. He recognizes that it seems to contradict his previous advice to have a specific objective in view. He also cautions that this general desire cannot be left to stand alone, for it will crumble. It must somehow be embodied in some practical way consistent with this desire. He does make the point, however, that this desire is rare and is seldom seen in worldly Christians. Considering that he was born in 1814 and died in London in 1863, how much more applicable is this sentiment today.

As I began to write this, we had just finished the politically charged impeachment trial of President Clinton, the situation in Iraq had worsened, the incident at Columbine High School in Littleton, Colorado held the country spellbound, the conflict in Yugoslavia had become much worse, and tornados shattered whole neighborhoods in Oklahoma and Kansas. Since then, we have had the attacks on the World Trade Center, the Twin Towers in New York, and the attack on the Pentagon. We have had the war in Iraq, and our city streets are still filled with prostitution, pornography and drugs, leading to drive-by shootings of the innocent occurring at a frequency making them almost routine.

How many sparks of virtue do we see amidst all of this? How many sparks of heroic virtue like that we saw in the young girl at Columbine High School who gave her life rather than deny Christ. Her courage was amazing considering her age and other factors. When she died for Christ, we were one martyr closer to the requisite number we must have before Christ comes to sit in judgment (Rev 6:9-11). One can only wonder how many students there, and in schools all over the country, have developed a heightened desire to be more spiritually perfect, and have someone to help guide them in their quest, because of the heroic virtue of that one young girl? How many of their parents and other relatives have such a desire to grow spiritually? It is probably not that commonplace. We should pray every day that such a desire becomes the norm among all of God's children. "I know that you live where Satan's throne is, and yet you hold fast to My name and have not denied your faith in Me..." (Rev 2:13)

This general desire to increase in perfection is like a fly-wheel on a spiritual generator. If you lose power from the external source, the fly-wheel has enough weight and speed to supply the momentum to keep the generator going until the external power is again available. We cannot depend on this general desire as a primary source, but it keeps us going when we hit the bumps and detours in the road.

If you have this desire to increase in perfection, you will be praying and looking for ways to make it a practical reality. This fact alone is very significant, for if this is the case, then you are not lukewarm. Lukewarmness would be inconsistent with this desire to progress spiritually. One of the most pitiable states in which we can find ourselves is that of being lukewarm toward God (Rev 3:16).

The Life Of The Soul

The life of the soul, in a very real sense, is the divine will of God. It is living each day seeking to do the will of God. Jesus told us that He is the Way, the Truth and the Life (Jn 14:6). He is the life of the soul, and if He is to be the life of your soul then your soul has to be receptive to His life within you. This means we must love him and keep His word (Jn 14:23). If your soul does not have Jesus within, it has no life.

How do we recognize when our soul has life? "Amen, amen I say to you, the hour is coming and is now here when the dead will hear the voice of the Son of God, and those who hear will live." (Jn 5:25) Jesus is our source of truth and life, and with that come the responsibilities to love and to obey the will of God. If we refuse these responsibilities, we choose to reject His life within us.

This sounds harsh, but think of the people you encounter every day. Do their lives exemplify living the truth and demonstrating love for others? How many spouses want to have everything their own way? How many commit adultery? How may are unfaithful in other ways to the responsibility they have to the covenant relationship they have entered? How many situation comedies do we see on television where one spouse lies to the other or tries to be deceptive to the other in some way, and where that unfaithfulness to the covenant is portrayed as comedy? What is funny about infidelity? How many people build themselves up by putting others down, or even abuse their spouse or children physically or mentally? How many would hurt another, physically or otherwise, for some worldly gain or a promotion? How many want children, provided they are not too inconvenient? How many young people are willing to obey their parents, but only as long as it is convenient? How many adults refuse to conform their lives to what God wants, as made known by the teaching magisterium of the Church, if it interferes with worldly gain or personal convenience? What they really want is for God to belong to them, on their own terms, not to belong to God on His terms. Jesus was, as usual, very explicit on our obligation to conform to the will of God. "Whoever believes in the Son has eternal life, but whoever disobeys the Son will not see life, but the wrath of God remains upon him." (Jn 3:36) We find this same caution in Luke, expressed a little differently but the message is there nonetheless. "That servant who knew his master's will but did not make preparations nor act in accord with his will shall be beaten severely; and the servant who was ignorant of his master's will but acted in a way deserving of a severe beating shall be beaten only slightly. Much will be required of the person entrusted with much, and still more will be demanded of the person entrusted with more." (Lk 12:47-48) How much more could anyone have than what we who are Catholic have been given through the sacraments and the teaching magisterium of the Church? Thus, more is expected of us by God than from anyone else on earth.

One of the things we say in the Act of Contrition before the priest gives us absolution is that we will, "with the help of Thy grace, sin no more and avoid the near occasions of sin." We are resolving to live, as best we can, in accordance with His will. It is not an empty promise, a mere perfunctory statement. It is a resolve made to God. It is a condition of forgiveness, and therefore is said before we receive absolution, not after. We cannot do this unless the motivation behind most of our acts is love. This means we have to focus on others, not self, for it is love for God which gives real life to all the relationships in our life. It is love that allows us to live the will of God.

391

Food For The Soul

We can consider the divine will of God for us as the one necessary and sufficient food for the soul, for all else of value derives from living according to God's will. In mathematics we speak of necessary and sufficient conditions which must be present for a proposition to be true. A condition may be necessary, but not sufficient. In order to have rain, we may say that clouds are necessary, but we know that by themselves clouds are not enough. Other conditions must also be present for there to be rain. To be true, the conditions must be both necessary and sufficient. So it is with the divine will and the soul. The divine will is the nourishment, the necessary and sufficient condition that brings life to the soul. Prayer is good, but prayer not made in conformance with the will of God has no force upon God. It is the will of God which give prayer its efficacy. God's will is always and only that which is for our spiritual good. Anything else cannot be God's will for us, so all that is good, all that is of spiritual value, must be in conformance with His will for us.

When we understand this dependency of our soul on the will of God as its necessary and sufficient condition for assigning spiritual value to all we do, for being the root source of nourishment for our soul, we see things a little differently than we did before. We seek the will of God in all we do and we trust ourselves less; in fact not at all.

We usually first approach God trusting Him a little and ourselves a lot. We try to figure things out ourselves without Him. We resist responding to the things He sends us in our life. We grumble and complain, agonize over the daily decisions of life. We commiserate with others of a like mind who have the same struggle. We do not understand why things do not come out right. Then the light begins to shine.

We grow a little and begin to realize our fallibility and God's omnipotence. We also begin to understand the extent of His love for us. We begin to see His hand in what happens to us each day. Little by little we allow Him to be a part of our everyday life. We learn to reach out to take His hand in trust and ask Him to lead us. We come to Him with our pending decisions, our problems, our concerns. We ask for guidance. We grow in prayer, and look forward to our periods of prayer. Our prayer becomes very personal, an encounter just between the two of us. Not memorized prayer, but prayer from the heart asking to Jesus to be a part of our daily life, asking Him to lead us in doing His will. We lay our most intimate and secret thoughts before Him. We are growing in love and trust, and that is exactly what He wants. It also means we are seeking His will in what we do. His will is becoming the food for our soul, the necessary and sufficient condition that keeps us spiritually alive. His will is becoming our essential spiritual food. The more we place our trust in Him the more we sense this intimate union taking place between our soul and God. He is becoming the source of our life in a not so hidden way. He is out in the open, so to speak, and our soul is rejoicing in Him.

This joy of awareness has nothing to do with physical health. A good friend of ours at church has some very serious physical problems, and came close to not making it through a couple of operations. Yet she is one of the most joy filled women I have ever met. She always has a smile and is always looking for ways to help others. She spends a lot of time with our Lord before the Blessed Sacrament and she and her husband are always there for Friday Eucharistic adoration. It is a joy for others just to be around her. Interestingly enough, her name is Joy. She is truly a model of someone who has placed the will of God first in her life, and draws on His will as the source of her interior life and strength.

Listening To The Voice

If we are to live in God's will, we must have a regular prayer life and must approach Him in love. We can come to Him as our loving Father or as our Brother, Lord and Savior. We can come to Him as the Holy Spirit, the Spirit of Truth. In any way we come to God in prayer, we come before the one who loves us infinitely. In prayer we grow in grace and love and we learn to listen to the voice of God and His inspirations spoken to our heart.

I mentioned earlier how I heard a voice one day calling me to pray for someone who was depressed. This was not an audible voice, but rather a sense felt interiorly to do something in response to a feeling I knew was foreign to me. I believed it was a call to pray for someone else who was experiencing what I was feeling. I knew this was a call to do something because I was busy washing dishes and had no reason to expect God to ask me to do anything else. I also knew I had to stop what I was doing and pray for that person. This little voice was not loud, but it was clear. It was not powerful, but it was specific. There was no doubt at all in my mind about what I should do.

As we grow in prayer and in our desire to live in accordance with the will of God, we develop a sense of presence and a sensitivity to when He is sort of tapping us on the shoulder. You may start to do something when suddenly you have a clear sense, or feeling, or awareness that you should not do this or that you should do something else. Often, when we feel a pull to do something it is to do something for someone else, to reach out to another person. When we do, we find that the reason for the contact is something we never could have anticipated.

I went on a business trip to meet with an Air Force major with whom I had spoken by phone but had never met in person. She is a very outgoing person; some might describe her as strong, or even tough, in getting her job done. When I went into her office she was on the phone and I noticed a picture of Jesus on her bulletin board. It was like one I had. Something told me to ask her about it, and at the opportune moment I did. She began to tell me about her experiences and I shared some of mine with her and before long it was clear she had a deep love for Jesus and Mary and a real thirst for the "living waters" Jesus spoke about to the woman at the well. She goes to Mass as often as she can, has a family she loves very much, and loves to share with others her love for Jesus and Mary. We spent our whole lunch hour talking about God and Mary. When it was time for me to go, she said, "Now I know why God made sure we had this meeting."

It was clear to both of us why God brought us together that day. She also has a group of friends who meet once a week to talk about spiritual matters. Not too long ago, her group and some members from our prayer group all went on a pilgrimage together. We still correspond by e-mail and her love for God has grown continuously. She is looking forward to the time when she can retire and devote her full time to her growing family. God often brings the people of His family together this way. If I had not asked about the picture, we would probably never have had the opportunity to share our love for God with each other. Listening to the voice brought God's people together so that now we can share with each other and support each other.

Some people are afraid to 'let go and let God'. The idea of abandoning their will to the will of God is scary. They are afraid they will turn into some kind of automaton or spiritual zombie. One person, remembering an episode in the original Star Trek television series, said he didn't want to be part of The Body of Landrieu.

In the Old Testament, in the Book of Kings, the Israelites has a similar kind of experience. God was their king and they followed His guidance. They looked around and saw other nations with human kings and, wanting to be like them, they asked God for a king. God asked them why they wanted a human king when they had Him for their king. They said they wanted to be like other nations who had kings. It was a huge mistake for Israel, but God allowed them to have a king and with the king they also got all the attendant baggage. They had Saul, then David, then Solomon, and then things pretty much went down hill. Solomon even began worshiping idols in his old age. It didn't work, and now Israel is like other nations, with all the attendant weaknesses. Perhaps one day they will again have God as their king. I hope this does come true for them, for to be a covenant people is exceedingly important, and as Catholics we share in that covenant history of Israel.

This response of Israel was mankind once again succumbing to the twin vices of peer pressure and pride. They were no longer content to merely be the people of God, a people set apart. They wanted that, but also wanted to be like other men, and they wanted to govern themselves.

Many, in fact most, of us are like this. We want to be in control. We do not understand the value of abandoning our will to the will of God. We see it as a form of giving up, of copping out, of shirking responsibility. We do not understand what it means to live a life in complete cooperation with the omnipotent God who loves us infinitely. The mere fact that He loves us infinitely and has asked us to love Him with our whole heart, mind and soul, absolutely eliminates any possibility of giving up or shirking responsibility, all of which are generated by fear or pride. God does not want to be loved by an automaton or a kind of spiritual zombie. Love is vibrant, dynamic, alive, engaged, giving, sharing, always growing and seeking, always deepening.

When we abandon our will to that of God, we accept His choice for the direction of our life, for we know He wants only what is best for us and only that which will bring us to the highest state of spiritual perfection we can reach. That means we must remain alive and engaged and deeply involved, for much will be required of us. It is not just sitting back and mindlessly following orders. That is not love, and God wants love of the highest order. Abandoning our will to the will of God is accepting His suggestions and decisions on their face, knowing they are the best for us. Some we may understand, some we may not, but we know they are always the best. It is accepting whatever He sends to us as a good, regardless of how it looks. That is sometimes extremely hard to do.

Sometimes God sends us situations that are extremely difficult to deal with, and expects us to respond with loving acceptance. It sounds calm, even sterile, when we say this, but it takes on a life of its own when it hits home. To speak of accepting hardship in general terms is one thing, but accepting as God's will the fact that your daughter was murdered in school or on the street, or your husband is out of work and you have four children at home, or your teenage son was arrested for drug distribution, or your wife just found out she has breast cancer, or your husband died of a heart attack at thirty-five, and so on, is extremely hard.

It is at times like these that we are tested most strenuously. It takes strong faith to accept such things as God's will and not become bitter or filled with rage or desire for revenge. We are so caught up in the event and difficulties of the moment that we are often unable to lay this burden at the feet of God and ask His help to carry it. We don't want to carry any part of it. We want it to go away. And yet we must bring this to Him, for that is most probably the only way we can get through it and survive.

We always ask 'why?'. Why is it the will of God that my child is murdered? How could this possibly be the will of God? There is usually no good answer in an earthly sense acceptable at the time. It is only when we get beyond the focus on this life that we can come to grips with it properly. The reason it happened may never be made known to you. That is something you have to be ready to accept. It means God has decided you do not need to know. It might be a form of punishment so you will not have to suffer as much in Purgatory. It might be the way God chose to bring the person home now because they were in immediate danger of losing their soul. The possibilities are endless. Whatever the reason, if we accept it as the best thing for us or for the person to whom it happened, we can deal with it because we know the primary motive behind everything God does is love. It has to be so, for God cannot act with any other motive. Even His justice is an act of love.

We also have to come to grips with the fact that God has two kinds of will. He has permissive will and active will. The active will of God is that by which He specifically directs certain things. The creation was the result of the active will of God. The permissive will of God is God allowing events to unfold because He will not interfere with the gift of free will He has given man. Sometimes, this means bad things happen, sometimes to good people. God will allow a young hoodlum to engage in a drive-by shooting, even if an innocent person is killed. That young killer still has to account to God for what he or she did. Our responsibility as a Christian, and even more so as a Catholic Christian, is to pray for the conversion of that young person. If you are the relative or parent of the one killed, that can be very difficult.

We sometimes, not often, see parents whose child has just been killed publicly proclaim their forgiveness for the person who committed the crime. Those of us who have never had to experience this have no idea how hard that is, and we must understand that it is impossible without the parent's cooperation with the grace of God to accept His will in this matter. No words can describe how hard that is.

When any kind of tragedy strikes, whether natural disaster or man inflicted, if we have grown spiritually and are able to abandon our will to the will of God, we accept what has happened and immediately seek the help of God to first deal with the situation, and then ask His help to move to the next stage of our life as He wills. No matter how hard the situation, we know He will always send the graces necessary to deal with it.

One of the most difficult things about dealing with a tragedy is that we deal with it largely alone with God. Even though we may have friends or doctors or family, it is ultimately something we have to wrestle with either completely alone or with God. It can be our finest hour on earth, or our greatest failure. In this culture of death, where we look for the easy street solution to everything, if we choose suicide or assisted suicide as our solution, we choose the ultimate failure, for at that moment we gain nothing, we reject God's alternative, we die spiritually, we break the fifth Commandment, we reject the opportunity to grow in humility and self-knowledge, we reject the grace to know God better, and we deny God His ultimate dominion.

In 1996, my father-in-law was diagnosed as having contracted a particularly painful and aggressive form of cancer called signet ring carcinoma. My mother-in-law had died a few years earlier, so when he was diagnosed, my wife, Mary Beth, brought him home from the hospital to live with us. There was no question in either of our minds that this is where he would come. As we expected, he was concerned about being a burden and said he wanted to go to a nursing home, but Mary Beth would not consider that and we soon dispelled any concern he had about being a burden. Events of the next several days soon overcame any other consideration.

My wife quit her job teaching at our parish school so that she could care for him full time. The disease progressed rapidly. Hospice visited regularly and supplied pain medication, but the medication was largely ineffective.

My father-in-law was not Catholic and had not been much of a church going person. In fact, he had been raised in an anti-Catholic environment. His faith was not particularly evident to others except that he always said grace before meals. He was a very big, strong, and quiet man, a former first string lineman in football, and very self-sufficient. His nickname was Tank. Now he was dependent, and growing more dependent each day. We were sensitive to this, and he took it well, recognizing there was no real alternative. My wife spent every day in his room with him caring for him, and many nights as well. She wanted to help him through his periodic times of extreme pain and to be there if he needed anything. She saw first hand how much he suffered and she wanted to do what she could to help. He could not hide his suffering from her, so she shared it with him, and they both grew. She saw a side of him she never knew existed. In many ways, she grew closer to her dad during this time than she ever had been in her life. Many times, when the pain became unbearable, he would break into spontaneous prayer of the heart for a half hour or more as a way to control the pain.

When other relatives came over, he would put on a good front for their benefit, and then release when they left. His self control was incredible. My wife's brother had no idea what Tank was enduring, even though my wife told him, because words were simply inadequate to describe it. Two days before Tank died, my brother-in-law learned first hand what she meant when he came over for a visit and Tank had one of his bouts with severe pain.

A few days before he died, my wife overheard Tank praying. He said, "Lord, I've done everything you asked me to do. I've forgiven ....", and he proceeded to give a list of names and other information, and then listed other things he had apparently been asked to do. Then he asked, "Why am I still here?"

A few days later my wife and I were praying near a statue of the Blessed Mother holding baby Jesus, and asked Blessed Mother to come get her child and bring him home. The next day Tank and my wife were talking. Suddenly he said he saw a woman standing nearby and asked who she was. My wife, thinking he may be hallucinating, asked if he was afraid and if he wanted her to make them go away. He said, "No, she's beautiful, and she has a little boy with her." He died the next morning.

Although Tank died about a month after he came to live with us, Mary Beth saw a side of her father she never knew existed. She saw a depth of spirituality that completely surprised her. Two days before he died he called all the family together to say goodbye. Then he told them, "No matter what, always trust God. He always knows what is best." When Tank died, he and Mary Beth were alone. He was having a convulsion spell, and he died in her arms.

These short few weeks were a very hard time for Mary Beth, but she would not trade them for anything. She learned so much about her dad and his real strength, and about herself and her strength. Our children, Nathan and Daniel, nine and eight years old at the time, also shared in their grandfather's final spiritual journey, spending time with him each day first thing after school and in the evenings. They loved him very much. When Tank died, Nathan and Daniel had the opportunity to tell him goodbye before they took him away. They had the chance to say goodbye in the setting which had been his home for the last few weeks. Afterward, Nathan said, "He was very strong." Mary Beth replied, "Yes, he was a big man." Nathan said, "No mom, I mean he was very spiritual strong."

The Spirituality of Suffering

The growth toward perfect love is a mystery which connects consecration to suffering, and both to the will of God. When we consecrate ourselves to God and to Mary, and really mean it, we offer all of ourselves to God, without condition, without holding back, and ask Mary to help us be faithful to this consecration. If a priest really lives his consecrated life of a priest, he lives a life dedicated to the Love of God, and to Love as it is intended to exist in all men. It is a life dedicated to being a shepherd, bringing those who walk away from God back onto the path toward God; a life dedicated to helping those who are already on the path toward God to expand their enlightenment of that path by recognizing the love of God in themselves and in others.

This is a sometimes delicate and distancing task since a priest, in the process of bringing someone back to God, cannot ever allow himself to lose his own anchor. He needs to always remain firmly rooted in God's love and anchored to his own path toward God. Therefore, he is always reaching out to others, seeking out the lost, encouraging them to turn toward God, reaching out a helping hand to others to join him on that journey toward God, but always by saying, with Christ, "Come, follow me.", never by saying "I'll stop my journey for a while and try to save you in the process." He needs to seek out the lost sheep, extend a helping hand while he himself moves forward, encouraging them to follow him and return to the flock; but he must never stop leading the flock himself. He cannot shirk this good shepherd responsibility by claiming to merely pray for his lost flock and expect Jesus to do everything else. He must go after them just as Christ ordered; just as Christ Himself did. He has to know his sheep, and they have to know him.

To accomplish this takes a very special consecration because of the ways available to a priest to bring the living Christ directly into a person through operation of the sacraments; specifically the Eucharist and Reconciliation.

Every sacrament gives sanctifying grace. That is the nature of a sacrament. Sacraments give us the grace necessary to have the strength to do something or to live a certain way in the future that helps us in our divinizing process. They are the source of grace and strength for the soul to face what is to come, as well as the instrument of transformation through the operation of the Holy Spirit. But two sacraments available to both laity and religious, the Eucharist and Reconciliation, go beyond that common character. Both are actually focused on the Eucharist. They provide grace to personally accept the new Covenant and to avoid sin in the future, but they also involve something over and above pure sacramental grace. They provide something quite unique and immediate, and something which requires that we, while individually receiving them, play an intimate and active part then and there at the moment of reception.

Neither sacrament is merely receptive on our part. It is through these two sacraments that I am able to experience the most complete and immediate union with Christ. It is through these two sacraments that I am truly able to live a life Through Him, With Him, and In Him, and to reach and fulfill that goal initiated at Baptism. It is through these two sacraments that I can, in a special way, share in the divinity of Christ as He shared our humanity. It is through the Eucharist, where the living Jesus Christ gives me His all - Body and Blood, Soul and Divinity, where He is completely consumed by me, that I am able to share in His life, in His divinity. It is through this sacrament that I am in Him and He is in me (Jn 17:23); where I pray that He will bring me into Himself and transform me. The Eucharist is the gift of His perfect love, the total giving of Himself, and through His Eucharist I grow in love for God, which is to become more perfect myself by sharing in His divinity, through participation, in conformance with His will for me. It is through these two sacraments that the priest shares that extraordinary privilege of standing in the Person of Christ Himself, of being *in persona Christi,* as he absolves the penitent sinner or says the words of Consecration during Mass.

Consider the huge mistake of Adam and Eve. They sought the source of sharing in God's divinity, but in a perverse and self-defeating manner, for their objective was not really to share in God's Divinity, but rather to achieve a separate and independent divinity of their own, thus making themselves independent from God, from Love. They sought this from an other external source instead of recognizing it as taking place within themselves and accepting this gift of love from God; instead of trusting in God and recognizing that the true and only source of divinization is the perfect Love which is God.

The ability to give the Eucharistic gift to men is an incredible privilege, one reserved to a priest, and dependent on that special consecration of his person when he is ordained. Likewise, the sacrament of reconciliation is offered to those who may not be able to accept love as they should, or have rejected God's love to some degree. They have placed themselves in a condition where they are separated from God to some extent and their ability to accept the love of God must be restored. They are made able to accept the Eucharist and to participate with God in His divinization of the soul through an immediate and present volitional act on their part. Not only do they receive the grace needed for future spiritual strength, but their soul is also enhanced or restored because of the immediacy of God's act of perfect Mercy, His perfect forgiveness, combined with their contrition and resolution to avoid sin.

Through the sacrament of reconciliation, Jesus forgives, He gives the actual grace to avoid sin in the future, and restores the capability of the soul to receive His love and to partake in His divinization through the Eucharist. It is a sacrament that Christ has given us so that we can now, this moment, accept His love, because of His forgiveness and absolution, even when our contrition is less than perfect and, because of our weakness, may be initially motivated more by fear than anything else. It is the only way in the gospels that Jesus specifically provided for the forgiveness of the sins of men (Mt 16:18-19; Jn 20:23). Through these two sacraments God pours out His love continuously for us before He is compelled to exercise His divine justice.

The other half of the spiritual coin is suffering. When we are able to accept our cross and offer it to Jesus to unite our suffering to His, as He called us to do in the gospel (Mt 11:29-30), we are necessarily offering our suffering in reparation for the sins of all men, because that is why Christ, to whose suffering we unite our suffering, also suffered. He suffered for no other purpose. His was a reparative redemption. When we ask Jesus to accept our suffering and unite it to His, we share, in a limited way, in His same reparative act. Our suffering now has the same purpose His did, and thus, because of His love for us, He allows us to participate in His redemption of mankind. If His suffering only had one purpose, ours joined to His must share in that same single purpose. This is a privilege we are offered by our loving Lord, not something to which we are entitled by right. Suffering, when offered to Jesus, and through our prayer united to His suffering, becomes a divine act allowed us by Jesus. Whether stubbing our toe or dealing with a major disease, it is not the magnitude of our suffering that is important, but rather whether we offer it to Jesus to be used by Him for His intention. We seldom understand the magnitude of this privilege. Christina Gallagher, a stigmatist in Ireland, once said that every time someone converts, it is because someone suffered for them.

Our suffering must therefore be a loving and selfless giving of ourselves to Jesus, a dying to ourselves for the love of God. In doing so we become more perfect because our love becomes less self-interested and thus more perfect. We more closely approach the goal Jesus gave us to be perfect as the Father is perfect (Mt 5:48). It is a call to perfectly imitate God, who is Love. "Come to me, all you who labor and are burdened, and I will give you rest. Take my yoke upon you and learn from me, for I am meek and humble of heart; and you will find rest for yourselves. For my yoke is easy, and my burden light." (Mt 11:28-30) It is a self-less love; it gives without seeking reward; it is unconditional because we don't know individually for whom we suffer; but we know they are all members of, or candidates for inclusion in, our Mystical Body. Our suffering becomes more perfect because it is united to and becomes a part of that perfect Love who is Christ, and because we are part of that Mystical Body whose head is Christ.

We do not do this alone. Jesus was always very careful about the words He used. He had a beautiful economy of words, always saying the perfect thing as simply as possible. Jesus asks us to accept His yoke, not His bridle or harness. A yoke is made for two oxen to pull a load together. It is often tailored to precisely fit the oxen, because oxen come in a variety of sizes and shapes, so they can pull with the least amount of discomfort. When Jesus asks us to accept His yoke, a yoke He tailored for us Himself, it is because He is the one there with us, pulling with us, taking the heavier part of the burden upon Himself.

St. Paul gives us further insight into this mystery of The Mystical Body. "As a body is one though it has many parts, and all the parts of the body, though many, are one body, so also Christ. For in one Spirit we were all baptized into one body, whether Jews or Greeks, slaves or free persons, and we were all given to drink of one Spirit. Now the body is not a single part, but many. ... But as it is, there

406

are many parts, yet one body. ... But God has so constructed the body as to give greater honor to a part that is without it, so that there may be no division in the body, but that the parts may have the same concern for one another. If (one) part suffers, all the parts suffer with it; if one part is honored, all the parts share its joy. Now you are Christ's body, and individually parts of it. ... Strive eagerly for the greatest spiritual gifts." (1 Cor 12:12-31)

Christ is the head of the Mystical Body and we are the members. It is one entity, one Body, and therefore all parts of the Body must in some way share a common nature. People don't have a human head and eagle's wings and a lion's body. All parts are human, even if the several parts are different in purpose and function and activity from the head. Likewise, the Mystical Body must have a common nature in all of its many parts. That nature must be derived from and imparted by God. The head of a body cannot have a nature different from the members. This Mystical Body is also unique. There are not two Mystical Bodies. There is only one. Jesus is the head and we, those of us on earth and those who are in purgatory or in Heaven, are the members. When we are injured (sin), God has to heal us by restoring our participating nature through the sacrament of reconciliation. If we die in mortal sin, we are cut from the body and cast away (Jn 15:6).

To be a part of this Mystical Body we must necessarily go through some process of divinization, partaking in the nature and life of Christ, and He must do this for us for we have not the ability to do this for ourselves. Arintero[90] tells us this happens through the effect of sanctifying grace received from the sacraments. The extent to which this divinization takes place is a function of the degree to which we seek Christ and try to become perfect in

---

[90]Arintero, Fr. John G. O.P., The Mystical Evolution, TAN Books and Publishers, Rockford, 1978.

Him, by conforming ourselves to Him so He can mold us and make us what He wants us to be. This means that the Church, The Mystical Body of Christ, is for us truly a family; the family of God, a family of all those - on earth, in Purgatory or in heaven - who partake in the divinity of Christ; a family of members, all of whom love each other and are able to say with conviction, "Our Father."

With specific regard to suffering, we can see from the excerpt of St. Paul's first letter to the Corinthians, above, how Christ allows us to partake in the continuing suffering of the Mystical Body of Christ. When a part of a physical body is injured, it is the head which communicates the suffering to the body, and the body sympathizes with the part which is hurt. It is also the head which to some degree controls the level of pain felt and the kind of healing process initiated. So too, Christ can say in the gospel that we should take up our cross because His yoke is easy and His burden is light (Mt 11:30).

Jesus can control the degree to which we suffer, and provides all the grace we need to allow us to bear this suffering. He shares this burden with us because we pull our burden by uniting with His yoke. Thus Arintero[91] says, "Therefore all those new organs through which Christ acts and suffers what He could not suffer in His own Person are properly His body and His fullness, for it is He who acts and suffers in them so far as they are Christians. Hence, [the sufferer] completed in his flesh whatever was wanting to the suffering of Christ, and he did this for the good of the Church."

This co-suffering is intimately connected to our participation in the reality of the Mystical Body. Christ could only suffer that which He was able to suffer within the confining limits of His human body. He suffered as much as

---

[91]ibid, p 158.

it was possible to suffer with that body, and certainly suffered enough since even the smallest suffering on His part would have been enough. However, in creating His Mystical Body, with Him as the head and us as the members, we are truly a part of His body and are sharing in His divine nature. Through this Mystical Body, Christ continues His redemptive suffering through our suffering. If the finger is injured, the body suffers the pain. The suffering affects all of our body, including the head.

If we lose a loved one or suffer some other emotional distress, the entire body suffers. The loss of a spouse or a child is excruciating. It tears at the very fiber of our being. We feel as if we have been ripped apart, that something vital to our being has been torn from us. This is how Mary felt when Jesus was crucified, so when we suffer this way we should have particular devotion to Mary and seek her help. However, as strange as it may sound, if the person we have lost had a close relationship with God, we can also experience this loss with a certain joy for that loved one. Consider these three scriptures.

"But to those who did accept him he gave power to become children of God, to those who believe in his name, who were born not by natural generation nor by human choice nor by a man's decision but of God." John 1:12-13

"Beloved, we are God's children now; what we shall be has not yet been revealed. We do know that when it is revealed we shall be like him, for we shall see him as he is." 1 John 3:2

"Amen, I say to you, among those born of women there has been none greater than John the Baptist; yet the least in the kingdom of heaven is greater than he." Matthew 11:11

The one we have lost we knew as a child of God, just as we are God's children. But in heaven, even if they are the least in the kingdom of heaven, they are greater than any person who has ever lived on earth; greater than Abraham, Isaac, Jacob or Moses. They are exalted above all of mankind. They stand before the throne of God and see Him as He is. If they are our spouse or child, we are the spouse or parent of a saint, even if not officially declared such by the Church. We must feel great joy for them, and rejoice in knowing they stand before God praying for us, preparing for the day we join them when we enter heaven, and then we will be reunited with them as we, too, share in the glory of heaven. That, alone, should give us the incentive to lead a life of grace so that we look forward with anticipation to our reunification.

If the one we have lost is our child, the loss is especially painful for it is also unnatural. Children are supposed to bury parents, not the other way around. Our loss is particularly acute because of this, but our faith can lead us to understand we, by cooperating with God in bringing new life into the world, have also given Him a new saint. We have given Him as much as we can give; the product of our love, the love of our life, flesh of our flesh.

But, when we suffer as a member of the Mystical Body, all the other members share in that suffering, and that suffering allows Christ, as head of the Mystical Body, to continue to suffer for us, and through us, in reparation for the sins of men. Our suffering, as we cope with this loss, will be the instrument of salvation for someone we may never know during our earthly life. But the soul saved by our suffering is a soul dearly loved by God, and one with whom we will have a special relationship in heaven.

This is what St. Paul was speaking of in 1 Cor 12:12-31. Therefore, if, when we suffer, we unite that suffering to the suffering of Christ and offer it to Him to be a part of His redemptive suffering for the sins of men, we are giving Christ the opportunity to suffer more for us and in so doing

He allows us, through our suffering, to share not only His divine nature, but the continuing act of redemption and reparation itself. He gives us the privilege, through our suffering offered to Him, to participate in His work of redemption because He has given us His nature through the sanctifying grace communicated to us through the Holy Spirit and has made us part of His Mystical Body.

However, it takes a volitional act on our part to bring the full fruits of this suffering to bear. We need to willingly offer up our suffering to Christ for Him to unite it to His own. If we do not freely offer our suffering to Him, as Jesus freely gave His in reparation for us, then the suffering remains only suffering, our suffering. It has no spiritual value. It never becomes anything but misery, and in that it is wasted on self pity instead of salvation for souls. Instead of being a source of our sanctification, it remains only our misery. But if we offer our suffering to Him, it becomes His suffering also, and that of the entire Mystical Body, and likewise becomes an instrument of reparation and redemption. What a resounding privilege!

When we unite our suffering to that of Christ, we are walking along the road to Calvary with Him, joined to His yoke as His partner in redemption rather than as part of the jeering crowd, and this is a privilege whose value is beyond our comprehension. It requires our willingness, and our trust, for He told us He would never give us a cross without the corresponding grace to be able to endure it. It is up to us to accept it as a redemption-participative cross, His gift with the grace attached, or endure it simply as an unwanted infringement on our physical and emotional freedom. We can accept it as His gift, or as a curse.

In some cases, throughout history, He has chosen certain souls and has asked them to be His victim souls, for He needed them at that time in history. These were people like Padre Pio, St. Francis of Assisi, Theresa Neuman, Little

Rose Ferron, and, in our time, people like Maria Esperanza and Christina Gallagher, and others. He has given these souls special suffering, the grace of bearing His wounds, but with this gift came extraordinary graces. St. Francis, before he became the first to receive the stigmata, prayed to feel in his soul and in his body the pain suffered by our Lord during His passion, and in his soul the love for mankind our Lord felt which enabled Him to undergo His Passion.

These are not your everyday souls, but for those of us who are "everyday", Jesus still allows us to participate in His redemption of mankind, if we are willing and accepting of what He sends us. How we receive it is entirely up to us. Whether it is only pain, or partaking in the redemption of mankind, is up to us. That the choice is up to us is the result of another of His many gifts, the gift of free will. Through our free will, our suffering becomes either mere pain or Divine privilege.

All these trials that we may beg God to take away (yes, I can keep begging Him to take them away) but meanwhile are accepting and offering them up to God, are the purest gift we can give to God. It is our version of, "Father, let this cup pass from Me; but not My will, but Yours, be done." (Mt 26:39) Even if it takes us to the point of feeling complete abandonment, we accept His will. We trust without understanding the reasons, knowing that His will is the best thing possible for us even if we don't understand how that could possibly be, and may never understand during this life. The one thing we must always keep in the forefront of our consciousness is that God is Love, pure Love, and He cannot do anything but love us, and anything He does for us or to us or with us has to be an act of divine love. We can always trust that to be true, no matter how difficult times may get. And, thus, we join trust with active submission to His will. It's a mighty and powerful combination.

This is how we find the real spiritual value of trust; when we encounter suffering. No matter how hard, no matter how dismal or abandoned you feel, you submit because you love and trust Him without question, and therefore you put into action your certitude of the goodness of our heavenly Father. We do this just as Abraham did when he was asked to sacrifice his son, long before mankind knew very much about God.

Suffering draws you out of yourself. You did not ask for it. If borne well, the energy it takes to suffer (think how tired you get) is prayer if we only let it be. We must surrender ourselves to that loving Energy that seems to sap us, for we are telling God, "Take me. Use me. Into your hands I commend myself." We need to accept it as we would accept Holy Communion.

In your state of helplessness, don't you reach all the more purely up to the Divine because of your complete trust in Him? Sufferers in their weakened state can prove to be the most active agents in the very process that seems to be sacrificing and breaking them. There is a grand task to fulfill, that of participative co-redeemer.

Sufferers are by nature and temperament driven out of themselves. They are compelled to depart from the prevailing forms of life. If we encounter suffering, our human tendency is to try to get away from it. If it is just suffering, we retreat inside ourselves, fill ourselves with self-pity or rage or whatever, and allow the physical effect to overwhelm us, for it is the suffering itself we focus on. The suffering thus has no spiritual value. We try to escape it any way we can. Some even choose suicide, for they fail to see the spiritual value of suffering. The only way to avoid this is to live as a child of God, conforming our will to His, and understand the spiritual value of being a member of the Mystical Body.

If we offer our suffering to God, and ask Him to join it to His, we are uniting ourselves to God spiritually with our gift of suffering, for the suffering becomes a way we give ourselves to God. Any gift goes from us, the giver, to the receiver, God. God will accept our suffering and may or may not alleviate it, and may send us more of the same or even one which is new and different. But if we keep giving, we are also in a continual state of uniting ourselves with God, and asking Him to embrace and comfort our soul. This He will always do, even if we are not conscious of it at all.

Any gift we give Him in love will be rewarded a hundred fold in love. He took His own suffering and turned it into the most glorious event in the history of creation. We need to trust Him to receive our suffering as glorifying Him, and use it for our own sanctifying glorification in Heaven. What happens here on Earth is incidental; what we receive in Heaven, and the level of sanctity we can attain through the suffering, is worth anything we endure. But it is up to us to make the conscious decision, the free will offering, to accept the suffering and offer it to Jesus as our gift to Him. It takes such great love, trust and abandonment to do this, and that is what He is looking for from us. It is our test, our fruit of the tree in the garden, to show we belong to Him, no matter what.

Complete Abandonment

One of the lessons De Caussade gives us is "God's constant care leads Him to give us each instant what is suited to us."[92] If we recognize this, we can abandon our will completely to the will of God with the firm assurance that God will provide for us every thing we need to live in Him. Therefore, in one sense, the book of our life is a documentary of the extent to which we have accepted the guidance of God in each of the events of our everyday life. If we try to live without Him, we are telling ourselves and Him that we know best.

It goes against many of our natural inclinations to submit our will to the will of God, to look for His hand in everything, to listen for His voice before we make the choices we do. We are trained from birth to be self-sufficient, to make our own way in the world, to "take on the day" as the expression goes. We are told it is our world to make of it what we will, to "do it my way".

Every generation tells the previous generation that the world is messed up and now it has to be straightened out. In truth, the only one who can straighten it out is God. God has made it so very simple to do this, and yet we find it so difficult to fight the world and stand with Him. Simple, but not easy.

What does the world tell us? "It is a cruel, dog eat dog world out there. Watch your back at all times. Money is power and freedom. Power is the key to survival. My individual rights supercede everything. If it feels good, do it. If I do something wrong, it is society's fault. If I want

---

[92]Fr. J. P. De Caussade, S.J., Self-Abandonment to Divine Providence, TAN Books and Publishers, Rockford, Il, 1959, pg 19.

something, I take it. If I have a troubled childhood, I can be excused for almost anything. Responsibility for my actions is for others, not me. I do not have to pay attention to God, and if I want, I have a perfect right to worship Satan." We seldom see anything that extols virtue or supports the value of a real family as the proper environment for raising children. Going to church is done out of obligation, to be entertained, or for "show."

When we look at the value system of the world, where do we find the simple commandments of God? We not only do not see Him placed first, we see society and the courts trying to eradicate Him from our public life, from our social consciousness. We are so very far removed from the time when mankind, or at least the part to which we claim a spiritual heritage, said, "We are a chosen people of God," and were proud of it.

We must regain that sense of belonging to God, of being His people, of being in His image and likeness. We must live like we believe it. We must change the way we think, individually and as a society, but it must happen one person at a time. We must look at our legal right to do what is wrong, and say, "No. I choose to do what is right." What are we proud of? Is it being a person revered by the world, or is it being a child of God and a member of His Mystical Body? When we think of who we are, what do we see? Do we see a person who lives in accord with God's will? Do we have His peace within? What is most important to us? Do I believe in God's constant care for me? What are the three most important things I should change in my life?

Without faith God is like vapor to us; something that wisps around in our consciousness but has no real substance. It is through faith that we gain the certitude that God is real and alive and concerned and interested in us as individuals, and that He loves us infinitely. It is through faith that we are able to interpret the things that God sends into our lives each day and through which we are presented the opportunity to live in His will. When we live a life of faith, love and hope, it is our prescription for sanctity.

When, through faith, we see things as God-sent and not just random happenings, we look for our own proper purpose and response, and we find that also in faith. Faith allows us to find the extraordinary within the ordinary, order amidst disorder. We also grow in love, in response to God's love for us. We cannot live in faith and respond to His love with anything which is not love.

Once we realize this, we must also recognize that to respond any way other than in accord with His will is to respond in a way that is not truth. He is truth. The Holy Spirit, the Spirit of Truth, will inspire us to act in only one way, and that is in accord with God's will. In considering responses to a given situation, if we consider which actions are in accord with God's will, the list narrows considerably. We must respond in a virtuous way, not contrary to love for God, and which incorporates a love for our neighbor at least equal to our love for ourselves. When we find that response, we have found the will of God.

Faith is illuminating. Very few of us choose evil deliberately, except for Satan worshipers and the rituals they conduct, so Satan must present things to us as something good and desirable. When faith illuminates the eyes of the soul, the soul is able to see through the deception offered by Satan because the soul is illuminated by the Holy Spirit, the Spirit of Truth. The Holy Spirit communicates to our soul the light of divine guidance, the light of Christ who is the light of the world. It is through this light, given to us in response to faith, that we can see the true value of each thing as it comes to us each day. It is through this light that we see the spiritual value of each thing we encounter, and can make our choices accordingly.

Through faith we believe in God, and therefore believe in His love, His goodness, and His omnipotence. Faith gives us courage to make hard choices, even those by which we become a martyr. Without faith this could not be done. Without faith the true value of martyrdom could not be realized and embraced.

I suspect that not many of us will be called to make this ultimate choice. Regardless of the extremity of the decision, we must make choices each day and must do so looking through the eyes of faith, through the eyes of the soul. The world sees martyrdom as folly, and assisted suicide as a good. The world see immorality as good, and virtue as foolish. The world sees love of others as misguided, and complete focus on self as the ideal. Worldly views are the complete opposite of the view we have if we truly believe that we are temples of God. Could anyone who truly believes his or her body is a temple of God fill that same body with junk, such as illegal drugs and other pollutants, or use their body for immoral purposes? We must live each day asking which alternatives are proper if we are a temple of God.

When God, in His wisdom, sends into our lives people or events to which we must respond, it is often difficult to see what He wants us to see unless we look with the eyes of faith. It is by looking at all things with the eyes of faith that we can respond to the inspiration of the Holy Spirit the way He wants us to respond.

There is a beautiful story, which I believe is true, about an incident which happened in Mother Teresa's home for the dying in Calcutta. A fashion model felt called to go to India to help Mother Teresa for a time. It was the way she wanted to repay God for the many blessings He had given her.

One day Mother Teresa was busy and asked the young woman to bathe a man unable to care for himself. The model went to the man, looked at him, and walked away. He was completely filthy, covered with sores, starving, skin and bones, and this young woman who was completely unaccustomed to such a sight could not bring herself to touch him. She asked what else she could do, and Mother repeated her request. The young woman could not, and Mother Teresa left what she was doing and gave the man a bath herself.

Later, the young woman, ashamed of herself and trying to come to grips with what had happened, asked Mother Teresa how she could touch that man who was so full of sores and dirt. Mother Teresa turned to the young woman and said, "I didn't give a man a bath. I gave Jesus a bath." Mother Teresa saw Jesus in everyone she encountered. Mother Teresa lived, in the most literal sense imaginable, what Jesus told us when He said that whatever we do for the least among us, we do also for Him. To Mother Teresa, everyone in need was Jesus. Her objective for these dying men and women was to make sure that they died clean, fed, and knowing that they were loved by at least her nuns.

The lesson the young model learned that day is one we all must learn. When we encounter another person we cannot pass judgment on them immediately, as we are so inclined to do. If someone does not stand favorably in our comparative gaze, we often consider that they are inferior and beneath our dignity. If they are higher in social status, and that usually means richer or more powerful, then we pay them due homage or look on them with envy. That is not the way of God. We have our dignity as a human being from only one source; the fact that God loves us.

Since God loves us all, we have no call to consider His love for another any less than His love for us. Because God loves others just as much as He loves us, then we owe respect to others for that sole reason, even if for no other. If we look back in history, we see numerous examples of people considered somehow less than others because of their economic status, color, or social class. That is not God's way and not how we will see others if we look at them with the eyes of faith. The poor beggar who goes to heaven will be on the same par as any king or president who also goes to heaven. The least in the kingdom of heaven is greater than any man ever born of woman, save Jesus. Jesus said we will always have the poor with us, and we will have the physically or mentally infirm, the sufferers of disease, and the like. They are all deserving of our love. What acts of love can I do today? What acts of love will I do today?

St. Peter taught us that we may sometimes respond heroically to extraordinary circumstances. In the garden, Peter was immediately ready to fight to save Jesus. He probably would have given his life for Jesus right there in Gethsemane. But later that night, when Peter sought anonymity among the people in the crowd, he was afraid and denied Christ three times. What happened to his the courage?

For most of us, it is in the ordinary routine of daily life that we will find our courageous sanctity, for it takes courage to do the loving thing, the right thing. Once in a while an ordinary, untrained citizen is called to heroism, usually in response to an emergency. Sometimes people do very extraordinary things in these circumstances. Some even have jobs that are exciting, or provide them with opportunities to do extraordinary things, or help others in many ways. But for the majority, our lives are filled with the ordinary, not the extraordinary. We travel the highways commuting to work during rush hour, which for many is usually more than an hour and anything but a rush. For many, our work is routine and we look forward to retirement. Our job is not much more than a means to a paycheck. We may look back on a week in the office and wonder what of real value was accomplished.

The ways we respond to our various duties and vocations are all opportunities for sanctity. Throughout each day, if we look for them, God will send us events and people and circumstances, each of which is designed to evoke a response from us in conformance with His will. Each time we act selfishly, we fail that call to virtue. Each time we act without love, we fail to answer our call to virtue. Each time we turn our head or look the other way when someone needs help, we fail in virtue.

Children seem to instinctively act out of love. That they do not in later years is a condemnation of how they are treated by the world. Jesus said we must be as little children in our dealings with Him. Children are open, trusting and loving by nature. They have to learn to be otherwise. We have so very many opportunities each day to respond to God's will as a child in dealing with other people, with love and trust.

Little things are always there in front of us. A dropped object we could pick up for someone; a book we could bring back to the office library for someone; a kind word about or to someone; an unkind word left unsaid; a beggar who needs a meal, and so on. It doesn't take much time, and in most cases not much effort. What is does take is caring.

Sometimes it is harder to live than to die. A friend of ours developed a serious medical problem and he could not work. His wife is the sole support of the family. After a year, she lost her job. Then they had an automobile accident and lost the use of their car for a time. Then their son, newly married, had an accident and lost his job. Then the wife's sister, who had not been to church in several years, was diagnosed with cancer. It seemed it would never let up.

Through it all, things progressed and life went on. The wife got a better job. The husband was operated on and returned to health, and to work. The sister, one week before she died, asked for a priest. She confessed, was anointed, and received the last rites. Through all these trials, the family never lost faith, never stopped praying, and offered all they endured to God.

It is through these kinds of responses to the ordinary things in our lives that God calls each of us to sanctity.

God Gives. Why Ask?

Someone once asked, "If God operates as He will, and if He will always give me only what is in accord with His will, why should I ask for anything in prayer?" This question goes to the heart of the relationship between man and God. Jesus told us many times in the gospel to go to the Father in prayer and ask for what we want. The one specific thing He did tell us to request is the gift of the Holy Spirit (Lk 11:13). We may ask for many things that are not good for us, as does any child. Parents often tell children they cannot have something requested because they know it will not be good for the child. It is the same with us in our prayer to God.

Our prayer of petition has another aspect which has nothing to do with what is specifically requested. By approaching God as our loving Father, we acknowledge our dependence on Him. Jesus teaches us to do this in several places, such as in Mt 6:25-34. Jesus combined a lesson on prayer of petition and living in God's will. He said do not bother God about your material needs if you have not yet sought your spiritual needs. We are instructed to first seek the Kingdom of God (Mt 6:33), and then seek the other things. Seek our spiritual needs first, and God will provide the rest of what we need. Focus on the relationship first, then the material needs.

Part of our prayer of petition, then, is to ask that God's will be accomplished in us regardless of what that might entail. We ask first for the grace to be His faithful child and for the Holy Spirit to come to us and sanctify our soul. We ask for the gift of enlightenment to understand His will and for the gift of fortitude to do His will. This is the kind of loving trust in Him God wants us to have.

In this same passage Matthew 6:33, Jesus also introduces us to the concept of the sacrament of the present moment, which is so powerfully developed in the writings of De Caussade. Jesus tells us not to worry about tomorrow, for there is enough evil right here, right now, trying to divert us away from seeking the Kingdom. Anyone seeking God can expect to be attacked by Satan, for capturing souls is the only way Satan can attack God. It is the only weapon Satan has. By placing ourselves in God's hands and seeking His will in all things, we cooperate with God in rendering Satan impotent.

Does all this mean we should not ask God for favors? Not at all. When we do ask, we should ask for whatever we desire, and at the end add, "In this and in all things, may Your holy will be done." One beautiful example of this is in the life of Blessed Margaret of Castello. She was born with many, many physical afflictions. At the request of her parents, she prayed for a healing, but at the end of her prayer she always added, "if it be your will." Her life story is beautiful and should be made widely known, especially among the young. She is one of the truly beautiful young saints of the Church.

God's Creative Will

When we consider God's divine will for us, which is always motivated by love, and our loving response to His will, we are mindful of a marvelous dynamic. Love is never static. True love is always dynamic, seeking, sharing, giving, and always looking the best for another. It is never self-focused. Even more marvelous, love increases the more it is shared, the more it is given. It is one of the few things we have that expands as it empties itself. It is self-generating, and the more creative we are in finding ways to give holy love the more love we have to give. The quickest way for love to die in the soul is to not love others.

God's love is not only infinite, it is also creative. When we act through His love, ours is also creative. A marvelous example of this creative expansion of love in the soul is seen in the life of Elizabeth LeSeur, born October 16, 1866, who documented her journey in a diary not found until after her death on May 3, 1914. Her diary was published as the book My Spirit Rejoices[93]. In this book you find a continuous outpouring of love for her husband, Felix, and for God. Felix loved Elizabeth very much, even though he derided her constantly, even in front of their friends, because of her love for God. He loved her, but was an atheist and could not abide her love for God, thinking it was ridiculous. He thought that by ridiculing her love for God she would eventually turn away from God and join Felix in his atheistic beliefs.

She prayed for Felix every day, and kept a journal of her love for God and for him. After her death at a fairly young age due to illness, Felix found her journal. Her writing

---

[93]Elisabeth LeSeur, My Spirit Rejoices, Sophia Institute Press, Manchester, New Hampshire, 1996.

moved him so deeply that not only did he convert, he became a priest and spent the rest of his life spreading the gift of her journal.

In this beautiful love story, we see God's will at work continuously, and we also see the dynamic of revelation of God's love. Elizabeth, loving God deeply, but not having anyone with whom she could discuss her love for God, recorded her love in her diary. Elizabeth, loving Felix deeply in spite of his atheism, offered her prayer and her life for him daily. Finally we see the net effect of her love manifested so profoundly in her husband when he read her diary. Through her love and her commitment to God and to her vocation as a wife, and her inspiration to record her love in her diary, God revealed Himself to Felix in the most powerful way He could, and thus God gained two souls instead of one, plus all those souls who have been moved to conversion or deeper conversion by her book. It was not through an intellectual analysis of theological principles that God revealed Himself to Felix, but rather through the revelation of love given and recorded in his wife's diary.

We must never take God and His love for granted, and never become complacent in our expressions of true love for God and for others. Real love is the most precious gift we have next to receiving the completeness of God Himself, for when we have love we necessarily have God. When we give real love to others, we are always doing God's will, and by giving His love to others we increase our own capacity for His love, and for doing His will. We expand the opportunities for God to reveal Himself to us.

Revelation is God revealing Himself to man. Public revelation is the revelation we find in scripture and in apostolic tradition. Public revelation ended with the death of the last apostle. But God, because of His great love for man whom He made in His own image and likeness, must maintain a dynamic relationship of love with man, as we see in Elizabeth LeSeur's diary. This means He must keep sharing His love, and therefore Himself, with each of us individually in a continuing revelation of Himself. This individual, private revelation is communicated to us in many ways, but most clearly through the communication of His will, and His inspiration in us to live in His will.

God's individual revelation is a revelation of love, not a revelation of mere words. It is not something He expects us to only tell the world about, or record for posterity, but rather something He wants us to live. His love is for each of us individually and is promulgated by the way we live and the way we respond to others. The full depths of His love may not be made explicitly known to us in a way that can be described, and may not be known to us fully until we are with Him in heaven, for then we will see Him as He is and will be one with Him. This communication of Himself to the soul because of His love for us is a communication of union, a communication of consummation.

Just as the Word of God is continually being generated within us, He is continually revealing Himself to the soul by His communication of love. Any like response we return to Him is immediately responded to by Him with an even greater outpouring of love to us. Every time we respond to Jesus with love, it is an open door for Him to share more of Himself with us.

This continuous revelation of love within our soul, and our response to that love, is shaping the 'dwelling place' He is preparing for us in His kingdom (Jn 14:1-3). The dwelling place is necessarily reflective of our relationship with Him, and therefore necessarily reflective of the love which flows between us and Him, and expressed in our love for each other. Your dwelling place is individual, unique, and like no other dwelling place in heaven. It stands as a monument to the response you have given to His love. It is determined by the depth of your love, not your time on earth.

One who found God only a short time before his or her death could develop a very deep love for God, and that is what God sees. The eternal God is not impressed with years but with love, for love is timeless. It is the one virtue which survives our bodily death.

In our prayer, in our response to liturgy, in our response to the Eucharist, we should keep always before us the dynamic of this relationship we have with God, this unique relationship, and we should pray that our response to His love will be what He wills, so that our dwelling place will be what He desires to build for us. Our response to His love is like the size of the spiritual mortgage we can afford. The more we love Him, the more fully we respond to His love, the bigger the mortgage we can carry, and the more beautiful our eternal dwelling will be.

The Beauty Of God's Will

The love of God is wondrous, and the manifestation of His will in His work among us is incomprehensibly beautiful. God must exercise His will in our life without interfering with our free will, without taking away our ability to choose or reject His will. God is infallible, omnipotent, and is motivated by pure and infinite love for each of us individually. That combination is what we have working for us night and day and each moment throughout the day, continuously urging us toward heaven. That is what we reject when we choose not to do His will.

The mind of man cannot comprehend the love God has for us, nor can it comprehend the extent to which God will go to help us choose His will. We often lose sight of the desire God has that each of us become saints. It is only our rejection of His will which prevents this from happening.

If you look at your life, consider the various happenings or people God has presented to you, and consider what it took for that to happen. I know a man who is several years older than his wife. They came from different states, went to different schools, and had virtually no chance of ever meeting, especially not on a social level. He was in college when she was born. He was from the deep South and was working in Texas when he first moved to her south-eastern coastal state, and actually lived not far from where she lived, but then she was only ten years old. Soon thereafter, he moved to the west coast. Several years later, he moved back to the east coast. She had moved to another county, and he now moved to that same county. He had three children from a first marriage that had been annulled. In the meantime she had become a high school teacher. Two of his children had her for home room, but he had still not met her. They did eventually meet by chance at a picnic given by a mutual friend. She paid him no attention, thinking he was married.

Later, because of a business concern she had, and on account of which she sought his advice during lunch, they learned more about each other. They began dating and he, a Catholic, found out she considered herself an atheist. In spite of this, and trusting in God, he proposed. They married in the Catholic Church one year after they met. Ten years and two children later, she was baptized, confirmed, received her first Eucharist, and they renewed their wedding vows, at a special Mass said for them by Fr. Steve Collins, a good friend of the family who had worked with her to prepare her for entry into the Church. After the Mass she turned to Fr. Collins, tears of joy streaming down her face, and said, "You didn't prepare me for how unworthy I would feel."

She is still the light of her husband's life, and always will be. Not long after she entered the Church, the older son of the husband entered the seminary and is now a priest. One day someone asked the husband why it took so long for his wife to convert. He said he loved her too much to push, she was far to brilliant to be pushed, and there was no way she could have that much love in her unless the Holy Spirit was hard at work, so he let the Holy Spirit bring her along at His own pace. All during the time they were dating, and every week after they married, she always went to Mass with him. When asked why, given what she thought she believed, she said she would rather be there with him than somewhere else without him.

There is no way I can look at this story without being in awe before the incomprehensible beauty of God's will bringing these two together, each needing the other, and both needing God. There are thousands of similar stories of His love. I know this particular story so well because it is the story of me and my wife, Mary Beth.

The Loving Will Of The Divine Spouse

When we consider the way God guides us toward the path of sanctity through the events and people we encounter daily, we must view these things and our response to them as opportunities for response between spouses. God does want us to be His spouse, He does want to be the Bridegroom of our soul. He does want us to respond to His gifts as gifts from one who loves us infinitely.

God gave us the model of marriage when He established His very first covenant as the covenant of marriage between Adam and Eve, and thus set in motion His divine will in establishing the model for how we should respond to Him. If we think of the perfect spousal relationship, we see a glimmer of how God wants us to consider the relationship between Himself and our soul. To see this, we have to move away from the physical and focus on the spiritual, on the movement of the will that is the seat of all acts of love. Love is giving and generous, not demanding and selfish. Paul gives us the characteristics of true love in 1 Cor 13:4-13. Among these characteristics is that one who loves rejoices with the truth. We also see that love never fails. When you read Paul's description of love, meditate on your relationship with God and then recognize all of the characteristics Paul lists as being of infinite degree in God and all of them directed at you by God as He pours out His love to you.

This divine action of God toward us is so very important, for only God can sanctify us. He could simply sanctify us without our consent, but it would not mean that much to either us or to Him. Therefore, He has chosen to direct His action toward us in such a way that it evokes a response from us. That makes it a relationship, not an action of control. He acts and we must respond. We act, perhaps through prayer, and he responds. Back and forth, back and forth, for all the days of our life, and the more we respond to Him the closer He will draw us into Himself and the more He will share of Himself with us. In this way He becomes the true Bridegroom of our soul. We become one with Him, with the Holy Trinity, by being consecrated in His truth (Jn 17:17-23).

When we look at His action in our life, we can sometimes see Him courting us, courting His future bride. He seeks union between His Spirit and our soul, He seeks for us a oneness with Himself in the Trinity. He encourages us to pursue Him until He captures us, captures our heart. Our responses to the gifts He sends us throughout our life, and the way we participate with Him in our prayer, all determine whether and how far along the path we move from acquaintance to betrothal to spiritual union. He will not make us His spouse, but He will encourage us and give us every opportunity to make that choice.

In seeking to satisfy God's will, His true bride will take His hand to respond to all that comes before the soul each day. The spiritual dimension of the day's events will be sought regularly until it becomes a habit. The soul will find contentment with what God sends, not looking at, or caring about, what is sent to other souls.

Some souls have a problem with curiosity. Curiosity tends to make you focus on other's gifts instead of your own, to focus on how others respond instead of how you should respond to your own gifts. Sometimes we see a soul envious of the gifts given to others. The only proper way we should ever respond to the gifts of others is with gratitude, for the gifts they receive are those they need to gain perfection, and the ones you receive are the perfect gifts you need to attain the perfection God desires in you. Any other gift would not be as good for you as the one you have.

Regardless of how it might look, the gift someone else receives could lead you away from perfection, or to a lesser level of perfection, than the gift you do receive. How do you know? Because of two things. God is infallible and He loves you infinitely. He cannot make a mistake and His love for you would never let Him give you less than He could give you unless you force Him to give you less by your rejection of His first choice. It is only by focusing on self instead of on God that we reject His choice of gifts for us.

Thus, the true bride of Christ will always accept the gifts of God without question, without challenge, and with great thanks, knowing that this gift, regardless of how it might appear to the world or regardless of how others might respond to your receiving this gift, is the best possible gift for you at this time and will bring a greater degree of sanctity to your soul than any other gift you could receive right now.

It takes a long time for a soul to reach the state where it can accept some of God's gifts in this spirit. That is why God will usually take a soul through the states of knowing Him and loving Him before asking it to accept certain gifts. Some gifts can only be accepted in the right way when one loves very deeply. The soul who is a true bride of Christ will accept each of these gifts, whether easy or difficult, as another jewel in the wedding ring God is placing on its finger. It will accept these gifts with simplicity, without curiosity and in complete trust in God's love. This soul will also know that God is showering it with grace with each gift it accepts, even if it does not sense the presence of the grace. It also knows that all of the grace needed to accept and properly respond comes with every gift. The true bride of Christ always says, "Yes, my Lord. May your will be done."

Fear Not, It Is I

Some of the more compelling passages of the gospels are those where Jesus tells the apostles, "Fear not. It is I." In Isaiah, Chapter 41, three different times God tells His people, through the prophet, to "fear not." Fear not, for I will help you, He says. Isaiah repeats this same theme in Chapter 43. In Daniel 10:19, He says, "O man greatly beloved, fear not, peace be with you; be strong and of good courage." But in Mt 14:27, Jesus says, "It is I. Be not afraid." He does not say, as He did in Isaiah and Daniel, "I will help you." He simply says, "It is I. Be not afraid." Their security rests simply in His presence among them. A motto of the Holy Father, John Paul II, used on the book jacket of Crossing The Threshold Of Hope[94], is *Be Not Afraid*.

Is there a relationship between *Be Not Afraid* and abandonment of one's will to the providence of God? I believe there is. When we abandon our will to the will of God, we submit completely to Him, accepting all that comes into our life as coming from Him, and therefore trusting in Him that nothing of what He sends is spiritually harmful. We are also relying on His great love for us as well as His omnipotence. This combination of His love and His omnipotence is, for us, a kind of spiritual blanket that protects us from evil once we have given ourselves to Him this completely.

A good example is St. Padre Pio. St. Padre Pio gave his will completely to God, and accepted all as coming from God. For a period of time, the devils would come to his cell at night when he was tired from a long, sixteen hour day of hearing confessions, and would physically attack him,

---

[94]John Paul II, Crossing The Threshold of Hope, Alfred A. Knopf, New York, 1994

beating him unmercifully, trying to get Him to do their will and reject God. In spite of this treatment, St. Padre Pio never was defeated. He remained a spiritual bulwark for all to see and imitate. God allowed this because he knew He would give St. Padre Pio all the strength needed to remain with God and not give in to the attacks of Satan. These attacks were quite ferocious, often drawing blood. But St. Padre Pio remained in the hands of God throughout and became an example for us, an example chosen by God. St. Padre Pio also made it evident to the devil that his actions were futile. Eventually, the devil gave up and the attacks ceased.

The vast majority of us will never have to do this kind of battle with the forces of evil, nor will we be asked to bear the stigmata for 50 years, as St. Padre Pio did. Each of us will be asked by God, in the way most beneficial to us, to serve Him according to His will for us. The examples of the saints are given to us so that we might serve God without fear, knowing He is with us, in us, loving us.

Every day there is a Mass broadcast from Mother Angelica's monastery over the EWTN network. One day a visiting priest was giving the homily and said, "The will of God is the greatest pursuit of humankind." A simple statement but profound in its implications. He said this the same day there was a shooting at the high school in Conyers, Georgia and it was the one month anniversary of the shooting incident at Columbine High School in Littleton, Colorado. What a contrast his statement made with the statement conveyed by these two incidents of children shooting children. It just shows how far we still have to go to even begin the pursuit this good priest was encouraging us to undertake.

Forgiveness and Examen

Forgiving others - which is doing the will of God, and examen, a term which means our examination of our own conscience, are intimately connected. Some people go to confession and never do much preparation. They mention a few things in passing, have little or no real resolve to avoid sin or the near occasion of sin in the future, and seldom mention the times they have failed to forgive. Confession is a marvelous instrument of grace and strength, a source of riches that God uses to help us as we struggle with forgiveness. We pray asking God to forgive us as we forgive others. Since we come to confession asking forgiveness for ourselves, we should be likewise willing to forgive.

What follows are some aids for making a good confession. They are approaches to an examination of conscience, often called an examen, which have been provided by different people on the internet. They are offered here for your assistance.

Someone asked: "Can anyone help me develop a fairly complete examination of conscience? Is there anyone who has developed a personal checklist or process? Something that can help me get past the obvious?"

Note the wisdom in this request. She seeks help to get past the obvious. Some suggestions given to her by the list members are:

1. See what the new Catechism says on the subject of examination of conscience.

2. Go through each of the 10 Commandments, and see how you might be failing to live these, not so much in the literal sense, but in a more complete sense. If, for

example, you look at the 6th Commandment, instead of focusing only on the act of adultery in its literal sense, you might think about all the ways a married couple could endanger the marriage, things which thus might eventually lead to an act of adultery. For example, in what ways have you failed to show love, forgiveness, acts of kindness, trust, or compassion? How have you failed to show support of all kinds - emotional, spiritual, physical, and the like? Do you lie to your spouse or to your children, thus breaking down trust?

When examining our conscience before confession, we can employ a number of means. One is to use the ten commandments as a base for the examination.

First Commandment example:

Do you place other things before God; not just idols but also money, power, things, self? How much of yourself to you give to them?

Keeping holy the Lord's day: How do you do this?

You may go to Mass on Sunday, but how much of you is there?

Is your heart there?

Do you tell God you love Him?

Do you participate in the Mass?

Do you pray for others there?

Do you come late or leave early?

Have you tried to learn everything you can about the Eucharist so you can more fully participate?

If you consider the two commandments of Jesus: love God fully and love your neighbor as yourself - how do you do this?

How have you failed to do this?

Do you love others as Jesus loved you?

Do you forgive others?

How do you know you forgive?

Is there anyone whom you need to forgive but have not yet forgiven? If so, why?

What opportunities did I have to show love for God and failed to take advantage of these opportunities? Same thing for love of others.

Pray the Lord's Prayer: Pray each phrase slowly, and, as you say it, what are you asking of the Father?

Do you live your life as if you believe what you pray for; as if you really want what you pray for?

How have you shown love toward others?

How have you shown love to someone you really don't like?

St. John says if we have no love for our neighbor, we cannot have love for God. Do you think you profess love for God but know you hate your neighbor? Ask for help through confession to resolve this.

What habitual sins do you have?

What are the occasions of those habitual sins?

What do you do to avoid those occasions?

What should you do to avoid those occasions?

Are you really contrite?

Do you really intend to avoid sin in the future?

If not, what are you placing ahead of God that is preventing you?

Why are you choosing sin instead of God?

The way an adult does an examination of conscience is quite different from what a child might do. What follows is an adult examen also founded on the ten commandments, found in scripture in Exodus 20:2-17 and Deuteronomy 5:6-21.

We will begin by looking at the first three commandments. Paraphrased, these are (1) To worship no God but our God, (2) To refrain from using the Lord's name in vain, and (3) To keep holy the Lord's day.

Prayer Before Confession

O Lord, grant me light to see myself as You see me and the grace to be truly and efficaciously contrite for my sins. O Mary, help me to make a good confession.

Preliminary

During the beginning of any examen, consider the nature of your sins. Recollect, as far as possible, the number of times you have committed them. Recollect also those circumstances, including motivation, which contribute to the sin, or which make a sinful act even more serious. Do I have habitual serious sin? Have I been guilty of irreverence for this sacrament of reconciliation by failing to examine my conscience carefully, or have I failed to perform the penance given by the confessor or disobeyed any of his directions? Have I neglected my duty to the Church or violated the precepts of the Church?

First Commandment

1. Am I ignorant of my basic catechism (Act of Contrition, Apostle's Creed, Ten Commandments, Seven Sacraments, the Our Father)?

2. Have I willfully received communion in any non-Catholic worship, or participated in a service in a way which gives scandal to the Catholic Church?

3. Am I a member of any anti-Catholic or secret society forbidden by the Church?

4. Have I knowingly read with approval any anti-Catholic literature?

5. Have I practiced any superstitions (horoscopes, fortune tellers, etc.)?

Second Commandment

1. Have I used God's name in vain by way of profanity?

2. Have I murmured or complained against God (blasphemy)?

3. Have I publicly and without evidence maligned priests or others consecrated to God?

4. Have I sworn by God's name (oath) either falsely or rashly?

5. Have I broken any private vow?

Third Commandment

1. Have I missed Mass on Sundays or holy days through my own fault?

2. Have I been late for Mass through my own negligence?

3. Have I been inattentive at Mass or otherwise failed in reverence for the most Blessed Sacrament?

4. Have I done unnecessary servile work (physical labor) or unnecessary shopping on Sunday?

5. Have I eaten meat on Good Friday or on Ash Wednesday, or otherwise failed to perform required acts of penance and mortification?

Fourth commandment: Honor your father and mother

1. Have I been disrespectful to my parents or neglected them?

2. Have I failed in obedience or reverence to others in authority?

3. Have I mistreated my spouse or children?

4. Have I been disobedient or disrespectful to my husband?

5. Regarding my children:

   – Have I neglected their material needs?

   – Have I failed to provide for their early baptism or their proper religious instruction?

   – Have I allowed my children to neglect their religious duties?

   – Have I tolerated their keeping questionable company or allowed them to go steady dating when they are too young?

   – Have I otherwise failed to discipline them?

   – Have I given them bad example?

   – Have I let boys and girls beyond a reasonable age sleep together?

Fifth, eighth, sixth and ninth commandments.

Fifth & Eighth Commandments: Do not kill; do not bear false witness against your neighbor

1. Have I quarreled with any one?

2. Have I cursed anyone or otherwise wished evil on him?

3. Have I taken pleasure in anyone's misfortune?

4. Is there anyone to whom I refuse to speak or be reconciled?

5. Have I lied about anyone (calumny)?

6. Have I rashly judged anyone as being guilty of a serious sin?

7. Have I engaged in gossip (detraction) or spread scandal?

8. Have I lent an ear to scandal about my neighbor when the information was of no concern to me or my family?

9. Have I been jealous or envious of anyone?

Sixth & Ninth: Do not commit adultery; do no covet your neighbor's wife.

1. Have I denied my spouse his or her marriage rights to a reasonable and loving sexual relationship?

2. Have I practiced birth control?

3. Have I abused my marriage rights in any other way, such as demanding forms of intercourse which are distasteful to my spouse or contrary to nature?

4. Have I committed adultery or fornication?

5. Have I touched or embraced someone other than my spouse impurely?

6. Have I sinned with others of the same sex?

7. Have I committed masturbation or otherwise sinned impurely with myself?

8. Have I harbored lustful desires for anyone?

9. Have I willfully indulged in or entertained other impure thoughts?

10. Have I knowingly failed to dress modestly?

11. Have I done anything to provoke or occasion impure thoughts in others?

12. Have I read indecent literature or looked at indecent pictures?

13. Have I watched suggestive films or programs because of their indecent content?

14. Have I permitted my children or others under my charge to do these things?

15. Have I used indecent language or told indecent stories?

16. Have I willingly listened to such stories?

17. Have I boasted of my sins?

18. Have I sinned against chastity in any other way?

Seventh and Tenth Commandments, and some final examen points.

Seventh & Tenth Commandments: You shall not steal; you shall not covet your neighbor's goods.

1. Have I stolen anything, including from my employer?

2. Have I damaged anyone's property through my own fault?

3. Have I cheated or defrauded others?

4. Have I refused or neglected to pay any debts?

5. Have I neglected my duties or been slothful in my work?

6. Have I refused or neglected to help anyone in urgent necessity?

7. Have I failed to make restitution after depriving another of their property?

Other Sins

1. Have I knowingly caused others to sin?

2. Have I cooperated in the sins of others?

3. Have I sinned by gluttony which, like lust, seeks only immediate sensory gratification?

4. Have I consumed alcohol beyond legal limit for driving and lost full control of my will or senses?

5. Have I used illegal narcotics, or abused the use of legal narcotics?

6. Have I been motivated by avarice, which is an inordinate desire for possessions?

7. Have I indulged in boasting or vainglory, which is doing good works for the glory they bring me, not God?

8. Have I received Holy Communion or another sacrament in the state of mortal sin?

9. Is there any other sin I need to confess?

Prayer for a Good Confession

O my Father, by my grievous sins I have re-crucified your divine Son to myself and have deserved your everlasting wrath in the fires of hell. Even more, I have been most ungrateful to you, heavenly Father, by my sins, you who have created me out of nothing, redeemed me by your Son, and sanctified me in the sacraments by your Holy Spirit. But you have spared me to make this confession. Receive me back as your prodigal child and grant me to confess myself well, that I may begin anew to love you with my whole heart and soul, henceforth keeping your commandments and suffering patiently whatever temporal punishment for my sins may remain. I hope by your goodness and power to obtain everlasting life in paradise. Through Christ our Lord. Amen.

Let us now take a slightly different view, and consider how we might prepare for a face-to-face meeting with our confessor. We should discuss serious sins, but also seek guidance in handling imperfections. Some imperfections may become serious sins later if not dealt with now. Driving 70 miles per hour in a 65 mile per hour zone may be an imperfection, but doing 100 miles per hour would be a serious sin. Lists are helpful, but they also tend to generalize or seem too rigid. In examining this list, some things are always serious sins and others may be imperfections. Consider whether, in you, a given item is an imperfection or a serious sin.

Consider:

How long since my last confession?

Have I committed any mortal sins? (These must be confessed by type and number. A mortal sin involves serious matter, full consent of the will, and awareness that the act is seriously sinful.)

Have I, or have I been:

- Missed Mass on Sunday or Holy Day of obligation without serious reason
- Received the Eucharist while in state of serious sin
- Committed impure acts alone or had sexual contact with another outside of marriage
- Engaged in heavy petting or other acts that placed myself or another in danger of committing adultery or fornication, including homosexual acts (gay or lesbian)
- Practiced contraception
- Had an abortion, participated in one, or paid for one for someone else or promoted abortion rights (by donation, volunteer work or other means)
- Abusive to self or anyone else; physically, verbally, or by drugs
- Withheld a mortal sin in confession
- Consumed alcohol to excess or ate to excess

- Refused to help the poor or needy who had a legitimate need
- Lied, cheated or stole any item
- Used the Lord's name in vain purposely, or cursed; used foul language
- Been selfish, proud, intolerant, overly aggressive
- Spoke unkindly to others or about others (gossip), or told harmful truths about another without just reason
- Excessively critical of others or deliberately angered another
- Unreasonably angry or refused to forgive another
- Failed to trust in God's forgiveness
- Dressed immodestly or provocatively
- Late for Mass or left early, or was irreverent in church
- Disrespectful of parents or superiors
- Failed to fulfill duties of one's state in life
- Given scandal, especially to children
- Watched entertainment or read books promoting immoral sex or violence
- Driven too fast or carelessly
- Failed to pray or failed to put God first

What Is Forgiveness?

The reason I keep coming back to this question is that it is so very important, and because forgiveness is one of the hardest things to accomplish well on a practical level. The hurt is still there, especially if the injury was occasioned by a breach of trust. That is why adultery is so devastating to a marriage. No matter how contrite the offending party might be, the breach of trust is shattering to the relationship.

Forgiveness is always associated with a relationship between two people, or between a person and God. When there remains a lack of trust, or a continued - possibly extreme - dislike, how does one forgive? Fr. Robert DeGrandis wrote several books on spiritual healing, and in one of them he said we can know we have forgiven the other person when we can honestly pray for their conversion and/or salvation.

That is an interesting thought, for Jesus on the cross said, "Father, forgive them." He did not say "I trust them again" or "I still trust Judas," nor did He say "It's OK, I like them now." He said simply, "Father, forgive them, for they know not what they do."

For God, forgiveness is purely a question of wiping out the eternal effects of sin in order to allow the person a continued opportunity for eternal life. It is an act of love and mercy. His love and mercy for all mankind compelled Him to sacrifice Himself for us all, even after He asked the Father, "Let this cup pass from Me." He accepted the will of the Father, put aside His expressed desire, and still said, "Forgive them." If He had not, we would not have been saved.

In imitation of Him, it therefore seems that true forgiveness is to sincerely pray for the salvation of that other, even to the point of making the ultimate sacrifice if necessary to accomplish that. Their soul is as valuable to God as ours, so it should be to us. We could never do this without the assistance of our Lord, for it is an act rooted in Divine love, not feeble human love and weakness. Real forgiveness is an act of Divine cooperation. We cannot do it on our own.

Isn't this what St. Maria Goretti did? As the assailant was stabbing her, she cried out "I forgive you." That led to her canonization and was enough to put into play the events that caused the complete conversion of her assailant. Her family also forgave him. He became a close friend of the Goretti family and stood with them at Maria's canonization.

Living Our Lives Through Christ

There is only one true adoration and service of God on earth and that is Christ's; there is only one true life on earth, and that is Christ's; there is only one vital good being done on earth, and that is the work of Christ. Our only hope of serving God, praying to God, or living for God, is to enter into that life and work of Christ - or as St. Paul says - to put on Christ, and we do that by doing the will of God for the love of God.[95]

Doing God's will means living our life in Christ by living the truth of the Mystical Body. What does it mean for us to be the branches of the vine who is Christ? We need to free ourselves from thinking of the boundaries of space and time that so dominate our individual mortal lives, and recognize first of all that the Mystical Body is not restricted by time or space. Christ is the head, and the members of the Mystical Body are the members as much now as they were 1,500 years ago, and will be in the future. We live the spiritual life of the Mystical Body through Christ, who is the ever-present, eternal, Only Begotten Son of God.

Consider St. Margaret of Castello, the daughter of nobility. She was born blind, hunchbacked, physically ugly and lame. She was rejected and abandoned by her own parents and for many years lived the life of a beggar. But she had a marvelously beautiful soul. She never lost her love for God and prayed for her parents every day of her life. She loved everyone she met and eventually became a Dominican. In spite of her appearance, she was loved by the people because of her love for them.

---

[95]Boylan, Dom M. Eugene, O.C.S.O., This Tremendous Lover, (Westminster: Christian Classics, Inc., 1989), pg 91.

We read the life of St. Margaret of Castello, a few pages at a time, after dinner each night, before leaving the table. My children were spellbound, and still speak of her to this day. She is a model of love, and a model of how we share in the Mystical Body of Christ. Her parents rejected her, but God sent a great deal of love into her life to fill the void left by her parents. She is, to me, one of the greatest saints of the Church.

It is Christ Who must make this kind of living the life of love a reality for us, for we can not do this for ourselves. The most important thing which could ever happen to us must happen to us by and through Christ. We merely cooperate through our conformance to His will for us. This is the real secret. We accept and conform, and Christ does the rest.

God's plan is that we each live forever with Him in heaven. He has one plan, and He has a unique implementation of that plan for each of us. Every time we deviate from His plan, He offers us the way back through the sacraments. The life of this plan is His love. It is a life whose vitality comes from love, finds expression through mercy and allows us to share in His life. It is the greatest gift we can possibly imagine, yet so many refuse this gift. They live, and die, in darkness, and thus spend eternity in darkness.

God's will is our sanctification. By conforming to His will, we live the life of the Mystical Body through which we share in the good works of all the members who have ever lived and who will ever live. The good we do is always the fruit of those things done in conformance to the will of God, for nothing else can be spiritual food for this Mystical Body. When we sin, we reject the operation of grace, but God's will is still there. "We can be sure that by doing the will of God we are bringing forth Christ in our soul, and entering into a still closer union with His Mystical Body. ...

that is the way we make ourselves perfect members of the Body of Christ and find our life in Him."[96]

Sometimes we get upset with ourselves when we do something and it does not turn out well. We undertake some task and offer the merits to God. We do this for love of God, and it turns out lousy. The cake falls, we get off-key when we have a solo to sing, we study hard and fail the test, we counsel someone who is suicidal and they commit suicide anyway, we do something other than what we hoped for, and we feel we have failed God since we offered this work to Him. We might especially feel this when we pray for the conversion of someone and they resist strenuously and appear to go in just the opposite direction.

It is the love with which we do the task, not the perfection of the activity, that is important to God. It is offering God our acts through obedience to His will that makes the act worthy, and the more perfectly our will is conformed to His, the more perfectly we are identified with Christ acting in us, so that we live our life through Christ.

Does a parent care how well an infant performs a task, or does the parent encourage the infant to try, and reward the infant with praise and hugs for making the attempt because that is what the parent asked of them? We know that if our children try enough, they will eventually succeed. So it is with God. If we continually try to live our life in conformance with His will, the more we try the more perfectly we will succeed. This is what He asks. It is our conformance to His will, doing what we do for love of Him, that unites us to the entire Mystical Body.

Christ is the vine, the only vine. His is the Mystical Body, the only Mystical Body. We have life in and from Him, or we have no life at all. We have been given the

---

[96]ibid, pg 89.

freedom by God to make the choice. We must choose for there is no middle ground; no grey area of indecision. This becomes more true every day. God already made His choice. We can live our lives through Christ, or we can live in eternal darkness. There is no middle ground, no compromise. Either Christ grows in us, or we die. We are the ground onto which His seed has been cast. We can strangle His life by our rebellion, or we can accept His life by our humility and obedience in imitating Christ.

The effect of self-will is sin and everlasting death. The effect of conforming our will to that of God is sanctification. These are our only options. It is up to us to make the choice, to decide to live His Life *in every moment*. We should live our life, *in every moment*, in preparation for our last moment. In the final analysis, the only thing that will ever really matter for us is the relationship we have with God at the moment we die, for at that moment choice ceases and time to repent has passed: eternal Life or eternal darkness hangs in the balance.

Spirituality and God's Will

We often seek God's will because we are trying to lead a spiritual life and want to remain close to Him. We look for road maps in the lives of the saints and others, and look for confirming signs that our present path is the right path. There are many examples of real folks seeking helpful advice on how to grow spiritually from those who are on the journey with them. Some of our guides are the saints, and others are the people we know and associate with daily. It is very helpful to be in a group where some people are farther along the path than you are, so you can grow from their example, experience, and your association with them.

In praying and meditating on the will of God, there is so much to consider and tie together. The Medjugorje messages about the power of prayer and doing God's will, and the writing of St. Teresa of Avila, especially the Interior Castle, offer many wonderful insights. Lucifer broke from God through his defiance of God's will, and Adam and Eve broke from God through defiance of God's will. Mary and Jesus have reunited us to God's will, or at least provided the means and the opportunity for us to be reunited to God's will, to have the desire for His will to dominate our human will. It is for us to make that choice and live it.

Lucifer had his opportunity. He was blessed among the angels. His very name meant light bearer. He had his test: submit to the will of God and be His servant. He failed that test, preferring himself to God. God created Adam and Eve, and made them a spiritual unit. He gave them their test. Eve was tempted, bit - so to speak, and then tempted Adam. The temptation Lucifer used to tempt Eve had its roots in the same pride which caused him to succumb: "Do not submit to God. Submit to no will but your own." The bait: knowledge from the tree will make you like God, and thus independent from Him and answerable only to yourself. It was not knowledge Eve sought, but independence from God. Adam was faced with the temptation, but unless he succumbed, mankind was safe. Adam and Eve were a spiritual unit, and both had to fail for mankind to feel the effects.

Adam failed, and as soon as he did, both he and Eve were stripped of many special gifts (the gift of integrity, the gift of immortality, the gift of dominion over nature, and most of the other gifts). It was only after they had been changed, fallen, that they had children, and so we all inherited their resultant fallen nature, the result of their sin. This fallen nature was the effect of their separating themselves from God by rejecting His will. Thus, we are born into this world with a human will which is weak, rebellious, inconstant and self-centered, but from which God did not remove the gift of free will. Our free will can be both a curse and the instrument of our salvation, for it is through an exercise of free will that we love God and live in accord with His will. Lucifer, and Adam and Eve fell by exercise of their free will, and it is through an exercise of our free will that we can either choose eternal damnation or, in cooperation with God's grace, become children of God. So, even when we confess, we still come back to our fallen nature, and must exercise our will over and over to remain God's child.

Mary was conceived immaculate, and lived her whole life in God's will. His will was her rule. When she gave God her Fiat, it was for all of her life, not just one event, and thus she was able to be the one fitting instrument in all the universe through which the Incarnate Word could come among men to fulfill His role as Savior. Thus, she served as the instrument to allow God and mankind to reconcile, to kiss, and she thus served as the instrument to unite heaven and Earth. If she had not been born immaculate, and if she had failed her test (had not given her Fiat), there would have been no fit instrument through which God could come among men as He did. She who was honored to bring God to mankind, undid the dishonor brought upon man by Eve.

Today, we approach Mary as our mother and the surest and most direct way to the heart of Jesus. Her love for Jesus is unequaled among all people, and her desire for each of us is that we love her Son with her heart, her love.

When we go to her and beg her help to love Jesus more, she will never refuse. Pray the Hail Holy Queen, and you immediately see the advantage of seeking her help and protection. She is mother of mercy, our life, our sweetness and our hope. United with Jesus in this role, she serves as our advocate before Him just as He is our advocate before our heavenly Father. Having lived in God's will all of her life, she has been given the role in eternity of helping us conform our lives to God's will, that we might join with her in praising God for all eternity.

In fulfilling her role she exercises all the power God allows her. We seldom consider the power she has been given by God to accomplish her mission. We think of her as sweet and gentle, which she is. But she is also a mother and will do all she can to protect her children. She is ever attentive to our needs, and stands before her Son as our vigilant intercessor. Jesus can refuse her nothing that is in conformance with His will, for His love for her is boundless. We must go to her, confident in her love and her desire to intercede for us. We must also have confidence in her power to help us.

I once felt what I believe was her power. I was on pilgrimage to an apparition site. Several events occurred, such as the spinning sun, but the thing I remember most clearly was felt, not seen. At the time the apparition began, I felt an incredible power come over me. When I was recording it later in my spiritual journal, the only way I could describe it was like being inside a nuclear reactor. The difference was that I knew it was a protective shield, her mantle, not something harmful. I was shocked by the experience. I had always thought of Mary as gentle, a mother, kind, but had never considered God having given her such awesome raw power as I sensed that day. It makes sense, considering her role as our Mother and protecting us from evil. This experience convinced me beyond doubt that if we live under her mantle, and do not try to take on the forces of evil alone, we have nothing to fear. I also came away convinced that the fastest way to lose our sense of balance is to move away from her protection and convince ourselves that we can combat Satan alone.

The role of the sacrament of Confession is essential to our fully sharing in the life of Christ. Confession is necessary because of our ever-present weakness. No matter what we do or how holy we try to be, we fall repeatedly, even when we are blessed with extraordinary grace for some special purpose. Confession is therefore a sacrament of mercy.

The Eucharist is a sacrament of Divine Life. We cannot approach the Eucharist unless we are in a state of grace, for to do so is a colossal insult to God. It repulses Him to a degree we cannot imagine when we receive the Eucharist in a state of mortal sin.

Recognizing this, our primary source of grace to live in accordance with the will of God is the Mass. God came among man for the remission of sin, to give man the power to become a child of God, and to reveal to us the infinite power of God's love. St. Leonard tells us in his little book, The Hidden Treasure[97], that the Mass is no mere copy, but is equal to the original sacrifice Jesus offered on Calvary. Jesus

---

[97]St. Leonard, The Hidden Treasure, TAN Books and Publishers, Rockford, 1952, pg 24.

is both priest and victim. Jesus' ultimate conformance to the will of His Father is repeated continuously and we are given the privilege to participate in and make this our own offer to the Father. We come before God at each Mass and offer Him the perfect sacrifice.

Is it not wondrous that the eternal Word of God, the Logos whose very word had the power of creation, is brought down among men by the power of the word of the priest, a power given him at the time of his ordination? Is it not equally appalling how many attend Mass with minimal or no attention - even gossiping, sleeping, balancing checkbooks, entertaining children, sometimes reading, completely unaware of what is happening at the altar, or their own role in the offering of the perfect sacrifice.

We often think of God as the giver, as the provider, which our loving God certainly is. But from those He loves and who love Him, He asks something in return. Many of us realize this and we do a little, and hope it is enough. It is never enough. The reason is that what we give is a measure of our love, and the more we love the more we not only want to give, but need to give. He wants all of our love, all we have to give, for then He can increase our capacity for love and we can love Him that much more. Through His love, we can love others more.

The issue is not how much of yourself you are willing to give. It is how much of yourself you are able to give to God. What stops you from giving all? Can you give your life if needed? Do you love God that much? For love of God, could you give your life for someone else? Even someone you don't know? Is there something of yourself you could offer God but don't? If the answer is yes, you have to ask yourself why. Are you afraid He might accept? You have to look deep within your soul and ask this, for He gave His all for you, and is offering you eternal life in an eternal happiness beyond your wildest expectation, and a share in

Himself. What is worth more to you than that? The more you give Him, the more you will receive from Him. In this sense, you are in some measure of control over the degree of your eternal happiness. Now, each of us should ask ourselves, "What is it again that is so precious to me that I wanted to hold it back and not offer it to God? What is so precious to me on earth that I would sacrifice a measure of my eternal happiness to retain it?"

How Do I Know?

The most common question in a discussion of God's will is "How Do I Know I Am Doing God's Will?"

This is a very important question since Christ told us that not all who call Him Lord, Lord, will enter heaven, but only those who do the will of His Father. This means focusing on God's will, regardless of our own will. It is not just loving submission, but actively seeking to do His will.

We know the will of God, in part, by studying the sound doctrine of the Church. Another is to read the gospels and the letters of Peter, James, John and Paul. We can also seek the guidance of a spiritual director. We can go through the gospel and write down everything Jesus told us to do. Another way is through prayer. Prayer is the most personal way. If we can achieve prayer of the heart, we can be guided by the Holy Spirit in our decisions. But, we have to listen carefully and recognize His still-small voice when we "hear" it. It may be inspiration, or may come to us through another person. St. Joseph was spoken to in dreams, and he responded by marrying Mary and later by taking the Holy Family to safety in Egypt.

I believe all are important ways we learn God's will, but following the guidance of the Church and our spiritual director are the two safest ways. The relationship we have with God through prayer of the heart can become very important, for, next to Holy Mass and the Eucharist, it is our daily and most personal encounter with God. Blessed Mother defines prayer of the heart as an encounter with God. We should conclude each prayer encounter with "Not my will but Yours be done."

We offer Jesus and Mary ourselves through consecration, just as we are, warts and all. We have to develop a habit of being completely, brutally honest about ourselves with God, for we cannot hide anything from Him. Even knowing this, it is not easy for most. It also does not mean laying guilt on yourself. Being honest about yourself is hard because pride keeps getting in the way. Not willing to face our warts leads us to put layers of cosmetics over our real selves. We need to strip this off. When we do, we see in ourselves, as best we can, what God sees in us. We then must pray for the courage to want to change, the conviction and fortitude to change, and this takes the gifts of the Holy Spirit. We need to ask for these gifts. Mary tells us that we should ask for these gifts each day before we do anything else. We must also avoid the trap of putting things on ourselves, through guilt trips, that do not belong there. This is a common way Satan attacks us.

One of the most important things in developing "sight of the soul" is to have absolute trust in God. Love and trust are essential. We must place our entire selves before Him; all our hopes and joys, all our desires and fears, all the things through which He knows us and we get to know Him. We must give Him ourselves completely; heart, mind, body and soul. We must understand that the greatest freedom we can have is to do the will of God. It sounds like a paradox, but it is true. In exercising freedom, we seek what we think is best for us. Only God knows what is truly best, perfect, for us. This is His will for us. Therefore, it is only through this complete submission to His will for us, and total giving of ourselves to Him, that we achieve the greatest freedom. Eventually, we need to bring our whole life into a focus that is directed toward God, toward our own personal sanctity, and learn to redirect our focus away from anything that pulls us away from God. We have to be able to recognize what those things are. Fasting helps us do this.

When we are faced with the everyday decisions of life, we have to rely on our conscience. When someone strokes our ego to tempt us to do something we know is wrong, we have to see past the adulation and look to the morality of the act. If we are tempted to cheat in school, or cheat on our spouse, falsify our tax returns, or lie to our parents, we have to recognize it as an attack on morality and trust our conscience.

If we are going to rely on our conscience we have to train it to be especially sensitive, particularly today when so much around us in music, movies, TV, videos, computer games, and other social activity is immoral but also considered socially acceptable. Even abortion is commonplace and considered a right. We are almost at the point where it is difficult to find anything in the popular media that is morally acceptable. Keeping your conscience fine-tuned when so many things assault it under the cover of being a constitutional right, morally acceptable under "today's new morality," or demanded by the "now" generation, takes particular effort and regular prayer. There is no such thing as a "new morality." There is only one valid morality, and that is God's morality, and God does not change.

The pressures societal norms create on children in school are unbelievable compared to what students had to face twenty or thirty years ago. Sexual promiscuity is often assumed as a normal part of dating, and drugs have become commonplace. Schools give out condoms and birth control pills, encouraging promiscuity, and the language high school students use today has never been so crass. We ask how things like the school shootings around the country could happen, and the answer is so clearly before us. Given the depths to which we have sunk, how could they not happen? It is sad to see the level to which society has sunk in the mad dash away from God, and the unwillingness of so many to accept morality as the underlying motive for their actions.

Many, having bought into the false notion that everything is relative, fail to see the truth of God as absolute and that His morality is eternal and as unchanging as is He. Given how popular the TV shows like Sex in the City are, can we say we are children of God? Is that how His children behave? Is that the kind of behavior they condone? Has shame been eradicated along with smallpox? Whose children are the producers and viewers of such programs? We say we are a nation under God. Are we? What evidence would convince us we are? Morality has become something defined by legal right and personal desire. If it is legal, it must be moral, so the logic goes. In Stafford County, Virginia, less than thirty percent of the population is affiliated with a church.

If we are to develop proper spiritual insight, we must condition and then inform our consciences with frequent Mass, confession, scripture, other spiritual reading, and regular daily prayer. We strengthen our consciences by continually questioning what we encounter, what we contemplate doing, always asking if it meets the standards refined by the spiritual insight we have developed. Is this something God would approve of us doing? Is it something He would ask us to do? This is particularly important for adults, who are the parents of the youth and the examples for many others besides their own children.

Humility and Obedience

I was raised in New Orleans, and Cajun food is a particular delight to my palate. When you make Cajun food, many of the dishes call for a base, or stock, known as a roux. It is fundamentally a mixture of a little water, some oil and plain flour. It is cooked slowly in a frying pan until it turns dark. The darker it is, the better. But it also burns easily so you have to use very low heat and stir continuously once you get it to a certain color. Making a good roux is not something you generally do on your first try. You have to cultivate the knack, you have to nurture the talent until everything about you is doing the cooking; your eyes, your nose, your ability to see subtle shades of color and texture. Making a good roux is so fundamental to so many Cajun dishes, we have a cookbook from New Orleans titled <u>First You Make a Roux</u>.

Boylan[98] tells us that the key to a spiritual life in conformity to God's will, the fundamental ingredient that makes it all possible is humility, and the way to true humility is not comparing yourself to other people, but to God. It is the recognition of what we have done, or what has taken place in us and with us and through us, because of God working in our lives. It is also looking honestly at what we have failed to do because we have not responded to His grace. How else could Mary, the most humble of creatures, have said the Magnificat? Without true humility, living the three theological virtues becomes impossible. True humility is therefore not walking around all day moaning about what a miserable worm you are and letting people walk all over you. It is recognizing who and what you are because God loves you, thanking God, and using those gifts to give Him, not yourself, greater glory.

---

[98]Boylan, Dom M. Eugene, O.C.S.O., Christian Classics, Inc., Westminster, 1989.

Fundamental to an understanding of humility is understanding clearly its opposite; pride. Boylan tells us,

"If we lack love for our neighbor, we are interfering with God's action in our soul. This is the symptom, not the disease. ... whatever is the root-cause of our tendency to refuse to abandon and deny ourselves and to put on Christ, is also the source of our failure to live fully the life of Christ. ... If we examine pride we shall see why it prevents God's grace from working in our souls. Pride is an inordinate love of self, which causes us to consider ourselves explicitly, or implicitly, as our first beginning and our last end."[99]

It is the *inordinate*, out of the ordinary, focus on self which puts us in the place where God should actually be in our lives. Notice he does not say pride is love of self. He says it is the inordinate love of self. We put ourselves before God; these same selves who probably say the Our Father wherein is found "Thy will be done." We make ourselves a mini-god for us. It is the fundamental disease of the "me-generation", those afflicted with the 'gimmies' and the 'I want' syndrome. "Pride brings the very law of God's being into operation to prevent His mercy from acting. Humility, on the contrary, not only removes the obstacle, but invites God's help."[100] What are the only two characteristics Christ ever used to describe Himself? He said in Mt 11:29 "I am meek and humble of heart." Fasting is denial of self, and prayer is encounter with God. Together, they make a powerful pair to foster humility. Fasting can take many forms besides fasting from food. We can fast from television, from gossip, or anything else we enjoy. We can also fast in other ways, such as ordering a food we do not like in a restaurant.

---

[99]ibid, pg 76
[100]ibid, p 83

If we have humility, and if we have prayer of the heart, we have everything. If we do this, Mary tells us that Satan cannot even come close to us. Look at how he attacked Adam and Eve. He convinced them to be self-focused instead of God-focused. Make yourself as a god, Satan told them.

We like to find apparent good within ourselves. When we find a good, whatever it might be, how do we view it? Do we view it as attributable solely to our own efforts, independent of God, or do we recognize God's role in our accomplishments? Do we put a limit on God's glory by attributing His good to ourselves? Can God tolerate us putting limits on Him or taking credit for His work? Do we internally say "Thank You" and accept the good we do, His and ours together because of Him working in us, or do we think, like in the Frank Sinatra song, "I Did It My Way"?

"Pride makes us consider our own selves as our last end; the proud man lives 'his own life, his own way, for his own sake above all else', for his own sake. This is the exact opposite from what should be done in the Mystical Body, where the member recognizes that all good works come from God, all operations are done by God's power, and all acts are directed toward God and for the sake of God."[101]

In the Mass we speak of God's glory. "All power in heaven and on earth is Yours, Almighty Father. All creation gives You glory." God does nothing except for His glory. He can not do otherwise, for He is all good and all love. Anything He did otherwise would have to be for something other than what is good and what is love, and He cannot be inconsistent or betray His own nature. He is the infinite one, He Who Is, the creator, and our loving Father. Given our state of being compared to that of God, it is our response to His love and His mercy that gives Him glory.

---

[101]ibid, pp 76-77.

When we deny Him glory by the way we live and act, we deny Him what is rightfully His. If we do not turn back to Him, He has no choice but to exercise His justice, for that is the only avenue we leave Him to preserve His glory in us. He can not have any creature be preferred over Him, even if it only exists in the mind of that creature. This was the first commandment. When we succumb to pride and place our will before that of God, we risk His justice.

When we have humility and recognize Him in us, and do what we are able because we are conforming ourselves to the will of God, when we accept in humility the Bread of Life, when in humility we accept Christ as our own personal way, truth, and life, then we give God the glory due Him.

There is nothing inordinate about offering to God all the good works we do, all our joys and sufferings, because He is our God. We owe Him our existence on a continuing basis, every moment of the day. We continue to exist only because He wills it. It is His choice for us. "We are like the sound of a man's voice; if he stops talking, the sound ceases to exist."[102] We really do owe Him everything we have and everything we are. In His love, He does not take back His gifts. He only asks we accept them, use them for His glory, and give Him thanks. Every time we see our child, or get our paycheck, or avoid danger, or have the opportunity to pray, or have the opportunity to attend Mass, or receive the Eucharist, or make a good confession, or help someone else convert, or bring someone closer to God than they were before, we should thank God, for each of these is one more of His gifts to us. Accepting and using these gifts properly is in part how we tell God we love Him.

On the spiritual side, "We do not realize that we owe the grace for every single act and also every single good

---

[102]ibid, p 77

466

thing in our spiritual life to God."[103] The opposite of this is the prideful rebellion we see among men everywhere. They always want to be in control, to make the decisions. The common theme is, "It's **my** body and I'll do anything I want with it and anything in it. It's **my** civil right; **my** constitutional right." My, My, My. We rebel against the will of God continuously. When we choose not to learn what God's will is for us, we keep our conscience uninformed, for otherwise we would have no excuse; or so we think. Ignorance is bliss, as the saying goes. If I do not try to learn, I have no responsibility for the consequences of my actions. If we choose not to conform to the will of God, we are saying we choose not to have Him cooperating with us in our life. We are saying that someone or some thing is more important; is placed before Him in importance in our lives. He backs off and lets the other powers rule. The only other power is that of Satan. But our loving Father is always there with a lifesaver. He is always there with the sacraments of reconciliation and the Eucharist. He never fully abandons us until we reject Him in our death. Then we truly die, for we have not accepted His way, His truth, His life. We have chosen eternal darkness.

We must consider the responsibilities of our role as members of the Mystical Body. Obedience to the will of God is crucial for a healthy existence as a member of this Body. Our acts, the merits of all the good works we do, are shared by all the other members of the Mystical Body, just as the benefits of food we eat with our mouth is shared by all the rest of the body. But this is the Mystical Body of Christ, and this Body can only accept good acts done in conformance to the will of God. Christ's Body cannot accept anything which is a spiritual pollutant. Therefore, "Every single act, even the slightest, done contrary to the will of God, cannot be shared

---

[103]ibid, p 79

by Christ, it is not part of the life of His Body, and therefore it has no real value."[104]

Think about this. Anything we do, anything at all, which is not in conformance with the will of God, not only has no merit for us, but has none for any other member of the Mystical Body. It produces no fruit, and must be pruned from our life. It is completely wasted time and effort. When we stand before God in judgment, when we stand there alone, the only thing we have to offer as our passport to heaven is the love we bring and the value of the good works we do. Any work done not in conformance with the will of God is something we do not have to balance our life. We need the merit of all the good we can possibly do so we can not only balance our life, but share that good with our many brothers and sisters in the Mystical Body, just as we share in the merits of their good works. If we do not do our part, we are letting the whole Mystical Body down. When we do not conform our lives to the will of God, we hurt ourselves and we hurt our brother and sister members as well, and Christ told us, "Whatever you do to one of these, you do also to Me." It takes on a whole new meaning.

All of this requires an act of the will. "All we do to deny ourselves and accept the will of God, accept Christ, and everything we do in opposition to that, all of it, depends on our own will. Therefore, willful disobedience to the will of God is the death blow to the life of Christ in us."[105]

The practice of humility is reduced to just two things: "an attitude of mind, and the expression of the attitude in action. The attitude is humility of soul, and its practical expression is the search for God by obedience to His will."[106] It is clear that humility is the gateway for reception of grace,

---

[104]ibid, p 80

[105]ibid, p 82

[106]ibid, p 82

grace is necessary for the three theological virtues of Faith, Hope and Love, and without these virtues we cannot conform our will to the will of God.

Finally, remember what Christ said in His first sermon[107]. "Blessed are the poor in spirit, for theirs is the kingdom of heaven." Poor in spirit is another expression for humility of heart. This is not a mere gateway to heaven; not a mere signpost. It is an entitlement. Christ said theirs <u>is</u> the kingdom of heaven; not theirs might be, or theirs will be sometime later. Theirs **IS** the kingdom of heaven. This is a very powerful incentive for humility.

---

[107]Mt, 5:3.

Mary and the Divine Will

At the annunciation, Mary told the angel "Be it done unto me according to thy word" and the world has not been the same since. Mary was born immaculate. That was necessary for the Divine will to be the predominant force of her life. Just as Adam and Eve were created unscathed, so was she. If she were motivated only by the imperfect human will, as most of us are, she would have been less proper a vehicle to receive the incarnate Word of God. When she gave her fiat, she gave it for her entire life, and on our behalf, not just permission for this one event. She gave it for every moment of every day, for her entire earthly existence. In a sense, she was spiritually much like Adam and Eve were at the beginning, and possibly much more. Adam and Eve had their test, and failed. With her fiat, she passed her test and gave her entire life, including every aspect of her human will, to God. Immaculate from the beginning, her fiat was her test, just as was the apple for Adam. One was a test of obedience, the other a test of total consecration.

As I consider the feast of the Immaculate Conception, to what extent can I consecrate the lives of myself and my family to God, and make us available for Mary and Jesus to aid us in living His Divine will? In what way do we live the Divine will in our daily lives? In what way can we improve the extent to which we live the Divine will?

We can also meditate on the greeting of the angel at the time of the annunciation. An angel of God greets Mary with, "Hail, Full of Grace." "Full of Grace" is the title given to Mary by God, not just a description. It is the name by which the angel addressed her instead of using her earthly name, Mary. Being filled with grace, God's grace, is more than just having some grace. It is being full of grace in the biblical sense of fullness, the completion of the infusion of grace, and thus the receptivity had to be there. Tradition says that this receptivity and fullness was from her beginning. Logic would also tell us this. It seems unlikely that an ordinary human, with a weak and sinful nature, could be brought to such a state of fullness unless the situation were completely unique, as unique as God Himself becoming man. This fullness of grace required a total submission of the human will to the will of God, for otherwise the free will which operates in all of us would have prevented her from receiving this fullness. The mere fact that she was addressed with this title by an angel of God, His messenger, and not with the salutation, "Hail, who will soon be full of grace", indicates a preexisting condition of fullness as well as a predisposition of complete subjection of her will to that of God, and this, in her, had to be done by God from her beginning. It required a special intervention, a special preservation, in preparation for the unique event to come, an intervention and preservation that the rest of us do not have and do not require.

Mary's condition glorified God, and thus she could say in all humility during the visitation that "God has done great things to me," while at the same time describing herself as the lowly handmaid of God. She recognized that what occurred in her from her beginning, and more recently, was not because of her greatness, but because of the infused grace of God in her. She was occupying a unique position among mankind, predicted from Genesis 3:15, and a unique preparation was necessary.

Jesus tells us that to those who have been given much, much will be asked. We often think of God as the giver, as the provider, which our loving God certainly is. But from those He loves and who love Him, He asks something in return. Many of us realize this and we do a little, and hope it is enough. It is never enough. The reason is that what we give is a measure of our love, and the more we love the more we, not just want, but need, to give. He wants all of our love, all we have to give, for then He can increase our capacity for love and we can love Him that much more.

How much of myself I am willing to give is not the question. It is, " How much of myself can I give?" Can I give all? Can I give my life if needed? Do I love God that much? Is there something of myself I could give God but don't? If the answer is yes, I have to ask myself why. I have to look deep within my soul and ask this, for He gave His all for me, and is offering me eternal life in an eternal happiness beyond my wildest expectation. What is worth more to me than that? The more I give Him, the more I will receive from Him. In this sense, I am in some measure of control over my eternal happiness.

Is there anything so precious to me that I want to hold it back and not offer it to God? If I understand God's love for me, could there be?

God and Not-God

Consider, not so much good and evil, but God and not-God. You may argue that this is a fine point, and I agree, but there is a reason for this consideration. If we recognize evil as that which is antagonistic to God, and then think of some things we or others say or do, we can see that there are some which are intrinsically evil. Other things we do are not overtly evil, but they are not of God, either. If we look at all this in relation to God, we can see that there is God on one side, and then there is evil, and those things we can label not-God, lumped together on the other side, but separated within themselves. Maybe that is why we are taught by Jesus to avoid evil, but to also be in the world but not of the world.

If you begin to think of what it means to be on the God side of the line, to stand for all the things He taught and asked of us, and continues to ask of us, then everything else is on the other side of the line. Lots of things on that other side don't seem too bad, are not evil in themselves, but are things which, if we allow them, draw us from God.

Some of these things have varied characteristics. For example, some secular music is demonic. Some is just poor quality. Some has quality but tends to be sentimental and thus draws us into daydreams rather than working for what we can realistically hope to attain. Music sentimentalizes relationships, but the reality is that a good wife is better than a fantasy perfect wife.

These not-God things may also be distractions in our daily activities, things which seem so pressing at the moment but which turn out to be so insignificant later, something we desire very much and to which we devote a large part of our time and energy and thought (new car or new fishing pole, new dress, new game, and the like). They are all things having no relation to God that attract our minds and hands, and consequently our hearts, away from God and doing His work.

To draw us away from God, Satan does not necessarily have to lure us into what we know is evil. He only has to lure us into something having nothing to do with God. If he can keep us obsessed with football, soccer, X-Box, the latest reality show on TV, soap operas, and all the many others things consuming so very much of our time, often including all day on Sunday, he can gradually move us farther and farther away from God, for we will think of God less, pray less, and less and less be concerned about the morality of what we do. Our vocabulary become more crude, our thoughts become more secular, and we gradually drift away from our anchor and stronghold, which is God.

Jesus told us that where your heart is there will be your treasure (Lk 12:34). Anytime you look into your heart, and the biggest and brightest treasure you see in there is not God and His will for you, you know you are in trouble. I suspect that, for many of us, it is not the overtly evil things that will most often divert us from doing the will of God and lead us astray, but those little ordinary things in life which are simply not-God.

The Final Lesson

We are often faced with the question of determining if we are doing the will of God. We ask what God's will is, how we can recognize His will amidst everything else we face, and what the relationship is between the will of God and God's love for us, especially at those times when His will seems to involve suffering. The most dramatic and evident example we can follow is the passion of our Lord. The most beneficial thing we can do is meditate on His passion and find how it applies to our own lives.

Many people who read the gospel account of the passion and death of our Lord look with dismay on His almost final words, "And at about three o'clock Jesus cried out in a loud voice, "Eli, Eli, lema sabachthani?", which means, "My God, My God, why have you forsaken Me?"(Mt 27:46) This is followed by "Jesus cried out in a loud voice, 'Father, into Your hands I commend My Spirit.'"(Lk 23:46) How can we reconcile these two cries coming so close together at such a time? Both cries were "in a loud voice", at a point three hours into the crucifixion when the effort to get even one breath must have been pure agony. Why a loud voice if He was only talking to the Father? Was He expressing despair when He cried out asking why He had been forsaken? Could Christ have experienced despair, as it appears on the surface, if He had previously said:

"I came down from heaven not to do My own will but the will of the one who sent me."(Jn 6:38), and "When you lift up the Son of Man, then you will realize that I AM and I do nothing on My own, but I say only what the Father has taught Me. The One who sent Me is with Me. He has not left Me alone, because I always do what is pleasing to Him." (Jn 8:28-29)

Could He contradict Himself by saying the Father "has not left Me alone" and then cry out "Why have you abandoned Me?" I suggest that Christ was teaching us, and was teaching us what the Father wanted Him to teach. This becomes more evident when we consider that the words He spoke, "My God, My God, why have you forsaken Me?" are the opening words of Psalm 22. He was pointing us to Psalm 22, all of it, as His final prayer, and to understand the significance of this event we must examine Psalm 22 in its entirety. We must learn from Him what our own prayer must be in the darkest of times.

In His final struggle, Jesus recognized the possible despair His disciples and friends might be feeling because of His crucifixion, so He was teaching them, and us, how to deal with it, how not to lose hope. His cry was to us more than it was only between Him and the Father, which is why it was uttered "in a loud voice." In these final minutes, at the end of the third hour, He had not the breath left to teach us other than to point, with His cry, to Psalm 22. Let us examine His final lesson, His final prayer, His Divine mind as our Savior during His final moments on the cross.

"My God, My God, why have you forsaken me, far from my prayer, from the words of my cry? O my God, I cry out by day, and you answer not; by night and there is no relief for me."

As we examine this Psalm in the light of the suffering of Christ's physical body, we should also consider it in a mystical sense, in light of how it applies 2000 years later to us in the Church today as members of the Mystical Body of Christ. We can see in the passion of Christ a sign of the passion of the Church itself as it struggles to bring truth and hope to a society determined to turn in on itself and away from God and embrace despair, a society which has embraced death as the answer to prayer.

For example, Christ was scourged brutally. The normal sentence for scourging was 40 stripes minus one, since 40 was considered enough to kill a normal man. Evidence from the Shroud of Turin shows Jesus suffered at least 120 stripes. His skin was ripped unmercifully, but it remained intact enough for His Body to continue to function. If we meditate on the scourging, we can consider an equivalent in the Mystical Body. We must ask ourselves what the equivalent of the skin might be. The skin is that organ which holds everything together, that keeps the vital organs in place and functioning. In the Mystical Body, we might say that the skin is the ministerial priesthood and the Mass. If these are attacked successfully, the heart of the Church, the Holy Eucharist, will not be able to remain in place. All will be gone, not there to maintain the body. The life source of the body will have been removed.

The passion of Christ teaches us that no matter how much the priesthood and the Mass are attacked, enough will remain to sustain the Church and the faithful who comprise the Mystical Body, because it is His church and no one can take it from Him. Jesus promised it would be attacked, but that the gates of hell would not prevail. Priests who understand this must do all they can to preserve the Mass, the Eucharist and keep life in the Mystical Body through fidelity to their vows. They do this by remaining faithful to the church, the Holy Father, and to the Mass. They do this by not deleting or changing the prayers of the Mass, however well-intentioned the changes may be, and by saying the prayers of the Mass so as not to change their theological meaning. For example, when the priest prepares the gifts for the Offertory, and the people respond, "May the Lord receive this sacrifice from your hands, ...", the priest should be silent. This is the people's prayer to the priest, not the priest's prayer. Neither the priest nor the people should change the prayer to, "May the Lord receive these gifts from our hands, ..." The gifts may be ours, but they are offered to God by the consecrated hands of the priest, not by the laity.

The function of a priest, the meaning of priesthood, is to offer sacrifice. The priest offers the sacrifice which we, the laity, provide. We are not the ministerial priesthood, and we do not offer the sacrifice. The priest offers the sacrifice on our behalf. It is in doing the little things improperly that we can lose the theological meaning and focus of the prayers of the Mass, and consequently, over time, we could lose the meaning of the Mass, and of the Eucharist itself. Then the prophesy of Daniel would be fulfilled, for the daily sacrifice, which is daily Mass, will be ended.

In Psalm 22 we find many lessons. It begins, not "God", but "My God." The relationship is invoked, not just the person. The cry of Jesus back then, clearly pointing us to Psalm 22 so we may read and fully understand this psalm as His final lesson in the light of what was happening to Him, and the cry of His disciples and friends then and now, is that of God's children through the centuries. Even today, as we struggle with our crosses, many of us pray the equivalent of:

You are My God, and you have a covenant with me, a covenant you formed. Why do you not rescue me? Why am I suffering this way, to the point of death, if I belong to you who are all-powerful? Do you still love me, my God? Have you broken our covenant? Could you break our covenant? Have I unwittingly broken our covenant and driven you from me? I cry out to you night and day and you ignore me. Why, my God, why?

"Yet you are enthroned as the Holy One; you are the glory of Israel. In you our ancestors trusted; they trusted and you rescued them. To you they cried out and they escaped; in you they trusted and were not disappointed."

Here, hope is remembered. Hope was alive in the fathers, and hope was fed and realized in them by God, a hope nurtured by faith and trust. God was their champion who came to their rescue. They were His people, and He was their God. The covenant was reality to them, it was lived, it was their spiritual survival.

If you, my God rescued your people before, why will you not rescue me now? Have I no faith? Am I not worth saving? Why do you leave me to be devoured by my enemies? Do you turn your gaze from me? Do you not remember me, do you not remember my faith, my love? How am I different from our fathers whom you helped?

These prayers, these cries to God, were heard then and are heard even today. As we encounter the trials of life, as we encounter spiritual darkness, we raise these cries to God. It may seem He has abandoned us, but if we have done our homework we know He is closer to us during these periods of darkness than at any other time. It is one of the ways He purifies our soul. He is helping us toward sanctity, even if His handiwork is not immediately evident.

One of the blessings God has given us is the rich body of spiritual writing from the saints. St. John of the Cross, for example, has written extensively about the state of spiritual darkness and the spiritual treasures it holds for us. These storehouses of excellent spiritual guidance from the saints help us find our own answers to the question which Jesus cried out from the cross, and which we sometimes find in our own heart.

How many ways do we hear the cry of abandonment today? We hear it from the parent who suffers the loss of a child, from one who suffers the premature loss of a spouse, one who loses a job, one who faces bankruptcy and its disgrace, one who loses his or her home to foreclosure, one who contracts a serious illness like cancer, one who is slandered and disgraced because of false accusations, one who is sexually mis-oriented, one who is hurt by someone who is supposed to love them, those who are unceasingly discriminated against because of accidents of nature or other things beyond their control - like color or religion or size or physical beauty or intelligence or social status.

For any number of reasons we hear this cry, not from the whiner who is just reaping the consequences of his or her stupidity, meanness or selfishness, but from the one who has been given a cross they feel is too heavy to carry. They have not yet learned to trust God enough, to rely on His strength, to look for the spiritual gift that accompanies the cross.

Sometimes it just takes time to accept the cross as a gift, especially when the hurt is so strong, as it is when your life is torn asunder by falsehood and meanspirited gossip, or when a young child suddenly dies. It is such an unnatural thing for a parent to bury a child. Even when we understand why, such as a condition of war, it still hurts deeply. When it happens suddenly, as in automobile accident or if they are murdered, the hurt is very sudden and deep, and is often accompanied by seething anger. It is usually much later before the person can seek solace from God and try to understand the mystery of the cross in their own lives.

"But I am a worm, hardly human, scorned by everyone, despised by the people. All who see me mock me; they curl their lips and jeer; they shake their heads at me: "You relied on the LORD--let him deliver you; if he loves you, let him rescue you."

Today, just as at Calvary, we can hear this same cry from people trying to deal with rejection in this world. We can hear them cry to Jesus: "I must be less than a man, of no real value, for they all reproach me. They measure me against their standards, and find I do not meet the test. They treat me as sub-human, a worm, they scorn me and laugh, even rejoice at my misery and my deficiencies. In their eyes, I have no worth, no value. I am homeless or malformed, perhaps slow of wit. Perhaps I am just old and useless in their eyes, and the delights of this world have passed me by.

They deride me most because I take delight in you. They challenge you to deliver me as once they challenged you on Calvary. Will you meet their challenge? What am I to you? What is any man that You, the infinite God, should be interested in him? Do you, my God, scorn me and deride me? Do you wag your head and look away from my misery? How can you if you love me? How can you if you made a covenant with me, if I am yours? I have not rejected you. Do you reject me? Where are you? Do you see me? Can you see me and not help me?"

We saw evidence of this sentiment among the disciples, in His abandonment by the apostles, during the passion of Christ. This was true even though the apostles knew from Isaiah 53 what the Messiah would have to endure, and that from His stripes they would be healed. But the pressure of the moment overcame them. We saw this very thing happen to Jesus as they scorned Him hanging on the cross, challenging God to save Him. Those disciples and apostles who heard the crowd must have felt these sentiments of scorn directed at themselves; guilt by association.

We saw reaction to scorn contrasted in two ways in particular, in Judas and Peter. Both sought to distance themselves from Christ. Judas was the traitor who sold Jesus for a few pieces of silver, and sealed his own fate with a kiss. He used a sign of love to betray Him who is Love. Judas was unable to reconcile his act by contrition, for his heart was of stone. He had rejected God. In hanging himself instead of asking forgiveness, he became the one, the only one, of whom Christ would say that it would be better if he had never been born. Peter, on the other hand, when confronting his own weakness and his denial of both the love Jesus had given him and his professed love for Jesus, "wept bitterly." His contrition was his salvation, and he was given the keys to the Kingdom. I sometimes wonder what would have been different if Judas had not been so quick to hang himself, if he had waited only three more days. Would he have repented and converted? We will never know, and neither will he. He has eternity to consider his lost alternatives.

Many of us today face tough situations in our own way. If you are Christian and live in a non-Christian country, or an atheistic country, you will face scorn, rejection and ridicule for your belief in Christ. You may be martyred for your belief. If you had to face that choice today, is your faith strong enough to die for Christ, as did a young girl at Columbine School in Littleton, Colorado, in April 1999? I am still amazed when I think of this girl. Only in her teens, she got on the school bus that morning, expecting the day would be just like so may others had been. Her mother kissed her goodbye, also expecting a routine day. Then, when she was in the school cafeteria, her whole world came apart. An agent of Satan, whom she did not know, came into the room with his guns, and, threatening the crowd, asked if anyone believed in Jesus. She didn't have time to think, or call her mom, but she knew there was only one way she could respond. She stood up and said, "I do.", and with those words became a bride of Christ, a young martyr at the end of the 20th century.

Is your faith strong enough to endure the ridicule of your coworkers? Is it strong enough to endure being denied a promotion because of your religion? Do you try to hide your religion from others so they will not be able to discriminate against you? How do you handle it when your children come home from school and describe what they endure because of their belief? Do you refuse to discuss religion at work or in your social life because you do not want others to know what you believe, or at least think you believe, or do you stand up for what you believe?

I live in a predominantly non-Catholic area. I have a good friend who is a priest. He was walking into a local grocery store wearing his clericals and a passerby gave him an insulting gesture, commonly called the New York salute, simply because he knew my friend was a priest. How would you respond to such an insult?

"Yet you drew me forth from the womb, made me safe at my mother's breast. Upon you I was thrust from the womb; since birth you are my God."

I cannot deny you, my God, even when you seem to ignore me. You are my God and I was always yours from the time I was born. My mother and father dedicated me to you, a dedication formalized by my baptism. All my life you have been my God. Do not depart from me, for I have not departed from you. I cannot turn the gaze of my soul from you even in my suffering, for I belong to you and I love you. Show me that you have not abandoned me, even if I cannot see you, even if I cannot feel you beside me.

Part of our coming to grips with the mystery of the cross is an unshakable belief that God is always with us and always loves us. Just as Psalm 22 shows us the mind, as well as the prayer, of Jesus during His final minutes on His cross, we must develop the conviction that He is always there, always beside us. We saw this in Psalm 139. How much closer to us could He possibly be? What must we do to prevent our separating ourselves from Him? We must remain in a state of grace. We must love Him and keep His word. As we encounter our crosses in this life, we must have the unshaken conviction that through it all He is within. He sent the cross, He will help us carry the cross if we let Him, and this cross, no matter how painful it may seem, is the thing we need most right now for our spiritual growth. If it was not, God would not have given it to us.

We must understand that when a cross is given for our spiritual growth, it does not necessarily mean we are being purified of evil, for that may not be necessary. It may come to us to help us grow in humility, or may be given to us

483

as a means for someone else to be saved through the salvific merit Christ imparts to our suffering. In such as case as this, God asks us to carry the cross because He knows we are strong enough in our faith to do so and He gives us His own strength to bear the weight. In any of these cases, God uses our cross as a means for our spiritual growth as long as we bear it in Christ, with Christ and through Christ.

To fully cooperate with Jesus, it is imperative that we let God work in us as He wills to help us overcome or bear the hurt which accompanies the cross. We do this with hope and must not let Satan drive us into despair. Every cross is a gift of love, and we must be certain of that truth. We must offer up to God our misery as our gift to Him. This is a hard concept to come to grips with. It takes time and much prayer, and total acceptance of His will.

"Do not stay far from me, for trouble is near, and there is no one to help. Many bulls surround me; fierce bulls of Bashan encircle me. They open their mouths against me, lions that rend and roar. Like water my life drains away; all my bones grow soft. My heart has become like wax, it melts away within me."

I am besieged by my enemies, the enemies of my soul. My enemies are Your enemies, for they are the idolaters, those who hate You and have replaced You with gods of their own making. They worship power and money and fame, even evil itself, and they hate me because of my love for You. They attack me on all sides. I have no strength left in my heart to fight them. They have sapped my strength and my courage. I am emptied and poured out. I have nothing left but You. Now, You must be my strength. If You fail me, I have nothing. You are my only hope. All I have left to give You is what You have given me.

How often have we, or those we love, had our back against the wall with no place else to run, no place to hide.

Our tribulation, whatever it may be, can no longer be avoided. We have dodged the bullets of insult, we have avoided the scorn of those whose entire concept of value is in earthly terms, we have arrived in that corner from which we cannot leave without taking up our cross. We must, even with trembling arms, reach out for the cross, even embrace the cross, ever mindful of from Whom it comes. In earthly terms, all hope seems lost. In spiritual terms, hope is always with us, for our hope is not of this world. In such a situation we resign ourselves and accept the condition, sometimes without knowing whether it is temporal or permanent. We may have a child who is bullied in school, or who may have made many errors and is now in jail. We may have a child born with an incurable condition, and we resign ourselves to the need for lifetime special care for this child. We must trust and hope in God, knowing, not just believing, that if He gives us this cross then He will also provide the means, the grace, to carry it.

We may not live to see the solution to every cross. It may seem that no solution is possible, but we also know that with God all things are possible. We must hope in Him who loves us, even if we do not live to see how it is resolved. We must not just reach out to take the cross with trembling arms. We must, with deep prayer of the heart, literally embrace the cross as God's gift. We must look for the spiritual bouquet which comes with every cross.

"As dry as a potsherd is my throat; my tongue sticks to my palate; you lay me in the dust of death. Many dogs surround me; a pack of evildoers closes in on me. So wasted are my hands and feet that I can count all my bones. They stare at me and gloat; they divide my garments among them; for my clothing they cast lots."

I have been brought to the edge of death. I have no prospect of anything else. Is that your will for me? My only hope is You. I am dried up inside, all my resources depleted, my strength gone. I am immobilized and completely at the mercy of my enemies and Yours. Only You can rescue me. Every possession of every kind has been taken from me. Now they deride me and try to strip all hope from me. All I have left is my love for You, my hope in You. Protect my hope, for my hope is You, my God. My soul feels empty and longs for Your embrace.

The fulfillment of this prophesy within Psalm 22 was clear to those Jews who were regulars in the synagogue and Temple. They could see the prophesy being fulfilled before their eyes as the Roman soldiers, unaware of the scriptures, cast lots for Jesus' garment. The impact must have been enormous.

Many times we are immobilized by circumstance. Often it is because of fear. Sometimes it is fear of physical danger, sometimes it is a psychological fear. Either way, it is fear, and real to the person experiencing it. Characteristic reactions to fear include flight, fight and immobilization. At times we can immobilize ourselves. This may happen when we are called upon to speak before a group, or undergo an oral examination, or testify in court. It may happen when we are confronted by evil in a place where we have no protection and no recourse, perhaps late at night on a dark street in a dangerous neighborhood. It could be a rape situation, or when confronted by a thief with a gun while we are working at a store or bank. We may face the prospect of losing everything we have because we must file bankruptcy, or because our spouse has to go into a nursing home, or because someone has filed suit against us. In a very real sense, they will cast lots for our possessions, dividing them among our creditors.

Any of these situations, and others, have the potential to immobilize us through fear. We even see children immobilizing other children though fear, often because the victim has something the perpetrator wants, or is what the perpetrator hates.

Fear has become an increasingly prevalent emotion in society today. A woman in Washington, DC was shot by a stray bullet from a drive-by shooting outside her house while she sat watching TV in her living room. Prisoners of war, even if not immobilized by fear, may be completely controlled by their captors. This was the case with many of the early Christian martyrs. It is true of those who have been, or still are, prisoners during war, and is true for many people today. It was true for St. Maximilian Kolbe. Many others are immobilized, either through incarceration or because of medical conditions which restrict freedom of movement. Some of those incarcerated persons are on death row. We should pray each day for their conversion so they can face what they must longing for God's embrace.

When we are faced with situations which deplete our strength and inner resources, and we have no place to turn, we must do whatever it takes to fall back on our Lord, to seek our refuge in Him. Even if we have lost, or face losing, everything, and are unable to take action on our own, our recourse and refuge is always the heart of Jesus. It may sound trite to some, but this is the reality faced by many. They have no place else to go, and sometimes that is why their cross has come to them. It may be the only way God can get their attention.

"But you, LORD, do not stay far off; my strength, come quickly to help me. Deliver me from the sword, my forlorn life from the teeth of the dog. Save me from the lion's mouth, my poor life from the horns of wild bulls."

My God, my trust is in you, my only hope is in you. Come to my defense, deliver my soul from the enemy. I only have one soul. It is the one thing I have of value to You, and I trust in you to deliver it from the dogs. Save me from those who would destroy my soul. My soul belongs to you. Take possession of my soul and protect it, for it is yours. My body is a shell subject to the enemy, but my soul is your eternal possession. While I hope in you, my enemies cannot touch my soul. Protect what belongs to you, and leave me not to the ravages of the dogs. Embrace my soul, my God, and shelter my soul in Your arms.

Sometimes we must give ourselves completely to the protection of God. We may reach out to embrace Him in love through our contemplative prayer, and it seems we embrace only emptiness. But we must have the certitude that He is there, that we do embrace Him, and that He returns our embrace. We must know that He does hear us when we cry out. It is our soul we must focus on, it is our soul we must preserve. Our enemy cannot do anything to hurt our soul unless we let him (Mt 10:28). No matter how powerful the enemy, our soul is the one thing over which he has no power at all. He can harm our soul only if we let him.

Our soul belongs to God, and no one can take it from God (Jn 17:12;20; Jn 6:39). However, because we have free will, we can give it away to the enemy. That is our choice and no one else's. As long as we remain in a state of grace, we belong to God, and if necessary because of circumstances, we may have to place all of our reliance in Him. If we do, we must focus on the preservation of our soul at all cost. We must pray constantly, "Into Your hands I commend my being."

"Then I will proclaim your name to the assembly; in the community I will praise you: "You who fear the LORD, give praise! All descendants of Jacob, give honor; show reverence, all descendants of Israel! *For God has not spurned or disdained the misery of this poor wretch, did not turn away from me, but heard me when I cried out."

My God, my God, You have heard me and You now come to my rescue. I cried for Your aid and You helped me. I sought You and You led me to Your arms. I knocked and You let me into the refuge of Your heart. My enemies surround me, they seek to destroy me, but You protect me in Your embrace. Your power overshadows me. I will sing Your praise to all the Church, to all who will listen. The Father has given me to You. You will not lose me (Jn 17:12; Jn 6:39). You enter my soul and make Your abode in me, and I rejoice in You (Jn 14:23). My joy in You confounds my enemies, confuses the proud (Lk 1:51-52). You are the only hope of the poor, the hope of all who love You. You heed my cry, the cry of one who needs You, for You, my God, are my Savior.

God always answers our prayer. He always hears our prayers and will help us, even if in ways we do not recognize. His ways may even seem to be abandonment, but we must have the absolute certitude that in the midst of our greatest distress He is there for us more powerfully than at any other time, showering us with every grace we need to protect our soul. In some cases He grants our request, in others He gives us an even greater cross, and in still others He gives us something entirely different. In any case, we should accept what He sends as being that which He knows is best for us, whether or not we understand it.

Our continual prayer should be that His will for us, all of His will for us, may be fulfilled in us. His will may puzzle us, for it may not seem logical, or even a good thing. That is where trust comes in. We must have faith that God will never, ever, do anything to us or for us that is not for our spiritual good. He does not play games with us. He wants us with Him for eternity, to live always in His love. He is the only one in whom we can always have absolute trust. To get to this level of trust takes time and effort. For many of us, it means testing the waters first. If that is what you are doing, let Him know. Tell Him, even though you know He knows.

Tell Him you love Him and are trying to conquer yourself. Ask Him to help.

"I will offer praise in the great assembly; my vows I will fulfill before those who fear him. The poor will eat their fill; those who seek the LORD will offer praise."

I praise You in Your Church, the Church You founded, the Church You will protect against the forces of evil until the end of time. I vow my allegiance to You in the company of Your people, and in the company of those who fear You, and before all who will listen. My voice is the voice of Your Church, we who love You and belong to You. You fed the poor as they wandered the desert seeking the promised land, and You feed the poor now, You who are our Eucharistic food. You fill us with Your love and clothe us with Your grace. I seek You so my heart will live, for it lives in You and for You.

In the midst of our everyday life, no matter the circumstances, we must praise God continually, for He is our God and all we have is from Him. All that He does is good. All He does is for His greater glory. Whatever our life circumstances, we praise God for being God, for loving us, for preparing a place for us with Him for eternity, for trusting us with His cross. We pray for the inspiration to discern His will, and the strength to do His will. We pray in full confidence that He will never leave us and will protect us from the only important evil, that which brings death to our soul. His strength is our strength, His love is our love, His prayer for us becomes our prayer to Him. We try to progress in prayer and holiness so that our life is lived in Him and through Him. One way we can do this is by simply thinking of God as often as possible throughout the day.

I taught at a Department of Defense graduate school. Before I went into a class, I would ask God to bless me and all of my students, and ask Him to help me help them. In the morning, I would go by the chapel on post before going to the office. There, before the Blessed Sacrament, I asked God to let this day be His day lived through me, and I opened myself to Him to use me that day in any way He desired. At home, before I left for work, I prayed a few minutes, asking God and Blessed Mother to watch over me and my family that day and to protect us from evil. I also prayed to the Sacred Heart of Jesus asking Him to bless all my works for that day. As I drove to work, I usually prayed the rosary, and made a point of thanking the Father for His gifts this day, perhaps for a beautiful sunrise or a glimpse of a flock of geese. Many of these things may seem trivial, but they are little ways you can bring God before your consciousness throughout the day. Each noon I went to Mass, which was the highlight of the day, but all the other little acts of worship served to put my mind and heart in a state where I was more receptive to the graces received during Mass, and more conscious of the benefits of the grace of Mass working in my life during the rest of the day.

"All the ends of the earth will worship and turn to the LORD; All the families of nations will bow low before you. For kingship belongs to the LORD, the ruler over the nations."

You have told us, my God, that your gospel shall be preached to the ends of the earth, and all who believe and are baptized shall be saved (Mk 16:15). You are the sign for all nations, foretold by Isaiah. You are the root of Jesse which You have set up as a signal for all the nations, the signal to be sought even by the Gentiles (Isaiah 11:10-12). You purchased for God, with Your Blood, the people of every nation (Revelation 5:9). And on that day when you claim Your dominion over us, all the nations will sing to You, our Savior, and You will be great in our midst (Isaiah 12). Truly You have kept Your inspired word, and You are great in our midst in Your Holy Eucharist. You have made us part of Your Mystical Body. Your word is true, and I know You will reclaim all that is Yours (Isaiah 11:10-11; Jn 6:39-40). I offer myself to You, my God, in my entirety and pray You accept me as Yours, a part of Your flock, a member of Your Body. I submit myself to Your dominion, all that I am and all that I have.

When Jesus looked down upon Jerusalem from the cross, upon the Temple where the Passover lambs were being slaughtered, He was mindful of these prophesies of Isaiah which were being fulfilled in Him. For Him, Jerusalem represented the world, and in the Temple He saw the Church He had founded on Peter to spread the gospel and bring God to all men everywhere. He knew He would soon, after the Resurrection, tell His apostles to preach His gospel to the ends of the earth (Mt 28:19-20). He knew that men would be converted throughout the earth, so that "All the nations of the world shall be converted and shall offer God true worship; all shall abandon their idols which have deceitfully led them into error, and shall bless the God of the ages in righteousness." (Tobit 14:6-7) They shall remember what He did for them and they shall be moved to accept the sublime gift of His sacrifice offered for them, and they shall be converted.

It is not often that we appreciate the importance of this gift, but if we meditate on the gospels, we realize that we only have two choices. Either we are with Jesus or we are against Him. There is no middle ground. If we accept Him, we accept Him who sent Jesus, and we accept the Holy Spirit, Him whom Jesus would send to us after the Ascension. We accept the Triune God. We must make the choice for or against Him, and must live that choice. The choice cannot be made only with the mouth. It must be lived in the heart. Declaring our fidelity only with our mouth and not with our heart is not making a choice, it is only telling a lie. When we choose Him, we choose all He commanded of us, and all He taught us. God is not a halfway house. We accept, we commit, or we lose for all eternity.

"All who sleep in the earth will bow low before God; All who have gone down into the dust will kneel in homage."

To You, my God, all the proud of the earth, all the sons of Satan who have been filled with earthly goods, shall bow, for Your dominion shall reach to the corners of all creation, and Your power and might shall endure for all eternity. It does not matter how little or how much I have of the treasures of this earth. I will try to be a good steward of all You give me and use what You give me in accord with Your will. All the creatures of the earth shall bow before You, for Your dominion is everlasting and all who sleep in You shall adore You for eternity. Temporal gain means nothing to me unless it is Your will for me, for You are my treasure, You are my hope, You are my love. With Your help, I will not forsake You, will not forsake Your word, for You are my hope and my strength. Nothing is more important to me than Your will for me.

The heaven and the earth belong to God, and all that is in them. His dominion has no limits. The prince of darkness appears to reign on earth, but his reign is a facade, a false kingdom, a house built on sand. Satan is the ultimate lame duck ruler. He is on the way out, and he knows it, and he knows there is nothing he can do about it. He lost the battle when He encountered Jesus in the desert at the beginning of our Lord's public ministry. Jesus did not fight him, or argue with him; He simply answered and dismissed Satan.

Jesus never argued; He only answered. To argue is to acknowledge the equality of the other. But no one is God's equal, and so He never argues. He answers, or He proclaims. Since the time Christ walked on earth, Satan began the slide down the slippery slope to Hell and he has been grabbing for everyone he can reach on his way down. If we accept Jesus, and live a live of prayer, and place ourselves entirely in His hands, we are protected. Satan may grab for us as he slides, or slithers, by, but prayer is like spiritual Teflon. Satan may try to capture us, but we have been made so slippery he cannot hold onto us, and we are protected from his grasp. God has dominion over our soul, and that is as it should be. That is what God wills for us.

"And I will live for the LORD; my descendants will serve you. The generation to come will be told of the Lord, that they may proclaim to a people yet unborn the deliverance you have brought."

To You, my God, my soul belongs. In You my soul has life. My children shall serve You, for the earth and all that is in it is Yours. All the covenants you made with our ancestors are fulfilled in You, You who are our new and everlasting covenant. You will come again and Your glory will be seen over all the earth. We live the advent of Your Second Coming, and look with anticipation to Your reign. You shower us with Your mercy now, and will exercise Your justice when You come again. You shall judge with equity and will recognize the faithfulness of Your servants. All will recognize You as their creator, both Your faithful ones and the unfaithful. The justice Your faithful ones have cried out for through the ages will be seen by all (Revelation 6:9-11). Into Your loving hands I commend my being.

"We wait in joyful hope for the coming of the Lord." How often have we heard these words at Mass? They teem with life and hope. We are not afraid of our God who loves us, at least not in the common context of fear, for our fear of God is a fear based on respect. We fear we will offend the one who loves us so much, we fear we do not do enough for Him, do not love enough, and this holy fear is well founded. We fear His justice, but have confidence in His mercy if we have truly loved Him. We are filled with joy at the thought of Him coming to rescue His people. We pray that when the angels "put the seal on the foreheads of the servants of God"

(Revelation 7:3), that we are among those so marked. We look forward to the day when God "will dwell with them and they will be His people and God Himself will always be with them as their God. He will wipe every tear from their eyes, and there shall be no more death or mourning, wailing or pain, for the old order has passed away." (Revelation 21:3-4)

Meditations

These meditations are provided to aid in your private prayer
and your response to God working in your life.

Mary At The Foot Of The Cross

I stand here at the foot of the Cross, almost in disbelief, looking at my Son whom I love so dearly. How could He suffer so much and still be alive? This is the second time I have had to offer my Son to His Father. The first time was preceded with such joy. But then Simeon spoke, and my heart was chilled, a chill that never left. And now, with the shouts of joy at His entry into Jerusalem still echoing in the streets, the prophesy of Simeon has come to pass. The sword which has hung over my heart for 33 years has struck; struck so very, very hard. I keep telling myself over and over; God's will be done, God's will be done. How can I stand here when He is up there, my beautiful Child? Everything in me is up there on the cross with Him.

I can still hear the cruel whips as they tore into His flesh, His cries echoing across the courtyard. I cannot stop thinking of the many times I held that body, my little baby, washing and cleaning Him, scrubbing Him when He came inside from playing or helping Joseph; watching Him grow strong and tall. His body was so perfect and unblemished.

As He grew to manhood, He would come inside after working all day with Joseph and sit beside us. In His gentle way He taught us the ways of God. After Joseph died, how I loved those times when we just sat and talked. He taught me so many things. Those times alone with Him are so precious to me.

When He left home, just a short three years ago, my heart was filled with anxiety for Him, for I had never lived a day without the prophesy of Simeon coming to mind. "Is the time now?", I would ask myself. Yes, it was now.

I look upon Him, who never hated anyone, His body now covered with the marks of hatred. Hate is so powerful, but it will never be as powerful as His love. I remember well the feel of His infant skin against my hands that night in Bethlehem as I held Him and hugged Him and kissed His little hands and fingers. Now, I see before me the world's response to His love. I can only hope that some day others will love Him as I do, as I always will.

As a child, He was into everything, always helping Joseph and me. How often did He bump His little head? I lost count. But each time He came to me for comfort and I would hold His precious head in my hands, kiss His brow, and give Him comfort. He would always put His little arms around me and kiss me back and thank me. Now, as my heart longs to give Him comfort, to hold Him and wipe His brow, to kiss His forehead once again, I am held back. I can only touch Him with my heart, for He is crucified. His forehead is now kissed by a vicious crown of thorns. This crown of hatred has not defeated Him, for in His sublime dignity, He looks at me through blood-streaked eyes and says "I love you."

Oh, how my arms ache to hold Him, to embrace Him and shield Him from these men who torture and mock Him, these men for whom He only has love. A little while ago, He looked up and said, "Father, forgive them for they know not what they do." All they did was jeer, even one who hangs with Him. Will His executioners ever understand?

I look at Him suffering so, listen to His groans of pain, and I can hear the joyful sounds of the crowd echoing across the valley as they begin the slaughtering of the Passover lambs. How ironic. They prepare for a feast honoring God for delivering them, while God's Son, the Paschal Lamb, is murdered at their request. He told me this would happen, and why, and I know it is God's will, but that does not make the hurt in my heart any less real, any less painful. It is only because He told me that I can bear to see Him in such pain and still live.

I was standing nearby when they threw Him down so cruelly on the rough hewn Cross. Splinters impaled His already lacerated back. They had just ripped His garment off, that seamless garment I made for Him just before He left our home three years ago. All the wounds from His scourging were torn open again. His whole body trembled from the pain. He looked into my eyes as He lay there, His body weak beyond description, His blood already soaking the Cross, and I could do nothing. It was so painful to do nothing. I thank our Father in heaven for not making my beloved Joseph witness this.

Then they stretched His arms out so unmercifully, driving those huge nails through His hands; those wonderful, beautiful hands. The pounding of those hammers will echo in my ears, and my dreams, for the rest of my life. I can still see His little hands that night in Bethlehem, the tiny fingers wrapped around my thumb and grasping at my lips as I kissed them. How can I describe how awestruck I was that night? The Son of God come among men. I could not stop looking at Him. I was so happy then, feeling His little hands touch my face. They were so soft, so pure, so clean. And Joseph was so kind to me, helping any way He could. I can still feel Jesus' little hands pushing against me as He nursed for the first time. He was such a joy.

As He grew, His hands were always helping, always serving. Whenever they were nicked by a wooden plank or a tool in the shop, He always let me care for His wound. He knew how much I loved to do this. I would hold His hand and wash it and bandage it if necessary. As I did, His eyes were always on me, those eyes which poured love upon everyone He met. Often, when I finished, He would hold my face in His hands, kiss my cheek and thank me. As He went from town to town in recent years, His hands spread love and forgiveness and healing everywhere He went.

I remember Jesus telling me about the crippled man at the healing pool. So many years and he had never been able to touch the water. My Jesus healed Him instantly. And the lepers; there were so many. Once He healed ten of them at once, and only one came back to give thanks. And the woman caught in adultery. I still wonder if she changed her life and sins no more. I pray she did. And Lazarus, and the centurion's daughter, and Peter's mother in law, and so many others, all healed, some by His touch, some by His mere presence, some even raised from the dead. But always healed and restored, never rebuked. Those who needed Him were never turned away.

Jesus told me once that sin is like leprosy of the soul. It eats away at the soul until finally nothing is left and the soul dies. He told me how He had been sent by the Father to offer healing to the souls of all men, but I did not fully understand. I am beginning to.

I look at His beautiful hands nailed to the Cross, the hands which blessed John, the youngest of His followers, and the others. John is here with me, the one whom Jesus loves so much, and whom I love as my own. The others have scattered. Even Peter, my dear, sweet, enthusiastic Peter. I want so much to hold the hands of my Son which move no more, bless no more, heal no more. His fingers, immobilized by the hatred of men, are now curled around those cruel nails.

One of the two thieves just begged for forgiveness. My Jesus, from the Cross, forgave him. He even promised this man would be with Him today in Paradise. Paradise. It is such a foreign sounding word right now.

Jesus just spoke to me. It startled me when He did. I didn't think He had the strength left. He gave John to me as my child, and me to John as his mother. But He called me woman! He only did that once before, at a wedding. In His agony, is He delirious? Does He realize who I am? Oh, now I understand, now I remember! He is giving me all of them as my children. He told me one day that I would be the mother of all God's children, and I just laughed. I thought it was just His teasing. I did not understand how this could be. Now I am beginning to understand. Is this why He called me woman at Cana?

He is so weak. His body slumps down and it is so hard for Him to breathe. It has been almost three hours now. How much longer can He suffer this? To breathe, He has to raise Himself by pushing against those horrible spikes piercing His feet. When He does, His torn back rubs against the splintery Cross, and He groans in pain. Every move He makes is agony for Him. My heart cannot take the pain I see in His face as He struggles so, but I cannot take my eyes from Him. I must share everything with Him, for that is all I can do. It is the only way I can help Him. His feet, which walked so far and carried Him to teach and help so many, can carry Him no more. Those beautiful feet. Last night, He washed the feet of His twelve companions. None but John are here to wash His feet now, to give Him comfort.

I can't bear it; my heart is torn apart. A moment ago Jesus cried out, asking why God had abandoned Him. His cry pierced my heart like another sword. But now, He is giving Himself to the Father. He is reconciled. It is finished. His body just slumped, lifeless at last. It is done. His pain is over, for which I thank the Father. Mine continues, which I offer to the Father.

John is taking me back to his house. It was so painful to have Jesus lowered from the Cross and laid across my lap. I held His cold, grey, lifeless face tightly against me, embracing all I had left of Him. That poor, tortured face will feel no more the cruelty of man.

As each spike was pulled from His hand and dropped to the ground, the soft thud echoed through my soul. His lifeless arm swung down like a cruel pendulum. The awful crown was pulled from His head and thrown down so casually, thorns breaking off, thorns covered with His precious Blood. He was slumped forward, His chest draped over the cloth used to lower Him to the ground; into my arms.

I kept wiping the blood from His face and body, removing fragments of thorns and splinters, until all the water I had was gone. I would have used my tears, but I had none left. He was so brutalized. I could hardly recognize Him. My baby, my child. What have they done to you? I moved automatically, almost in a trance.

I can hardly believe it has actually happened. The whole sky went dark, so very dark, when He died. Heaven itself cried out in pain. We heard people in the crowd say that the veil in the Temple, the veil that enclosed the sanctuary of God, was torn from top to bottom when the sky darkened. Top to bottom; no man could do this to a veil so high. What does it mean? What now? What will we do? What will my dear Peter do? How will I live without Jesus, without my Child?

To add insult to injury, a young soldier even thrust a spear into His dead body, almost like testing meat to see if it is cooked enough. Had they not done enough, insulted Him enough? Was that really necessary? I will pray for that soldier.

We are almost to John's house. We stopped here to rest for a moment at the crest of the hill on John's street. I am so weary. Looking back at Calvary, I can see the empty

Cross, the cloth used to lower Him still draped around the outstretched beams. The sun is low, almost to the horizon. The three crosses are silhouetted against the evening sky as Passover begins. How barren Calvary looks, almost innocent. No noise, no evidence left of the horrible cruelty just done except for that empty Cross.

Will the world recover from what it has just done? Will it ever understand what has just happened? My Son is dead. My beloved Son. The Son of God.

The Door of Longinus

At the crucifixion, a young soldier, Longinus, thrust a spear into the Sacred Heart of Jesus. Water spilled forth, washing Longinus, and Blood followed, giving Longinus the grace of conversion. Having been touched by the healing contents of Our Lord's Sacred Heart, Longinus eventually became a martyr, giving up his own life for the one he helped crucify.

Longinus opened a Door into the Sacred Heart of Jesus, which stands open, ready to receive all. We each have many opportunities to cross this threshold, to enter through this Door, to be immersed in the Love within. How we respond to that invitation is dependent on how much we love. This Door can be wide, but it is often hard to pass through.

To find the Door of Longinus, we need to care enough, for the colder we are the more the Door will shrink, the less visible it will be. Even if we are lukewarm, the Door will be too indistinct, too small to pass through. The more passionately we burn with love for Jesus, the more visible the Door will be and the wider it will become, until, when we love enough, it glows like a furnace, calling us, and stands wide to receive us with ease.

We cannot buy our way in. There is no sum of money sufficient to accomplish this. Judas found out the value of money. Money, it is said, greases the ways of the world. It acts just the opposite for Jesus. No matter how many philanthropic works we do, no matter how many works of charity we perform, if we do not act out of love, we have accomplished nothing. The Door is still hidden, still too small.

We cannot bribe our way through the Door. We have nothing material Jesus wants. All our worldly attachments must be left behind, for there is no room for them in His Sacred Heart. He wants nothing except our love. Real love can never be used as a bribe. It is always given freely. Nor can we threaten our way through the Door. There is no force in the universe as powerful as the force of God's Love. Nothing can threaten or conquer His Love, or make His Love respond to anything worldly or unholy.

We can each enter through this Door of Longinus at will. The key to the door is love. If we love Jesus enough to surrender our will to His, to ask His pardon for our sins, to ask His help to sin no more; if we burn with love for Him, desire Him more than everyone and everything else, with our whole mind and heart; if we give Him all we have, all we are, placing all in His loving hands with trust; if we love our neighbor because we see Him in that neighbor; if we come to Him for all things, and accept His decisions; then the Door of Longinus will open wide, and we can enter and make the Sacred Heart of Jesus our perpetual home.

Meditating On The Mystical Body

First meditate on these scriptures:

Romans 12:3-8. (The Mystical Body). ... so we, though many, are one body in Christ and individually parts of one another. ...

1 Cor 6:15. Do you not know that your bodies are members of Christ?

1 Cor 12: 12-31 (The Mystical Body). As a body is one though it has many parts, and all the parts of the body, though many, are one body, so also Christ. ... Now the body is not a single part, but many. ... But as it is, God placed the parts, each one of them, in the Body as He intended. ...But God has so constructed the body as to give greater honor to a part that is without it, so that there may be no division in the body, but that the parts may have the same concern for one another. If one part suffers, all the parts suffer with it; if one part is honored, all the parts share its joy. Now you are Christ's Body, and individually parts of it. ... Strive eagerly for the greatest spiritual gifts.

Gal 1:22-23 (Mystical Body). And He put all things beneath His feet and gave Him as head over all things to the Church, which is His Body, the fullness of the One who fills all things in every way.

Eph 3:4-6. When you read this you can understand my insight into the mystery of Christ, which was not made known to human beings in other generations as it has now been revealed to His holy apostles and prophets by the Spirit, that the Gentiles are coheirs, members of the same body, and copartners in the promise in Christ Jesus through the gospel.

The Mystical Body is made up of all of God's people as the members, and Christ as the head. We who are members of the Mystical Body have a true, not just symbolic, connection with the rest of the Mystical Body through the operation of the head of this Body, Jesus Christ. We must be a member of the Mystical Body to go to heaven, and that is why Christ was the one who had to open the gates of heaven. He went to the place of the dead after He died; so He could bring the news of their liberation and prepare to bring them to heaven. Christ had to first die before He could take His position as the head of the Mystical Body, for until He died He was in a physical human state, not a mystical state.

God chose from all eternity to operate through the Mystical Body, and gave us physical bodies which function as they do so He could help us understand the Mystical Body. God helps us to understand the Mystical Body, and how we relate to that Mystical Body, by comparing its function to that of our physical bodies. The way the Mystical Body operates and the way we need to view ourselves as a part of the Mystical Body can be seen from the way our physical bodies work.

Control:

The head (brain) controls the physical body by controlling the automatic involuntary processes we take for granted, like breathing and heartbeat, and the operations which are voluntary and deliberate, like walking and throwing and reading. The brain sends out signals to the body through the network of nerves and the muscles respond. The brain also controls the body defense mechanisms and the way the body processes the nourishment it receives through the head when we eat and drink.

Christ, as head of the Mystical Body, controls the Mystical Body. He directs the function and operation of the

Mystical Body, down to the most minute level, and all of its members; its members being the members of His Church and all those who are in heaven or purgatory.

Healing:

In our physical bodies, we depend on our immune systems, controlled by the head (brain) to fight off disease, and to rush to the aid of a member when that member is injured, such as when a finger is cut. When a finger is cut, it is not just the finger which is injured, but the body. The body is endangered when infection enters the body through a wound. Therefore, when a finger is cut, blood rushes to the place of the wound to wash it out and to begin the repair process. The blood also carries the white corpuscles to fight off infection. The substance in the blood combines chemically with oxygen in the air to form a scab which covers the wound and prevents dirt and infection from entering the body through the wound.

When we abuse our bodies through conduct we know is wrong, such as homosexual conduct, promiscuous sexual conduct, and illegal drug use, we place ourselves at very high risk of destroying our immune system and preventing it from protecting us because we place ourselves at high risk of contracting AIDS.

As a member of the Mystical Body, when we are spiritually injured through sin and moral weakness, our defenses against sin are weakened and we cause injury not only to ourselves but to the Mystical Body, for we may infect another soul with our error communicated to that soul by word or example. But through the function of Christ as head of the Mystical Body, we can draw spiritual healing from the Mystical Body through the sacraments, prayer, fasting and other forms of sacrifice, and conforming our will to the will of God. This is particularly the function of the sacraments of reconciliation and Eucharist. Through these means, our spiritual well-being is restored and we are no longer a source of injury to the Mystical Body. Reconciliation is like a shot of penicillin or a swarm of white blood cells, used to fight disease which has entered a part of a physical body. That part must be either cured or cut off and discarded for the sake of the health of the whole body. The cure of our spiritual disease is the sacrament of Reconciliation.

Once restored to health through reconciliation, we are nourished to full strength through The Eucharist and the other sacraments, the Eucharist being our needed spiritual food. It is the one food we can never get too much of. If we refuse to conform our will to that of God, if we refuse the sacraments of reconciliation and the Eucharist, if we persist in our self-centered manner of behavior, we are in mortal sin. This means we are in mortal danger of being cut off from the Mystical Body and cast into hell, separated forever from the light and the life.

Nourishment:

In the physical body, nourishment is taken in through the head in the form of food and drink and is used, under control of the brain, for the health of the physical body. The nourishment is distributed, by the flow of blood, throughout the body to keep the various parts in functioning order. When a part is deprived of nourishment, such as when a part of the body becomes gangrenous or has a tourniquet put on for too long, that part of the body is deprived of nourishment and dies. When this happens, it must be cut off and discarded or it will cause the infection and disease to spread through the rest of the body, eventually killing the body. The welfare of the body demands that all the parts be healthy or the part which has died be removed and discarded.

Each of us, as members of the Mystical Body, has an obligation to nourish this Body, and we do so through prayer, fasting, Eucharist and sacrifice (which sometimes may include suffering). Just as our bodily nourishment is taken in through the head, the nourishment for the Mystical Body is offered to Christ for Him to use and control as He knows best in order to maintain the spiritual health of the Mystical Body. A major part of the strength and food we receive is from the sacraments, especially Reconciliation and the Eucharist.

Strength:

In the physical body, a muscle derives strength from other parts of the body, such as the blood which brings it food for energy, and through exercise. Without food and exercise, our muscles grow weak and do not serve the needs of the body when called upon to perform a necessary task.

In the Mystical Body, we need to nourish our spiritual muscles through the sacraments, especially Reconciliation and the Eucharist, and exercise ourselves spiritually through prayer and fasting so that we may have the spiritual strength to resist sin. To properly participate in the Mystical Body, we must deny our own selfish desires which are contrary to the will of God, and consecrate ourselves to Christ and Our Mother, Mary, to let them lead and guide us in the way they know is best for the health of the Mystical Body, which is also always best for our own spiritual health. We must try to know ourselves so that we might know our strengths, but, very importantly, our weaknesses. It is through our weaknesses that Satan attacks us. A general always tries to attack the enemy at his weakest point of defense. We contribute our strength to the strength of the Mystical Body; we draw strength through prayer, from the power of the Mystical Body, to compensate for our weakness. This is why Christ can say to us My yoke is easy and My burden light; we draw on that strength by abandoning ourselves to the will of God.

We who are married should pray for help from other God-filled and good spouses who are members of the Mystical Body, living on earth or otherwise, for the strength and power to likewise be a good spouse and parent for ourselves and for our spouse. We who are priests should seek power from other Mystical Body priests to help us in whatever ways we perceive we are weak or otherwise need special help to keep from injuring the Mystical Body; and so on.

Why would Christ not just do all this directly Himself? Clearly, He could; but in His infinite Love He allows other members of the Mystical Body to assist Him in this task. He does this by using their love for Him and for us, just as He *allows* us to join our suffering to His. But all is directed and controlled by Him, and all is done for the good of the Mystical Body. Through the Mystical Body, we can join in the suffering of others while at the same time sharing the sublime Love and presence of God through Christ as the head of the Mystical Body.

Full participation of the Trinity:

We speak of the Mystical Body as being Christ as the head and ourselves as the members. But we can also see the operation of the full Trinity permeating the function of the Mystical Body, each acting in accordance with His principal activity. God the Father, as omnipotent Creator, creates the Mystical Body through the Incarnation and the necessary integration of us as members through His divinization of our souls. In this way, Our Father provides the means and the operation by making us all His children, and establishes His Only-Begotten Son as head of the Mystical Body, with His adopted children as the members.

Christ, as Redeemer and Him through whom we reach the Father, is the head and controller of the Mystical Body; the One who conquered suffering and death, death of the soul as well as of the body; the One who gave us His beloved Mother as our Mother to nurture and guide us to Himself; the one who nourishes the Mystical Body with His own Body and Blood, allowing His priests to share as His instruments of consecration and distribution of this heavenly nourishment. The Holy Spirit gives life to the Mystical Body through His guidance and inspiration, and dispensing of His gifts to the members of the Body in the degree to which they seek, merit and ask for His gifts. In this regard, merit is not so much a question of accomplishment but of abandonment to the will of God and participation in His divinization of our souls. The Holy Spirit gives the power of love, and the breath of life, to the Mystical Body, the Mystical Body nourished by the Precious Blood of Christ. Thus Christ tells us to seek a transfusion of His Precious Blood so we can draw on His life and His strength.

Power of the Mystical Body:

It is said that the greatest power is the power of love. The tremendous power of the Mystical Body is the power of love, for love is the one thing that Satan can never be or possess. Satan cannot ever draw on the strength of the Mystical Body which is the strength of love. Satan can only hate, and hate is a dissipating condition. It is also said that hate feeds on itself. Therefore, hate can only continue to exist where there is reciprocal hate; hate returned measure for measure. Vengeance, jealousy, envy, and all the other seven deadly sins are sources for hate. But when hate comes up against love, and there is no reciprocal hate to feed upon, the more one hates the more one is drained and diminished.

The more you love, the more you are filled and fulfilled, and the more your capacity for love increases. Through the action of God divinizing our souls, our capacity of love becomes infinite as our souls, more and more, take on the nature of God. That is one reason why Satan, no matter how much he tries, must ultimately fail when confronted with the most powerful weapon of all, love; especially love of God and our neighbor. This is also why Mary must ultimately be victorious over Satan. The power of love, communicated to us through Mary and the Trinity, in communion with the saints, must prevail over hate if we but reject hate and allow love to work in us. This love is the real power of the communion of saints; the <u>common</u> <u>union</u> of all who have accepted God's love who in return give their love to Him and also to us as fellow members of this Mystical Body. The saints take great delight in having us join them in this journey of love, and will help us as much as they are able and allowed by our actions.

God, our Father, out of love for us, in one sense created us with more freedom than He Himself has. He must be consistent with His own nature and completely trustworthy, and must always love us. He cannot cease to love us. But He created us with the freedom to love Him, or to reject Him, and did this so that those who loved Him and lived in accord with His will might be greatly rewarded in heaven. To fully participate in the Mystical Body, we need to have complete and absolute trust in God and His love for us. We need to place ourselves in His loving arms and be content to let Him care for us, trusting completely in His love for us.